THE FALL OF THE
U.S. CONSUMER ELECTRONICS
INDUSTRY

THE FALL OF THE U.S. CONSUMER ELECTRONICS INDUSTRY

An American Trade Tragedy

Philip J. Curtis

Quorum Books
Westport, Connecticut • London

338.76213
C98f

Library of Congress Cataloging-in-Publication Data

Curtis, Philip J.
    The fall of the U.S. consumer electronics industry : an American
trade tragedy / Philip J. Curtis.
        p. cm.
    Includes bibliographical references and index.
    ISBN 0–89930–880–5
    1. Zenith Radio Corporation. 2. RCA Corporation. 3. Radio
supplies industry—United States. 4. Television supplies industry—
United States. 5. Electronic industries—United States.
I. Title.
    HD9696.R364Z463   1994
 338.7'621381'0973—dc20   94–8538

British Library Cataloguing in Publication Data is available.

Library of Congress Catalog Card Number: 94–8538
ISBN: 0–89930–880–5

First published in 1994

Quorum Books, 88 Post Road West, Westport, CT 06881
An imprint of Greenwood Publishing Group, Inc.

Printed in the United States of America

∞™
The paper used in this book complies with the
Permanent Paper Standard issued by the National
Information Standards Organization (Z39.48–1984).

10 9 8 7 6 5 4 3 2 1

Copyright Acknowledgment

Chapter 4 includes an article entitled "Enforcing the Antidumping Laws: The
Television Dumping Case" by John J. Nevin. Reprinted from *Journal of Legis-
lation,* Volume 6, pages 24–43 (1979). Reprinted with permission. © 1979 by
Journal of Legislation, University of Notre Dame.

Dedicated to the thousands of American workers who lost their jobs as a result of the predatory attack of a foreign cartel described here—a protected attack made possible by heavily lobbied federal law enforcement failures.

Contents

List of Exhibits and Appendices

Acknowledgments

There are a number of friends I must acknowledge and thank for their helpful suggestions in my efforts to write in plain language without "lofty legalese" about the important litigation covered in this book. But I must particularly thank the following friends without whose patient help and encouragement this effort would not have been possible:

Joseph S. Wright, retired former President and Chairman of the Board at Zenith. As described in the book, he has been a most-valued mentor to me for over forty years.

John Nevin, Mr. Wright's successor at Zenith, whose talent, hard work, and selfless devotion to the Zenith cause is evidenced by his article reprinted here in Chapter 4.

William H. Roberts, an outstanding partner in the leading Philadelphia law firm of Blank, Rome, Comisky & McCauley. He and his late senior partner, the beloved Edwin Rome, were counsel with whom I had the privilege of working in the *Matsushita et al. v. Zenith* litigation. Bill Roberts is one of the most talented lawyers I have had the good fortune to work with in my forty years in the legal profession. He is not only an outstanding lawyer but also an impressive, well-rounded scholar and gentleman. Any client would be singularly fortunate to have him as an advisor and counsel.

Frederick L. Ikenson, a leading Customs lawyer in Washington, D.C., did a brilliant legal job in Zenith's countervailing duty and related Customs litigation. I enjoyed a valued privilege in working with him as co-counsel in that case and in our legal attack on the government's political settlement of the 1921 Antidumping Act case described in this book. Fred has been a valued friend whose brilliant scholarship and abilities in Customs and related international trade matters were selflessly given to the Zenith cause.

John Borst, Jr., my successor as General Counsel at Zenith when I retired, was my assistant and co-counsel during the *Matsushita* litigation. John did much of the hard work and was a tremendous help throughout the many years; also, during the writing of this book he graciously allowed me access to my former litigation files in storage at Zenith.

Last but not least, Ms. Barbara Phillips was my valued secretary for years before I retired. She selflessly did the word-processing work on this manuscript in an expert and devoted way. She did this at home after working at her present job—a feat beyond the endurance (and talent) of most legal secretaries and paralegals.

I also want to thank Pat Choate, author of the well-known book *Agents of Influence* (Alfred A. Knopf, New York, 1990) and his friend, Dan Baker, for their encouragement and suggestions.

Introduction

This is an inside history of the once-great pioneer consumer electronics industry in America. It is told in the context of the decades-long battles waged by Zenith Electronics Corporation, a leading independent pioneer in the industry, against a powerful international conspiracy that once monopolized worldwide radio—and later television—manufacture. Ultimately, one of the formidable American architects of this early trade conspiracy, David Sarnoff of RCA (Radio Corporation of America), would, for generous license fees, facilitate the complete capture of the American television manufacturing industry by cartelized Japanese companies. This twenty-year operation was the first of many highly successful Japanese mercantilistic programs in the United States.

The story begins in the American industrial past with the notorious "trusts" that locked up markets and ruthlessly extorted the American public in the later part of the nineteenth century and early 1900s. The great "robber barons" were finally brought under some semblance of control by America's pioneering antitrust laws, just as the age of electricity and radio began. The emerging technology-based industries provided new opportunity for the so-called robber barons intent on evading or avoiding the antitrust laws.

The key patents of electricity and radio were bought up and combined into patent pools, which were used to crush competition in the new electrical industries. America's first large multinationals—General Electric (GE), Westinghouse, and American Telephone & Telegraph Co. (AT&T)—prospered wildly with almost complete monopolies in the electrical power, lighting, telephone, and radio manufacturing industries. These fields were carefully divided among the multinationals by the massive pooling of thousands of patents in the United States and the interlocking of foreign patent pools that divided the world markets into territorial monopolies. The monopolies were parceled out among foreign and domestic co-conspirators and were controlled by the combined patent power of all participants protecting the lines of business assigned to each territorial group.

RCA was formed in 1919 by GE and Westinghouse, with the cooperation of AT&T, to handle the new radio business. David Sarnoff, a brilliant and ruthless young Russian emigré, seized control of the RCA radio patent pool by negotiating a consent decree in 1932 that separated this company from its parents, GE and Westinghouse. Through interconnecting foreign cartels, Sarnoff and RCA locked up the radio manufacturing business worldwide and, with domestic and foreign partners, controlled the lucrative industry for over thirty years by means of a scurrilous patent package–licensing scheme.

Zenith, a scrappy young entrepreneurial company, finally destroyed RCA's illegal cartelized hold on radio and television with a landmark antitrust suit that began in 1946 and ended in 1957 on the eve of trial in a settlement favorable to Zenith. The government was impelled to subpoena Zenith's evidence and break up the conspiracy for the rest of the industry. Zenith had taken on the combined Goliath of RCA, GE, and AT&T and had won, but the victory was short-lived.

RCA's vindictive Sarnoff continued to exploit the American broadcast receiver industry by preparing for the next great battle in the television manufacturing business. He helped to organize (and lucratively licensed) the struggling Japanese electronics industry. He built it into a vast cartel, exporting out of a tightly closed Japanese market, that would decimate the entire American radio and television manufacturing industry in just twenty years.

This book tells the unbelievable story of how one of America's most notorious industrialists helped prepare the Japanese for their first successful industrial market capture attempt in the United States, and how one valiant American company fought this injustice for a full three decades. The last battle of the legal war was lost by a heartbreaking 5-to-4 Supreme Court ruling in 1986 at the frantic urging of the Reagan administration. Japan's powerful new political influence apparatus was seen for the first time in this struggle, and it significantly affected the outcome of this crucial case.

The Japanese would go on to capture the entire U.S. consumer electronics industry, using the methodology first seen in the great radio and television assault.

Sarnoff taught the Japanese much more than the structure and methodology of operating a predatory cartel in the United States. He and his associates also assisted in their study of the importance of purchased political influence in American big business as a means of preventing effective enforcement of federal laws condemning "contracts, combinations, and conspiracies" restraining free trade and competition in the interstate and foreign commerce of the United States.

This tragic history of a great American manufacturing industry is distilled here largely from the unpublished evidence adduced by compulsory pretrial processes in Zenith's litigation struggles. The first encounter was successfully pursued against the worldwide cartel originally formed by GE, Westinghouse, RCA, and AT&T. The later battle was unsuccessfully waged against a successor Japanese cartel, profitably backed and fed by RCA and an army of perfidious Washington lobbyists—including former government officials and insiders—generously funded by enormous lobbying fees. Such unprecedented foreign lobbying in Washington produced the tragic 5-to-4 decision in the Supreme Court at the urging of our own government and the government of Japan.

This is not a "Japan bashing" diatribe. It is a critical exposé of the American legal tricksters and merchants of political influence who sold their skills to the Japanese cartel for very high fees. It is also an exposé of U.S. government officials who were used by these perfidious legal tricksters to help perpetrate fraudulent defenses to an old-fashioned predatory dumping scheme that had been universally condemned by the world's leading trading nations since early in the twentieth century.

1

The Age in Which the Electronics
Conspiracies Began

The post–Civil War era produced a dynamic industrial revolution in America. Obscure inventors were experimenting with new technologies and finding remarkable new ways of doing things. The opportunity for profitable exploitation of these new markets inspired entrepreneurs and investment bankers to create commercial enterprises in new, anticompetitive forms that came to be known as combines or trusts.

Many American companies in this period considered open competition among competitors to be an unmitigated evil. To eradicate this evil, the use of a new device called "pooling" emerged. This arrangement was common in Europe, where pools were known as cartels. The dominant companies in an industry would organize themselves into a pool, in which they jointly divided the market among their members. They fixed prices, shared profits, and—by joint efforts—destroyed competitors. This effective device was used extensively by the railroads, which ballooned into one of the most powerful economic entities of the day.

Pools, however, had one weakness. Like that of any conspiracy or gang, a pool's success depended upon the voluntary cooperation of its members. Pool regulations, like betting contracts, were not enforceable in the courts because they went against the public interest. American corporate lawyers soon devised ways to eliminate this weakness. They employed the trust—a combination of companies dominating an industry, legally bound together by a board of trustees. The trustees controlled the companies through stock ownership conveyed to them by each participating corporation, in exchange for trust certificates. Participating companies shared proportionately in the trust's profits.

A variation, the holding company, was invented by corporate lawyers to accomplish the same monopolistic purpose achieved by the trust. For example, the corporation laws of New Jersey were conveniently amended in 1889 to allow New Jersey corporations to own stock in other corporations. Conspiring competitors could buy up other companies to form powerful combines. These groups could easily eliminate uncooperative members of any industry and exploit the public by fixing prices.

The most famous of these combinations and trusts was John D. Rockefeller's Standard Oil Company. Beginning in 1870, Rockefeller and other so-called robber barons organized the Standard Oil Company of Ohio and transferred their independent businesses to this corporation. Using their combined power, Standard Oil obtained preferential rates from the railroad combines and forced remaining competitors to either join the combination or leave the oil business. Standard Oil acquired almost all the refineries in Ohio, Pennsylvania, New York, and elsewhere. The powerful trust controlled 90 percent of the U.S. oil industry and was able to fix the price of both crude and refined petroleum.

Rockefeller's ruthless "gang warfare" on competition was awesome. Competitors were either acquired or driven out of business by various tactics, which included (1) territorial price cuts in the target competitor's area funded by high prices in the areas controlled by the combine, (2) espionage, (3) use of bogus "independents" to attack the target companies, (4) extraction of discriminatory rebates from suppliers of goods and services, and (5) pressure on suppliers to cut off, overcharge, or otherwise cripple competing companies. The scheme produced huge, protected profits for the gang and its members.

John D. Rockefeller's trust approach became a profitable corporate fad that was widely emulated. Huge trusts, pools, and holding companies emerged in many basic industries such as steel, tobacco, salt, sugar, whiskey, and farm machinery. J. P. Morgan and Company and other investment banking houses garnered unconscionable fees for funding and engineering such arrangements. In many ways, this was the early precursor of Wall Street's merger and acquisition industry.[1]

It was during this era that the great electrical conspiracies were born. A brief review of the history of the General Electric Company is helpful in understanding how the so-called electronics conspiracies all came about.

ORIGINS OF GENERAL ELECTRIC

In 1873, Charles A. Coffin began a small shoe and leather goods manufacturing firm in Lynn, Massachusetts. By 1882, Coffin had achieved some success; and a friend, Henry A. Pavear, invited him to join a group of local businessmen in a wild new venture of manufacturing and selling electric dynamos and lights. This exciting new technology had been illuminating the famous boulevards of Paris since 1867, and it was spreading rapidly to other cities and smaller towns.

Pavear and Coffin organized a small group of fellow shoe manufacturers in Lynn to buy out the American Electric Company of New Britain, a tiny firm that had put together the dynamo and arc lamps used in the recent Boston electric light exhibition. The apparatus had been developed and patented by two high school teachers, surnamed Thomson and Houston. The inventors and their patents came along with the purchase of the company.

Coffin knew nothing about arc lighting, dynamos, or electric generators (as they were called), but he was a personable, ambitious salesman. He knew that arc lighting worked and could be sold as an amazing new product that would revolutionize American cities. In one year Coffin sold thirty-one electric generating stations, supplying 2,400 arc lamps. To encourage small, undercapitalized entrepreneurs to start central generating plants, Coffin offered to equip them for part payment in cash and the balance in securities of the local company. Twenty-eight such ventures were launched in 1884, and forty-seven in 1885.

Coffin was quick to recognize the mutual advantages of acquiring stock ownership in his station customers. He adopted the philosophy of the day in business circles: avoid cutthroat competition at all costs. He preached that conciliation and cooperation among competitors was in the best interest of all. By the end of 1889, Coffin's Thomson-Houston Company had grown from $300,000 in annual sales to $3,500,000, an explosive growth rate even by today's standards.

Coffin quickly moved into the electric trolley business. However, competitors and their patents stood in the way of his plan for quicker growth. There was Professor Sydney Howard Short, whose company operated the Short Electric Railway Company of Cleveland. It owned important patents covering an improved street railway apparatus as well as a system involving a new underground electrical conduit system that eliminated the cumbersome overhead trolley and wires. Coffin, with the help of his eager investment bankers, persuaded competitors like Short to become a part of his rapidly growing company instead of competing against him. He acquired their inventions, facilities, and most important, their combined patent power.

Coffin's lust for rapid growth turned toward the newly organized Edison General Electric Company. Edison's patents were troubling to Thomson-Houston, and they offered real competition. In many larger cities there were two rival electric lighting systems, Edison's and Thomson-Houston. Rather than solving the patent problem by the simple expedient of a patent cross-licensing agreement, Coffin saw the strategic advantages of eliminating competition between the two companies by means of merger or combination. The combined patents of both companies could completely dominate the industry. Thus, America's first multinational corporation, the great General Electric Company, was born.

The merger produced even greater advantages. Coffin acquired the esteem of the world-renowned inventor, Thomas Edison, and his business ventures. Also, Coffin was able to entice to the new board of directors two of America's most powerful investment banking firms: Lee, Higginson and Company of Boston; and Drexel, Morgan and Company of New York, later to become the powerful J. P. Morgan and Company. J. P. Morgan would soon become the source of capital and acquisition skills for many of the infamous trusts and monopolies of the period.

Coffin accomplished this remarkable merger campaign in less than ten years—an incredible feat for an obscure shoemaker. Only the Westinghouse Company of Pittsburgh, the successful venture of the brilliant engineer George P. Westinghouse,[2] remained as a competitive challenge to Coffin. Meanwhile, Coffin became president and chief operating officer of General Electric Company when it began its merged corporate operations under that name in 1892.

GROWING PUBLIC OUTRAGE
AGAINST BIG BUSINESS TRUSTS

While Coffin and his investment bankers were conducting their merger blitzkrieg to eliminate competition in the infant electrical industry, the country was awash with public outrage over the trusts and business combinations that were rapidly monopolizing whole industries from steel and machinery to salt, sugar, whiskey, and tobacco. The ruthless industrial gangs were absorbing or destroying independent businesses at such an alarming rate that the public became aroused and demanded that state and federal legislators outlaw such "combinations and conspiracies," which were generally perceived to be against the public interest.

The prevalent philosophy of the new so-called big business ventures was that if cutthroat competition (allegedly so destructive of profits) were eliminated, great corporate combines with the power to stabilize prices could benefit the economy. Big mergers and combinations of competitors created new "efficiencies" and benefited the public, because it was in the public's best interest for the combines to regulate prices at reasonable levels that would provide the profits necessary for growth and prosperity. J. P. Morgan and his fellow investment bankers were leading proponents of this business philosophy. Morgan helped to create the infamous steel trust, U.S. Steel Corporation, an amalgam of former competitors that removed the threat of cutthroat competition in the steel industry. Morgan and his cohorts contended that such combinations were efficient and benevolent monopolies. U.S. Steel became the country's first billion-dollar trust.

The ruthless capture of basic industries by the robber barons' organized gang tactics became known to the general public through the press. For example, in February 1888 the *New York Times* ran leading articles criticizing trusts on every day of the month except one. In one week during February 1988, the *Chicago Tribune* ran twenty-three articles exposing trusts and their evils to public view.[3] Editorials, political cartoons, and magazine articles nationwide exposed and condemned the industrial conspiracies and gangs and the perceived abuses of their ill-gotten power. Farmers, independent businessmen, and workers of all types were up in arms over this new economic tyranny, which they perceived as a strong-arm exploitation of the public by self-appointed robber barons uncontrolled by the democratic processes that were supposed to govern America.[4] The grass roots rage of the public flared.

By 1890, fourteen states and territories had produced constitutional prohibitions against trusts and thirteen states and territories responded to the public clamor with antitrust statutes. These efforts failed to achieve significant results because lawyers quickly exploited loopholes and other infirmities in the laws, such as jurisdictional limitations and the ability of corporate counsel to (1) create business forms escaping the laws, and (2) enlarge corporate activities into interstate commerce, thereby escaping state power to regulate them.

The public clamor was first led by the politically powerful farmers' organizations; it was joined by most other segments of society, including small business. Finally the clamor became so loud and pressing that Congress was forced into action. Some of the states, notably Kansas and Missouri, had attempted to eliminate the evils of the burgeoning industrial gangs; but their jurisdiction, limited as it had to be to their borders, doomed the effectiveness of these local laws. Louisiana made a brave but ineffectual attack on the Cotton Oil Trust in 1887. California failed in an attack on the Sugar Trust. Nebraska lost what proved to be a futile challenge to the Whiskey Trust. The Attorney General of Ohio was able to cause the repeal of the charter of the Standard Oil Company of Ohio, but an order of the Ohio Supreme Court commanding the local oil company to sever its connection with the infamous Standard Oil Trust was never enforced.

These ineffectual local attacks on the trusts were further frustrated by the holding company pyramid scheme when New Jersey amended its corporation law to permit any corporation to own the stock of any other corporation. The simple scheme was easy to implement and provided a complete defense against the growing number of state antitrust laws. Under the New Jersey model, which was emulated by other states to lure incorporations for revenue purposes, corporations A, B, C, and so on could give 51 percent of their stock to a holding company, corporation X, which then gave 51 percent of its stock to holding company Y. Thus, with only 25 percent of the operating companies' stock, holding company Y controlled them completely. Indeed, Y could transfer controlling stock to Z, which needed only 12.5 percent to control the entire industry. No state could attack these pyramids, which were burgeoning in many important industries, because they were legal in the state of incorporation. Congress alone could meet this challenge and could conjure up no defense for inaction, however sympathetic individual members might have been to their big business sources of political contributions and power.

SHERMAN ANTITRUST ACT OF 1890

At the time, the Republican Party was the loyal friend and advocate of the new "big business." It was the champion of high tariffs to protect "big business America," whose philosophy and religion were based on the revelation that if big business were relieved of the destructive disease of cutthroat competition, it would become fair and benevolent. Great corporations, the Republicans believed, if allowed the power to unite and dominate prices and the market without government interference, would benefit the economy and thus the country. Big mergers and combinations, they sincerely believed, provided efficiencies and were therefore justified. J. P. Morgan was the hero of this philosophy and religion. GE's Charles A. Coffin was a devoted disciple. As previously noted, Morgan had made Coffin's rise possible and, appropriately, was a GE board member. Morgan had convinced the once fiercely independent Andrew Carnegie to join the Steel Trust by paying him twice what Carnegie thought the stock in his steel company was worth. This master stroke created America's first billion-dollar enterprise, the monopoly known then as the Steel Trust.

In addition, the Republican formula for American business required high tariffs sufficient to keep out foreign competition, which might totally wreck the allegedly benevolent price-fixing plans and efficiencies of America's new and great business combinations.

But in the midst of the growing public clamor against the trusts, the Republicans in Congress proceeded to react with an effective defensive strategy by admitting that a federal law was needed to curb the excesses that were so enraging the voters. A leading Republican, Senator John Sherman of Ohio, stepped forward to lead Congress in this crusade to fashion a federal antitrust law that would quell the public outcry.

In November 1888, the Republicans had elected Benjamin Harrison to the presidency and had gained a decisive majority of the seats in Congress.[5] Senator Sherman was a high tariff advocate—an extreme "big business" conservative. He sincerely believed in the Republican philosophy described earlier in this section. He was an ideal Republican to control the proposed legislation, lest rival Democrats force through some radical bill that big business could not possibly abide. Some Democrats were preaching the philosophy that prices and supplies in the market should be fixed by competition, unfettered by big business combinations; thus, a free and open market, where success depended on efficiency and not undisciplined market control by friendly competitors, could best promote industrial progress and protect the public from the evils of industrial conspiracies between would-be competitors. In short, the Republican majority postured by attacking the politically indefensible excesses of the hated trusts, while the Democrats demanded that unfettered competition be effectively protected against the cunning, undisciplined schemes of the robber barons like J. P. Morgan and his associates.

There is no room here for an adequate review of the rich legislative history behind the Sherman Act wherein conflicting philosophies were expressed in fiery speeches, many demagogic and Machiavellian in the worse sense.[6] Whatever one's persuasions might be politically and philosophically on antitrust matters, the clever partisan direction Senator Sherman and his cohorts gave the congressional exercise is to be admired.

Sherman was a highly intelligent, gifted, and experienced legislator. He served a total of six years in the House and thirty-two years in the Senate. He also served in the cabinets of Presidents Hayes and McKinley, as Secretary of the Treasury and Secretary of State, respectively.[7] Although he was not the actual author of the Sherman Act as finally passed, he introduced the first Senate resolution that led to passage of the act—which appropriately bears his name.

The deftness with which Senator Sherman directed the final act to passage in its now undetectably Republican form is revealed in a speech he made in the Senate. It presents his view that specific anti-competitive types of conduct should not be spelled out to horrify big business. He would leave it to the courts to assess any challenged conduct on a case-by-case basis, according to the "guiding policy" of the bill. He cleverly stated:

I admit that it is difficult to define in legal language the precise line between lawful and unlawful combinations. This must be left for the courts to determine in each particular case. All that we, as lawmakers, can do is to declare general principles, and we can be assured that the courts will apply them so as to carry out the meaning of the law, as the courts of England and the United States have done for centuries. This bill is only an honest effort to declare a rule of action, and if it is imperfect it is for the wisdom of the Senate to perfect it. Although this body is always conservative, yet, whatever may be said of it, it has always been ready to preserve, not only popular rights in their broad sense, but the rights of individuals as against associated and corporate wealth and power. [21 Cong. Rec. 2460 (1890); 21 Cong. Rec. 2455 (1890)]

The Sherman Act, as amended, is set out in Appendix I of this book.

The Sherman Act not only got the Congress off the hook (temporarily at least) with a public and press that had been aroused by the excesses of the robber barons, but it ricocheted to the courts the power to interpret the act on a case-by-case basis. To provide a wide area of discretion for the courts, the act, seemingly written in clear and unambiguous language, was later said to contain legal "words of art" whose interpretation could provide judges holding the "pro big business philosophy" ample elbow room to accommodate the clever defenses of big business. There was also discretionary room for judges holding the opposite philosophy: that competition, unfettered by cooperative agreements between competitors, should rule the marketplace and be protected against injury by the schemes of gangs of so-called competitors. Thus, either plaintiffs or defendants could be favored, depending upon the philosophy of the judges. Because the Republican Party was the dominant party, it could control appointments to the courts and thereby—most likely—ensure that its philosophy would prevail.[8]

It should be noted that in the foregoing, perhaps overly broad, description of the two competing philosophies, one may have been unfairly labeled Republican and the other Democratic. There have been, and will always be, good and even great judges appointed by Republicans who have been honorable protectors of competition. There have also been judges appointed by Democrats who have rendered decisions in favor of antitrust defendants that would absolutely delight J. P. Morgan or Charles A. Coffin. Mere party labels guarantee neither integrity, courage, nor intelligence.

The Sherman Act was written more as a statement of policy—like a constitutional provision—than as a statute proscribing specific wrongs. It was an ingenious political action claiming to create for an aroused public an economy that would be both properly disciplined and free. Although business pressures against enforcement are always powerful, no credible politician of either party has been foolhardy enough to urge repeal of the act. Indeed, it was passed in the Senate, then comfortably Republican, by a vote of 52 to 1; and no votes were cast against it in the House. It has been badly bent at times by Supreme Court decisions, often 5 to 4, but over time it always bounces back to proper shape in response to the public interest. Public attitudes ostensibly change from time to time; but that common-sense feeling of what is right and what is wrong—which explains the greatness of our jury system, which is often maligned unfairly in so-called complex business cases—is also often reflected in the decisions of the Supreme Court in Sherman Act controversies. In this respect, the act closely resembles our constitutional provisions and their varying interpretations throughout history. The American system of democracy effectively corrects even Supreme Court blunders, although it often takes periods of frustration and hardship before the error is finally rectified.[9]

To illustrate briefly, one of the first important antitrust cases reached the Supreme Court in 1895: *United States v. E. C. Knight*, 156 U.S. 1 (1895). The case was a government attack on the infamous Sugar Trust. A Pennsylvania-based company, American Sugar Refining Company, acquired 98 percent of the sugar business in the United States by paying off its competitors. The Trust raised prices alarmingly, and the government charged it with conspiracy to restrain trade and monopolize interstate commerce in sugar.

In an unexpected opinion, Chief Justice Fuller, writing for the Court, conceded that a monopoly over the manufacture of sugar had indeed been achieved by conspiracy, but he in effect repealed the Sherman Act by holding that the manufacture of sugar or anything else was a purely local process wherever it took place and was subject solely to state law. Before the Sherman Act could take hold, he said, there had to be a direct restraint on the movement of manufactured goods across state lines. Manufacture affected interstate commerce only indirectly, he reasoned, and the Sherman Act, based as it constitutionally had to be on the power of Congress over interstate commerce, condemned only direct restraints on the transit of goods across state lines.

Of course, the Sugar Trust's products were sold all over the United States and it concededly was a monopoly created by buying up most competitors; and it had acquired the power to control sugar prices, which it exercised to the detriment of the public. Fuller said that the only constitutional reach Congress could and did give the Sherman Act was limited to tinkering with transit across state lines. To accomplish its illegal purposes, no monopoly or conspiracy needed to tinker with transit under Fuller's sophistic analysis. No state had been able or could be enabled to curb the giant combinations that were doing business all over the country. The Sherman Act was indeed mortally wounded by Fuller's ridiculous sophistry.[10]

The irony of such Republican-type sophistry in the *Knight* case was that it was authored by a "loyal" Democrat from Illinois appointed by President Grover Cleveland, who had met Fuller in Illinois prior to the 1888 elections. Cleveland had been impressed by Fuller's loyalty to the Democratic Party and his reputation as a good lawyer. Illinois had been a state of particular concern to Cleveland in the election.

Within two years, the Court began to steer away from the defiantly foolhardy evasion of the Sherman Act it had subjected the country to in the *Knight* case. The Court resuscitated the act by determining that various price-fixing schemes were indeed violations of the Sherman Act. In *United States v. Trans-Missouri Freight Assn.*, 166 U.S. 290 (1897), the Court flatly rejected the argument that a combination of eighteen railroads was in reality a "reasonable restraint of trade" and therefore not prohibited by the Sherman Act. The Court sweepingly held that the act proscribed *all* restraint of trade conspiracies between competitors, whether "good" or "bad."

Justice Peckham's majority opinion effectively responded to the seductive argument of the railroad combine that their scheme would actually benefit the public by lowering rates. He pointed out that the concerted power to lower rates or prices exercised by any combination of competitors would permit big business conspiracies to ruin small entrepreneurs, who had a right to be free from the dictatorial predation of any gang of undisciplined competitors.[11] Defending American individualism and freedom, Justice Peckham observed that nothing good could come of turning independent businessmen into members of combines under threat of destruction or by any other means. Independent American entrepreneurs should not be forced or enticed under threat of destruction into becoming mere servants or agents of any industrial combine.

Two years later, Justice Peckham again spoke for the majority in ruling against another industrial combine selling iron pipe: *Addyston Pipe and Steel Co. v. United States,* 185 U.S. 211 (1899). Six competitors had entered into a marketing agreement to eliminate competition between them. The conspiracy had been formed under the legal theory of the *Knight* case, which held that the Sherman Act could not reach a conspiracy of manufacturers because manufacture was local and never carried out during transit of goods across state lines even though the manufactured product was sold throughout the country.

In 1904 the landmark antitrust case of *Northern Securities v. United States,* 193 U.S. 197 (1904), established that holding companies were no longer exempt from the Sherman Act, contrary to the theory of their inventors. Ironically, the decision was engineered by a Republican president, Theodore Roosevelt. Roosevelt had acquired firsthand knowledge of the dangerous evil of big business conspiracies. He had been a New York state assemblyman during the investigation of the famous robber baron Jay Gould, and in 1882 he campaigned for reelection on the antitrust issues of the day. In 1899 he had written, "I have a great quandary over trusts. . . . I intend to see that the rich man is held to the same accountability as the poor man and when the rich man is rich enough to buy unscrupulous advice from very able lawyers, this is not always easy."

After becoming president, Roosevelt saw an opportunity to pursue three of the most notorious (or famous, depending upon your philosophy) tycoons of the day, who were flaunting their disrespect for true Sherman Act principles with the thought that their lawyers could completely detooth the statute if the government dared to challenge them. The Northern Securities Company was a holding company created after a no-holds-barred struggle on the New York Stock Exchange for control of the Northern Pacific Railroad. The fight had run the railroad's share price up to $1,000 and ended in a stalemate among the famous combatants: J. P. Morgan, James J. Hill, and E. H. Harriman. The three powerful competitors settled by dividing the spoils according to the holding company strategy described earlier. The combine created a railroad monopoly and seized control of every foot of railroad track west of Chicago. Roosevelt was surrounded by cabinet members fully sympathetic to the big business philosophy, and he quietly—without cabinet consultation—directed his Attorney General to pursue the combine under the Sherman Act and break it up.

It was a rip-roaring, Theodore Roosevelt–type fight all the way to the Supreme Court and within the Court. The government prevailed in another 5-to-4 decision of monumental importance at the time, because it was the first opportunity for the Court to test the famous holding company device under the Sherman Act. The Northern Securities lawyers pulled out all the stops. Their sophistry was appealing or appalling, depending upon one's antitrust philosophy. Their reasoning, gleaned from the Sherman Act legislative debates, seemed convincing, especially in the light of the Knight case. The lawyers argued that the holding company was completely beyond the reach of the law because it merely controlled its subsidiaries' stock and was in no way engaged in interstate commerce! Justice Harlan, writing for the majority five, declared that by its very nature the combine restrained interstate commerce; and he ordered the Northern Securities Company dissolved.

Justice White wrote a dissent full of anguish, saying the majority ruling approved regulation of stock ownership—to him an abominable power the Congress did not and could not authorize. Justice Holmes also wrote an eloquent dissent, arguing that Congress had not authorized the action of the Court's majority. It is in this dissent that Holmes's famous aphorism first appeared: "Great cases, like hard cases, make bad law." He appeared to be rationalizing with regret as he wrestled with his conscience.

Although Roosevelt was delighted with the government's victory, he was furious at the dissent of Justice Holmes in siding with the holding company. Roosevelt had appointed Holmes to the Supreme Court because he believed him to be an antimonopolist and defender of a free market unimpeded by anticompetitive conspiracies. Expressing his rage and disappointment in Holmes, Roosevelt said, "I could carve out of a banana a judge with more backbone than that."

Justice Holmes seemed to redeem himself in another big trust case in 1905, the government's Sherman Act case against the Beef Trust: *United States v. Swift*, 196 U.S. 375 (1906). The case is a landmark because of its important analysis of the scope of the Commerce Clause under the Sherman Act and, by analogy, other similar regulatory statutes of Congress that have followed. With the help of highly paid lawyers, the great and wealthy meatpacker Swift and Company joined in a conspiratorial arrangement with other meatpackers in a scheme to fix prices in the Chicago stockyards. Swift's illegal price-fixing scheme was carefully crafted to support his claim that all the livestock entering the stockyards, regardless of where they had been driven from, were bought and sold locally. All such sales activity being local, he reasoned, was not in interstate commerce and therefore outside the reach of the Sherman Act.

This time, Justice Holmes, writing eloquently for a unanimous Court, pulverized the sophistry in Swift's legal arguments. Admitting that under the cleverly crafted scheme the packers had literally restrained trade in only one state, Holmes viewed the activity as a whole and arrived at the common-sense view that the conspirators had effectively restrained trade in many states, thereby bringing their conduct well within the proper reaches of interstate commerce. His famous analysis of interstate commerce—the so-called stream of commerce doctrine—applied the Commerce Clause of the Constitution exercised by Congress to the realities of modern business. Despite the politically soft-shoe approach by Congress at that time to the true constitutional reach of its power over commerce, Holmes explained with his characteristically simple eloquence just how sweeping that power was:

When cattle are sent for sale from a place in one State, with the expectation that they will end their transit, after purchase, in another, and when in effect they do so, with only the interruption necessary to find a purchaser at the stock yards, and when this is a typical, constantly recurring course, the current thus existing is a current of commerce among the States, and that purchase of cattle is a part and incident of such commerce. [*Swift & Co. v. United States*, 196 U.S. 375, 396–397 (1905)]

There now was recognized a true national market with a federal referee using the rules of the Sherman Act to protect it from local as well as national restraints on competition.

There was reason to believe that the line of cases after the *Knight* debacle, from *Trans-Missouri Freight* to *Swift*, gave Sherman Act protection against all conspiratorial restraints of competition—that the "pro big business" sophistry about every conspiratorial restraint concocted had to be tested for reasonableness within the discretionary power of the courts was specious and fallacious reasoning. Where interstate commerce was affected, all conspiratorial restraints on competition, locally or otherwise imposed, were condemned by the Sherman Act, despite the fact that some of them were described as "good" and "efficient" by counsel and as "economic experts" for the conspirators.

But what Theodore Roosevelt had characterized as "highly paid lawyers giving unscrupulous advice" did not lose heart. They knew they could bend the Sherman Act. Lawyers will always seek to bend the statute for their "big business" clients. Because the composition of the Supreme Court changes, every antitrust holding (especially the too-frequent 5-to-4 decision) is as mortal as the Court's members. For stability, the Court often says it is bound by precedents and that only Congress can change the law. However, when five members or more decide to overrule a previous case, they do so either furtively by implication or with a defiant refusal to follow a prior erroneous holding.

Justice Edward White, in his 10,000-word dissent in *Trans-Missouri Freight*, had attacked the majority holding that all conspiratorial restraints on competition "good" or "bad" came within the Sherman Act proscription. Inspired by "pro big business" arguments found in the legislative history, White had futilely argued in his dissent that a rule of reason should be applied to Sherman Act restraints of trade on a case-by-case basis.

Thirteen years after this dissent, White was sitting as Chief Justice when the famous Standard Oil combine came before the Court in 1911 [221 U.S. 1 (1911)]. Now he finally was able to inject the controversial rule of reason into the Sherman Act. Of course, Congress had not condemned only "unreasonable restraints of trade"; it had (as Judge Peckham said in *Trans-Missouri Freight*) condemned "all" conspiratorial restraints on competition in plain language. White got around the plain language by treating the words "restraint of trade" as "words of art," with a meaning to be found not in the plain meaning of the language but in the common law transplanted to America from England during and after colonization. Although he had been Chief Justice for only about six months when the Standard Oil case was decided, he strongly dominated the Court and was able to convince six fellow Justices that the rule of reason of the common law should be injected into the statute.

At the time, the prevailing view of most consumers and public interest groups was that *all* agreements among persons engaged in the same trade or industry whereby competition was eliminated or reduced—either by price fixing, control of output, pooling of profits, division of markets, or other anticompetitive devices—should be declared unlawful. Whether the format of the conspiracy was designed by a "benevolent" membership allegedly fighting "the evil of ruinous competition" or was allegedly inspired by other "good" motives was immaterial.[12]

The press of the day was full of exposures and condemnations of all such plots against the consuming public. How in a great democracy could anyone successfully defend turning over to any group of competitors the unrestrained dictatorial power to regulate commerce without having ever to face the voters or their government "of the people, by the people, and for the people"? Such economic tyranny was not tolerable in a free and democratic nation. Europe and other nations had been "cartelized" and competition otherwise frustrated. America had brilliantly devised a new democratic freedom from such economic tyranny. But White wanted to preserve for big business a limited right to regulate competition, provided that the conspirators' acts were reasonable under the common law of England and early America.

Although all members of the Court recognized the Standard Oil Trust as a violation of the Sherman Act, two concurring opinions were written. Justice Harlan's observation in his separate *Standard Oil* opinion that White was unnecessarily injecting in the main opinion a judicial amendment not found in the plain language of the Sherman Act was, indeed, accurate. A fundamental rule of statutory construction needing no citation of authority is that courts should never grope through legislative history to put a different interpretation on plain words whose meaning is clear. Nor should they look to congressional debates for guidance in such cases. Either side of any statutory interpretation can usually find support in some speech by some member of Congress, who is usually representing special-interest constituents. Committee reports are of a higher caliber. But even they cannot properly change the plain language of the law. As Justice Peckham said, only Congress, not the courts, can properly amend statutes.

Of course, *Standard Oil* involved about as grossly illegal and criminal a course of conduct as any robber baron could conceive. The lower court had ordered the breakup of John D. Rockefeller's evilly constructed empire into its component parts. This involved over forty large companies and a myriad of offshoots that would have been competitors had there been no conspiracy. The antitrust violations were so grossly illegal and indefensible that all nine Justices had to and did uphold the breakup order.

Although there was no need to do it, Justice White saw his chance to inject the rule of reason into the act by describing his basis for rejecting the oil company's appeal. Writing for himself and six other Justices, he described Standard Oil as being guilty of an "unreasonable" restraint of trade. The mere act of all these competitors combining and conspiring was no longer a violation; there had to be an unreasonable restraint on competition—which, of course, there was in every respect. But White clearly implied that competitors could restrain trade by agreement if the restraint was reasonable and protected otherwise legitimate contractual provisions. Such ancillary restraints were recognized as reasonable under the common law—the judge-made law of England, reflecting the customs and business mores of the people—that the colonists brought to America. The common law flexibly reflected the beliefs of the people, which new experiences and new conditions changed from time to time. Much of the common law was also codified or altered by state and federal statutes.

When the Supreme Court, under Chief Justice White, unnecessarily injected the so-called common law into the restraint of trade language of the Sherman Act, it catered to the big business philosophy of the day. But it failed to define what version of the common law on restraint of trade was to be found in the United States in 1890, when the Sherman Act was passed. It failed to recognize that there were at least three versions of the meaning of a common law "restraint of trade" in the American courts prior to 1890.

Under one view, all agreements between competitors that eliminated competition by fixing prices, controlling output, dividing markets, or otherwise, were unlawful (1) whether or not the prices or market conditions noncompetitively established were reasonable, and (2) whether or not the motives of the conspirators were honorable and the arrangement was employed to stop a perceived evil such as "ruinous competition." Under another view of the common law, minority groups of competitors were allowed to conspire to restrain trade if they did not control the entire market. Under a third view, even competitors achieving monopoly power were permitted to fix prices or otherwise restrain trade by agreement if they did not abuse their power. Even when they fixed prices, they were acting legally if the prices fixed were reasonable. Rectification of industrial conditions the conspirators considered necessary justified such restraints. There were other refinements wherein ancillary restraints were allowed to protect legitimate purposes of the main contract.

The failure of Justice White and his concurring majority to define which common law version it was injecting into the statute really should have been recognized as rendering the act "void for vagueness."[13] As a criminal as well as civil remedy statute, under White's vague reference to the "common law" it did not sufficiently inform the public of what it prohibited. Indeed, Congress has always seen fit to define any terms it uses when those terms need a definition other than the ordinary meaning of the plain language of the statute. There are definitions of terms in the antitrust laws, but they do not include "restraint of trade"—which always occurs when competitors conspire.

As a practical matter, the "rule of reason" doctrine gives the courts a measure of discretion that frequently can accommodate the prevailing economic philosophy or political prejudices of the courts at any particular time. It again brings to mind the famous warning of a great English judge, Lord Camden:

The discretion of a Judge is the law of tyrants. It is always unknown. It is casual and depends upon constitution, temper, passion. In the best it is often caprice; in the worst it is every vice, folly and passion to which human nature is liable. [*Hindson v. Kersey* (1765), cited, 8 How. St. Tr. 57 fn.]

Our own Justice Black said in 1958:

"Reasonable"—that irrepressible, vague and delusive standard which at times threatens to engulf the entire law, including the Constitution itself, in a sea of judicial discretion. [Dissenting in *Green v. United States*, 356 U.S. 165]

The Supreme Court in the past has been able to gloss over the fallacy of the "rule of reason" by holding that price fixing and other obviously flagrant conspiracies to destroy competition are illegal per se and cannot be justified by good motives and benign intentions of industrial gangs plotting against the public interest. Even in that tattered form, however, the rule of reason remains alive and is still subject to renovation by the newly constituted Reagan Court. As we shall see in reviewing the *Matsushita* case in a later chapter, the Sherman Act may face judicial repeal at any time as effectively as it encountered it in *E. C. Knight* in 1895, wherein Justice Fuller declared that all manufacture was local and not covered by the Sherman Act because it was not "in interstate commerce." But it took several years for the *Knight* Court to regain its senses and modify that doctrine, which had left the public at the mercy of the robber baron monopolists of the day.

The "judicial legislation" mentioned in Justice White's opinion in *Standard Oil* became partially eroded over the last eight decades in various cases in which gross violations such as price fixing were so indefensible that they had to be described as "unreasonable per se." But for years counsel for defendants argued that even in gross price-fixing cases, the rule of reason required the courts to determine whether the prices had been fixed at reasonable levels under White's formula. Like a powerful weed, the rule of reason through the years has resisted total extermination in the Supreme Court. Where the challenged conduct is so plainly indefensible and injurious to the public interest such as price fixing, the reasonableness test becomes laughably inappropriate and its attempted application a foolish waste of the Court's time. Price fixing remains one of a shrinking number of gross violations that are treated as per se violations. Defense counsel, however, never lose heart. If the current antitrust climate further deteriorates in the Supreme Court under successfully lobbied administrations, it is possible that Justice White's "rule of reason" amendment to the statute might be applied even to price fixing and the public will have to demand reform again.

GENERAL ELECTRIC AND THE NEW ANTITRUST LAW

Growing and attempted rigorous enforcement of the Sherman Act was beginning to cramp Coffin's drive for dominance in the rapidly growing electrical industry. At the time of the famous Standard Oil case in 1911, to avoid exposure in a public trial GE wisely and quietly engineered a so-called consent decree in a government Sherman Act case against it for price fixing. This quiet settlement shielded from the public any knowledge of GE's criminal activity.

Congress was driven to further antitrust action in 1914 when the Clayton Act was passed to supplement the Sherman Act. The Clayton Act sought to prohibit *specific* anticompetitive acts such as predatory price discrimination and exclusive contracts that prohibited merchants from buying competitors' goods. Theoretically, it reached the evil at inception before the practices had developed into full-blown Sherman Act violations.

By 1913, Coffin needed a well-rounded lawyer to guide GE's growth by acquisition or alliance with competitors in the new regulatory environment. Coffin was attracted to Owen D. Young, whose smooth and scholarly handling of utilities cases against GE impressed the company. Young became Coffin's legal strategist and advisor in the clever and bold cartelization of major portions of the electrical industry in the United States and throughout the world. He developed the argument that patents, then being accumulated by GE, would legally authorize cooperative conduct by competitors that otherwise would flagrantly break the law. Young worked on theories that would insulate the antitrust laws from any application to agreements and activities abroad by companies doing business in the United States under the protection of our laws. Their reach, he reasoned, should stop at our shorelines.

Coffin's dreams of expansion by cooperation or merger with competitors were not confined to the American market. GE obtained counterparts of its growing U.S. patent accumulation in many foreign countries. Coffin had sought business and commercial relationships abroad almost from the beginning. A foreign department was organized at GE in 1897. By 1900, GE had sold power plants to Mexico, India, Argentina, Japan, and Canada. GE opened an office in London and equipped the new subways in London, Paris, and Tokyo. During World War I, GE profitably expanded its munitions manufacturing business as well as the sale abroad of its other products. By 1915, GE employed over sixty thousand workers, a gargantuan enterprise for that period.

Vigorous sales and lobbying efforts at the Navy Department persuaded the Secretary of the Navy, Josephus Daniels, that GE's new turbine drive could successfully propel the navy's warships. In 1915 the *New Mexico,* an electrically propelled battleship, was successfully launched and operated.

By 1918, Coffin, Young, and their cohorts had built GE into a formidable commercial power in the electrical field. The company had close ties to all leading commercial companies in the electrical field in England, France, postwar Germany, Holland, Scandinavia, Japan, and South America. GE divided the world into major industrial areas for monopolies and protected these from outside competition by massing all the patents of the combined companies. The stage was set for the formation of one of the most effective conspiracies in global restraint of trade ever devised: the GE, Westinghouse, AT&T cartel.

NOTES

1.   For an in-depth technical treatment of the subject, see H. Thorelli, *The Federal Antitrust Policy* (1955); H. Seager and C. Gulick, *Trust and Corporation Problems* (1929); A. Walker, *History of the Sherman Act* (1910).

2. George Westinghouse was a very important factor in the manufacture of electrical apparatus. His company's exploitation of the alternating current (AC) system in the country's first AC central station at Buffalo, New York, during 1886–1887 threatened Thomas Edison's direct current approach, which was limited then to about two miles. Stanley, a Westinghouse inventor, had designed the AC system; it gave the central station in Buffalo a very large radius and made effective, wide-scale power transmission a practical reality. Coffin's powers of persuasion, however, could not seduce George Westinghouse into being absorbed by another Coffin merger. Patent disputes and expensive on-going litigation finally persuaded Westinghouse to enter into a patent sharing agreement with GE in 1896. Under the agreement GE was allotted 62.5 percent of their combined business, which at that time included central station equipment, trolley systems, electric motors, and electric lamps.

This bold combination between the two leading corporations in the field was a bald "contract, combination and conspiracy in restraint of trade"—indeed, it was a monopolization—in flagrant violation of the new Sherman Antitrust Act five years after its passage. Avoidance of competition either by contract, combination, or conspiracy was Charles A. Coffin's forte at GE. It was his "rule of law"—any other rule was for his lawyers to evade or avoid.

3. W. Letwin, *Law and Economic Policy in America: The Evolution of the Sherman Act* (1965).

4. For an in-depth technical treatment of the subject, see Thorelli, *Federal Antitrust Policy*; Seager and Gulick, *Trust and Corporation Problems*; Walker, *History of the Sherman Act.*

5. There was a 47-to-36 Republican majority in the Senate and a 172-to-156 Republican majority in the House.

6. See E. Kintner, ed., *The Legislative History of the Federal Antitrust Laws,* vol. 1 (1978).

7. See John Sherman, *Recollections of Forty Years in the House, Senate and Cabinet—An Autobiography* (1895).

8. When Senator Sherman, in the quoted speech, avoided conflict by conferring on the courts the discretion to determine the meaning of the Sherman Act in each case, he should have stopped to consider the often-quoted (and possibly overstated) warning of a great English jurist, Lord Camden: "The discretion of a judge is the law of tyrants. It is different in different men. . . . In the best it is oftentimes caprice; in the worst it is every vice, folly and passion, to which human nature is liable." Lord Camden, *C. J. Hindson v. Kersey* (1765), cited 8 How. St. Tr. 57 fn.

9. Indeed, it took a civil war and the Thirteenth and Fourteenth amendments to correct the Supreme Court's incredible blunder in the infamous *Dred Scott* decision of 1857. In this decision the public was informed that a Negro brought from a "slave state" by his "owner" could be viewed in a free state not as a person but as a form of subhuman chattel without any rights.

10. It wasn't until 1914 that the Supreme Court in the Shreveport Rate Cases, *Houston R. Co. v. United States,* 234 U.S. 242, openly corrected the error of the *Knight* case that steps in the flow of commerce can be separated and analyzed in isolation. Indeed, the *Knight* fallacy of considering manufacture as a purely local, intrastate matter not covered by the antitrust laws—although the product is sold in interstate commerce—has been repeatedly overruled by implication in Supreme Court cases. Finally, in *Mandeville Island Farms v. American Crystal Sugar Co.,* 334 U.S.

219 (1948), a full and complete analysis of the *Knight* error was made by the Supreme Court; *Knight* was recognized as having been completely overruled in the Shreveport Rate Cases and others that had preceded and followed it.

11.   This sage observation escaped the perception of five members of the Supreme Court when the predation of the Japanese electronics cartel came before them in 1986. The cartel received immunity from the Sherman Act in a 5-to-4 decision of the Supreme Court at the urging of the Reagan-Mccse Justice Department. The case is the last of the three Zenith cases covered in some depth in later chapters of this book.

12.   The revered Adam Smith, in his classic 1776 treatise on the virtues of free trade, scornfully warned of a weakness afflicting business tycoons of any generation: "People of the same trade seldom meet together even for merriment and diversion, but the conversation ends in a conspiracy against the public, or in some contrivance to raise prices." Adam Smith, *An Inquiry into the Nature and Causes of the Wealth of Nations* (1937), at p. 128.

13.   A fundamental legal doctrine sensibly requiring that a law must clearly inform the public of what it proscribes.

2

Zenith Challenges the Patent Racket

WHO WAS THIS CHALLENGER, ZENITH?

For background, it is helpful to trace very briefly the history of Zenith and the "Commander," its founder. That history, in some measure, involves a history of radio and television in America from radio's birth as an amateur toy to the electronic miracle of television.

Guglielmo Marconi, founder of the great Marconi Wireless and Telegraph Company in England, fascinated the world in 1901 by flashing the letter "S" without wires or cables across the Atlantic Ocean by means of wireless telegraphy. The stunning possibility of communication over long distances without wires or cables inspired hundreds of young amateurs to put together crude broadcasting and receiving apparatuses in garages and basements across America.

One young amateur, R. H. G. Matthews, had qualified as an amateur radio operator in 1912. Another, Karl Hassel of Sharpsville, Pennsylvania, qualified as an amateur in 1915. Before both enlisted in the navy during World War I, Matthews had begun a tiny business in Chicago building broadcast and receiving apparatuses for other amateurs. Hassel had matriculated at the University of Pittsburgh, where he was the most knowledgeable radio amateur on campus and was asked by the university to operate a newly constructed wireless station at the school.

Matthews and Hassel met each other as new navy recruits at Great Lakes Naval Training Station near Chicago. Upon discharge at the end of the war, they became partners in a new venture, the Chicago Radio Laboratory, building and selling radio sets in Chicago. The factory was a table in Matthews's kitchen. Their first notable venture was building a long wave radio receiver for the *Chicago Tribune* that was able to pick up the news dispatches about the Versailles Peace Conference from a long-wave station in France. This gave the *Tribune* a 12- to 24-hour lead on conference stories that other papers were getting belatedly from the congested trans-Atlantic cable. This feat accomplished, the partners were able to build a 14- by 18-foot factory and radio station near the then well-known Edgewater Beach Hotel in Chicago. The call letters of the new station were 9ZN, and the new business put out a catalogue advertising radio sets for amateurs under the trademark Z-Nith, later changed to Zenith, derived from the station's call letters.

The next notable achievement of the Matthews-Hassell venture was the construction of a wireless system that enabled the North Carolina & St. Louis Railroad to become the first railroad in the world to successfully dispatch trains by radio. Transmitters and receivers were set up in Tullahoma, Tennessee, and Gunterville, Alabama, to handle traffic over the rough country between those rail points. The project was successful, although great concern was expressed locally when the station's radio waves unexpectedly set off the burglar alarm at a local bank during a directors meeting and allegedly caused a dentist's drill to set off a high voltage shock, to the great alarm of both dental patient and dentist. Nearby telephones were also put out of service until the unexpected difficulties of the new venture were resolved.

By the end of 1919, the new partnership was taking on the appearance of a potentially promising business. It was producing and selling at least one complete radio set a week and had gained a measure of favorable local notoriety. To the general public the primitive radio sets of the day were products for amateur radio "hams," "nuts," or "doodlers." The vast potential of the strange device was not generally appreciated. Of course, Marconi had focused the attention of his famous Marconi Wireless and Telegraph Company on wireless communications with ships and between nations. Entertainment broadcasting for the general public was not yet within the vision of the great electrical companies, American or foreign.

But the ranks of the amateur hams grew like weeds. In 1916 Frank Conrad, a Pittsburgh ham, began an amateur broadcast of news and music for other hams from his garage during evening hours after work at Westinghouse. A leading executive at Westinghouse encouraged Conrad to broadcast news and music on Wednesday and Saturday nights for two solid hours. The response by the growing number of amateurs in Pittsburgh was so enthusiastic that the Joseph Horne Company, a local department store, bought a supply of Conrad's "crystal sets" and advertised their sale to the "amateur" public for ten dollars a set. The store's supply was quickly exhausted and many more sets were ordered. Harry P. Davis, a top executive at Westinghouse, persuaded his company to develop and sell Conrad's radio transmitting and receiving apparatus. The later-famous Westinghouse radio station, KDKA, was set up in Pittsburgh. Its initial broadcast of the Harding-Cox election returns created a sensation. From then on, radio broadcasting grew wildly.

In the Midwest, meanwhile, Chicago Radio Laboratory was successfully promoting its radio apparatus for the growing army of hams and amateur enthusiasts. Orders for sets became so great that a new, mammoth, 3,000-square-foot radio factory was built by the Matthews-Hassel partnership. Beginning in 1919, the University of Wisconsin began broadcasting news, market reports, and weather information as a public service for radio amateurs. This helped to stimulate the Matthews-Hassel venture.

McDONALD JOINS THE PARTNERSHIP AND
MOVES ZENITH INTO NATIONAL PROMINENCE

Eugene McDonald had served during the war as a lieutenant commander in Naval Intelligence. After reverting to reserve status, he had a measure of success promoting the sale of automobiles in Chicago. On New Year's Eve, 1920, he drove into a gas station; while his car was being serviced, he noticed several men listening to music coming from a mysterious box. In reply to McDonald's expression of curiosity, one of the men told him the box was a new radio bringing in a program from station KDKA in Pittsburgh. Upon inquiring where he could buy such a gadget, he learned it had been made by the Chicago Radio Laboratory, the Matthews-Hassel venture.

Two days later, McDonald visited the Matthews-Hassel factory in Chicago and ordered for $75 a radio plus tubes, batteries, and headphones. Hassel delivered the radio and installed it in McDonald's room at the Illinois Athletic Club. McDonald was so enthusiastic about the potential of the product that he offered not only to put money in the Matthews-Hassel business but to join it as an active participant. Agreeing, Matthews and Hassel had a young attorney, Irving Herriott, represent them in the negotiations. McDonald took a liking to him. He told the partners, "I like the cut of Herriott's jib. Let him represent us both."

There was a worrisome legal problem confronting McDonald's direct entry into the Chicago Radio Laboratory. Matthews and Hassel had an important patent license agreement with Edwin Armstrong, one of America's greatest inventors in the radio field, and they were building their receivers under the teachings of Armstrong's patents. The license was not transferable and no new licenses were available. McDonald, although not a partner, raised capital for the partnership and worked with the company, planning promotion and sales activities that would bring Zenith to the attention of the national marketplace.

A new broadcast transmitter was installed by Matthews and Hassel in the old radio shack at the Edgewater Beach Hotel using the call letters WJAZ. By 1923, McDonald's ambitious plans called for the formation of a new corporation. The radio receivers still had to be made by the Chicago Radio Laboratories partnership under the Armstrong license; but the new corporation, operating under the name Zenith Radio Corporation, became the exclusive sales agent of the partnership. Later arrangements made it possible to merge the partnership into the new company; and with McDonald at its helm, Zenith began promotional activities that made the company and its product nationally well known.

McDonald's dynamic flair began to draw widespread public attention for Zenith in 1923. He organized and became the first president of the National Association of Broadcasters. When the United States Navy announced that its famed Arctic explorer, Donald B. MacMillan, planned a historic exploration of the Arctic in the summer of 1923, McDonald convinced MacMillan that the expedition could benefit from the installation of Zenith short-wave radio equipment on MacMillan's ship, the *Boudoin*. Short wave at that time was generally regarded as of no commercial value, but experiments proved that it was enormously superior to standard navy long-wave equipment, for which very long distance radio transmission and receiving were required. Also, long-wave apparatus worked satisfactorily only at night; and in the far north region of the Arctic, the expedition would encounter long periods of daylight during the summer.

For the benefit of the expedition, Zenith's station WJAZ in Chicago set up special news programs including messages from friends and families of men in the expedition. Broadcasts from WJAZ were picked up directly by the *Boudoin*. Return messages were picked up and relayed by enthusiastic youngsters from all parts of the country. The free publicity gained by Zenith as a result of these efforts spread from coast to coast, and its business grew steadily. In 1925, when the U.S. fleet scheduled a goodwill tour to Australia, McDonald persuaded Admiral McLean to install Zenith short-wave equipment on the U.S.S. *Seattle,* flagship of the fleet. Again, its great effectiveness in long distance communications was impressively demonstrated. In that same year, Admiral MacMillan selected McDonald to serve as second-in-command of the MacMillan–National Geographic expedition to the far north. When the expedition sailed, it left behind the heavy long-wave and receiving equipment installed by the navy. In its place McDonald had installed Zenith short-wave transmitting and receiving apparatus to provide continuous communications during the around-the-clock daylight of the Arctic summer that silenced standard long-wave navy equipment. The outstanding performance of the Zenith equipment in these navy ships resulted in the general use of short-wave communications equipment by the navy. The navies and merchant marines of the world soon followed suit.

While McDonald was busy with all this and other activity demonstrating the excellence of Zenith Radio's products and receiving national public attention, his command of the Zenith factory was not neglected. Intense loyalty to Zenith and the quality image of its products was carefully nurtured in and through his executive staff to factory workers at every level. "The Quality Goes In before the Name Goes On," still at the heart of Zenith's advertising, was not just an advertising slogan. It was impressed into the personnel almost as a religious vow by McDonald, who preached that quality was the most essential ingredient of every product bearing the Zenith name. He had a nearly fanatical belief that the public wanted quality merchandise and would loyally respond to any company that produced quality products. He also nurtured loyalty, pride, and devotion to duty in competent employees who were proud to become career members of the Zenith Pioneers Club.

McDonald set up a quality control system of unique effectiveness. He hired a former Marine as head of the Quality Control Department, who reported to him directly. McDonald gave him the authority to close down the plant if the plant manager attempted to ship receivers that did not meet Zenith's high standards. Every set had to be independently tested by Quality Control before shipment. Sales growth was burgeoning so fast that the demands for ever-increasing shipments strained the plant manager to the point at which quality workmanship could suffer from frantic efforts to ship in response to the Sales Department's demands that orders be filled to appease the pleas of Zenith distributors. On a number of occasions, McDonald's Quality Control Manager shut down the factory to prevent shipment of receivers that were below rigid test standards. The story circulated that McDonald would fire the Quality Control Manager if he even became friendly with the Factory Manager!

Frequently, McDonald would visit retail establishments in various parts of the country, pose as an ordinary customer, and buy a Zenith radio—which he would ship to the Engineering Department for careful examination. Any found not measuring up in every respect were traced to the workers who had produced them, and the cause of any defect in quality, however minor, was effectively eliminated.

There were many "firsts" produced by the Engineering and Research departments at Zenith through the 1920s. In 1926, Zenith produced the first radio receivers that did not need cumbersome and troublesome batteries, which marred the appearance of any household room. The new, attractive Zenith radio operated directly from AC electric outlets. Attractive cabinets housing Zenith radios became desirable household furniture as well as high quality receivers.

The following randomly selected letters McDonald wrote to Zenith distributors as early as 1925 illustrate his almost fanatical devotion to quality and his belief that the buying public wanted, deserved, and would buy Zenith quality products and would be as proud of owning them as the loyal Zenith employees were in producing them.

February 26, 1925

[Name of Individual Distributor]
Dear Mr. _____:

In this letter I shall attempt to cover three subjects—the Model X and the battery eliminator, the reason for your not getting more deliveries, and advertising. They are three subjects which normally would require separate letters but I shall roll them up into one.

Not a day passes that we do not receive protests from some of our distributors either by telegraph or long distance telephone because of insufficient deliveries. We know that most of you who are dealers get the same from your customers. Therefore, a word of explanation will not be amiss at this time.

Through the entire history of our company up to two years ago, our products for the summer months would be excellent. Yet the moment we started to push up production for fall and winter requirements, try as we would, the quality seemed to go down and the returns of imperfect goods increased. We then created at our factory, an Inspection Department, *not controlled by the factory.* An ex-Marine, Mr. G. B. Baca, was put in charge of this final Inspection Department. He was in no way responsible to the factory manager. He and his department were outside the factory manager's control. He had only one person to answer to—the writer of this letter. I create the standard—he maintains it. No matter how much we demand increased production from the factory, Mr. Baca and his department reject apparatus and refuse the stamp of approval until it has reached the desired standard.

It may startle you to know that our rejections of Super-Zeniths have run as high as 80 percent in a single day because the factory was trying to push up production too rapidly. The question of quantity, however, did not interest Mr. Baca and his department. He was concerned with only one thing—the standard of quality. It was his duty to reject imperfect apparatus and it would have been the same to him had he been obliged to reject all of the day's production.

We opened an additional factory last fall and while that helped considerably, we were not able to catch up with our orders. We are right now 29,000 Zeniths behind in our deliveries. From one standpoint it is a condition not to be proud of. We should like to be able to fill immediately every order on hand. We know that prompt service would increase the demand just so much more. It was gratifying to me, however, to receive the report at the end of January that of the entire output of the month, only 16 Zeniths had been returned because of imperfection.

While in New York last week I was told that one of our large competitors was obliged for fifteen days in January to stop manufacture for the purpose of rebuilding the great number of machines that had been returned because of imperfection. And I also know it to be a fact that another competitor's returns amounted to over 3,000 in the month of January.

To an opportunist the temptation would be strong to push up production rapidly, slight the quality and get the money while the season is on. But we are not opportunists. We are not in this business for just the present and for next year. We are building a name—a reputation—and it is our hope that we shall always be behind in our orders because of increased demand for quality product.

No doubt you are pointing out to those who have not yet received deliveries that they will be well repaid for waiting. We cannot build Supers as rapidly as 3Rs and 4Rs. We, therefore, impress upon you the need of selling 3Rs and 4Rs wherever you can. In districts away from the immediate vicinity of broadcasting stations, the Super-Zenith is not needed. We will deliver to you Super-Zeniths in direct proportion to the 3Rs and 4Rs that have been and are being sold to you. The Super-Zenith needs no salesmanship. But just because it is easy to sell, do not neglect the vast market for sets at the prices of the 3R and 4R—the vast 3R and 4R market existing in all sections that are not immediately influenced by broadcasting station.

Model X can be sold only at $475.00 because it will be without the battery eliminator. And here again I have opportunity to disclose to you more inside information on the Zenith policy. We have produced in our laboratory a battery eliminator that gave excellent results. We built ten of them. They were used in various parts of the country and were thoroughly satisfactory. We endorsed them fully and the order was issued to put these battery eliminators into production. We spent thousands of dollars advertising the Model X with the battery eliminator. Much to our disappointment, when the eliminators came through the factory they had the hum of the 60-cycle characteristic of all battery eliminators that have as yet appeared on the market. While the hum was not audible, in fact less than that of any other eliminator, we were fully aware it would distort the quality of reproduction and lessen the Zenith standard. Since these eliminators did not reach the high standard, we decided regardless of our investment not to put them on the market until they were right. Purchasers of the Model X can have it equipped with storage battery and battery charger. When then, the battery eliminator is perfected as we hope it will be sooner or later, you can furnish it to those customers because it will be built to fit the Model X.

With all good wishes, I am

> Cordially and sincerely yours,
> ZENITH RADIO CORPORATION
>
> E. F. McDonald, Jr.

EFM/F

June 6, 1925

[Name of Individual Distributor]
Gentlemen:

May we direct your attention to page 685 of the June 1925 issue of the *National Geographic* magazine?

It is a story of MacMillan's last expedition, told by this scientific publication, interspersed with the most wonderful collection of Arctic pictures ever gathered together.

In this article, MacMillan pays tribute to the merit and wonderful performance of Zenith on that expedition.

In passing, let me say that the prominent role Zenith so far played in the Arctic will be little in comparison with that to be assumed in the coming expedition. From the last MacMillan expedition, Zenith received five and one-half million lines of publicity. From the new expedition we confidently expect many times that enormous number of lines.

Because of the perfect performance of Zenith on the last MacMillan expedition, Commander MacMillan has again selected Zenith exclusively to get his messages back from the Frozen North where he will be in 24-hour daylight during the entire trip.

Unless all our calculations go awry, Zenith will add another chapter to radio history by transmitting from that far remote part of the world, over enormous distances, IN DAYLIGHT. That will be daring something which has never been attempted before. At this particular time the undertaking is fraught with considerable risk to our reputation, especially now that the eyes of the world are eagerly turned on the Arctic region in quest of Amundson from whom no message has come in several weeks. General interest in the Arctic will be more than usually intense when the spotlight is thrown on this new radio feat of ours.

We want you to profit by every word written on this new MacMillan Polar Expedition which sails from Boston June 17th.

Cordially yours,
ZENITH RADIO CORPORATION

E. F. McDonald, Jr.

EFM/F

BACKGROUND OF THE ZENITH CHALLENGE

While Zenith was struggling from a kitchen-table operation to a prominent position in the new radio industry during the early 1920s, a great pall of fear hung over the independent radio entrepreneurs. The fear of patent infringement attack by GE, Westinghouse, and AT&T through their radio patent enforcer, RCA, permeated the industry.

It is estimated that over 500 small, independent companies emerged in the United States as radio manufacturers during the early 1920s. Only a handful survived, mainly because—like Zenith—they had obtained a license under the patents of Edwin Armstrong before that great American inventor was persuaded to sell his patents to Westinghouse in 1920. This acquisition enabled Westinghouse to bargain its way into the GE–AT&T patent cartel whereby all the patents of all the parties were placed in a radio patent pool administered by a new company, the Radio Corporation of America, which was owned 60 percent by GE and 40 percent by Westinghouse. RCA was originally only a jointly held patent licensing cartel and sales company selling radios made by the joint owners, GE and Westinghouse, on a 60 percent–40 percent basis.

As will be explained later, the entire field of electrical apparatus was parceled out among the American cartel members. AT&T got control of wire communications, and GE and Westinghouse controlled the wireless or radio field operating through the jointly owned subsidiary, RCA. GE and Westinghouse were also assigned control over all electric power apparatus and all electrical industrial and railroad apparatus.

In the radio field, literally hundreds of patent infringement actions were threatened and/or filed by the GE, Westinghouse, AT&T patent trust. The potential competition of a vast number of independent entrepreneurs in the radio manufacturing business was ruthlessly eliminated. Luckily, the Armstrong license Zenith had obtained before Armstrong sold his patents to Westinghouse saved Zenith from the gigantic wave of patent attacks launched in the early 1920s.

Cries of conspiracy, monopoly, and restraint of trade were increasingly heard in Congress. GE's Owen D. Young and his cohorts decided to preempt the rising demand by emulating the licensing programs of European cartels. These programs provided manufacturing licenses to reputable independent competitors, which would quiet political cries of monopoly. Zenith was offered the first such license in 1927. A limited number of other successful independent manufacturers were given the same "privilege." The license, however, was financially burdensome; and not only was it crafted to give RCA a generous return on the sale price of every radio receiver sold, but it required the licensees to grant back to RCA any patent the licensees' research departments might develop or acquire. In addition, every development the licensee might be working on in the radio field was exposed to the scrutiny of RCA engineers.

The license fee was set at 7.5 percent of the sale price of the entire radio. All parts, including expensive cabinets, were included in the royalty base. The scheme made the licensees "riskless subsidiaries." RCA got a percentage of the selling price of every receiver, whether the licensee made or lost money or used any of the pooled patents.[1] The basic scheme proved to be diabolically clever and immensely profitable to RCA and its owners, GE and Westinghouse. The plan worked for the next thirty years before its illegality was finally exposed as a result of Zenith's litigation.

ZENITH DECLARES WAR ON THE RCA PATENT RACKET

In 1946, as Zenith was converting its wartime operations to consumer products, the company was again faced with paying expensive tribute to the RCA patent racket. Zenith's package license was, in effect, an agreement not to sue under the thousands of patents garnered into a frightening litigation weapon by RCA. The power of this worldwide patent monopoly lay not in the strength of any particular patent but in the threat of expensive, devastating infringement actions against any manufacturer who dared to refuse to sign the infamous RCA package license.

Zenith knew that the basic radio patents had all expired or were about to expire. RCA's patent package had been fed with thousands of "improvement" patents that were narrow in scope, of little importance, and most of highly questionable validity. Zenith's patent counsel advised that none of these patents be used in the company's postwar products. Zenith advised RCA that future licensing was no longer required. To David Sarnoff, head of RCA and the radio patent racket, this was an act of war.

Zenith's crusty founder, "Commander" McDonald, considered the package license scheme to be no different than garden-variety extortion. McDonald decided not only to fight the racket but to take the offensive, rather than await a patent attack. McDonald and his general counsel, Irving Herriott, retained a prestigious New York patent firm, Pennie, Edmonds, Morton, Barrows & Taylor, to represent Zenith in the impending patent war. That firm immediately brought an action in the Delaware federal court for a judgment against RCA, AT&T, Western Electric, GE, and Westinghouse, declaring that all the patents in the RCA package license were unenforceable because they were pooled by unlawful conspiracy. The intent of this conspiracy was to monopolize an industry in violation of antitrust laws.

The defendants filed answers and counterclaims alleging infringement of 40 patents in the RCA pool: 24 patents specified by RCA, 10 by Western Electric, and 6 by GE. The defendants began a legal war of attrition designed to break Zenith with crippling pretrial expenses in what are known as pretrial proceedings under the Federal Rules of Civil Procedure. The defendants filed a series of dilatory motions and began conducting pretrial discovery to fully occupy Zenith on purely technical and patent issues.

Pretrial conferences with the judge were held on these collateral matters, and briefs had to be prepared and filed. Written interrogatories were also filed, as well as demands to inspect relevant company files. All this time-consuming and very expensive diversionary activity cleverly sidetracked Zenith from the antitrust defense, the heart of its lawsuit. In a desperate move to open discovery on the antitrust defense—an issue that could make unnecessary all the technical patent issues—Zenith's patent counsel filed elaborate written interrogatories designed to force the defendants to admit their illegal activities. This tactic would reveal the worldwide conspiracy to monopolize patents, cartelize and divide up world markets, and apportion the fields of the electrical business in the United States among the defendants.

This radical discovery move brought on a fateful pretrial conference with Chief Judge Leahy of the Delaware federal trial court. The judge handed down a ruling that was devastating to Zenith. A copy of Judge Leahy's fatal ruling is set out in Appendix II.

The truly back-breaking burden imposed by the court at the defendants' suggestion was the requirement in the last paragraph of the opinion that there be forty full-scale trials on at least forty patents then being asserted by defendants *before* any consideration of the antitrust claims could be heard. A final judicial determination of the highly technical issues of validity and infringement of forty patents would require tremendous time and resources. In addition, new patents were issuing almost daily to the cartel's patent acquisitions departments and could be continuously added to the case. Leahy's ruling would coerce any sensible company to surrender and sign the RCA package license.

Judge Leahy's ruling brought memories of Charles Dickens's classic description of endless litigation in England during the last century:

This is the Court of Chancery: . . . which gives to monied might the means abundantly of wearing out the right; which so exhausts finances, patience, courage, hope, so over-throws the brain and breaks the heart that there is not an honorable man among its practitioners who would not give—who does not often give the warning, "suffer any wrong that can be done you rather than come here." (*Bleak House,* p. 2)

Zenith's legendary founder, "Commander" McDonald, was a fighter. He hired Joseph S. Wright, an able and highly respected lawyer at the Federal Trade Commission in Washington, D.C., for the next round. Wright had been elevated to head an important new division of the General Counsel's office at the Commission shortly after World War II. His Division of Compliance was charged with policing compliance with Trade Commission cease and desist orders. Congress had set up the Federal Trade Commission in 1914 as a bipartisan law enforcement body to stop unfair methods of competition and unfair and deceptive acts and practices. The Commission had successfully attacked monopoly, price fixing, and other restraints of trade in important industries. Wright was the government's bulldog, and Zenith needed a man with bite.

From 1948 to 1952, fresh from World War II military service and graduate courses in trade regulation and federal procedure at Georgetown University Law School, I had worked under Joe Wright on many cases and had been in charge as a "straw boss" of his antitrust section of the Division of Compliance. Several months after Wright took the position with Zenith in Chicago, he came through Washington. While visiting old friends at the Commission, he mentioned to me that if I was interested he could use my services in a life-and-death legal struggle Zenith was having with the RCA Radio Trust. Joe had been a valued mentor to me at the Commission, and I was intrigued with his enthusiastic general description of the struggle between Zenith and RCA. I had been planning to leave the Commission anyway after four years of interesting work.[2] Out of curiosity and a desire to work for Wright again on what seemed to be an intriguing case,[3] I went to Chicago at Wright's invitation and met "Commander" McDonald and his General Counsel, Irving Herriott. They hired me as an assistant to Wright, and I reported for duty in February 1953.

Joe Wright introduced me around in the Zenith headquarters offices and we met with Irving Herriott in his Chicago Loop law offices. Here we gloomily reviewed the "death sentence" Judge Leahy had pronounced in his opinion in the Delaware federal court, and we briefly discussed two possible moves to escape the Delaware trap. The potential escape hatches were as follows:

1. Make desperate attempt to have the Court of Appeals issue an "extraordinary writ" forcing Judge Leahy to allow Zenith to proceed immediately

with its antitrust claim. As will be noted, the odds on winning this were conservatively over 100 to 1—hardly worth the effort.

2. Try to break loose in an additional patent case RCA had filed against Zenith and Rauland in Chicago in 1948. The case was designed to punish Zenith for buying a radio tube manufacturer, Rauland, to ensure a supply of tubes to Zenith if RCA attempted to cut off the supply and thus close down the Zenith plants.

Wright gave me a general assignment to study the litigation files at Zenith; visit with the Patent Department head, Frank Crotty, and the Foreign Department; and come up with suggestions. Meanwhile, I worked with Wright on the futile task of petitioning the Third Circuit Court of Appeals to rectify Judge Leahy's "abuse of discretion." This latter effort was doomed to failure because the Leahy order was not appealable and because an extraordinary writ of mandamus is rarely issued by appellate courts—and then only where a trial judge has grossly prejudiced a litigant by depriving him of a right the law clearly gives him. Judge Leahy had cleverly put Zenith's antitrust issues on a timetable behind all the patent issues; ostensibly he did not attempt to eliminate them, RCA argued. The Court of Appeals, as expected, summarily dismissed the Zenith petition as an attempt to appeal from an "unappealable interlocutory order" (i.e., one made during pretrial proceedings). Any alleged erroneous deprivation of rights that might occur prior to and during trial would be reviewable after the trial.

In reviewing the Chicago case files, it appeared that RCA's David Sarnoff had attacked Zenith and Rauland with a raft of tube patents, which had not been asserted in Delaware. The infringement case had been filed in Chicago in 1948 against both Rauland and Zenith within 24 hours after Zenith acquired the Rauland stock. It vindictively opened a second front, so to speak, that would further help bleed Zenith to death. Ironically, at the time RCA filed the case, Zenith's lawyers had sought to have the Chicago case moved to Delaware. Fortunately, RCA vigorously opposed this effort and Judge Leahy had effectively ruled in their favor! In hindsight, some higher power appeared to have rescued McDonald from what turned out to be the folly of his lawyers. The Chicago suit eventually provided an escape hatch from destruction in the Delaware litigation.

There was only one major problem with the posture of the Chicago case: the antitrust issues were framed there precisely in the form in which they were framed in Delaware. How could the Chicago court be persuaded to disagree with Judge Leahy and the Court of Appeals for the Third Circuit? That was the legal problem that had to be solved if Zenith was to survive.

The patent lawyers were working on an amendment to Zenith's Chicago pleadings aimed at shoring up and emphasizing the patent misuse and antitrust aspects by shaping them more effectively as grounds for injunctive relief against RCA's assertion of its illegal package license. Burton K. Wheeler's partner, George Herman,[4] had prepared a proposed 172-page brief outlining the nature and scope of the alleged conspiracy. From public records; congressional, FTC, and FCC hearings; and other public sources he had garnered evidentiary materials indicating the criminal conspiracy Zenith was challenging. No antitrust discovery proceedings had yet been attempted. But Herman's admirable effort was premature until the Chicago court either overruled Leahy or recognized that the Zenith case in Chicago was somehow different from the Delaware case and could therefore go forward simultaneously with the Delaware litigation.

By early April 1953, I had met and talked with almost everyone in the company having knowledge of any aspects of the RCA litigation.[5] In my search for ideas that might help resolve our litigation quandary, I spent a great deal of time talking with John Miguel, the courtly head of Zenith's Foreign Department. He helped me locate files that graphically showed how Zenith had been shut out of foreign markets by a number of foreign patent pools similar to RCA's American pool, which was at the heart of our litigation in Delaware and Chicago. In particular, I was shocked at how Zenith had been shut out of a lucrative Canadian market where demand for its product was high. Miguel told me that Zenith was foreclosed from shipments to Canada on account of a Canadian patent pool the patent lawyers felt helpless to combat, because of the Canadian patent law and the position of the Canadian pool that licenses for importation could not be issued without jeopardizing their Canadian patents. On April 24, 1953, I wrote the following memorandum to Mr. Wright advising him of my limited inquiry into the matter:

April 24, 1953

To: Mr. Wright   Re: *The Canadian Patent Pools*

Information contained in Zenith files indicates that certain dominant American companies in the radio and electronic field, operating through foreign subsidiaries, have by concerted action effectively closed the

Canadian border to imports by Zenith and other American manufacturers and excluded Zenith from what appears to be a very lucrative market in Canada. This concerted action, although taken in foreign territory, would appear to be flagrantly violative of the Sherman Law and redressable in any federal court where jurisdiction of the parties can be obtained.

My brief study of the matter indicates the following:

In recent years management has made efforts to get into the Canadian market but has been met in every instance by a blockade of patents concertedly set up in the form of a patent pool operated by Canadian Radio Patents Limited, an organization apparently controlled by the dominant American Electrical Companies operating through Canadian subsidiaries. Licenses available from the pool are strictly conditioned upon manufacture within Canada. Imports from the United States have been effectively prohibited by the pool.

In addition to various memoranda and letters relating to the subject, the files contain copies of three published reports, Report of "The Tariff Board" Reference Number 104—Radio Industry, dated April 21, 1939, a Department of Commerce bulletin on the Canadian radio market dated October 3, 1939, and a Report of the Commissioner, Combines Investigation Act, dated October 10, 1945, and entitled "Canada and International Cartels."

[The lengthy excerpts from these reports are omitted here. They were included in the memo to indicate that the American Radio cartel was in full control of the Canadian business through a jointly owned patent pool that blocked imports from the United States and resulted in monopoly prices for radios in Canada.]

Zenith has from time to time communicated with Radio Patents Limited in an endeavor to find a way into the Canadian market. Replies from the pool have made it clear that exports from the United States will not be permitted and any license available to Zenith would require manufacture within Canada. The latest letter from the pool in the file is dated January 17, 1952, signed by S. D. Brownley, Secretary-Treasurer, which states in part:

The Canadian patents (covered by a license) listed in Schedule "A" are those covering inventions originating with such companies as General Electric, Westinghouse, Northern Electric, Marconi, Rogers (including Philips), RCA, and certain patents owned by CRPL. We also have the right to extend licenses under the Canadian patents of Philco and Hazeltine. . . .

An earlier letter from the pool, dated December 4, 1951, describes the pool and its licensing activities as follows:

CRPL is a central patent licensing agency administering patents in the field of radio and television receivers and other electronic equipment covering inventions originating with such companies as RCA, General Electric, Northern Electric, Canadian Marconi, Westinghouse, Rogers Majestic (including Philips), Philco, Hazeltine Corporation, and others.

Canadian Radio Patents Limited has issued licenses to all applicants wishing to manufacture radio or television receivers under the patents administered by CRPL in accordance with the requirements of the Canadian Patent Act with respect to manufacture of the patented product in Canada.

The companies presently licensed by Canadian Radio Patents Limited are currently manufacturing radio and television receivers in Canada in quantities ample to meet the public demand. In fact, manufacturers' inventories of radio and television receivers as published by the Dominion Bureau of Statistics indicate that Canadian production is far in excess of present demand.

Canadian Radio Patents Limited is willing to grant licenses to any further applicants wishing to manufacture radio and television receivers in Canada in accordance with the requirements of the Canadian Patent Act under the patents administered by it but, in protection of its own rights and those of its licensees, it is prepared to take action against receivers offered for sale in this country that are an infringement of the patents administered by it and are not manufactured in Canada by its licensees.

The letter also refers to a general notice to the trade which the pool publishes as a warning to all concerned that only the companies listed in the notice are licensed in Canada and that the pool will take legal action against importers, vendors, purchasers, or users of receivers which the pool considers infringe any of the pooled patents. This is obviously a bold ultimatum to the effect that distributors and purchasers must do business with companies listed on the notice or face harassment and litigation. Copies of similar notices had been obtained from the pool in 1950.

Another letter from the pool dated September 12, 1951, refers to a revision of the license to include RCA and Philco patents:

Although our licensees are covered under the RCA Canadian Patents and also those of Philco, neither of these groups were included in the Schedule "A" as originally printed. However, as previously indicated, the coverage offered to our licensees is all of the present and future patents in these fields covering inventions originating with such companies as RCA, General Electric, Westinghouse, Northern Electric (Western), Marconi, Rogers (including Philips), Philco, Hazeltine and certain patents that have been purchased of various inventors and companies by Canadian Radio Patents Limited.

Three prior letters from the pool dated September 6, 1951, December 5, 1950, and December 15, 1950, also set forth the terms and conditions under which the pool would be willing to grant a license to Zenith. In the December 15 letter, it is stated that a license would include television receivers.

I have discussed this matter at length with Mr. Miguel and he informed me that many requests for Zenith radio and television products have been received from Canadian dealers, but that Canadian Radio Patents Limited has effectively prevented Zenith from exporting to Canada. Early in 1951, Consolidated Industries Ltd., a Winnipeg distributor of electric appliances, obtained a Zenith distributor franchise. After stocking Zenith radio products and advertising, however, Canadian Radio Patents Limited, by threatening suit for infringement, forced Consolidated to discontinue handling Zenith products.

Although the present structure of Canadian Radio Patents Limited and Thermionics Limited is not definitely known to us, it is reasonable to surmise "the Radio Group," RCA and its American co-conspirators, armed with their patent monopoly, are in full command of the radio industry in Canada and are the authors of the restrictive arrangements which wall Canada against American imports.

Unless it can somehow be validly argued that American law is not applicable to this situation or that the Canadian Patent Act requires the patent pool to refuse to license importers, those activities appear to disclose a combination in total restraint of foreign commerce with Canada well within the interdiction of Section 1 of the Sherman Act. That the antitrust laws are applicable to restraints upon foreign commerce imposed by American companies abroad seems reasonably well settled. "Acts abroad affecting either our international trade or domestic economy, if violating any of the trade regulatory laws of the United States, may be enjoined and the offenders prosecuted in this country." 3 Toulmin's Antitrust Laws, page 160, citing *U.S. v. General Dyestuff Corp.*, 57 F.Supp. 642; *U.S. v. Hamburg*, (CCA 2) 200 Fed. 806, 216 Fed. 971, reversed on other grounds, 239 U.S. 466, 36 S.Ct. 212, 60 L.Ed. 387; *U.S. v. Pacific & Arctic Ry.*, 228 U.S. 87, 33 S.Ct. 443, 57 L.Ed. 742; *Thomson v. Cayser*, 243 U.S. 66, 37 S.Ct. 353, 61 L.Ed. 597; *U.S. v. Aluminum Co. of America*, (CCA 2) 148 F.2d 416; *U.S. v. General Electric Co.*, (DC N.Y.) 40 F.Supp. 627; *U.S. v. National Lead Co.*, (DC N.Y.) 63 F.Supp. 513, affirmed and modified, 332 U.S. 319, 67 S.Ct. 1643, 91 L.Ed. 2077; *U.S. v. Sisal Sales Corp.*, 274 U.S. 268, 47 S.Ct. 592, 71 L.Ed. 1042; *U.S. v. B. C. Knight Co.*, 156 U.S. 1, 15 S.Ct. 249, 39 L.Ed. 325; *U.S. v. New York Coffee & Sugar Exchange*, 263 U.S. 611, 44 S.Ct. 225, 68 L.Ed. 475; *U.S. v. Bausch & Lomb*, (DC N.Y.) 34 F.Supp. 267; *U.S. v. Allied Chemical & Dye Corp.*, (DC N.Y.) 42 F.Supp. 425; *DeBeers Consolidated Mines, Ltd., et al. v. U.S.*, 325 U.S. 212, 65 S.Ct. 1130, 89 L.Ed. 1566.

In *Branch v. Federal Trade Commission*, 141 F.2d 31, 35, Mr. Justice Minton, while sitting as Circuit Judge in the Court of Appeals for the Seventh Circuit, referred to this principle as follows:

... If that commerce (foreign commerce) was being defiled by a resident of the United States to the disadvantage of other competing citizens of the United States, the United States had a right to protect such commerce from defilement, even though the customer who is the victim of such a defilement and a non-resident may look to his sovereign for protection. For protection of the competitors within the United States, the United States is the sovereign to look to. The right of the United States to control the conduct of its citizens in foreign countries in respect to matters which a sovereign ordinarily governs within its own territorial jurisdiction has been recognized repeatedly. *Blackmer v. United States,* 284 U.S. 421, 436–438, 52 S.Ct. 252, 76 L.Ed. 375; *Cook v. Tait,* 265 U.S. 47, 54–56, 44 S.Ct. 444, 68 L.Ed. 895. Congress has the power to prevent unfair trade practices in foreign commerce by citizens of the United States, although some of the acts are done outside the territorial limits of the United States.

Examination of the standard license agreement of Canadian Radio Patents Limited indicates that the restrictive condition prohibiting importation will probably be defended as being a reasonable restraint required by the Canadian Patent Law. Under the so-called "working provisions" of the Canadian Patent Act, Section 65, et seq., if a patentee has abused his patent rights in specified ways the Commissioner of Patents is empowered to grant an applicant the right to work the invention or may revoke the patent if necessary to prevent the abuse. Among the abuses listed are: (a) failure to work the invention in Canada; (b) importation to the detriment of its working in Canada. Section 65(2)(b) provides that this importation into Canada of a patented article in sufficient quantities to meet the demand in Canada is not a working of the patent. Importation appears to be considered as an abuse, however, only where it prevents or substantially hinders the working of an invention within Canada. To interpret these provisions as requiring that no importer can be licensed under a Canadian patent seems unreasonable. There is nothing in the Patent Act to support such a startling argument. Certainly it is not the policy of the Canadian Government to prevent the sale of American goods in Canada. It cannot be said with any degree of conviction that to allow importation into Canada by Zenith under a license would constitute an abuse of Canadian patent rights under Section 65 of the Patent Act.

There is a strong likelihood, in my opinion, that we can establish that the Canadian patent pools are controlled by RCA, General Electric, Western Electric, Westinghouse, and the American Telephone and Telegraph

Company and constitute a combination in restraint of foreign commerce within Section 1 of the Sherman Law; that as a direct result of the conspiracy, Zenith is being excluded from the Canadian market and is entitled to treble damages and injunctive relief which could be appropriately sought by supplemental pleading in the Chicago suit.

In accordance with your instructions, full information on the structure and operation of the Canadian patent pools will be obtained in Canada.

P. J. Curtis

PJC:mw

There was no mention in either the Delaware or Chicago cases of Zenith's commerce with Canada being in any way restrained by the conspiracy. If we filed an orthodox antitrust case in Chicago seeking damages and injunctive relief, RCA and its cohorts could not claim it was in the Delaware suit. We could, therefore, proceed in Chicago to try all the antitrust issues, thus avoiding the patent morass that had us fatally pinned down in Delaware.

Joe Wright responded to my memo with his characteristic speed, decisiveness, and enthusiasm. He sent me to Ottawa (1) to confirm from the public records of the patent pool that GE, RCA, and the others were running the Canadian cartel, and (2) to research the Canadian Patent Act claim of the pool that they could not license imports from the United States without forfeiting their patents under Canadian law. In Ottawa I found that the shareholders of the pool were still the members of the American Radio Group (as they were known in foreign cartel circles) and that the legislative history of the Canadian Patent Act and other legal authorities strongly supported our feeling that the Canadian Patent Act defense was a clever hoax that could not stand up in court.

After I returned to Chicago from Canada, Joe Wright and I discussed the matter with Herriott and our eastern counsel. We were met with a cool reception—which was certainly understandable, because the Zenith lawyers had been pursuing the "patent misuse" defense for over seven years in both the Delaware and Chicago cases. Although it wasn't said, I could see that to inject in the Chicago case at this late date an orthodox antitrust action claiming a conspiracy to shut Zenith out of Canada and other markets added on to the charges of patent conspiracy to monopolize the U.S. market could be viewed as a desperation move by Zenith lawyers, whose failure for over seven years to even mention such a cause of action for damages was enough to expose it as a specious afterthought. The Rip Van Winkle seven-year sleep might never be credibly explained or excused as an oversight.

Herriott seemed to reflect this dilemma when he posed several questions to me: "When you are in Canada, doesn't Canadian law govern you?" and "Haven't you read the *American Banana* case?"[6] The questions indicated to me that my memo and Wright's position on the matter had received some defensive research attention in our New York patent counsels' offices. My answer was the cases cited in my memo and in a second memo written after my trip to Canada.[7] Some confusion in our patent lawyers' offices apparently was caused by the fundamental rule that the legality of any act or conduct is determined by the law of the place where it occurs. Illegal gambling in Illinois is legal when done in Nevada, for example. That is plain common sense. But where companies doing business in the United States, under the privileges and protections afforded by our laws, conspire in Canada or other countries to restrain or prevent exports from the United States to such foreign markets, our foreign commerce is adversely affected; the Sherman Act is obviously violated by such conspiracies to restrain our shipments from the United States to foreign markets.

There is a logical exception to that rule where a foreign government orders such conduct. There it is said to be caused by foreign government compulsion—the exception the Canadian Patent Pool was deceptively trying to use as a cover for its illegal blockade of imports from the United States. That exception was recognized in the *American Banana* case Herriott had mentioned to me. It was not applicable to Zenith's case. Neither the Canadian Patent Act nor the Canadian government had compelled the pool's blockade of Zenith's shipments to Canada. That pool had been created by agreements between GE, AT&T affiliates, RCA, and others. It therefore was our position (Wright's and mine) that Zenith could sue for treble damages and an injunction under the antitrust laws.

The matter of how to break loose in the Chicago case from the "death sentence" Judge Leahy had imposed on our antitrust case in Delaware was the subject of a key meeting of Zenith counsel in Herriott's Chicago office on June 24, 1953, prior to an important pretrial conference in the Chicago court scheduled for the following day. Present in Herriott's office were the chief Zenith patent counsel from New York, Willis Taylor and R. Morton Adams; their Washington advisory counsel, Burton K. Wheeler and George Herman; and Joe Wright, Francis Crotty (head of Zenith's Patent Department), and me.

Wright made a persuasive pitch for filing a draft we had prepared of an orthodox antitrust pleading, with a jury demand, seeking damages for Zenith's exclusion from Canada and other foreign markets added on to the injunctive relief from the "package licensing" assault against Zenith that was already requested in both the Delaware and Chicago patent suits. This radical proposal was met with a polite, cool, condescending reception, understandably created by the embarrassing fact that the litigations were now over six years old and the radically "new" case might appear to be nothing but a specious, desperate afterthought concocted to escape Judge Leahy's ruling in Delaware.

The solemn meeting ended with a painful decision by Herriott: "Gentlemen, we are walking on eggs. Let's just file tomorrow our more detailed pleading amending our Chicago pleading and argue that this is what we thought we had pleaded in Delaware, but Judge Leahy did not see it in our inadequate pleading there. Then we will ask Judge Igoe to let us go forward here with the antitrust issues."

At 9:00 A.M. on the following day, June 25, 1953, we all assembled in Judge Igoe's conference room adjoining his chambers in the old Chicago Federal Court House. We encountered our opposition in the anteroom before the conference; Herriott served on RCA's counsel, John T. Cahill, accompanied by his right-hand partner in the case, John E. Nields, our patent counsel's "new" amendment to our Chicago pleadings.

Counsel assembled around a long conference table with Judge Igoe, in his black robes, at one end and an impeccably dressed Herriott at the other end. Judge Michael Igoe was not an Oliver Wendell Holmes–type of judge. His wisdom was not in the world of academe but in the area of common-sense justice. Short in stature, his appearance was dominated by an Irish face and perceptive eyes that could smile with favor on an advocate with an honorable cause or wither with outrage any lawyer he perceived to be attempting to deceive him with a meritless argument. His white hair contrasting with his black robe set him off as a dignified, very fair jurist. Before his appointment to the bench, he had been an active U.S. attorney for the federal district encompassing Chicago, officially designated as the Northern District of Illinois, Eastern Division.

The meeting opened with Herriott graciously arguing that he had served and was filing an amendment to Zenith's pleadings, setting out in more detail what he thought Zenith had pleaded in the Delaware patent case. He made a plea that Zenith's antitrust issues should go forward here because they had been indefinitely deferred until after the radio set patent issues were tried in Delaware. RCA had brought the radio tube patent infringement case here and, he argued, Zenith's antitrust defense and suit for injunctive relief here would dispose of both cases.

Cahill stood up in a pose of righteous indignation. Waving the new amendment Herriott had just served on him, he declared with outrage:

I have just read this new pleading. It is nothing but a rehash of everything Chief Judge Leahy and the Court of Appeals have disposed of in Delaware in a very orderly and fair way. Mr. Herriott is attempting to have your honor overrule Chief Judge Leahy and the Court of Appeals for the Third Circuit. We have had no notice until this morning that any such outrageous move was to be attempted here. This case should be stayed until Judge Leahy tries the case in Delaware. Then only the tube patent infringement case will remain here. The burdensome, concocted antitrust defense will be disposed of in Delaware in the orderly manner Judge Leahy has ruled it should be.

Judge Igoe turned a withering stare on Herriott and lectured him along the following lines:

You are mistaken if you think you can persuade me to overrule Judge Leahy. I have no such authority and quite frankly I have read Judge Leahy's opinion and I agree with what he proposes to do. This case is not going forward until the antitrust issues in Delaware are disposed of.

The conference had only been in session for about thirty minutes or less, and the judge curtly asked, "What else do you have, Mr. Herriott?" In a state of shock, Herriott explained that his only purpose was to move the court to allow Zenith to go forward with its antitrust issues. He ended with an unfortunate remark: "I will file our amendment in the Clerk's office after this conference." Cahill, gloating with his "righteous" indignation now vindicated, complained that he had been dragged from his busy schedule in New York to this conference only to find that its sole purpose was to give him another pleading that duplicated the Delaware Zenith pleadings.

Judge Igoe gave Herriott a final lecture:

You don't have to file this thing in the Clerk's office. You have filed it with me and served it on Mr. Cahill. I have as much right as the clerk has to accept your filing. I have set this whole day aside at your request only to find that you want me to overrule Judge Leahy, which I am neither empowered nor inclined to do.[8]

We all filed silently out of the conference room and the Court House. Out-of-town counsel caught cabs for the airport; Wright, Crotty, and I walked with Herriott to the corner of LaSalle and Adams by the old Rookery Building, where we parted—Herriott walking to his LaSalle Street office and Wright, Crotty, and I walking to our car in a parking lot one block further west on Adams Street.

Herriott was leaving later in the day for a vacation with McDonald at the Commander's fishing lodge in Canada. Before we left him, I noticed how ashen and ill he looked. The last thing I recall him saying to us as he looked at the gray sky over the Board of Trade building at the south end of LaSalle Street is, "God, what can I tell the Commander about this?" We wished him a restful vacation and went back to Zenith in a state of disappointment bordering on despair. That was the last time I saw Herriott alive. He spent his vacation with McDonald at the Commander's fishing lodge in Canada, came home at the end of the summer, fell ill, was hospitalized, and died in November 1953.

Within two months of Herriott's death, Wright, newly appointed as Vice President and General Counsel, retained Thomas C. McConnell as trial counsel for Zenith in the Chicago case. His entry as additional counsel in a case that was stayed indefinitely until completion of the Delaware litigation was a routine matter of no noticeable significance at the moment except to those who knew McConnell as a fearless, brilliant trial lawyer. Within days of his retention, however, Zenith was able to break loose from the deadly hold the RCA–GE conspirators had imposed on its antitrust case in both the Chicago and Delaware courts.

A NEW FRONT IS OPENED IN CHICAGO

On February 11, 1954, Wright and I met with Tom McConnell in his office at 134 South LaSalle Street in Chicago. After reviewing the "miserable state of affairs" that had befallen our antitrust case, we went over the draft of our proposed pleading—the one Herriott had refused to file. It was a draft of the new orthodox antitrust conspiracy action for treble damages for Zenith's exclusion from Canada and other foreign markets and for the expenses incurred by Zenith as a result of the unlawful patent package license scheme RCA and its co-conspirators had employed against us.

Tom McConnell had no difficulty in quickly understanding and agreeing with what Wright and I had been unable to persuade Herriott and the New York patent counsel to do in the Chicago suit. He called in his secretary, and that very same day our draft was put in final form with cross-claims against GE and Western Electric. Late that afternoon, the new pleadings with a jury demand were served on RCA, GE, and Western Electric and were filed as an amended counterclaim in the Chicago case.

All hell broke loose in the enemy camp after the pleadings had been served and filed. The New York legal brigade representing RCA, General Electric, and Western Electric attacked the new pleadings with a desperate fury. There was John T. Cahill and John Nields of Cahill, Gordon, Reindell & Ohls representing RCA; Whitney North Seymour of Simpson, Thatcher & Bartlett representing General Electric; and Dewey, Ballantine partners entering appearances for Western Electric. All were among the most prestigious old-line New York law firms. Seymour had been president of the American Bar Association. Thomas E. Dewey, the Republican candidate for the presidency in 1948, headed the firm representing Western Electric. Top Chicago firms were also added to the brigade. There was Weymouth Kirkland of Kirkland, Green, Martin & Ellis, the *Chicago Tribune*'s well-known counsel, appearing for RCA. His firm was perhaps the most prominent in Chicago. Western Electric named Sidley & Austin, a leading Chicago firm, as its counsel. Walter Cummings, a prominent partner in the firm and son of the head of one of Chicago's big banks, was the partner in charge of the case. Hamilton K. Beebe and Cyrus Mead III were retained as additional Chicago counsel for General Electric; and RCA added to its Chicago counsel Johnston, Thompson, Raymond, Mayer & Jenner with partner Thompson, a former Illinois Supreme Court Justice, their lead Chicago counsel.

This impressive crew filed motions frantically opposing the filing of our antitrust case. Pleas were made to dismiss it on every grounds imaginable. At hearings before Judge Igoe, Tom McConnell branded our opposition as a coterie of New York lawyers attempting to overpower and deceive our Chicago court with high-powered trickery designed to prevent trial of our lawsuit on its merits. "If it's never tried on the merits, that will be too soon for them," McConnell said, "because they have no respectable defense to the conspiracy charges."

Their attempt to dismiss our new pleadings was rejected by Judge Igoe. After their answers to our pleadings were filed, we moved the court to lift the stay on the proceedings the judge had imposed at the

June 26, 1953, hearing at which Herriott's plea to proceed had been rejected. On June 15, 1954, after a hearing on our motion, Judge Igoe ordered that the new case could proceed immediately under the Federal Rules of Civil Procedure. Frantically, counsel for RCA and GE filed in the court of appeals an elaborate petition for a writ of mandamus directing Judge Igoe to vacate his order of June 15, 1954, allowing the case to proceed, and further directing him to stay the Chicago case until the Delaware litigation was determined. Elaborate briefs were filed and an impassioned oral argument was held before a panel of three federal appeals court judges: Major, Finnegan, and Schnackenberg.

The court of appeals reviewed the history of the Delaware and Chicago cases in an illuminating opinion (217 F.2d 218) written by Judge Schnackenberg for a unanimous court. After referring pointedly to the fact that RCA itself had filed the patent infringement suit in Chicago against Zenith and its tube-making subsidiary, Rauland, two years after the Delaware patent suit was at issue, the court further noted that RCA had successfully blocked the early efforts of both Zenith and Rauland to move the Chicago suit to Delaware and then had persuaded the Chicago court to stay that action until the Delaware litigation was concluded. Then, the court observed, after Zenith and Rauland had filed new counterclaims in Chicago asserting antitrust treble-damages issues not raised in Delaware, RCA reversed its previous position that the whole controversy was in Delaware and attacked the Chicago judge for allowing the new action to proceed in accordance with the Federal Rules of Civil Procedure. The Court of Appeals flatly held that Judge Igoe had properly ruled on the matter and that the attempt to get the appellate court to order him to stay the Chicago suit was an obviously improper effort to delay the case by appealing from an unappealable order.

Judge Finnegan wrote a withering concurring opinion in which he lambasted the distinguished array of counsel for RCA, General Electric, and Western Electric for using a petition for a writ of mandamus, an extraordinary writ, to punish the trial judge for not ruling in their favor. The petition, Judge Finnegan said, made Judge Igoe a defendant in the appellate court—a great burden on a trial judge. The court called their petition a "vehicle for delay" and their arrogant stance before Judge Igoe an ultimatum to the judge: "Rule sympathetically, else plead forthwith as a respondent." Judge Finnegan further noted that RCA's argument in the Delaware case was a "standing refutation of that which they sought before us" (1974 CCH Trade Cases 67,886–67,887).

It was a resounding victory for Zenith. The deadly grip RCA, GE, and Western Electric had on Zenith in Delaware had been finally broken in the Chicago action—a litigation RCA itself had filed in 1948 to punish Zenith for assuring itself of a tube supply source other than RCA by acquiring the Rauland tube plant in Chicago. In retrospect, the fateful failure of Zenith's patent counsel in 1948 to have the Chicago suit moved to Delaware had proved to be a blessing in disguise. Had not RCA been so successful in opposing that Zenith blunder, our escape path would have been cut off by our own counsel.

The importance of their defeat inspired the prestigious array of counsel for RCA, GE, and Western Electric to make a final move in the Supreme Court for salvation from having to face the antitrust conspiracy charges head-on. They retained Adlai Stevenson, the prominent titular head of the Democratic Party who had run for president against Eisenhower in 1952. Stevenson was a lawyer but had to be admitted to practice before the Supreme Court before he could lead the new charge there. The embarrassment of the matter reached the press when Stevenson, after admission to practice in the Supreme Court, filed an emergency motion there to stay the Chicago case while a further petition to have the Supreme Court review the court of appeals holding could be prepared. The motion for a temporary stay came before Justice Minton and was promptly denied. The subsequent petition that the Court agree to review the matter by issuing a so-called writ of certiorari was also denied by the Court.

These desperate moves signaled the importance of the case, and the press began to cover the story prominently. In some accounts it was noted that RCA, GE, and Western Electric now had retained both Republican Dewey and Democrat Stevenson to help the already prestigious array of counsel against lonesome Zenith. It was a David and Goliath scene. The best talent, political as well as legal, that money could buy had been arrayed against Zenith to no avail.

However, in one sense Zenith's victory was no more than a permit to undertake an enormous task—prying out of RCA, GE, and Western Electric and their co-conspirators documentary and other evidence that would be admissible at a trial to prove the alleged gigantic conspiracy. All the processes of the court were now available to Zenith in this undertaking. But time was of the essence. The controversy was now going on eight years old, had drained Zenith financially, and not one iota of evidence on the antitrust issues had yet been adduced in the case!

We started by having issued under the Federal Rules comprehensive demands and subpoenas for documents from our opponents' files, interrogatories, and notices for the examination of witnesses under oath. As expected, every move was met with attempted delays and withholding of evidence on every conceivable technical grounds. A few examples will illustrate the wearisome ordeal we continuously encountered until the case was finally settled in September 1957. It was a three-year nightmare requiring persistent hard work, numerous hearings, preparation of briefs, and patient cross-examination of hostile witnesses, all carefully coached and afflicted with memory problems. The coaching appeared to be along traditional lines: "Do not volunteer anything—do not answer any question unless you, the witness, have direct personal knowledge of the answer as recorded in some document that is or may be presented to you—Anything else you may think you know is hearsay and is inadmissible and not to be divulged in any answer under oath." That such instructions were probably given became obvious throughout the depositions.

The document production by RCA illustrated the difficulty expected and to a sufficient degree overcome in the main with the help of the trial court. Our demands for relevant documents in the RCA files covering the period of the conspiracy from 1919 to the date of our counterclaim and beyond was also met with what is known in the trade as "sandbagging" and "the wallpaper treatment." The army of counsel "screening" documents to be produced (or not produced, for "legal reasons") seemed to have been given standing orders: "Swamp them with plenty of nothing until they give up in exhaustion and despair."

One of our first memorable encounters with this strategy was in New York when we were examining documents from RCA's files. I undertook this assignment with Frank Crotty, head of the Patent Department at Zenith, who had a good general knowledge of RCA history and was a careful, perceptive examiner of corporate files. We received a message from RCA counsel that their documents would be produced in a hotel room on Third Avenue in New York and *not* at RCA's headquarters at Rockefeller Plaza, where the files were being screened by a brigade of RCA "legal screeners." When we entered the Third Avenue hotel and viewed the document room, we immediately became aware of the game RCA was playing.

The hotel itself was an ancient Third Avenue fleabag, so to speak. The room was apparently a less-expensive back room that had not been cleaned or decorated for human habitation for many, many years. There was a small window covered with years of New York grime and jammed shut so that we could not open it. Hanging from the center of the ceiling on a black, twisted cord was an original light fixture that must have been installed when the building was first built. The large light bulb looked like the type Edison first produced. It had a pointed drip tip on the bottom. I remember having seen one like it in the basement of my great-grandmother's house when I was about 8 years old. My great-grandmother had kept it as a conversation piece until it finally burned out.

The document room had the sepulchral stench of many decades of living and, possibly, dying. The "air conditioning" was a contradiction in terms. This had apparently been for years an abandoned storage room. Counsel for RCA must have thoroughly searched New York City and could find none worse for our accommodation. In the middle of the room was an antique "kitchen table" piece of furniture with three wooden chairs. Numerous cartons of documents produced for our inspection were stacked around on the ancient linoleum floor. Along with all the facilities, RCA counsel provided us with a junior lawyer who would ensure that we would not destroy or purloin anything and who would send to headquarters any documents we needed to have copied.

Crotty and I spent many miserable weeks sorting through this production of "wallpaper" and many more cartons of predominantly "low-grade ore," replacing those we examined initially. Nothing could be overlooked, however low-grade or irrelevant many gobs of the trash seemed to be, because now and then a relevant nugget would be found buried in the irrelevant or peripherally relevant rubbish.

After a good deal of argument and confrontation with opposing counsel, it became clear that they were withholding a large number of documents, allegedly on legal grounds. The documents included the following:

1. Communications to and from counsel for the various conspirators negotiating agreements relative to the conspiracy.
2. Communications to and from various officers of the conspiring corporations and their legal departments.
3. Documents relating to the infamous government consent decree of 1932 that had freed Sarnoff and RCA from General Electric's and Westinghouse's ownership of RCA's stock but left untouched the monopolization of patents and the division of markets and fields of business of the various conspiring companies and foreign cartels.
4. Documents containing "confidential" competitive information.

5. Documents dated after February 1954, the date of the filing of our new counterclaim.

6. Documents referring to broadcasting and point-to-point communications.

Zenith brought the withholding problem before Judge Igoe in appropriate motions for a direct order to produce. An interesting aspect of the withholding on the claim that certain documents were privileged because one of the authors happened to be an attorney was provided by RCA's chairman and president, David Sarnoff himself. At his deposition the following exchange occurred:

Q. Do you know who the other counsel were who were dealing with the Attorney General on behalf of General Electric? [negotiating the infamous 1932 consent decree]

A. I think for the Westinghouse it was Cravath, and for the General Electric I don't recall, but—oh, yes, I think they had White and Case, and we finally—I had independent counsel when it came to making the trade with General Electric and Westinghouse, so that that independent counsel could give his opinion on the equity so far as the independent shareholders of RCA were concerned, and that was the office of John W. Davis. There was no dearth of lawyers, I can tell you.

Q. I can see there were quite a few around, and very good ones, too, apparently.

A. This is an aside, if you will permit it. It has always been a question to me why all these contracts, which were all written by lawyers, why the lawyers are not on the witness stand to answer with respect to them.

Q. This is a great mystery to me, but your counsel do not want that to happen.

A. I am willing to yield the seat to them. . . .

Q. Were the negotiations on these contracts handled by the businessmen in your organization, or did the lawyers take over with that?

A. There was no contract made that a lawyer was not in on, because he had to draft the contract and study the language and so on. However, generally speaking, they were between the businessmen of the company and the businessmen of General Electric and Westinghouse, but there were lawyers on both sides at all times.

Q. The reason I ask that question is that some of the documents are so formidable in their language and in their technical use of words, that I wondered if they were not out of the hands of the businessmen in your organization and had got into the hands of the lawyers in setting up these various arrangements.

A. I think, generally speaking, on the General Electric side Mr. A. G. Davis, who was a patent lawyer and a vice president of General Electric, carried on these discussions. While he carried them on in his business capacity, he was also a lawyer. On our side I don't recall who handled these international matters particularly, but whoever was the export manager might have handled the business end of it, but the actual discussion generally took place between A. G. Davis for General Electric, or Mr. Terry for the Westinghouse, and whoever was counsel for the RCA, staff counsel at that time, Adams or Van Cise—I don't remember the names of the people. If you are smelling the labor of lawyers in those contracts, I think your smelling power is normal.

Q. They seem so foreign from what you usually expect a businessman to stipulate in agreements that it would seem to me that it was someone acting as a lawyer and thinking as a lawyer, and that was apparently Mr. Davis.

A. Yes, he was the star performer on the other end.

Q. He was a patent lawyer, wasn't he?

A. Yes, he was vice president in charge of the Patent Department for the General Electric, but he also handled their negotiations. When they were getting into anything new, he was generally the fellow who sat in. Also on the business end at that time was the head of International General Electric, Mr. Burchard, and a good deal of the staff of these international companies were so-called commercial lawyers, because they had been brought up that way, and the foreign contracts were always difficult for a layman to read or understand.

Q. It seems to me that the lawyers had got themselves in a position where they were almost indispensable in the operation of a corporation because of the constant question you would have to ask as to construction.

A. I think that is true today of any business, even domestically as well as foreign. I don't know any corporation today that can run its normal business, whether it is contracts for distribution or tax questions or financial questions or filling out forms; I would say the legal profession was doing very well in industry in America.

Q. We are talking now about an age which was supposed to be before this present time when you got to depend on your lawyer so much, 1922, 1923, 1924, 1925; that was more or less a free period.

A. The lawyers apparently succeeded in getting themselves into the top positions as negotiators in all these companies. The negotiations were carried on by lawyers. They may have been carried on in their capacity as businessmen, but they were lawyers nevertheless.

Q. They sort of left their footprints all over this picture, didn't they?

A. I should think so, yes.[9]

On August 10, 1955, Judge Igoe issued a written opinion rejecting much of the legal rationalization counsel had advanced as excuses for withholding many relevant documents (1955 CCH Trade Cases, 70,712). The judge restricted the boundaries of legally protected privileged communications with lawyers. Agreeing with Sarnoff's lay but common-sense opinion inadvertently volunteered at his deposition, the court said:

Communications between businessmen are not privileged because one of them happens to be a lawyer. Nor does the privilege extend to directors and officers of one corporation with other corporations and negotiations between corporations. Nor to communications by a client to an attorney to be imparted to a third person or party. Conspiracies formed and conducted by lawyers for corporations are not beyond the reach of the law. (*Radio Corporation of America v. Zenith and Rauland,* 1955 CCH Trade Cases, 70,712, 70,713–70, 714)

It was indeed ironic that in response to Tom McConnell's astute interrogation, David Sarnoff unwittingly provided answers that exposed the fallacies of his counsels' "attorney-client privilege" excuse for failing to produce damaging documents. Judge Igoe had an innate talent that enabled him to cut through the elaborate briefs and sophisticated arguments of high-priced counsel and provide just rulings on seemingly complex matters. Sophistry neither impressed nor confused him.

PRETRIAL DISCOVERY IN EUROPE

As the summer of 1955 approached, we decided to expand our search for evidence to Europe. Understaffed though we were in our forays in New York, we decided to seek evidence from the American Radio Group's co-conspirators in Europe. We reasoned that the interrelated English, French, Dutch, German, and Scandinavian patent pools—counterparts to the RCA patent pool in the United States and Canada—had files on the overall conspiracy that we might obtain by the use of what is known as letters rogatory. Federal law empowers federal trial court judges to issue letters of request to appropriate foreign courts asking those tribunals to cooperate by ordering witnesses within their respective jurisdictions to appear and testify as well as produce relevant documents there in aid of litigation in the United States. The letters are mere requests; they promise that the issuing U.S. court will likewise cooperate with the foreign court should that tribunal ever need similar assistance.

At Zenith's request, Judge Igoe issued letters rogatory to the High Court of Justice in London and the appropriate courts in Germany, Holland, and Scandinavia, asking for help in issuing their appropriate processes so that we could examine named participants in the European patent pools and their documents relating to those pools.

McConnell, Wright, and I, and another young lawyer who assisted us initially in the venture, departed for London in June 1955. We had retained a firm of London solicitors to "pave the way" for us foreigners in the High Court of Justice. After our arrival in London we were informed by our British solicitor, a Mr. Stinson, that our efforts were being violently opposed in the British court by (1) RCA, (2) General Electric, (3) the top officials of the Marconi Wireless and Telegraph Company, and (4) its successors in interest in the radio field such as Electric and Musical Industries Limited (EMI) and English Electric. The letters rogatory had named certain British company officials because they were mentioned in various RCA documents as participants in the British radio patent pool or cartel.

A hearing on the matter before the High Court of Justice had been scheduled. As required by court rules, our solicitor retained a barrister to represent us in the proceeding. British solicitors are licensed to give legal advice and assistance, but they must select a barrister to present a matter to a British court. British lawyers, or solicitors, are elevated to this exclusive class by being allowed to "take the silk"—to wear the exclusive black robe of the barrister.

A day or so before the June 1955 hearing date, our solicitor, Mr. Stinson, introduced us very briefly to our barrister, whom Stinson had already "sufficiently instructed" on our matter, according to custom. On the morning of the hearing, Stinson met us at the High Court of Justice and escorted us to the courtroom, a high-ceilinged, ancient sanctuary whose walls were lined with shelves of law books recording centuries of precedents. A dark crimson, velvet drape covered the wall behind the judge's bench—an impressive, elevated, dark wooden structure accommodating behind it a line of high-backed, antique judges' chairs. We Americans were allowed to sit in the well of the court, facing the bench. When the judges assembled in their wigs and robes and were seated, we could look up at them, it seemed, as if we were in an orchestra pit staring up at a stage high above us where a collection of impressively robed and white-wigged, seemingly supernatural jurists sat in divine judgment on our cause.

After our barrister in his flowing silk robes had addressed the court, briefly explaining our predicament, a tall, heavy man also in flowing silk robes rose to address the court on behalf of the RCA–GE interests. He announced that he also represented the list of titled British citizens who together with their British companies were apparently under attack in America by a "Chicago company" and their "Chicago lawyers." Al Capone wasn't mentioned, but it wasn't necessary to make his point. He described what we were up to as a so-called discovery procedure entirely foreign to the British system of justice. In stentorian tones, he said that we were seeking to subject prominent British businessmen to an attack during which their companies' files would be rifled in search of evidence of alleged violation of an American law called "anti-trust"—entirely foreign to British law—and that we proposed to subject his clients to a hostile, primitive procedure called "grilling" in Chicago. He emphatically suggested that the British High Court of Justice should never authorize or condone such uncivilized behavior directed against honorable British citizens doing business in the United Kingdom in accordance with British law.

As I looked up at the judges, their faces wrinkled by years of judicial service, they appeared to be pained and horrified by the revelations of our opponents' barrister. With saddened eyes, the judges seemed to be staring down at us as if we were Chicago gangsters boldly intent on attacking the cream of Britain's peerage in the very capitol of the Empire. Tom McConnell facetiously whispered to Wright and me, "We'll be lucky if we escape from here without being put in a dungeon at the Tower in chains."

Of course, we knew beforehand that GE and RCA had important, long-standing connections in England. They had made sure that we would be opposed by the best, most influential barrister they and their British co-conspirators could find. Their selection, a former prestigious Attorney General of England, Sir Hartley Shawcross, had been much more than was needed to doom our efforts to failure in the London court. We felt fortunate in being able to leave the High Court of Justice without being arrested. But there was no surprise when the opinion of the court, issued shortly after the hearing, expressed regret that it could not accommodate Judge Igoe's request in his letter rogatory because discovery proceedings in American courts were foreign to the British system of justice.

To salvage something out of this trip to London, we demanded that RCA produce for examination in London several of its American executives located there. The Chicago court had jurisdiction over RCA officials. Their names had appeared in documents produced by RCA in New York, identifying them as having been engaged in RCA's patent licensing activities in Europe. We had included their names in proper deposition notices, and arrangements were made to take their testimony before a consular officer at the U.S. Embassy in London.

As it turned out, the most important of these witnesses was Commander Cornelius "Rip" Mayer, RCA's European representative. His office address had been listed as 55 Pall Mall, London. We were told by John Nields, one of RCA's counsel, that Mayer was in Switzerland and could not appear in London until July 14, 1955. Out of curiosity, I took a cab to 55 Pall Mall and discovered from building management personnel there that RCA had completely vacated the offices "only two weeks ago" and had moved everything out. I surmised that our discovery mission may have inspired the move.

On July 14, 1955, Mayer did appear at the U.S. Embassy in London. We began his examination before a so-called Commissioner, an employee of our embassy, whose function in our case was merely to administer the oath to witnesses—a function similar to that of a notary public. As expected, Mayer was a reluctant, hostile witness, fully instructed by RCA counsel, who volunteered nothing, remembered little or no detail about anything, and repeatedly denied (as if horrified by the thought) that RCA was a participant in the British patent pool that blocked imports of radios and television receivers from America. He was forced to admit, however, that he had very recently moved his office from London to Switzerland—coincidentally, while we were arranging for the European depositions. He had moved his RCA London office and all the files to a newly formed Swiss RCA subsidiary in Zurich. He also admitted that RCA's Vice President and General Counsel had very recently come from New York to discuss certain matters with him at the Savoy Hotel in London. Those certain matters, he reluctantly said, were in general this case, the background of it and what he might be asked in cross-examination. He refused to be specific.

Mayer admitted that for years he had represented RCA in Europe on licensing matters, that he had been hired by the Foreign Licensing Department of RCA in New York and briefed on patent agreements held by RCA with companies in Europe. His memory of any or all of those matters, however, was almost nonexistent. All his files on those matters were now in a newly formed RCA Swiss subsidiary in Zurich. Of course, RCA had not produced them even though they had been fully covered in our document demands in New York.

After 244 pages of arrogant, evasive testimony and outright refusals by Mayer to answer numerous questions, Tom McConnell suspended the deposition until we could examine Mayer's files—the ones that had been spirited away to Switzerland and were presumably under the protection of Swiss law. The following colloquy occurred at the close of Mayer's testimony on July 14, 1955:

By MR McCONNELL: I have got to the end of this line with this witness till I can see his files. I would suggest this: We want his files. We want the files that he took from London over to Zurich. All we can do is ask him for them. If he does not want to produce them, we will have to take other steps to get them. We are willing to go to Zurich. Let this witness go home and go to Zurich. If he will produce his files there, I will continue this examination there. Otherwise, I am going to ask that he come back here with his documents.

By MR NIELDS: We will have to consider that, Mr McConnell. It is a strange business to ask for Mr Mayer to appear some months ago and never mention anything about his documents, and wait till you get here and ask for documents, and reach an agreement that you can examine him in one day, a large part of which has been wasted with irrelevancies; but we will consider the matter and advise you.

By MR McCONNELL: May I say, in response to that little speech, that we asked for the production of documents which were included in this man's files. We did not get them.

By MR NIELDS: You will not be able to point to a single place in the record where you did any such thing.

By MR McCONNELL: I can point to one right now, and that is the notes that were sent supposedly by the Commander to Mr Shackelford which are reposing in his files in Zurich, which were never produced by you people down in New York. If you had produced those things, we would not be asking to see his files; but you did not.

By MR NIELDS: Let us make this perfectly clear. If your statement is that what you are asking to be produced in Zurich is material that you have asked to have produced in the United States, we will see to it that it is produced in the United States.

By MR McCONNELL: You heard my request. It is on the record. I have made the request. If you want to take time to consider it, that is all right. I am requesting one of two things—either this witness remain here for further examination, returning with his documents, or that he be made available to us in Zurich for further examination. I think we have gone far enough with it today. It is 4 o'clock.

By MR NIELDS: We will consider and advise with respect to both requests.[10]

That night it was decided that while McConnell continued with another RCA witness in London, Wright and I would immediately fly back to Chicago with the Mayer deposition transcript and appear before Judge Igoe with a motion to compel RCA to produce in the U.S.

Embassy in London all the Mayer files that had so boldly been removed to Switzerland in an effort to escape the processes of the Chicago court. We were well aware that Swiss law prohibited Swiss corporations from producing records in response to the processes of any foreign court. We felt confident that should RCA counsel seek to obstruct justice by such an outrageous maneuver, Judge Igoe would not tolerate it.

At our request, the court reporter prepared and certified the transcript of the Mayer deposition "on an emergency basis." Wright and I then flew to Chicago, immediately prepared the motion with an attached affidavit and transcript of the Mayer testimony, served it on local counsel, and brought the matter on before Judge Igoe.

Following Wright's effective presentation of the matter and after reading the motion and affidavit, Judge Igoe asked RCA counsel for an explanation of what Wright had asserted their client had done to hide Mayer's files in Switzerland. Judge Thompson, RCA's local Chicago counsel from the firm of Johnson, Thompson, Raymond, Mayer & Jenner (later known as Jenner & Block), was in Europe, so Bert Jenner, a prominent partner, appeared for RCA. He made an impassioned plea for a delay until Thompson returned from Europe in September. He made the outrageous claim that all the documents we sought were technical documents having nothing to do with our lawsuit.

After hearing both sides and on the basis of our affidavit and Mayer's testimony, Judge Igoe expressed justifiable anger at what had occurred. He said that perhaps the U.S. Attorney ought to be called in to see if RCA was engaged in a deliberate effort to obstruct justice. He ruled that the Mayer documents should be returned to London for our inspection immediately and placed in the custody of a Marine guard there. He signed our proposed order to that effect, and Wright and I left for the door of the courtroom. Despite the fact that the judge had ruled, Jenner made a final, embarrassingly desperate personal plea to the judge. He said if he could not even get a delay of the matter until September, he would be in great trouble and disfavor with his senior partner, the eminent Judge Thompson. Judge Igoe said that Thompson's disfavor would probably extend more to him than to Jenner, that he had decided the matter, and that no further argument was in order.

Wright and I left the courtroom before Jenner could attempt any further histrionics. We went to my office a block away and tried to get McConnell on the telephone in London. We learned that he had left for the continent and would not be back in London until the following week. We decided that I should return to London as quickly as possible with the court order and, if possible, make sure the documents were made accessible to us at the embassy before any additional shenanigans were attempted. Fortunately, there was a late afternoon plane direct to London and I was able to get on it.

I arrived in London on a Saturday morning and checked back in at our hotel, the Grovenor House, where I learned that McConnell would not be back from the continent until Monday. Finding it impossible to reach McConnell, I immediately called John Nields at the Savoy Hotel, where RCA counsel were staying. Nields was RCA's senior New York counsel in charge of the London legal contingent. A woman answered Nields's phone and told me that "John" would not be back until very late evening. I told her that I was a lawyer in the case (I didn't say on which side) and that I had to discuss an important court order that had just issued in Chicago—that I had just arrived from the States and had to reach her husband immediately. She told me that John was at his solicitors' office at Slaughter & May "on an emergency matter" and would be there most of the weekend. She said she had a private number for him there but was under strict orders not to give it to anyone. I then told her that I was a lawyer for Zenith, and that she should call John immediately and have him call me; that if I did not hear from him that morning, I would take the afternoon plane back to Chicago and we would report the matter to the court.

Within a half-hour, Nields called me from the offices of Slaughter & May, RCA's solicitors, and I explained to him what had happened in court. He said they had received the news and that the files had just arrived at Slaughter & May's offices, where he was in the process of "inventorying" them. We could have access to them after he had examined them and moved them to the embassy. I told Nields that the order directed that *we* should have immediate access to the documents and that no provision had been made permitting him the privilege of screening or otherwise tampering with them outside of our presence. I said I would come to Slaughter & May immediately and begin our examination of the files there until we could get them to the embassy, pursuant to the court order. Nields at first refused. He said the embassy personnel handling the matter were off for the weekend, that Slaughter & May was closed to the public during the weekend. He insisted that I would have to wait until "next week" for anything further to be arranged.

I told Nields that I would come to Slaughter & May immediately and that if he would not let me in, I would fly back to Chicago as soon as possible and report the matter to the court. With bitter reluctance, he asked me not to do that. He agreed to let me in if I came to their offices.

I immediately took a cab to Slaughter & May. It was Saturday morning, and everything was closed for the weekend. The public entrance was locked. I rang the doorbell. Nields responded, opened the door of the reception area, and led me to a large back office where crates of documents were stacked around a large conference table. I gave him a copy of the court order, which he said he had already received by radio. Jenner had obviously transmitted the order to him—probably via the RCA Communications Network.

I called our solicitor, Mr. Stinson, and had him arrange to send one of his assistants to me so that we could both be with the documents until they could be transported to the embassy. I stayed with the documents all that weekend, separating out for copying any documents relevant to our case. After Stinson's young man arrived, I had him guard the documents for a few hours that night while I got a late dinner and some sleep at my hotel.

When I began to inventory the document production, I noticed that Nields had been going through several large cartons on the conference table. I insisted on starting my examination with them, despite Nields's plan to allow me to start with a large number of other boxes near another table. One of the cartons Nields had obviously been examining caught my attention. It contained hundreds of formal reports to RCA headquarters in New York, written by Mayer to Sarnoff's patent licensing department in the International Division. Mayer, a commander in the Naval Reserve, had put these communications in a sort of neat navy form with a convenient designation. He had headed the documents with an "L.M." (London Memorandum) designation and had numbered them consecutively. There were some 1,400 such numbered memoranda in the carton. Anyone screening the documents before production would have had a problem if he removed anything. The omission could readily be noted and an explanation properly demanded. Everything therein had relevance to RCA's elaborate activities in Europe with the patent cartels over a number of years. I felt fortunate to have access to them.

In the face of all our formal demands on RCA in New York these important documents had not been produced there, although the originals had obviously been sent there. It did not seem unreasonable to speculate that Mayer's highly sensitive files had been concealed from us and had been spirited away for protection in the newly formed Swiss corporation in Zurich while we were preparing to go to London. Any such scheme had gone awry as a result of Judge Igoe's prompt and effective emergency action in Chicago.

Mayer Is Returned to the Stand

Tom McConnell returned to London on Sunday. He had been traveling on the continent when Judge Igoe's order was issued, and he was unaware of the apparent bonanza that the order had suddenly produced. We made arrangements with RCA counsel to bring Mayer back to London for further examination beginning on the following Tuesday morning. I continued to examine the documents at Slaughter & May's offices until we could have them moved to the U.S. Embassy on Monday morning, when they were placed under guard there. I was able to arrange to have copies made of selected documents for use in our examination of Mayer.

Pertinent parts of the reopening of the Mayer deposition are reproduced in this book as Appendix III.[11] They illustrate why it was necessary to have the documents, in light of such a hostile, evasive witness whose memory extended only to what he could not credibly deny when confronted head-on with his own files.

Documents produced from Mayer's Swiss files made it clear that after World War II, when Zenith was making antitrust charges in Delaware, RCA and its counsel began erecting a facade that would conceal their illegal participation in the British patent pool that prevented imports from the United States. They drew up a phony license agreement purportedly licensing RCA British patents to pool members and pool licensees. But that license was a complete sham. It had no restrictions and was purportedly issued for a royalty of only one pound—which was never paid, because EMI (Marconi's successor) had already put all of RCA's patents in the British pool and paid RCA a percentage of the substantial "royalties" the pool collected under typical pool package licenses prohibiting imports. Since technically EMI, as RCA's agent, put the RCA patents together with its own into the pool, RCA could deceptively say in any investigation that it was not a member of the pool and received no royalties from the pool! This was the deception Mayer had apparently been coached to attempt; it explained why McConnell had to chase him so hard and confront him with his own documents to get him to admit the truth. Mayer knew from RCA counsel that the arrangement with the pool violated U.S. antitrust laws, as his documents showed. In his persistent sparring with McConnell, he was obviously acting under orders.

This episode also explains why RCA fought so hard in both the Delaware and Chicago cases to prevent discovery on anything from 1919 through 1945, when RCA was a charter member of the pool under the original Marconi–General Electric cartel arrangement.

Our examination of Mayer extended to 887 pages. He was confronted with 155 multipage exhibits from his newly produced files in order to refresh his faltering memory and expose his many incorrect denials. The related cartels in Germany, Holland, France, and Scandinavia were also covered, as many of Mayer's revealing London memoranda to RCA headquarters in New York were used to pry the truth out of this hostile, evasive witness.

The lengths to which RCA had gone to prevent disclosure of damaging evidence were also revealed in the following secret letters we discovered in Mayer's newly revealed London-Swiss files.[12] Mayer's testimony about these exhibits is set out in Appendix IV.

September 23, 1953

RCA International Division
License Department

Trip Reports: Japan
                East Asia and Europe

To: J. J. Benevie
      W. S. Bopp
      J. T. Bray
      Meade Brunet
      D. M. Crawford/L. C. Melas
      A. F. Dollar
      H. C. Edgar
      A. D. Gordon   Please destroy Page 1 of Report
      E. A. Laport   entitled "Trip Report—East Asia
      J. E. Lothian   and Europe" and Page 6 of Report
      F. A. McCall   entitled "Trip Report—Japan"
      M. J. Matson   and substitute attached pages.
      C. G. Mayer
      T. H. Mitchell
      B. F. Moore/C. P. Baswell
      L. R. Schorr/A. H. Jacobs
      R. F. Simokat
      C. W. Slaybaugh
      E. F. Sutherland
      W. W. Watts
      T. P. Wynkoop

RADIO CORPORATION OF AMERICA
RCA International Division

INTER-COMPANY CORRESPONDENCE

To: J. J. Benevie   Date: 10/20/53
     W. S. Bopp
     J. T. Bray
     Meade Brunet
     D. M. Crawford/L. C. Melas
     A. F. Dollar
     H. C. Edgar   Subject: Trip Report Japan 1953
     A. D. Gordon   *Dr. Shackelford and Mr. H. A. Straus*
     E. A. Laport
     J. E. Lothian   Trip Report East Asia and Europe 1953
     F. A. McCall   *Dr. Shackelford*
     M. J. Matson
     C. G. Mayer
     T. H. Mitchell
     B. F. Moore/C. P. Baswell
     L. R. Schorr/A. H. Jacobs
     R. F. Simokat
     C. W. Slaybaugh
     E. F. Sutherland
     W. W. Watts
     T. P. Wynkoop

    We should appreciate it very much if you would return your copies of
the above trip reports which were sent to you on September 23, 1953.

                                                        B. K. Shackelford

---

RADIO CORPORATION OF AMERICA
RCA International Division

INTER-COMPANY CORRESPONDENCE

To: Mr. C. G. Mayer   Date: 10/30/53
      55 Pall Mall
      London S.W. 1

Subject:

Dear Mr. Mayer:

We received your note of October 23rd stating that you were enclosing your copies of the Dr. Shackelford–Straus trip reports. However, with your note we received two pages—Page 1 "After the writer left Japan," etc. and a page 6 beginning "For the first time outside of the United States, the entire radio industry has now been organized patent-license-wise." I checked with Mr. Straus' office and they said they sent you full copies of the reports. Would you please see if you do not have the rest of it?
Thank you.

Yours very truly,

L. M. Neyhart

C. G. Mayer   5 Nov. 1955
Miss Lena Neyhart
NEW YORK

Re your note dated 30 October, regret through misunderstanding returned only substitute sheets sent out with note of September 23 as referred to in your note of October 20. Herewith full Report sent out with note dated September 15.

C. G. Mayer,

Encl. Report (via Surface Mail)

As expected, we were never able to get a copy of the apparently very revealing "trip report" made by Dr. Shackelford, head of RCA's Licensing Department, and a top assistant, Mr. Straus, after they had toured the world, including the Far East and Japan, in 1953. Based on the statement, "'After the writer left Japan,' etc. and a page 6 beginning 'For the first time outside of the United States, the entire radio industry has now been organized patent-license-wise,'" we surmised that it would have greatly shortened the preparation of our proofs for trial had the report not been destroyed or otherwise permanently kept from us. The report also may well have disclosed the creation of the Japanese electronics cartel, the building of new plants furnished with RCA technical aid and patent licenses, and the predatory dumping scheme for the takeover of the American market—Sarnoff's last spiteful as well as lucrative accomplishment.

The Mayer documents vitally complemented what we had been able to pry out of RCA, General Electric, and Western Electric in the United States with the help of the federal court in Chicago. We also took depositions in Germany, Norway, Denmark, and Sweden that were helpful in our trial preparations. In Holland, however, our attempt to get the Dutch court to honor Judge Igoe's letters rogatory met with the same fate as we had encountered in the British High Court of Justice. We had sought to adduce evidence from N.V. Philips Gloeilampenfabrieken, the largest of the American Radio Group's European co-conspirators.

Operating out of Eindhoven, Holland, Philips had been generally assigned the field of radio and television in central Europe and Scandinavia. All the counterpart patents of all its American and European co-conspirators had been assigned to it for use in the pools controlling its allotted territories. We knew the Dutch government was reputedly highly protective of this great Dutch company, and we had heard—rightly or wrongly—that Queen Wilhelmena was an important Philips stockholder. It was not surprising, therefore, when the Dutch court held that although the court was always anxious to cooperate with the courts of the United States, our antitrust laws were foreign to their jurisprudence, which unfortunately precluded cooperation in our case.

However, we had obtained copies of the basic RCA-Philips long-term contract of 1925. That agreement, together with the General Electric–Marconi original agreement of 1919 and the complementary agreements A and B between General Electric, RCA, AT&T, and Westinghouse, are classic examples of how General Electric and its co-conspirators divided up the world as well as fields of business. Owen D. Young, David Sarnoff, and their co-conspirators and counsel housed their scheme in ponderous, legal language. All the actual agreements would fill several very large volumes.

Zenith's rapid progress in our trial preparations apparently alarmed the legal brigades of RCA, General Electric, and Western Electric. With their defenses and dilatory strategies in disarray, they decided to attack Judge Igoe and have him removed from the case on the grounds that he had displayed "personal bias and prejudice" toward them. Counsel wildly cited Section 144 of Title 28 of the United States Code, a law not conceivably applicable to the court's conduct, as authority for their bold demand. In support of their position, they filed what was purportedly an affidavit based only on the so-called information and belief of Frank Folsom, then president of RCA under the chairmanship of David Sarnoff. Why Sarnoff was not the affiant, we never understood. He knew the case like the back of his hand, in our judgment, and had been a principal architect of the conspiracy. Frank Folsom was a newcomer and subordinate to Sarnoff, as far as the conspiracy was concerned.

Briefs were filed, a hearing held, and Judge Igoe issued a written opinion dated March 26, 1956, in which he carefully examined the papers and arguments. Treating Folsom's affidavit "as true for the purpose of deciding the case," he held that on the basis of the facts and governing law, he could not properly remove himself from the case. He rejected the attack on his integrity as a desperate effort to delay the trial by getting "another judge in the hope that he will rule differently on matters already decided during the course of several years of litigation." Judge Igoe's opinion, an important, clearly written recitation of what had gone on in the Chicago case, is included in this book as Appendix V (*R.C.A. v. Rauland and Zenith,* 1956 CCH Trade Cases, 68,306).

As we continued our trial preparation on all fronts, the legions of opposing counsel continued to file distracting, dilatory motions. We had to return from Europe in the summer of 1956 to meet and brief three diabolically complex motions, which each of our opponents concocted allegedly to show that a different statute of limitations applied to each of them and that, therefore, we could not recover our claimed damages against any one of them. This was another obtuse legal diatribe totally without merit. But it had to be analyzed, met, and exposed for what it was. The court, with admirable restraint, took apart the complex motions and elaborate supporting briefs in a carefully written opinion issued on July 17, 1956 (1956 CCH Trade Cases, 68,475).[13]

As the end of 1956 approached, our opponents' diversionary tactics required our tiny team to split up. While McConnell and Wright were pinned down in depositions in the United States and Frank Crotty continued to prepare digests of important documents produced by the three counterdefendants, I went to Scandinavia to develop further evidence of how the European cartels (with our opponents' vital collaboration) had dominated the radio industries in Norway, Denmark, and Sweden and had blocked Zenith's efforts to export to those markets.

I had found in the Zenith files correspondence through the years with potential Zenith distributors in Scandinavia as well as in England, Europe, Australia, and Canada. These distributors were anxious to import Zenith products but were restrained from doing so by threats from the respective patent pools. With the help of letters rogatory and arrangements with the State Department, I was able to locate and take the testimony of several important witnesses in Norway, Denmark, and Sweden.

Among these witnesses was a Mr. Steen, a very knowledgeable international trader who was experienced in importing products into Scandinavia and who could rebut RCA's contention that aside from the patent pool's blockade, Zenith could not have imported into those countries anyway because of local customs and other regulations. Steen was traveling between various markets and could only accommodate me if I could arrange for his deposition at the U.S. Embassy in Oslo, Norway, the very next day. RCA's counsel, Jerome Doyle, and his crew of fellow counsel were staying at my hotel, so I was able to serve a notice for the Steen deposition on him immediately. I also arranged at the embassy for the deposition to be taken on the following day. There was nothing else scheduled. Doyle and his crew would have had a day off if the Steen deposition had not been scheduled.

That night, however, I got two telephone calls: one from Doyle, who arrogantly said he would not honor my notice because it was not "timely," and a later call from an embassy employee informing me that the Steen deposition could not be taken on the following day because I had not given "sufficient notice to RCA." I told the embassy employee that he was not a judge—that his only function was to swear in the witness; that I would be at the embassy at ten o'clock the following day with the witness and that if he refused to swear in the witness and allow me to take the deposition as scheduled, I would report the matter to the federal court in Chicago as a contempt of court and an obstruction of justice that was obviously engineered by RCA counsel.

Around 9:00 A.M. the next day as I left my hotel for the embassy, I noticed Doyle and several of his associates sitting in the lounge bar off the lobby. Doyle waved and with a mocking smile said something like, "You're wasting your time, dummy." My witness, Steen, showed up at the embassy and a consular officer swore him in. It was a delight to get his testimony without Doyle being there to interpose sham objections to questions and otherwise frustrate the examination. Steen was a good, knowledgeable witness. With no interference, I was able to finish my examination in a relatively short time.

After I had returned to Chicago following completion of the depositions in Sweden, Norway, and Denmark, RCA counsel filed motions to
suppress the testimony of our witnesses Steen, Broberg, and Noren—all
of which was damaging to our opponents. Included as Appendix VI is
the court's opinion issued on May 23, 1957, after briefs and a hearing,
which soundly rejects counsels' last attempt to damage our case (1957
CCH Trade Cases, 73,047).

DEVELOPMENTS IN CANADA

In the spring of 1956, we were able to get access to the files of the
General Electric Company subsidiary in Canada, Canadian General
Electric Company, and the Canadian cartel set up in Canada by General
Electric. It was joined in by affiliates of AT&T, Westinghouse, and the
principal European cartel members: the British companies and Philips
Gloeilampenfabrieken, the huge Dutch concern that dominated the
radio markets of central Europe and Scandinavia. Judge Igoe's letters
rogatory to the Canadian court received a more friendly and understanding treatment than they had encountered in London. With the aid
of Canadian counsel, I filed an affidavit in the Canadian court in support of the letters rogatory, asserting that we were seeking evidence for
use in the trial in Chicago and were not engaged in what the British
High Court of Justice had described as a primitive discovery exercise
unknown to British law. The Canadian court recognized the distinction
and cooperated. We were granted access to the Canadian pool's relevant
records.

In addition, we obtained access to Canadian General Electric's files
and were able to take depositions of fifteen key witnesses. These
included three Canadian wholesale distributors who had tried through
the years to import and sell Zenith receivers in Canada but had been
stopped by repeated threats from the pool. We were able to take over
1,500 pages of testimony, using approximately sixty key documents
that thoroughly proved our case.

The only defense attempted by RCA was the legal excuse that the
Canadian Patent Act required the pool to refuse to license imports from
the United States under pains of forfeiture of their Canadian patent
rights. Not only did RCA documents show that this defense was meritless, but treatises on Canadian patent law and the legislative history of
the Canadian Patent Act clearly refuted it. Canada had been forced to
amend its patent law in 1923 by removing a prohibition on imports in
order to be admitted to the International Convention, a mutually benefi-

cial treaty between the leading trading nations. The British law was copied in the amendment, and certainly no one had ever claimed that the British patent law required a refusal to license imports from the United States. The British pool—or, more appropriately, the British, American, European pool in London—prohibited imports wholly by agreement between the conspirators without any feigned claim that a patent law made them do it.

Among the internal documents produced by RCA in the litigation showing the fallacy of the Canadian Patent Act defense, the following two are representative:

• Manton Davis, head of RCA's Law Department, wrote the following to Ira Adams, head of RCA's Patent Department, on January 21, 1924, right after the Canadian Patent Law had been changed to allow importation:

> From the attached correspondence it would appear that the patent attorneys of G.E. are of the opinion that as a result of recent modifications of Canadian patent law, the situation has been changed and that, although Mallory's [representing Westinghouse] statement was correct under the old law, it is incorrect under the law as recently modified. (PD2477-78)

• By letter dated January 23, 1924, Adams responded and acknowledged the change in the law:

> Now in respect to importation, it formerly was the law that importations into Canada later than one year after the date of the patent grant would invalidate the Canadian patent if the importation was carried on by the party owning the Canadian patent or someone having an interest in that patent. This has long been a thorn in the side of the U.S. manufacturers who own Canadian patents and it was a great relief to those manufacturers when the Canadian laws were changed last year in this respect. When I wrote you about this situation, I was fully advised in regard to the Canadian law and knew that the law against importation had been repealed. (PD2479-80)[14]

PRETRIAL PREPARATION

As the summer of 1957 approached, the court set a tentative trial date for June, later moved to September. In the period of about two years of intense pretrial discovery, a total of 22,966 pages of depositions had been taken in which 961 multipage documentary exhibits were used. Hundreds of thousands of documents had been produced under the court's processes; many had been selected for copying and use with the witnesses. A broad breakdown of this activity illustrates the scope of the effort:

RCA Witnesses Examined: Forty-five RCA executives were cross-examined with the use of 575 documents from the RCA files. Chairman David Sarnoff was on the stand for days. His deposition covered 609 pages and 100 documentary exhibits were used. Commander Mayer's deposition covered 886 pages in which 155 exhibits were employed. The examination of Benjamin Shackelford, head of licensing in the RCA International Division, covered 558 pages and 93 documentary exhibits were used. The deposition of Henry Johnson, Operations Manager, License Department, RCA International Division, covered 644 pages and 63 exhibits. The examination of John G. MacKenty, for years a master advisor to Sarnoff and his Licensing Department and, after retirement, a consultant to the RCA lawyers on the myriad international agreements of RCA, covered 289 pages and 36 key exhibits.[15]

General Electric Witnesses Examined: The depositions of 23 General Electric executives covered 2,080 pages in which 122 documents were used.

Canadian Depositions: In Canada, we took the depositions of 16 witnesses reported in 1,511 pages. The testimony of the then operating manager of the Canadian pool covers 345 pages in which 48 key documents were used.

Other Foreign Depositions: Over 2,000 pages of depositions were taken in Australia, France, Germany, Holland, and Scandinavia, plus the over-2,000 pages of testimony taken in England.

While all these depositions and discovery activities were going on, RCA, GE, and Western Electric took the depositions of 28 Zenith personnel covering 10,243 pages. Commander McDonald's deposition covered 2,406 pages; Hugh Robertson's (Zenith's Executive Vice President) testimony covered 2,243 pages. Both were kept on the stand for weeks—we believed, as a form of punishment. Certainly, nothing in the way of evidence helpful to the RCA cause could be discerned in this punitive exercise.

When the frantic evidence-gathering period was over, we had very limited time to plan for the actual trial before a jury. The mountain of evidence would have had to be greatly refined for any effective presentation, even at a juryless bench trial; for the jury trial we faced, there had to be an even greater effort to present the evidence in the most simple and understandable way. Our opponents could be expected to try to complicate, obfuscate, and bury the real issues in a sea of complexity and distortion. We had to keep everything simple, try our case, and not permit them to lure us into a defensive trial of their case.

The major deposition exhibits in the main represented a vast distillation of the huge quantity of documents produced under the processes of the court. Frank Crotty and his efficient clerical staff at Zenith had prepared well-indexed notebooks giving quick access to all relevant documents on a subject-matter basis. We rented office space in a building directly across the street from the Federal Court House in Chicago so that all potentially important documents would be quickly accessible for cross-examination of adverse RCA witnesses as well as for use in our case in chief.

Our plan was to put on as streamlined a presentation as possible to establish a prima facie case. To hold the jury's interest, we would call as adverse witnesses certain key RCA personnel whom, under the rules, we could cross-examine effectively on "their documents." The controversial Sarnoff, a key architect of the historic conspiracy, would obviously be of interest to any jury, as would the elusive RCA European representative, Commander Cornelius "Rip" Mayer, and a few others. Parts of depositions would be presented in question-and-answer form using surrogate witnesses in order to make it easier for the jury to follow the testimony. Simplified visual aids would show the basic structure of the various cartel agreements. To prove up the impact of the conspiracy and monopoly on Zenith, we had the courageous and dynamic founder of Zenith, E. F. MacDonald, Jr. And Sam Kaplan, the brilliant treasurer of Zenith who had risen from clerk in the mailroom to become the top financial officer of the company (after working his way through Northwestern University and serving as an accountant), was available to quantify our monetary damages. From the Zenith Research and Engineering departments there were leading scientists and engineers who could be called upon to explain technical aspects of the case for the jury.

RCA's only defense to the vicious exclusion of Zenith products from Canada was the so-called Canadian Patent Act defense. Such questions of foreign law were provable in the federal courts as facts, but the determination of foreign law facts was for the court—not the jury—to decide. To prevent this spurious issue from confusing the jury during the trial, we brought a pretrial motion to have the issue presented to the court ahead of the jury trial and determined so that any attempt to confuse the jury with it could be forestalled at the outset. After a bitter oral argument, the court was persuaded to adopt this procedure.

Although the apparent legal complexity of the case and the mass of evidence in deposition and documentary form would appear to render the case highly inappropriate for any jury trial, analysis of the basic scheme of the conspiracy could be presented so that any qualified jury could understand it and, with proper instructions on the law from the judge, would have little difficulty in rendering a proper verdict.

NOTES

1.   As will later be shown, the license was specifically limited to the U.S. market because the foreign counterpart patents of the "American Radio Group," as it was known in foreign circles, had been transferred to the related foreign cartels for use in protecting their territorial monopolies in Europe, Scandinavia, Canada, South America, and Australia from imports. RCA shared generously in the revenues from the foreign pools' licensing in their specific territories.

2.   The popular conception of "easy" government jobs did not fit my experience as a young lawyer working for Joe Wright and the hard-driving W. T. Kelley, then General Counsel of the Commission. It was not uncommon to work at night as well as on Saturdays and Sundays to meet court dates on briefs and related matters.

3.   I had been impressed by Joe Wright's down-to-earth common sense in legal matters and his well-deserved reputation among the Commission and outside lawyers for having a steel-trap mind. One veteran, describing Wright's ability to analyze complex cases, often said, "I am amazed at how often Wright's legal analysis in complex cases turns out to be right."

4.   Burton Wheeler was a former senator from Montana who opened a law office in Washington, D.C., after leaving the U.S. Senate. Wheeler's firm had been retained early in the case to advise the patent lawyers on the antitrust aspects of the Delaware and Chicago cases.

5.   I remember being impressed by the large number of long-time Zenith employees at all levels. They were devoted to Zenith and their work.

6.   *American Banana Co. v. United Fruit Co.,* 213 U.S. 247 (1909).

7.   See, for example, *United States v. Sisal Sales Corp.,* 274 U.S. 268 (1927).

8.   Extracted quotes are from notes taken at the pretrial conference in the judge's chambers.

9.   Deposition of David Sarnoff, May 10, 1955, pp. 312–13, 316–19, United States District Court, Northern District of Illinois, Eastern Division, No. 48 C 1818.

10.   Deposition of Cornelius Mayer, July 14, 1955, pp. 244–46, taken at the American Embassy, London, W.1., England; United States District Court, Northern District of Illinois, No. 48 C 1818.

11.   Continued deposition of Cornelius Mayer, August 16, 1955, pp. 458–80, 560–62, 604–7, taken at the American Embassy, London, W.1., England; United States District Court, Northern District of Illinois, No. 48 C 1818.

12.   Cornelius Mayer deposition Exhibits 33A thru 33E, United States District Court, Northern District of Illinois, No. 48 C 1818.

13.   Similar "technical" attacks on our pleadings had already been formally disposed of by the court. See, for example, 1956 CCH Trade Cases, 68,490.

14.   For both extracts, the PD numbers are RCA Patent Department document identification numbers.

15.   We had located MacKenty in Martha's Vineyard, and I was able to take his deposition in the local courthouse there. He was a wily, intellectual-type historian,

fond of semantics but sufficiently honest when confronted head-on with documents to make our deposition effort worthwhile. He did become unnerved and upset when I cross-examined him on RCA's license and technical assistance agreement with Russia, which he excused by saying that our government had approved it.

3

Trial Is Imminent

REVIEW OF THE PROSPECTIVE TRIAL EVIDENCE: BACKGROUND AND ORIGIN OF THE CONSPIRACY

The background and origins of the conspiracy needed but a cursory review of undisputed facts concerning (1) the invention of radio and, later, television, and (2) how the scattered but essential discoveries of many independent entrepreneurial inventors were brought together into interrelated patent pools. The pools divided world territories and lines of business into patent monopolies that dominated all aspects of the radio and television business in each of the pools assigned geographical and lines-of-business areas.

The scientific pioneers of radio came from many different nations. But the first major points of development were in England and Germany. James Maxwell, known as the scientific father of wireless, was a professor of natural philosophy at London University and Cambridge. He presided over the famous Cavendish Laboratory established in 1871. He had published his "Dynamical Theory of Electro-Magnetic Field" in 1864.

From 1884 to 1893, while Charles Coffin was developing General Electric and its predecessor companies, Heinrich Hertz in Germany was the first scientist to produce and detect wireless waves. At about the same time, Oliver Lodge, a physicist at the University of Liverpool, designed an effective system of wireless reception. The system was comprised of a spark gap for collecting waves and a coherer for detecting them, a relay for magnifying the currents, an inker for registering Morse dots and dashes, and a trembler for tapping back the coherer.[1]

Guglielmo Marconi: Commercial Innovator

The son of a wealthy Italian father and a mother from the Irish "aristocracy" who moved in the best circles in England, Guglielmo Marconi was raised in Italy and educated by tutors. He developed a fascination for electricity and worked constantly on perfecting homemade radio equipment. He improved the Hertzian oscillator by building transmitting equipment that, from an elevated aerial, discharged across a spark gap to earth. He improved on Lodge's coherer and by 1896 was receiving Morse Code messages over a distance of two miles.

His family believed that he would have a better chance of commercializing his developments in England; so his mother took him to London, where he was introduced to government officials and wealthy capitalists interested in radio. He was only 21 years old. The Engineer in Chief of the British Post Office, William Preece (an inventor himself), set up a Marconi demonstration for the Post Office engineers. Marconi showed that messages could be transmitted up to 8 miles. In 1897, the British Marconi Company was formed.

Two years later, an American subsidiary, Marconi Wireless and Telegraph Company of America, was set up. From then until the formation of the Radio Corporation of America in 1919, the Marconi companies were the dominant concerns in British and American radio—or wireless, as the English call it. Marconi had the backing of a number of wealthy Englishmen who were interested in radio, and the company had a very distinguished directorate. When ship-to-shore radio communications became important, Marconi dominated the business internationally.

Marconi's contributions to the commercialization of radio were mainly as an innovator, not as an inventor. He and his company set out to acquire, in one way or another, most of the principal patents in the radio art. The most important inventions covered by those patents were not his, but his patent acquisition efforts placed his company in a position to dominate any of its rivals in the world. In this regard he was very much like Charles A. Coffin, the Massachusetts shoemaker who acquired his competitors and their patents, rolling them all into a dominating General Electric Company.

By 1915, General Electric's work on wireless produced the famous Alexanderson alternator, invented by a Swedish engineer General Electric had hired. General Electric then had a complete system of continuous wave transmission. But Marconi and AT&T were in dominant positions in the communications area at the time. General Electric had many interests in Europe in the power and electrical fields, and the patented Alexanderson alternator became a subject of negotiations between Marconi and General Electric in both London and America during 1915.

The commercial philosophies of (1) Coffin and General Electric, (2) General Electric board member J. P. Morgan, a leading financial architect of many trusts, and (3) Marconi and his British and American companies were very similar (i.e., dominate an industry by making cooperative pacts between competitors; monopolize patents to protect those pacts; and center the controlling power in one company or group of companies in which lines of business could be parceled out and unwelcome competitors eliminated, controlled, or absorbed). Thus, General Electric's complete system of continuous wave transmission featuring the Alexanderson alternator was of great interest to the Marconi group. Marconi and General Electric courted each other as natural allies. The British Empire and the Western Hemisphere—mainly the United States and Canada—were natural territories wherein the united power of dominant American companies could be combined with that of the Marconi group to dominate the radio field in both England and America. The natural territories and lines of business of the groups could be parceled out exclusively to each, to be protected from competitors by their combined patent power. Each group would stay out of the other's territory and mutually protect each other from potential outside competition. Hundreds of pooled patents would effectively guard each group's territorial and line-of-business monopoly.

World War I delayed the consummation of this tempting liaison, but by the end of the war the courtship was renewed with vigor. By 1919, Coffin had had his new general counsel and successor-in-training, Owen D. Young, on the job for six years, clearing all important contracts and studying ways to evade or avoid the troublesome Sherman Antitrust Act. Marconi renewed negotiations with GE to acquire rights to the Alexanderson alternator. Related patented GE developments led again to discussions of the mutual advantages of combining the patent rights of the American Radio Group (GE, Westinghouse, AT&T) with the huge patent holdings garnered by the Marconi interests, so that Marconi could further strengthen its domination and control of the radio business in the British Empire. In exchange, GE and its American co-conspirators would be given the combined patent rights of both groups for domination of radio in the United States and Canada.

To effectuate this scheme, a series of interrelated agreements created the following structure:

- General Electric formed RCA, the Radio Corporation of America, as a radio sales company. Its stock was owned 60 percent by General Electric and 40 percent by Westinghouse (AT&T's original stock interest was sold back). RCA had no radio manufacturing rights until the "unification" in 1930, when some manufacturing facilities of both General Electric and Westinghouse were transferred to RCA for "efficiency" purposes. Until then, 60 percent of radio receivers and related products sold by RCA were manufactured by General Electric and 40 percent by Westinghouse.

- RCA acquired the assets of Marconi's American subsidiary, American Marconi Company, and the U.S. counterparts of all Marconi's radio patents. This took the Marconi group out of the United States. General Electric obtained the Marconi Canadian patents and put them in Canadian Radio Patents Limited, a patent pool formed by General Electric to control radio in Canada and prevent imports.

- The American Radio Group (GE, Westinghouse, AT&T, and its subsidiaries and their affiliate, RCA) then divided the communications field in America between them as follows:

Telephone Group	Radio Group
(Wireless Communications)	(Wireless Communications)
AT&T and its subsidiaries	RCA, General Electric, and Westinghouse
A. Principal Fields	A. Principal Fields of RCA Radio Purposes
1. wire telephony	1. radio and television receivers
2. wire telegraphy	and tubes
	2. licensing manufacturers of such
	receivers and tubes under all the
	patent rights of the Group.
	3. broadcasting
	4. wireless communications for toll,
	that is, wireless telegraphy and
	telephony
	B. Principal Fields of General Electric
	and Westinghouse
	1. all electric power apparatus
	2. all industrial apparatus
	3. all railway apparatus

Thus, for the United States and Canada, the combined power of the British Marconi group was added to the combined power of AT&T and its subsidiaries, General Electric, and Westinghouse. The entire patent power of all for the radio purposes field was placed in RCA, the jointly owned sales subsidiary of General Electric and Westinghouse, which manufactured all RCA receiving sets and tubes on a 60 percent–40 percent basis. Conversely, the British Empire was exclusively allotted to the Marconi interests.

Between 1919 and 1921, GE was able to organize a huge international cartel that effectively restrained interstate and foreign trade in radio (and later television) manufacture, patent licensing, and independent research and development. This situation remained in effect until the 1957 settlement of the Zenith case immediately followed by a U.S. government criminal prosecution of RCA and related civil cases against GE, RCA, and Westinghouse finally broke it up. Agreements known as A and B united the patent power of the dominant electrical and communications firms in the United States. Their combined power was added to the Marconi pools in England, France, Germany, Central Europe, and Scandinavia, dividing the leading world markets into territories and lines of business that were parceled out to each national combine by the respective pools for the purpose of controlling commerce in each national territory. Competitors in Europe could not invade the United States or Canada; conversely, General Electric and its American and Canadian affiliates and licensees could not ship or license anyone to ship to Europe.

GENERAL ELECTRIC AND AMERICAN MARCONI; RCA AND DAVID SARNOFF

The acquisition of American Marconi by General Electric brought to RCA through General Electric and the American Radio Group not only the valuable assets of Marconi in the United States and Canada, but the American Marconi personnel as well. Edward Nally was the aging ceremonial head of Marconi's U.S. subsidiary; but the chief operating executive was the cunning, intensely ambitious, irrepressible David Sarnoff, who briefed Owen D. Young and his mentor, Charles Coffin, on how American Marconi was run and how RCA could best exploit the acquisition.

Sarnoff had arrived in New York as the offspring of immigrant Russian-Jewish parents. Although he had little formal education, he was a bright, shrewd opportunist who was intent on promoting himself out of poverty and feeding an abnormal ego. He did this by exploiting an unusual and cunning talent for negotiating himself into success and prominence by whatever means available. In 1906, at age 15, he was hired by American Marconi as an office boy and junior radio operator; but he quickly came to the notice of Guglielmo Marconi himself during Marconi's frequent stays in New York and became an adept radio operator who was proficient in sending and receiving Morse Code. By age 26, Sarnoff had become head of the Commercial Department with a staff of 725, installing and servicing radio apparatuses on 582 ships. Marconi had a monopoly in ship-to-shore communications and had a lock on that business with the United States Navy during World War I. Sarnoff rose to the position of chief operating officer of American Marconi in an amazingly short period of time.

On his way up in RCA after the acquisition, Sarnoff began telling stories that glorified himself as a hero. These tales were effectively spread to the public by a prolific public relations department. As an example, years after the *Titanic* hit an iceberg and sank on April 14, 1912, Sarnoff spread the story that he had singlehandedly received a message on his radio receiver from a rescue ship near the *Titanic*: "*Titanic* hit iceberg. Sinking fast." Going for three days and three nights without sleep or food, according to Sarnoff, he received and passed on messages from the rescue ship *Olympic* containing the names of survivors and other details. Actually, he was only one of quite a number of amateur radio operators who received news of the disaster and the names of survivors. As a matter of fact, Sarnoff's radio apparatus was at a station in Wanamaker's department store at the time. The disaster message was transmitted at night, when the store and station were closed. It appeared that Sarnoff was one of many amateurs who heard of the disaster and belatedly, after the store opened, joined other amateurs in picking up radio messages about the disaster and the names of survivors.

Carl Dreker, a longtime RCA engineer and associate of Sarnoff, scoffed at the myth that Sarnoff had picked up the first disaster signal. Like a number of Sarnoff's myths, fact and fiction became more and more blurred into fantasies as he told and retold them in false self-advertising. Indeed, throughout the years he had himself proclaimed as the father of radio and television rather than as the feared enforcer of the radio cartel, the true role assigned to him by Owen D. Young when American Marconi assets and personnel were placed in RCA by General Electric after the acquisition.

Knowing Sarnoff's propensity to lapse into story-telling, we pre-pared for his cross-examination at the trial with documents to expose the fallacy of some of the tales he would be tempted to recount on the stand to impress the jury. One of his favorite myths was a fable about President Roosevelt proclaiming himself to have been the mother of RCA and Sarnoff the father. This story fit in with a bigger fable that GE had created RCA at the request of the U.S. government. Charges of monopoly and restraint of trade were thus deflected. If the worldwide cartels were really the product of the federal government, the conspir-acy could not properly be criticized.

The tale of Roosevelt's "motherhood" of RCA seems first to have had critical exposure in 1940 in hearings before the Senate Interstate Commerce Committee on the nomination of Thad H. Brown as a Fed-eral Communications Commission member. Antitrust violators were excluded by law from holding broadcast licenses, and the hearings fea-tured evidence concerning the infamous 1932 consent decree entered by agreement in a government case brought in 1930 to break up the conspiracy. The decree, negotiated at the end of President Hoover's dis-astrous term, was allegedly the result of corruption and undue influence by RCA and, particularly, Sarnoff.

The 682-page hearing record was full of evidence pointing to the alleged corruption of the Delaware federal court in approving the decree that had made Sarnoff's RCA free from the stock ownership and control of GE and Westinghouse and, in effect, put the entire radio monopoly in the hands of Sarnoff. As a result of the decree negotiated by Sarnoff, RCA acquired the sole right to license manufacture in the United States of the huge mass of radio and television patents owned by AT&T, GE, Westinghouse, and the U.S. counterparts of patents of the great European cartels. The license rights were "nonexclusive," but RCA employed only a package license under all the patents without naming them individually—thereby rendering useless any theoretical right any of the co-conspirators had to license their own patents. In fact, under the decree, GE and Westinghouse had to pay RCA, their former sales subsidiary, royalties on their own manufacture of radio apparatus even under their own patents!

Without digressing into the details of how a trial delay enabling Sarnoff to complete this, his greatest coup, was corruptly arranged by Sarnoff and certain Washington real estate operators and influence ped-dlers, Sarnoff's testimony included a total refutation and bitter denial of the sworn statements of Edward Keller, one of the real estate dealers involved in the scandal.

In describing a secret Sunday trip Keller and Sarnoff took to Boston in 1932 to meet with one of two influential senators who could perhaps "get to" the judge and/or the administration, Keller had related under oath that Sarnoff personally told him the Roosevelt motherhood story, indicating that he could "fix" the case once Roosevelt was elected. Keller described Sarnoff's story in detail. Sarnoff denied Keller's statements as lies in the following eloquent diatribe under oath on August 7, 1940:

Mr. Sarnoff: Insofar as Congressman O'Connor there refers to any arrangement or discussion between Paley and myself, I am sure that any such reference to the President of the United States cannot touch his honor, but I do want to deny categorically any such discussion was ever had between us and Mr. Paley or with the President of the United States.

I regret exceedingly that there has been thrown into this political discussion the name of President Roosevelt. I say this because I think it is very unfair. Yesterday in the affidavit of Mr. Keller, to which I assume subsequent reference will be made, there was a statement on that boat trip to which we have referred—and I quote from the record:

> On my boat trip with Mr. Sarnoff, from New York to Boston, Mr. Sarnoff informed me that he and President Roosevelt had been very close friends since the inception of radio, and that Mr. Roosevelt had said to him, "Dave, you are the father of radio, but when I was Assistant Secretary of the Navy, I mothered it for you," and that he believed Mr. Roosevelt would be elected in November and that if we were able to postpone this case until after the Roosevelt inauguration that he would have no trouble in dealing with Mr. Roosevelt personally.

Mr. Chairman and gentlemen, I brand this as a lie. No such statement was ever made by me to Mr. Keller or to anyone else. Furthermore, the facts themselves contradict it. The inception of radio was in about 1919. The Radio Corporation was organized in 1919. This boat trip took place in 1932.

I never met President Roosevelt in my life until after he had been President of the United States for some time. I think the first time in my life I ever met President Roosevelt was toward the latter part of 1933 or the beginning of 1934. I never discussed this case or any other pending case with the President.

I think it is a libel on the President, to say nothing of it being a libel on me. I brand it as an unadulterated falsehood.[2]

Yet at the taking of Sarnoff's deposition in the Zenith case on December 6, 1954, nearly fifteen years after his congressional testimony, Sarnoff responded to questioning in the following way:

Q. How about Mr. Roosevelt, F.D.R.?

A. I did subsequently and Mr. Roosevelt used to be fond of saying when they talked about Mr. Young being the father of RCA and a little later when I grew up, this paternity was handed down I suppose in the form of an honorarium and at times I was referred to as the father of RCA—although I was only a boy when it was formed—Mr. Roosevelt said to me, "If you and Owen Young are the fathers of RCA, I am the mother of RCA."

Q. When did that talk take place and where?

A. In the White House on a number of occasions.

Q. Can you give us one?

A. I can't give you the date. I used to be there—it was during his lifetime, during the period of his presidency. He was fond of telling the story of his participation in the organization of RCA, sometimes at dinner before others, and he used to wind up with that observation, "If he is the father of RCA, I am the mother of RCA."

Q. You say he said that on several occasions?

A. Yes.[3]

Thus, Sarnoff's memory had been fully restored for our case fourteen years and four months after his sworn testimony of denial in the Senate Interstate Commerce Committee hearings. This shocking inconsistency would have been of interest to the jury when Sarnoff was called by Zenith as an adverse witness subject to cross-examination at the then-impending Zenith trial.

The myth that RCA was formed at the request of the government and, by implication, was licensed to ignore the Sherman Act was repeatedly told throughout the years by Sarnoff and his mentor, Owen D. Young. We expected that Sarnoff would testify at the trial that RCA was formed at the request of the U.S. government and that President Wilson had designated Admiral Bullard to sit as a member of the board of RCA.

The so-called official government sponsorship of RCA and designation of Admiral Bullard as an RCA board member has the following background. There was pending in the House of Representatives in 1919 a bill known as H.R. 10831. The object of the proposed legislation was to protect against control of the communications business by foreign interests and against the licensing of aliens to own and operate stations. The bill also provided that certain restrictions of the law would not apply to those corporations whose bylaws provided for attendance at stockholders' and directors' meetings of a navy officer of or above the rank of captain. This bill never passed, and at no time after 1921 was any navy officer assigned to attend RCA board meetings. The *Report of the Federal Trade Commission on the Radio Industry* (1923) shows that Admiral Bullard retired from the navy to accept "employment" with RCA, but that he had no official relationship with the navy whatsoever in connection with his RCA employment.

The official attitude of the Navy Department was effectively expressed by Secretary of the Navy Danby in a letter dated December 16, 1921, to the Secretary of State. In this letter Danby refused to sanction a proposed agreement between Federal Telegraph of Delaware (controlled by RCA) and China whereby Federal of Delaware would acquire exclusive communications rights. A copy of the letter was sent to RCA, according to the FTC report. The following pertinent excerpt from that letter appears at page 5 of the FTC report on the radio industry:

The Navy Department fears that any commitment on the part of the Government to an arrangement favorable to a monopoly by a single commercial company, though limited to a particular service, would but lend a means toward extending monopoly to other services such as development and distribution of apparatus in general, and this is considered absolutely undesirable, particularly in the field of supply and service to ships.

At page 16 of the FTC report, the failure of General Electric to obtain official approval for the formation of RCA and any immunity from federal law is described:

The officers of the General Electric Co. called Admiral Bullard's attention to the fact that its business was to develop electrical apparatus and to sell to its regular trade, and that the only customers for the devices in question were the Marconi companies. They explained to Admiral Bullard the status of the pending negotiations and pointed out that if these negotiations were terminated the company would have no other outlet whereby it could realize on the investment and developments which the company had made. A discussion was had as to the formation of a new radio company which would have the support of the General Electric Co., and which would therefore be in a position to make the inventions of apparatus available for American communication.

It was pointed out that the most important radio company was the Marconi Co. of America, and that by a patent license from the British Marconi Co. its operations were limited to the United States. It was also shown that the British company owned considerable stock in the American company, and that through such influence radio communication to and from the United States would be largely dominated by the British company. Following these conferences with Admiral Bullard and Commander Hooper, the General Electric Co. ceased negotiations with the British Marconi Co., and proceeded to work out with the officials of the Navy Department a proposed contract under which a new company controlled wholly by American citizens might be formed.

A proposed contract was worked out with the Navy Department which never became effective [emphasis added]. The proposed contract contained a stipulation providing that the new company would be so constituted that control thereof should always remain in the hands of American citizens. Secretary Daniels, at the time of the negotiations, was in Europe and the execution of it was delayed until his return. On May 23, 1919, Secretary Daniels requested the officers of the General Electric Co. to meet him in Washington and discuss the contract. The Secretary stated (1) that he was in favor of Government ownership of radio; (2) he doubted his power to execute such a contract because at best it would be an exercise of a war power to project a peace program, which he did not desire to do except with the consent of Congress; (3) that if Congress did not approve of the program of Government ownership of radio, and did authorize the Navy to deal with the matter, a contract such as had been worked out would be acceptable. *Congress not having authorized the Secretary of the Navy to deal with the matter, the proposed contract was never executed* [emphasis added], and the General Electric Co. proceeded to make arrangements with a view of forming a new company which would take over its inventions.

Certain officials of the War Department were not in accord with the officials of the Navy Department, who desired to officially sanction such a company. Maj. Gen. George L. Squier is authority for the statement that he did not believe the War Department would have taken the same stand in the matter. He also pointed out the uselessness of the Radio Corporation as a selling agent for radio apparatus when the General Electric and Westinghouse companies already had efficient sales organizations.

Having failed to obtain official dispensation from either Congress or the navy, the Radio Group unsuccessfully attempted to get immunity for the trust from two attorneys general—Dougherty and Palmer. Conferences were held and a "brief" together with copies of the basic cross-licensing agreements were submitted for clearance. Even Attorney General Dougherty refused to express an opinion on the legality of the agreements under the antitrust laws. The two letters were introduced as Respondent's Exhibits 27 and 28 in the FTC proceeding, together with the brief of the Radio Group submitted to the Department of Justice. In the brief it was brazenly argued that radio is a natural monopoly and that all patents should be owned by one company in the interest of "national defense"!

Against this background, Sarnoff testified as follows at his deposition in the Zenith case on December 6, 1954:

He [Mr. Young] received the approvals he sought from his own board, and then organized the plan or team to effectuate that idea. So keen was Mr. Young about making certain that this plan had the approval of the Government of the United States, that Mr. Young, himself not only being a man of great experience and wisdom but also a lawyer by training, said that the contracts relating to that setup or the plan relating to that setup was one that he wished to submit to the Government for approval before he would proceed.

My recollection is that all the contracts, all the arrangements, all the understandings relating to that setup were spelled out by Mr. Young or his representatives to the proper authorities of the United States Government, including Mr. Roosevelt [then an Assistant Secretary of the Navy] and the others I have mentioned, and that they had received their blessing before the plan had actually been consummated.[4]

Sarnoff, a born raconteur and fabricator of tales, seemed to have been afflicted with a compulsive habit of concocting myths to glorify himself. He had from time to time made outrageous claims that he parented not only RCA but radio and television as well. We all looked forward to the illuminating show Tom McConnell's prospective cross-examination of Sarnoff at the trial would provide the court and jury. McConnell was a well-recognized master at cross-examining witnesses who could not remember "yesterday's lies" or inconsistent statements or who were afflicted with convenient lapses of memory that could be embarrassingly revived by their own documents.

THE "PACKAGE LICENSE" WEAPON WIELDED BY RCA

The linchpin of the conspiracy that held Zenith and the other independent radio and television manufacturers in bondage was the form of domestic license RCA had imposed on those Sarnoff, for a rewarding fee, permitted to be in the business. It was a broad license under any and all patents RCA had a right to grant in the United States during each five-year term of the license. Particular patents were never specified. The royalties were a percentage of the total selling price of the radio or television receiver (including the cabinet), whether or not any patents were used and despite the fact that most of the parts (such as the cabinet) were not conceivably covered by any patent. It was a total package. Arguments about coverage or noncoverage of any part of the product by any specific patent were irrelevant as far as RCA was concerned. You either took the package or faced extinction in interminable infringement suits against you and/or your customers under any or all of the vast array of patents flowing into the RCA patent pool from every source.

The diabolical necessity of maintaining the package license, which was so effective in the United States and in all the interrelated foreign territorial pools, was demonstrated in 1956 in a deposition taken by Joseph S. Wright from Ray Luebbe, General Counsel of GE. In 1946, in an attempt to break up the patent packaging scheme of RCA, Zenith had unsuccessfully sought a separate license from GE under certain GE radio patents. In cross-examining Luebbe, Wright asked if anyone at GE had ever talked to anyone at RCA about whether GE could license anyone separately under GE's patents. Luebbe, with surprising candor, replied "Yes." Wright then asked "Who?" and "When?" Luebbe responded that he had been present at a meeting in 1946 with Philip Reed, then Chairman of GE, and Sarnoff of RCA, the head of the radio patent pool of the American cartel. Luebbe testified that Sarnoff successfully warned GE that it would be unfair (a breach of the patent cartel arrangement) for GE to grant a license to Philco (which was also seeking a separate license agreement) because it "would undercut RCA's licensing situation." RCA had flatly denied any such attempt to break up its patent packaging license scheme.

As we prepared for trial, RCA had patent licensing rights under an estimated 10,000 to 15,000 patents emanating from its own laboratories, from those of its licensees and other independent inventors whose patents it purchased, and from GE, AT&T, Western Electric, and Westinghouse, as well as the patent holdings in the United States of all the foreign interrelated cartels of Europe. A total of sixty-two of those patents (some added, some dropped) had been asserted against Zenith in the Delaware case alone.

Origins of the Scheme

The patent licensing scheme was a diabolically cunning way to exploit the territorial monopolies of the cartels. Its interesting origins were traced in many RCA documents. A few scattered examples illustrate how the package licensing scheme was devised and how the anticompetitive restraints on independent research and development were fostered.

In response to the request of the RCA board of directors, a formal report to the board on licensing was made on January 31, 1922, by a committee dominated by David Sarnoff. Printed on Sarnoff's stationery, the report was broken down into five sections: (1) Requests for Licenses, (2) Disadvantages of Licensing, (3) Advantages of Licensing, (4) Grant Back of Patent Rights of Licensees, (5) Conclusion.

Under "Requests for Licenses," the report states that although RCA had received a number of requests for licenses under the Armstrong patents, no licenses had been or would be granted until a licensing policy was determined. The following observation is then made: "At this point it should be stated that if the corporation is to adopt a licensing policy, it would seem wise to grant licenses under all of its patents." This was the mandatory form of package license RCA later illegally adopted as the only license it would issue.

Under "Disadvantages of Licensing," the report mentioned the danger of a licensee developing a position of strength in "unpatented" devices and "upon expiration of our principal patents" continuing in business without paying royalties. RCA's program of acquiring patents from every source and the funneling arrangements with foreign cartels removed this threat.

Under "Advantages of Licensing," licensing would result in "recognition of the validity and scope" of the RCA patent pool and litigation could be eliminated except that "those not licensed would be attacked with infringement suits." Over 670 infringement suits eliminated unlicensed entrepreneurs without any having to go to trial! "Substantial royalties could be derived from licensing," the report very conservatively noted.

Under "Grant Back of Patent Rights," responsible manufacturers would result in their development of improvements [sic], observed Sarnoff. Therefore, RCA would require as a condition of the license that licensees "grant back to RCA licenses under any patents the licensee acquires." This is the origin of the infamous "grant back" clause in all licenses issued to Zenith before the litigation.

Most important, "RCA would be less liable to the charge of being a monopoly if it granted a limited number of licenses" (S441).[5] On this important consideration, a memo on the point further states:

It is also pertinent to bear in mind that through its agreements and affiliations with foreign operating companies, the corporation has excellent protection to its business of international radio communications. And having a virtual monopoly by reason of these affiliations, it does not seem desirable to endeavor to rigidly enforce a patent monopoly in the U.S. if suitable licensing arrangements can be made. The majority of people are interested more in the amateur and entertainment feature of radio than the commercial and communications side of it and to set up and rigidly enforce a complete patent monopoly without licenses would, in all probability, result in sentiment being turned against the corporation. (Y696–712)

Thus was born the licensing ruse set up to camouflage the antitrust law violations at the heart of the cunning scheme.

In a letter to Edwin M. Herr of Westinghouse dated October 13, 1925, Sarnoff refers to the RCA board's resolution appointing a committee of the conspiring companies to study and recommend a licensing policy. Sarnoff was instructed to prepare a statement of recommended policy and action. His statement and recommendation, which are attached to the letter, describe the infamous and cunning license policy that was put into play in 1927 when Zenith and other leading independents were licensed and allowed to continue in business under the yoke of the conspiracy.

In his recommendations to the Patent Policy Committee, Sarnoff points out that it is a basic principle that a company holding patents fundamental to an industry should license some recognized competitors—that it is impracticable for one manufacturer of an article of general application to supply the entire public demand with a single brand from only one source or supply. He explains that this was the reason for licensing the Masda Lamp Patents: that no manufacturer could maintain a complete monopoly "even on a patented article."

Sarnoff points out that before RCA had consolidated its position, it was not necessary to license; no outstanding competitors had yet developed, and the RCA set had no advantage over other sets. He notes that this situation had changed: RCA was firmly established, and Victor and Brunswick (leaders in the phonograph and record industry) had been acquired. In short, the Radio Group members were in a position in which licensed competition could not harm them but would help them, both by producing hugely rewarding royalties and by creating the deceptive impression that they were not dreaded monopolists but public-spirited patriots.

Under "Urgency of the Licensing Problem," Sarnoff refers in the letter to a suit then pending on an Alexanderson patent testing whether the manufacture of tuned radio frequency and neutrodyne sets then being made by the independents could be stopped. He states that the defendants would make capital if the suit was viewed as an attempt to eliminate all set competition. This would not be so if they granted licenses; and if they lost the suit, their ability to license would be impaired. Suggested royalties and terms of proposed licenses are then described and the prospective licensees are listed.

The document is an important statement of why the company should license and what the limitations of a suggested licensing policy should be. In terms of philanthropy and a general desire to advance the industry, as opposed to feathering one's own nest, the statement is made that a manufacturer whose patents are fundamental to an industry should license:

Because the needs of the market will inevitably encourage competition even at the risk of infringement and because the courts hesitate to enforce patent rights when the effect is to perpetuate a monopoly and prevent competition. (H739)

If our claim should be declared invalid, we would be deprived of any opportunity to extend licenses and collect royalties, while at the same time, retaining the odium which would attach to any effort practically to eliminate all said competition. (H740)

Both from a legal as well as from a commercial standpoint it would seem safer to determine upon our course in the matter of licensing before the validity of the patent is decided. (H738–749, H741)

It is interesting to consider Sarnoff's reference to the Masda Lamp Patents licensing scheme. Among the number of antitrust cases brought by the government against GE throughout the years (beginning with a 1911 price-fixing case that was closed out with a consent decree) was the so-called General Electric lamp case. In this case the government proved up a GE conspiracy to monopolize the manufacture and sale of light bulbs, glass bulbs, lamp bases, and related products in the United States, aided by the so-called Phoebus cartel agreements with leading foreign companies in the field of incandescent lamp manufacture. That conspiracy—which began in 1919, when the radio and television conspiracy was also born—is in structure and purpose an almost exact counterpart of the GE–RCA electronics conspiracy involved in the Zenith case. In a monumental opinion handed down in 1949 by the very able Judge Foreman, the United States District Court in New Jersey found that the aggregation of criminal conspiratorial activities of GE in the United States and abroad was a flagrant violation of the Sherman

Act, Section 1 (a conspiracy in restraint of domestic and foreign trade) and Section 2 (an attempt to monopolize and a monopolization of the incandescent electric lamp industry) (82 F.Supp. 753).

Sarnoff's reference to the Masda Lamp licensing practices indicated his knowledge of how to structure such a conspiracy and how—by enslaving selected independent manufacturers as package licensees—a deceptive appearance of benevolent "advancement" of the art and the "public interest" would camouflage the crimes.

Although in recent decades the illegality of mandatory package licensing became abundantly clear in principle as an illegal extension of individual patent monopolies, for years RCA had been remarkably successful in hiding behind an infamous antitrust consent decree that a fading Hoover administration had negotiated with Sarnoff in a civil antitrust case in 1932 in Delaware. In that infamous episode, Sarnoff, while still ostensibly working for Owen D. Young, had been able to strip GE and Westinghouse of their stock control of RCA. This enabled him to set himself up in Rockefeller Center as a new "independent" entity armed with all the domestic cartel patent powers and interrelationships with the foreign cartels, and the combined, dominating patent arsenals of all in the consumer radio products field. It was a familiar story in the industry that Sarnoff's favorite description of his accomplishment in negotiating the consent decree was this: "the Government handed me a lemon and I made lemonade out of it."

Sarnoff made the lemonade in a grand style of personal aggrandizement. Whether by hypnotizing Justice Department political appointees or persuading them by other means, Sarnoff came out of the negotiations that led to the consent decree with complete control of RCA, two radio networks, the radio manufacturing facilities of GE and Westinghouse, international ship-to-shore communications facilities, a majority of clear channel stations, and the sole right to license all the cartel's radio patents in the United States, which it employed in the package licensing scheme. Sarnoff's mentor, Owen D. Young, was forced out of his RCA leadership role in radio and out of his office at the newly constructed "palace"—the 65-story Rockefeller Center on New York's Fifth Avenue, where Sarnoff enthroned himself in the grandeur of a 53rd-floor corner suite paneled in white oak with an adjoining personal barbershop, lavatory, and private dining room. Sarnoff's day-to-day contacts with his mentor and the legal architect of the conspiracy, Owen D. Young, were no longer necessary for his advancement; so they ceased. Sarnoff surrounded himself with loyal men: Manton Davis, his

General Attorney and Counsel; Otto Shairer, head of the all-important Patent Department; George DeSousa, Treasurer, who had hired Sarnoff as an office boy at American Marconi; and Lewis MacCormack, Corporate Secretary.

The scandals surrounding Sarnoff's "accomplishment" in the consent decree occupy volumes of testimony before congressional investigative committees[6] and other reports on the alleged corruption of Delaware court personnel preceding the entry of the 1932 consent decree. Although that decree ostensibly changed the "exclusive" provisions of the patent rights exchanges between the domestic and foreign conspirators to "nonexclusive," as a practical matter the change provided a deceptive distinction without any difference. Subsequent attorneys general, however, were for years held by the courts to be contractually estopped by the settlement agreement from any attempt to rectify the injustice to the public.

ZENITH'S CONCERN OVER THE GOVERNMENT'S CONCERN

During its breakaway moves in the Chicago court in 1954, Zenith had drawn the attention of the Antitrust Division of the Department of Justice under Stanley Barnes. In November 1954 Barnes filed a civil suit against RCA in the New York federal court that mirrored Zenith's antitrust, monopoly allegations. Other related civil actions against GE, Westinghouse, and Philips followed much later, as did a criminal prosecution of RCA well after the Zenith litigation was settled in 1957.

However, as Zenith's Chicago case was moving rapidly into 1955, we had the haunting fear that another counterproductive government consent decree might be engineered by Sarnoff. It might prejudice our case with the same kind of deceptive cry that Sarnoff had made about the 1932 decree: "We have always complied with any request the government made of us." Zenith's general counsel, Joseph S. Wright, was therefore anxious to comply with requests by the government to cooperate in its new investigation of the cartelized monopoly. He had properly expressed to the Justice Department Zenith's willingness to cooperate. In a letter to Wright dated November 10, 1954, Stanley Barnes, Assistant Attorney General in charge of antitrust matters, stated: "It would be appreciated if the next time you are in Washington you would get in touch with Mr. Hallabaugh [a Barnes assistant]."

A meeting followed with Barnes and his staff. The frustrating history of the RCA monopoly and the nature of an adequate remedy to protect the public interest were discussed in some depth. Wright wrote to Barnes following the meeting, emphasizing the dangers of another inadequate consent decree. That letter accurately describes in detail the nature of Zenith's fears:

January 7, 1955

Honorable Stanley N. Barnes
Assistant Attorney General
Department of Justice
Washington, D.C.

Dear Judge Barnes:

Mr. McConnell and I appreciated very much the courtesy you extended us on January 5, and the opportunity of meeting you personally and attempting to answer some of the questions which were in the minds of your very capable staff members.

During the course of our discussions we explained a fundamental problem that is involved in considering appropriate relief against the conspiracy alleged in the government's complaint, which is a problem very similar to that facing Zenith as a private litigant. The RCA package license system has never concerned itself with individual patents—it frankly grants "protection" from patent infringement actions under any patents in the field which RCA has the right to sublicense. We do not know exactly how many patents this might be at any particular time, as patents expire at the end of their terms and new patents are being issued to the parties to the cross-licensing agreements every day and American patents of the foreign signatories are likewise "funneled" into the mass. When Zenith refused to execute a new license in 1946 we had no idea what patents RCA would choose to assert against us either on the apparatus we were making at that time or on the improvements of our apparatus which are constantly being engineered. Altogether sixty-two patents were selected by RCA, GE and Western Electric to assert against us in the Delaware case. Thirty-nine of these patents have now been dropped following our showing of invalidity through anticipation of the alleged invention in the prior art or related considerations.

In other words, from this mass of patents which has been estimated to be in the neighborhood of 15,000 there were asserted against us sixty-two patents which were undoubtedly the patents which RCA thought were the strongest and on which they were willing to rely in court. Sixty percent of these patents have already been withdrawn as worthless even prior to the trial, and our patent counsel assure us that most, if not all, of the remaining patents can be beaten at the trial purely on considerations of patent law. Of these remaining twenty-three patents, eleven have by now expired and all but a very few will have expired by the time the litigation is terminated.

Some of your assistants were wondering whether this kind of a patent action would not finally adjudicate the extent to which RCA could assert its patent power over the industry, so that once having litigated these patents Zenith would then be in a position of knowing that in the sale of its standard radio and television apparatus only the few remaining patents could be asserted. The answer is very definitely a "no," since RCA takes the position that it is not barred from asserting any of its patents not definitely adjudicated as invalid against receivers which are in any way different from the ones we were making when the suit started.

No one now knows, and I don't know how anyone could find out, the extent to which the remainder of the 15,000 patents in the pool are invalid. If the Delaware litigation proceeds to an adjudication, we would be very bitterly disappointed if the court were to sustain as many as six patents out of the sixty-two asserted. We know that these sixty-two patents were very carefully selected by RCA, GE and Western Electric for the purposes of our case, and it would be a reasonable assumption that this process was designed to pick only the best of the patents for the suit. If more than ninety percent of these "best" patents prove worthless, how can anyone assume that there is not at least as high a "mortality" rate in the remainder? While it would be helpful to some companies to provide "selective"—as distinguished from "package"—licensing, in that there would not then be an estoppel against showing invalidity of unlicensed patents which RCA might assert in an infringement case, this would not provide any relief to a concern which does not have the resources to spend several million dollars in litigation over the mass of other patents which are unlicensed.

Mr. Cahill himself is a well-qualified witness as to the perils of patent litigation with RCA. When we advised RCA in 1946 that we would not renew our license, he went directly to the president of Zenith with the suggestion that he consult independent counsel who would confirm that Zenith's proposed course involved the risk of treble damages, costs and attorneys fees amounting to a great deal more than the proposed royalty payments. Fortunately, Zenith had both the courage and the resources to resist this coercion, but it is the only company in the industry that did.

We are convinced that any decree in the government's suit which terminated the cross-licensing agreements between the telephone company, GE, RCA and the foreign sources would give little effective relief to our industry if it still left RCA free to use the great mass of patents of which it is now the record owner to force its competitors either to take out a package license or subject itself to the risk of harassment by litigation over a mass of patents of which we suspect at least ninety percent to be invalid.

A further relevant consideration is this: That mass of patents owned outright by RCA has been manufactured for the principal purpose of perpetuating RCA control over the industry. RCA has a large patent department engaged in the business of manufacturing patents in collaboration with its extensive research laboratories and we can prove that its purpose was to take out a mass of patents, regardless of their validity. This patent factory has been supported wholly by the proceeds extracted from the rest of the industry pursuant to the illegal scheme. In our litigation in Chicago we are prepared to show that the current mass of RCA patents has been created pursuant to the objective of the conspiracy and that it is the very fruit of the conspiracy. If we are successful in this position, as I am confident that we will be on the basis of even the fragmentary discovery which we have now had, we will be entitled to a decree which will prevent RCA from asserting any of its existing patents against us—in effect the kind of a dedication of patents that was involved in the GE lamp case in so far as our own interests are concerned.

It seems to us that dedication is the only adequate remedy to dispose of a huge mass of patents which (1) has been created as an enforcement weapon of an illegal conspiracy, and (2) which is composed for the most part of invalid patents created to fence in the industry.

We did not discuss the subject in our conference on Wednesday, but you have undoubtedly been advised by representatives of RCA that its system meets with the approval of everyone in the industry with one or two exceptions and that RCA is in fact a sort of public service institution which makes it possible for a lot of small concerns to remain in the radio business; that without the beneficent licensing policies of RCA, these small concerns would be unable to continue in the industry. There are a few companies in our business who will take that position. However, to accept that argument and follow it to its logical conclusion is to permit RCA to *enforce* a monopoly position in research and development supported by the entire industry because some concerns are willing to pay for a shield from the necessity of research and development on their own account, and to rely on RCA to conduct all the research and development and supply all the engineering service necessary to keep them in a competitive position.

Others of us in the industry would prefer to do our own research and development—or at least to have the choice to do so, which we would not have if RCA's position is perpetuated. We are firmly convinced that competition in research and development is the lifeblood of the entire radio industry and we are willing to take our chances in competing with RCA and GE and Westinghouse in that respect. We have gotten along without any RCA engineering or laboratory services for many years and we are known in the industry as a pioneer in the engineering and development of high quality radio and television receivers without the slightest bit of help from "the great white father."

As to those companies in the industry which would prefer to rely on RCA for engineering and research, there is no reason why RCA could not continue such service for them on a fee basis, regardless of any antitrust decree which might be entered. Zenith, for one, would much rather conduct its own research and development, and we feel that both the industry and the public at large will derive more benefits from competition in research than from the present system, with its requirement that the industry finance a monopoly of research in RCA. To leave RCA with the power to force the industry to pay twenty or thirty million dollars a year to support RCA's research is to deprive us the means with which to carry on our own research. The really great inventions of our industry have not come from the large corporate laboratories, they have come from individuals like Armstrong, De Forest, Farnsworth, Parker and others, either working alone or in small companies. Freeing the industry of RCA's domination should be a great stimulus to this kind of invention.

Zenith is now in the position of getting all the facts regarding RCA's violations of the antitrust laws, and within six or eight months we will be able to complete our discovery on both the domestic situation and the foreign restrictions as well. When that record has been established it will be possible for the courts to frame appropriate relief on the basis of all the facts. Our only present concern is that the Department of Justice is not persuaded to take hasty action to accept a consent decree that would leave RCA free to continue its domination of the industry with the cover of government approval. Such a decree would certainly be urged by RCA, just as the 1932 decree has been urged, as a reason for denying Zenith relief in a case which has already cost us over a million dollars and eight years of strenuous litigation.

With kindest regards, I am

Sincerely yours,

Joseph S. Wright

JSW:moh

The response of the Justice Department to this letter was, indeed, reassuring:

UNITED STATES
DEPARTMENT OF JUSTICE
WASHINGTON 25, D.C.

January 25, 1955

Joseph S. Wright, Esquire
General Counsel
Zenith Radio Corporation
6001 West Dickens Avenue
Chicago 39, Illinois

Dear Mr. Wright:

This will acknowledge receipt of your letter of January 7, 1955.

I very much appreciate the cooperation which Zenith has extended to us and in particular your courtesy in coming in with Mr. McConnell on January 5, 1955.

In reference to the last paragraph of your letter, please be assured that the Department has no intention of entering into any consent decree with RCA, which is the result of hasty or ill-advised action. We are aware of the dangers attendant upon such a procedure.

My thanks again to you and Mr. McConnell.

Sincerely yours,

Stanley N. Barnes
Assistant Attorney General

THE SETTLEMENT BETWEEN ZENITH AND RCA ET AL.

During the summer of 1957, as we were making final preparations for trial scheduled for September 1957, a high official of GE came to Chicago seeking to open settlement discussions with McDonald. A preliminary meeting took place at McDonald's fishing lodge in Canada, where he was on his usual summer vacation. Other discussions followed in Chicago. On Sunday night, September 7, 1957, the litigation was settled in a document hastily prepared by RCA counsel to avert the opening of the trial on Monday morning.

98   THE FALL OF THE U.S. CONSUMER ELECTRONICS INDUSTRY

The initial settlement draft prepared by RCA counsel provided for payment of damages to Zenith in the amount of $10 million (estimated damages for exclusion from Canada) and a worldwide five-year, royalty-free license to Zenith for the radio-television receiver field under all the patents of RCA, GE, AT&T, Western Electric, and Westinghouse.[7] One nettlesome problem so concerned RCA that it held out for some provision that would protect it from attack by its other licensees in the United States, who might seek to renege on their royalty obligations under their RCA licenses because of the Zenith settlement.[8] In what appeared to us to be window dressing, RCA proposed that the settlement agreement provide for arbitration of "claims" for the difference in value of Zenith patents and RCA patents with low minimum and maximum amounts specified that would not radically affect the settlement agreement.

Zenith accepted the basic settlement proposal on September 9, 1957, and the separate arbitration agreement dated September 27, 1957. There was, however, a concern about what specific issues were to be arbitrated. Supreme Court Justice Minton, a first preference for arbitrator, declined the invitation to act as arbitrator. The parties agreed to the appointment of the recently retired federal district court judge in Chicago, the well-known and respected Judge Barnes.

Preliminary meetings were held with Judge Barnes. We reached the point of submitting to him the specific issues he was to hear and determine. I prepared an internal memorandum analyzing the settlement and related arbitration agreement in which I argued the following points: (1) "Enforceability" of the patents (i.e., whether or not the alleged antitrust violations rendered the patents unenforceable under the law) was an issue to be given priority in the arbitration; and (2) The value, if any, the arbitrator could assign to Zenith's use of RCA patents would be zero, if the arbitrator found the patents to have been misused in violation of the antitrust laws.

Under the first point, I argued that the following specific provision of the arbitration agreement effectively left enforceability (i.e., the antitrust issue) an issue for the arbitrator to determine: "The arbitrator shall proceed on the assumption that all patents asserted hereunder are *valid* and shall interpret the claims thereunder *according to the standard principles of construction laid down in the United States statutes and court decisions*" (emphasis added).[9]

Thus, only "validity" was an issue specifically excluded from arbitration. "Enforceability," the technical term relating to the antitrust issues, had not been included with "validity" and was therefore, under standard rules of construction, included with the issues for arbitration. The standard rule has a Latin phraseology: *Inclusio unius est exclusio alterius* ("including one excludes the other[s]"). Thus, by specifically including "validity"—a technical term limited to whether or not an invention is patentable (e.g., is it found in "prior art" or is it merely an "improvement" obvious to anyone skilled in the art?)—other issues such as unenforceability for antitrust violations were automatically included with the issues to be arbitrated.

Under the second point, no value could be assigned to patents being misused because of antitrust violations. This construction of the settlement agreement was further bolstered by the rule that in construing a contract, any ambiguity is to be resolved against the party who prepared the contract. RCA counsel had prepared the contract, and any attempted construction by them of any alleged ambiguity contrary to our construction would not prevail.

Joe Wright and Tom McConnell fully agreed with this analysis. Tom first broke the news to Leslie Hodson of the Kirkland, Ellis Chicago firm representing RCA. Hodson had come to our offices on his way to the airport one afternoon to discuss the arbitration. He said he was on his way to a meeting of RCA counsel in New York "to finalize" on the issues to be argued before the arbitrator. McConnell clearly explained that the first and foremost issue we intended to address was the antitrust issue—the question of the enforceability and value of the RCA patents. The cries of surprise, anguish, and outrage emanating from the stricken Hodson were heard throughout our offices. He left for the airport in a state of tearful rage. The practical result of that meeting and a confirming letter from McConnell to our opponents was a complete abandonment of the arbitration. Obviously, RCA decided not to have Judge Barnes determine the antitrust issues. If RCA felt it had somehow eliminated the issues in the settlement agreement, the question of construction of the arbitration agreement would have had to be presented to Judge Igoe in the federal district court. The result of this dilemma was RCA's abandonment of the arbitration.

Sarnoff's bitterness was driven to new depths by this turn of events. As shown in later chapters, his consuming hunger for retribution and a desire to replace his now-lost huge royalty income from U.S. licensees was partially sated by his profitable collaboration with the Japanese cartel in its campaign to destroy and replace the ungrateful American industry he had allowed to exist for so "reasonable" a royalty.

Meanwhile, after the Zenith settlement, the Justice Department accelerated its antitrust activity against RCA, GE, Westinghouse, and co-conspirator Philips of Holland, whom it found within its jurisdiction in the United States. Its process reached Philips through the so-called Hartford Trust in Hartford, Connecticut, where Philips had scampered to escape Hitler's onslaught during World War II. In addition to the civil action filed in the New York federal court in November 1954, the Justice Department brought civil suits against GE, Westinghouse, and Philips in 1958. A New York federal grand jury indicted RCA on February 21, 1958, for criminal violation of the Sherman Act. RCA slipped out of the criminal case by pleading nolo contendere (unwilling to contest the case) on October 28, 1958. The plea was accepted, and New York District Judge McGohey imposed a fine on RCA of $100,000 without appearing to understand the gravity of the offenses charged.

On November 5, 1958, a year after the Zenith settlement, RCA avoided trial of the government's civil action against it by entering into a complex consent decree partially dedicating on a royalty-free basis 100 patents in its pool to members of the domestic radio and television manufacturing industry. As a condition of receiving such royalty-free licenses, industry members were required to make their relevant patents available to other licensees of this government pool. The consent decree was designed to break up—for the rest of the industry not affected by the earlier RCA-Zenith settlement agreement—the monopolistic patent pooling scheme that Zenith had escaped in its litigation and settlement.

In 1962, five years after the Zenith settlement, GE, Westinghouse, and Philips consented with the government to the entry of injunctions forbidding agreements to restrict the export of radio and television sets from the United States to Canada (participation in their Canadian patent pool).

There were at least three major criticisms to be leveled at the results of the government actions:

1. They were thirty years late. One of Sarnoff's greatest "achievements" was his success in frustrating and delaying the government's compliance with its constitutional and statutory duties to enforce the antitrust laws.

2. By accepting RCA's nolo contendere plea in the criminal case, an apparently uninformed judge treated the case like a minor prosecution for a careless misdemeanor. Imposing a $100,000 fine on a multi-billion-dollar worldwide enterprise was ridiculously inappropriate.

3. Most important, the consent decree and nolo pleas to the indictment frustrated a primary congressional purpose written into the antitrust statutes: that is, to compensate victims of any antitrust conspiracy by providing

that when the government successfully proceeds against conspirators, a final decree after trial or after a guilty plea in a criminal action permits victims to recover threefold their damages on the basis of the government case merely by proving up their actual damages. The successful government case is prima facie proof of the violation in any private damages suit by any victim.

On January 30, 1959, the House of Representatives' antitrust subcommittee of the Committee on the Judiciary commenting on the Consent Decree Program of the Department of Justice reported:

Much of the success of the private antitrust action, however, has in turn been due in large measure to the antitrust litigation of the United States Government. It has been estimated that approximately three-fourths of all private suits have followed in the wake of victorious Government actions in fully litigated cases. . . .

It is clear that the substantial immunity from private antitrust actions is a primary consideration in defendants' willingness to negotiate consent decrees. . . .

Because of the protracted nature of antitrust litigation, with the expense and complexity of proof of the legal and economic issues involved, it is difficult at best for a private citizen to prosecute to conclusion an action under the antitrust laws. When the private litigant is deprived of the use of the Government's decree as prima facie evidence, moreover, a private action becomes virtually impossible to maintain. The almost inevitable consequence of the acceptance of a consent decree by the Department of Justice in an antitrust action, therefore, is to reduce the effectiveness of Section 5 of the Clayton Act and to deprive private suitors, who have been injured by unlawful conduct, of their statutory remedies under the antitrust laws.[10]

The report fittingly describes the reason why RCA, GE, Westinghouse, AT&T (Western Electric), and Philips so successfully engineered the consent decrees and why RCA avoided trial and pleaded nolo contendere[11] in its criminal case. However, Zenith had fought the good fight all alone and obtained its settlement prior to any consent decrees and the prosecution of RCA. The government suits were anticlimactic, in Zenith's view, although we were grateful that the government did not fight us on behalf of the conspirators.

NOTES

1. W. H. Eicles, *Wireless* (1933), pp. 28–29.
2. Testimony before the Senate Interstate Commerce Committee given on August 7, 1940. "Hearings of the Senate Interstate Commerce Committee on the Nomination of Thad Brown" (1940), pp. 292–93.

3.   Deposition of David Sarnoff, taken by Zenith counsel on December 6, 1954.

4.   Ibid.

5.   "S441" is an identification number placed by Zenith on copies of documents produced to Zenith by court order. Other lettered numbers cited in this chapter represent similar document codings. The documents are not public records.

6.   See, for example, the 685-page "Hearings of the Senate Interstate Commerce Committee on the Nomination of Thad Brown" (1940).

7.   The licenses were for five years, but the RCA license was renewed and no further patent conflicts were experienced by Zenith from any of the defendants.

8.   Zenith had paid no royalties to RCA after the expiration of its license agreement in 1946. Had Zenith lost the case, it would have owed at least those royalties (in the area of $16 million) plus any punitive damages (in the area of $48 million) that might have been assessed by the court.

9.   *Black's Law Dictionary,* 5th ed. (West Publishing, 1979), p. 687.

10.   "Report of the House of Representatives Antitrust Subcommittee on the Judiciary," dated January 30, 1959, at p. 23.

11.   Unlike a guilty plea, nolo contendere (unwilling to contest), like a consent decree in government civil actions, is not a confession of guilt usable in subsequent private actions by injured victims. It enables the court to find a defendant guilty only for the purposes of the government's case.

4

"It Ain't Over Till It's Over"

Following the settlement with RCA in 1957, Zenith concentrated on the advancement of its radio and television products. Zenith's first efforts on television had started in 1940, when all necessary transmitter, receiver, and studio equipment—including cameras—were constructed in Zenith laboratories. Interrupted by World War II, the work had been resumed in November 1945.

In 1950, Zenith had developed a practical alternative to the impractical CBS (Columbia Broadcasting System) field-sequential color TV system. By the end of 1953, the Federal Communications Commission (FCC) approved the NTSC (National Television System Committee) system of color television that Zenith and other industry members had been instrumental in developing. When the FCC demonstrated the first color receiver compatible with black-and-white TV in October 1953, Zenith was one of only three manufacturers that was able to demonstrate its own color tube in its own color set. Zenith responsibly cautioned the industry that color development was at an interim stage and was not ready for production.

RCA's David Sarnoff, however, could not resist the temptation to cash in on the industry's NTSC standards adopted by the government. Falsely claiming to be the inventor of color TV, RCA began mass production of color receivers. Only one in three color tubes RCA produced was found to be usable. As Zenith's Eugene McDonald had warned, color TV was not yet ready for mass production. By October 27, 1956,

Time magazine described Sarnoff's new color receivers as "the most resounding industrial flop of 1956."

Sarnoff's color TV fiasco contrasted sharply with the growing success of Zenith's high-quality products. Zenith took over the number one position in black-and-white TV in 1956. By 1961, Zenith's development work in color TV reached a point that permitted mass production of a greatly improved and simplified color receiver, which was reliable and easy to repair. Zenith entered the color TV market, and sales took off like a rocket.

Sarnoff experienced much resentment as a result of his losing fight against Zenith, his initial flop in color TV, and his need to wiggle out of the government's civil and criminal cases against RCA. His notorious sense of cunning was, if anything, further sharpened.

WHO OR WHAT WAS HAZELTINE?

Sarnoff welcomed and encouraged Hazeltine, an independent radio and television patent producing entity with an adjunct government business as a defense contractor. As a licensor of an array of approximately 500 radio and television patents, Hazeltine had the public appearance of being an RCA competitor in the patent license business. This enabled RCA to deny its alleged monopoly; it could point to "independent" Hazeltine as its vigorous patent licensing competitor.

Despite the fact that the government had listed Hazeltine as a co-conspirator in its indictment against RCA, it did not join Hazeltine as a defendant in either the criminal case or the related civil actions. We were never able to learn why Hazeltine was allowed by the government to continue with its package licensing and conspiracy with the foreign cartels.

In May 1959, Lawrence B. Dodds, counsel for Hazeltine, made a personal call on Zenith to deliver an ultimatum. Dodds announced that Zenith was infringing on four of Hazeltine's patents; and unless Zenith signed the Hazeltine patent license, a package license under all of its some 500 patents, Hazeltine would file suit for infringement. Zenith refused to sign the proffered package. Zenith did not believe it was infringing on any of the four patents asserted, and it further believed that under the antitrust laws, the demand that the mandatory package license under all of its some 500 patents was illegal. Hazeltine claimed that the Supreme Court had legalized the practice in *Automatic Radio Mfg. Co. v. Hazeltine Research Corp.* [339 U.S. 827 (1950)].

On October 20, 1959, Hazeltine filed suit against Zenith in the Chicago federal district court alleging patent infringement. Zenith answered the complaint by denying the validity and infringement of the patent in suit and set up the defense of misuse and violations of the antitrust laws. Files subpoenaed from Hazeltine Research Corporation and its New York parent, Hazeltine Corporation, revealed not only the close, clandestine relationship Hazeltine had with RCA but the important and active role Hazeltine had in the foreign cartels involved in our RCA litigation. On the basis of these revelations, we filed a counterclaim for treble damages as a result of Hazeltine's unlawful efforts to force its package license on Zenith and to keep Zenith out of Canada and other foreign markets.

As discovery proceedings continued on both the patent and antitrust issues into the fall of 1961, Zenith began to successfully market color TV receivers. Counsel for Hazeltine boldly informed Zenith that it was infringing on at least nine Hazeltine color TV patents. Thus, the ghost of the vanquished RCA struggle had been resurrected in the form of a cleverly disguised surrogate. Hazeltine was simply a weapon in Sarnoff's continuing war against Zenith.

Although Hazeltine had successfully defended the package license scheme against a licensee in the Supreme Court in 1950 in the *Automatic Radio* case, that case did not apply to anyone coerced into a package license or to anyone refusing tender of such a license, as the Court was later to hold. Theoretically, Hazeltine could successfully extend that holding in the Zenith case, thus freeing up RCA to reconstitute its old monopoly with newly manufactured and acquired patents.

Another reason for this scurrilous lawsuit soon became obvious. As soon as Zenith began to set up distribution of its products (including receivers) in Canada after the RCA settlement, the Canadian patent pool signaled it would welcome Zenith as a pool member if Zenith would manufacture in Canada and contribute the Canadian counterparts of Zenith's U.S. patents to the patent pool. Zenith's refusal of this bold offer was met with assertions that Zenith was infringing on Hazeltine patents in the Canadian pool.

Hazeltine was thus fighting in principle for legalization of the old RCA conspiracy, foreign and domestic. The government's unexplained failure to make Hazeltine a co-defendant in its civil and criminal cases took on the prospects of a potential disaster to Zenith. Hazeltine was portrayed as a "scientific enterprise" engaged in valuable research for the advancement of science and the American electronics industry. Hazeltine would argue that Zenith was 600 times larger and a ruthless pirate plundering the patent properties of a struggling, "public-spirited" Hazeltine research organization. Viewing Zenith in such a role, the courts could conceivably favor Hazeltine despite Zenith's valid legal arguments.

Hazeltine fought with a surprising endurance and fury, making every possible argument that would legalize package licensing and patent cartels, domestic and foreign. It took two Supreme Court reviews and fourteen years before Zenith prevailed in 1971.[1] Zenith recovered $22 million in damages and an effective injunction. The Hazeltine threat was permanently removed.

The true reason behind what we believed was RCA's Hazeltine gambit would be revealed in the coming war over television. The nagging Hazeltine case tied up important legal resources and significantly delayed Zenith's response to the ambush that lay ahead.

SARNOFF'S REVENGE

Occasionally, documents[2] produced by RCA in Europe in the Zenith case disclosed that Sarnoff was focusing unusual attention on Japan, beginning in the mid-1950s. Teams of Japanese scientists and engineers were welcomed in visits to RCA headquarters in New York. Their in-depth conferences with management and their inspections of RCA facilities and laboratories indicated that Sarnoff's philosophy and industrial skills were being studied by Japanese experts with a frenzy. Teams of RCA patent licensing experts and technical personnel were in turn being welcomed in Japan. The documents contained clues to the coming assault on the U.S. television industry, but their significance was overlooked in Zenith's frantic antitrust trial preparations.

Other documents produced by RCA disclosed a very early tutoring of the Japanese by Sarnoff and Young on how to cartelize the Japanese industry in the same manner as GE had cartelized the American market. For example, as early as December 9, 1921, Sarnoff memoranda recommended that there be a "consolidation" of competitors in Japan in the same way as GE and its competitors were operating in the United States. Sarnoff's interest in harnessing such a cartel with lucrative foreign patent licenses is plainly revealed in one of the memoranda: "RCA would be glad if such a group in Japan would be its representative in that country and would be pleased to represent the Japanese group in the United States."

Following up on this scheme, Owen D. Young wrote to a "Doctor Dan," an important contact in Japan, urging the Japanese "to stabilize" the industry in Japan. Young very frankly stated: "I explained to you that we had mobilized in RCA the patents and technical resources of AT&T, Western Electric, United Fruit, Westinghouse and GE and that to make such a mobilization effective all these concerns have taken a substantial financial interest in RCA."

Still other documents disclosed that an elaborate Japanese cartel was in fact formed in general conformity with the Young-Sarnoff instructions, and for years was part of the foreign cartel system engineered by Young and Sarnoff on behalf of "the American group."

RCA's lucrative patent licensing scheme in the United States was facing destruction through Zenith's Chicago litigation, its settlement, and the subsequent criminal and civil antitrust prosecutions by the government. In a brilliant and cynical move, Sarnoff more than replaced the threatened patent licensing fees extracted from American manufacturers with a generous percentage of the entire production of the new, super-efficient Japanese cartel, which had a protected monopoly in Japan and was successfully beginning to prey upon the markets of the United States and other nations. This operation would produce for RCA as much as *$200 million in licensing revenue yearly* by the time GE reacquired RCA in 1985.

In 1986 a close Sarnoff business associate and a retired RCA vice president, Kenneth Bilby, published a book entitled *The General: David Sarnoff and the Rise of the Communications Industry.* This was done with the aid of a Harvard professor in a project of the Harvard Business School to eulogize Sarnoff after RCA had generously endowed two professorships in his honor in 1971. Bilby claimed to have had access to the RCA files to augment his memory, and he made some significant disclosures in his book. For example, in recounting how Sarnoff's pride had suffered as a result of the Zenith case and the loss of his licensing income in the United States, Bilby wrote:

Then he [Sarnoff] did his best to bury the [Zenith] litigation, even the memory of it. He seldom spoke of it within the Company. He refused to cooperate when various business magazines sought to probe unrevealed aspects of the Zenith settlement. His official press biography glossed over the long royalty battle. Later, he turned abroad with considerable success in Japan and Europe to recoup lost domestic patent income. (p. 216)

To a greater degree than any other American company, RCA "reverenced" the patent. It was the company's building block even if originally tainted with illegality, providing royalty income that in several depressed years during the thirties spelled the difference between profit and loss, a stream of bottom line dollars that flowed into the research laboratories and nourished new technologies like color. Over the years, a corporate culture emerged that held the licensing activity of RCA sacrosanct and its principal disciple was Sarnoff. The slogan "world leader" was soon abandoned. The decision had been made to license the world rather than sell RCA products to its customers.

In the pursuit of foreign licensing income, Sarnoff focused first on Japan. (pp. 221–22)

Sarnoff made a triumphal tour of Japan in 1960 at the invitation of the Japanese Federation of Economic Organizations. With technical assistance from RCA, Japan was building its electronics industry with great speed and targeting the huge U.S. market for consumer electronics products. Leading Japanese industrialists welcomed Sarnoff on his 1960 tour. The *Japan Times* eulogized him as the hero of the new Japanese television industry. Emperor Hirohito received him in private audience and conferred on him the Order of the Rising Sun, the highest decoration that could be given to a foreigner. Sarnoff responded in an address to the Japanese Federation:

To me Japan's progress in electronics is best symbolized by its growth in television. Almost alone television initiated the upsurge in Japanese consumer sales. One in every five TV sets installed throughout the world last year was in Japan. I am delighted that Japan is pioneering in color on a national basis. I am told that eight stations on three networks have been authorized to begin colorcasting and that many manufacturers have started production of color receivers. To me there can be no finer opportunity than color television for a fusion of Japanese artistry and technical progress.[3]

From the very beginning, development of the Japanese radio and television industry had been engineered and orchestrated by RCA. Sarnoff established in Tokyo a technical center modeled on his famous RCA laboratories in Princeton, New Jersey. Soon his trademarks of flagrantly illegal tactics and lawless commercial weaponry would be seen over and over in an epic battle to gain control of the American radio and television manufacturing industry.

THE JAPANESE TELEVISION CARTEL

By the mid-1950s, Japan's unique industrial policy and planning ministry, the Ministry of International Trade and Industry (MITI), took steps to organize the consumer electronics industry along lines broadly suggested by Sarnoff and his RCA specialists. RCA advocated the pooling of industrial interests in this industry so that RCA could license the powerful cartel and participate in its revenues through no-risk licensing agreements. The first step was to quietly enact a Japanese law in 1957.

The Electronics Industry Development Emergency Law authorized MITI to create a new Japanese electronics industry. The law elaborately outlined programs for the organization, financing, and direction of this new industry. A variety of government subsidies was provided. Free or extremely low interest loans from the Japanese Development Bank were made available to nurture the new industry.

This industry was to operate in much the same manner as America's infamous trusts—and on an international level. The industry would quickly carve out large market shares in the United States by using a predatory dumping scheme. Extremely low-cost sets in large numbers would be sold for as long as it took to drive out American competition. Prices in Japan, tightly closed to import competition, would be maintained at a very high rate to offset losses in the targeted market. The vast increase in production would lower the per unit costs considerably, and an overall total profit would result. To prevent competition between cartel members, promising American customers were exclusively assigned to particular cartel members; this ensured that their prices would only be low enough to undersell American competitors. Japan's prodigious savings rate, government loan guarantees, and subsidies provided virtually limitless, patient capital.

The passage of the landmark legislation that created a government-sponsored cartel coincided with the settlement of the Zenith-RCA litigation, but it was little noticed by Zenith or industry observers.

From 1958 to 1965, Zenith witnessed a Japanese commercial attack on the domestic radio market that reduced a once-healthy and highly competitive U.S. radio industry to a shambles. Many U.S. radio plants were closed and their work forces terminated. Companies that did not go out of business delayed their demise by moving production facilities to countries where labor was cheap, or else they procured their radios or parts from Japanese producers. Many American suppliers to the industry were forced out of business. This was the first technology-based consumer product assault by Japanese producers, and it would be seen in television and many more American industrial sectors selected for attack in the coming years.

By 1968, there had been a complete takeover of the U.S. radio market by the Japanese cartel. In February 1969, the trade publication *Association News* reported: "There is a joke that as Radio Corporation of America has ceased producing radios, they should omit 'Radio' from their firm name." RCA was getting a no-risk royalty return as a percentage of every Japanese radio made and sold in Japan and every set shipped to the United States. Sarnoff and his engineers had helped build the new Japanese factories and were continuing to service them with technical aid. The rest of the U.S. radio manufacturing industry, however, was driven out of business.

This was a first step in Sarnoff's revenge against his ungrateful, former American licensees. It should be noted that Zenith was the last American radio manufacturer to be driven out of the radio business by Sarnoff's new creation.

During the 1960s, the new color TV market was developing at a rapid rate. Zenith's full attention was given to the development and marketing of the new TV products and the exploding market for them. Zenith was a dynamic new force in TV manufacturing. An exceptional dedication to quality above all else drove Zenith to the number one position in the American TV market. A vigorous group of independent distributors, all loyal Zenith veterans in sales and service, were the envy of competitors.

By 1961–1962, the growing Japanese attack on the U.S. television market caused Zenith's management to study the Japanese strategy. It was apparent that a highly organized cartel was operating in Japan in much the same anticompetitive way as the old American trusts. The Japanese television industry was obviously fixing prices in Japan at levels at least 40 percent to 50 percent and more above prices it was charging in the United States. Zenith reasoned that American competition in Japan would force these prices down to reasonable levels and destroy the cartel's ability to engage in predatory dumping in the United States. Zenith decided to enter the Japanese market on a large scale. Now Zenith was about to experience the key component of Japan's industrial policy: the ironclad protection of Japanese industries involved in government-sponsored export programs. Imports from the United States would be blocked in every way.

Zenith contacted C. Itoh and Company, a huge Japanese trading company, for help in opening Japan to Zenith products. The potential popularity of Zenith products with Japanese consumers was apparent in trade fairs and demonstrations in Japan. C. Itoh took steps to market the product. However, market-entry barriers of every kind thoroughly frustrated the effort. Ultimately, an apologetic letter was received from C. Itoh, crudely explaining in translation, "MITI would not allocate the foreign currency, because Zenith products are exceedingly popular in the market here."

Characteristically, Zenith did not give up. Nichimen, another major Japanese trading company, was contacted and elaborate marketing plans for export to Japan were made. Although prospects were promising at first, the Nichimen efforts were blocked as effectively as C. Itoh's had been. The following excerpt from a final letter from Nichimen to Zenith, dated May 16, 1963, explains vividly the closed condition of the Japanese market:

After several publicity and news releases on the intention of our company to market Zenith's product line, there was an abrupt halt to the entire program. Although the reasons for this halt have never been officially explained to me, I feel they were due to the following reasons:

1. The Japanese Electronic Industry Association's pressure to the Government;
2. The Japanese Electronic Industry's pressure to the leading chain and department stores;
3. An attempt to pressure our company and persuade us by various means not to indulge too aggressively in the distribution of these products.

A final all-out effort was made again with C. Itoh in 1963. At Zenith's request, the trading company made an elaborate market analysis and proposal for the distribution in Japan of Zenith's advanced, highly popular color TV receivers. A high degree of interest was generated at the retail level in Japan through displays and demonstrations. However, every effort to import and market the product on a commercial basis was met by the same kind of immovable barriers that had frustrated prior attempts. After months of frustrating delays of every kind, Zenith was finally forced to give up the effort.

By 1968, the Japanese had seized the entire U.S. radio industry and were moving in the same manner into the TV market. Concentrating on the small-screen market, they captured an 11 percent market share of the entire market in 1968, their first year for the product. It was apparent that unless something was done to open up the Japanese market to American competition, or unless our federal anti-dumping, antitrust, and countervailing duty laws were enforced, the entire consumer electronics manufacturing industry in the United States would be destroyed.

The dumping margins, the difference between the high prices in Japan and the low prices offered by the cartel in the United States, were so great that no amount of cost cutting by American manufacturers could possibly save the industry. In addition to the Sherman Antitrust Act, there were three federal laws prohibiting such dumping: the Antidumping Act of 1916 (a criminal and civil remedial statute modeled on the Sherman Act), the Antidumping Act of 1921 (a law directing the administrative imposition of dumping duties to alleviate injury found by the International Trade Commission to have been sustained by domestic industry as a result of dumping), and the Countervailing Duty Statute (authorizing the government to offset foreign government subsidies unfairly aiding the massive dumping by foreign producers in competition with American manufacturers).

A number of independent manufacturers filed a petition with the Treasury Department in 1968, pleading with the administration to enforce the Antidumping Act of 1921. The Treasury and its Customs Bureau lethargically responded with an "investigation." Zenith's president, Joseph S. Wright, pleaded with administration officials and Congress to expose the unlawful conduct of the Japanese and put a stop to it as federal law demanded.

Chief among the American cohorts of the Japanese stood David Sarnoff and RCA. Their opposition to the industry petition was well known in industry and government circles, and they refused to participate in the proceeding.[4]

After the Treasury Department had had the petition for two full years, a so-called disclosure conference was held by the Customs Bureau at the urging of petitioners. This was a carefully guarded exercise wherein attorneys for the petitioning companies were told of the progress of the investigation without learning of the highly confidential pricing information the Customs Bureau had obtained from the Japanese manufacturers. Customs officials described briefly their conclusions about the Japanese market pricing of Matsushita, the largest of five Japanese manufacturers being investigated. They recited a raft of so-called downward price adjustments that had been allowed on Matsushita's home market prices to radically lower the dumping margins. When confronted with explaining each item on the long list of claims of allowances, which had obviously been made to shrink the dumping margins, Customs officials became officious and hostile. They repeatedly stated that they did not consider it necessary to discuss with "outsiders" the investigative processes of the office. Zenith's attorneys expressed outrage at the number of allowances, especially the absurd packaging differential. Here, Customs allowed an adjustment because Japanese sets were allegedly more expensive to package for shipment in the Japanese market than those shipped to the United States!

The commodity tax issue was much more important, and it raised the question of Japanese government subsidies. How could a 15 percent commodity tax as a percentage of the price of factory shipments to the Japanese market be the same as that same tax on lower-priced sets shipped to the United States and remitted by the Japanese government? How could they justify arbitrarily adding the amount of the tax in Japan to U.S. imports to "balance out" a "comparison of prices" to determine dumping? The allowances claimed by the lawyers for the Japanese interests involved were dubious and scurrilous. That Customs was more than willing to accommodate these practices without question was horrifying to the American producers. This was one of the first observed instances of unmistakable disloyalty on the part of U.S. trade officials.

The list of allowances included in the calculations of the prices in the Japanese market ran to the absurd. There was a "Distributor Prompt Payment Discount," a "Standard Distributor's Trade Discount," a "Set Discount," a "Retailer Cash Discount," a "Transaction Discount," and a "Retailer Discount." When questioned as to what had been done to validate the alleged allowances, Customs once again informed us that the confidential investigative processes of their office were in effect none of our business and that they did not intend to discuss them. Zenith's reasonable argument to simply use RCA's license royalty fees (a percentage of the sales prices in both markets) as the price bases was met by the same wave of the hand, officiously dismissing the suggestion.

Customs officials then discussed the results of their investigation of the export pricing to the United States. Unlike the Japanese home market pricing, there were no discounts, rebates, or other allowances admitted or discovered that would lower the prices claimed on the U.S. import documents. There was not even a warranty allowance for defective sets! Zenith's counsel repeatedly asked whether the records of the large American chains—like Sears and Penney's—were subpoenaed to determine the true prices paid and to prove the validity of the claim that absolutely no discounts, allowances, or rebates of any kind were made on their huge-volume purchases. Customs stated with finality that it was the firm policy of the Treasury Department not to investigate U.S. buyers of Japanese consumer products.

Incredibly, the commodity tax (a value-added tax) in Japan was added to the U.S. export price, although it had been "remitted" on the exports. This was done, Customs said, to balance out the comparison! Adding the Japanese market tax to the U.S. price to balance out the comparison was an obvious distortion and camouflage of the lower U.S. price. The granting of the tax remission on U.S. sales was a subsidy that should be equalized by a countervailing duty imposed by the United States in accordance with the Countervailing Duty Law. Customs dismissed these arguments as being contrary to Treasury policy and refused to discuss the matter further.

Customs officials then announced that their investigation had disclosed dumping margins of only 8 percent on some black-and-white TVs and 11 percent on some color TVs. In submissions to the government, Zenith had convincingly demonstrated that 19-inch color TV receivers were selling in Japan at price levels over $500 and that the same sets were being sold in the United States for less than $300. In more expensive models, the dumping margins were even greater.

In closing, Treasury announced that it was the intention of the Bureau "to accept tentatively" what was termed official letters of assurance from three unnamed Japanese companies "technically" found to be dumping, and to close out the investigation. Letters of assurance are broadly analogous to consent decrees. In them, anyone accused of dumping formally pledges that although they do not admit dumping, they are no longer dumping and will not do it again. Zenith and other industry representatives were deeply shocked.

This blatant siding with foreign interests dumping products in the U.S. market by the U.S. Customs Bureau had never been witnessed before. Zenith's president, Joe Wright, surmised that it was possible that our government had entered into an agreement with the government of Japan to trade off our industry for some unknown international purpose. All we could do was try to have the law enforced by continuously exposing the grave threat to our industry, which was exacerbated by a refusal of the government to enforce federal laws. Wright wrote letters, called on government officials, and pleaded with members of Congress in frantic efforts to get American antidumping laws enforced. The Customs Bureau, the State Department, and the Department of Justice were continually hounded with frantic appeals for some reasonable attempt to enforce relevant federal statutes. Nothing happened. The first terrifying instance of disloyalty and abandonment of a domestic industry by an American government was occurring. It would not be the last.

In September 1969, Wright wrote a letter to Treasury Secretary David M. Kennedy, urging reasonable efforts to enforce the Antidumping Act. He urged the government to impose a countervailing duty on imports that unfairly benefit from foreign government subsidies in competing with American products. The Secretary agreed to look into the matter with his counsel, Donald L. E. Ritger.

Ritger began the first meeting with Zenith in February 1970 by expressing the "grave international concerns" the Japanese had over strict enforcement of U.S. dumping and countervailing duty laws. Ritger went on to recall recent golf outings with Japanese representatives and related how he found their enthusiasm for this American pastime "so entertaining." This was entirely new in 1970, to hear high-level American trade officials openly describe social engagements with foreign interests who were charged with violating U.S. laws en masse. Such ominous prattle was merely a glimpse into an all-out assault on the American trade law establishment by powerful Japanese interests.

Referring to Wright's letter to the Treasury Secretary, Ritger said that he wanted this case completed as soon as possible, but there was a shortage of personnel at Customs. I suggested to Ritger that merely rushing the dumping investigation to completion on the basis of answers to questionnaires submitted to the Japanese would serve no useful purpose if their answers were inaccurate. Customs could easily get the truth from the large American discount chains and buying groups who were handling the bulk of the dumped imports. Customs had the power to inspect the records of these American companies without the enormous problem of sending agents to Japan to spot-check whatever records the Japanese felt willing to show them.

Zenith produced an investigative report of Mentor International (an American company), a private Japanese-market investigating group stationed in California and retained by Zenith. The report indicated that rebates were secretly being paid to large American buyers and were being concealed through falsified Customs entry documents. Ritger asked if there was any hard evidence of this. Zenith replied that the Mentor report and the vast disparity between prices in Japan and prices in the United States were enough to trigger at least a spot-check of some of the big American buyers. Ritger admitted that an investigation of big buyers in the United States might be productive, but he went on to emphasize that we were dealing with a matter "very sensitive" to government relations with Japan and that to launch such an investigation would delay the prompt disposition of the case. The message was obvious, that the Treasury Department was following political directions that favored Japanese interests. Even the rock-solid arguments that proved Japanese government subsidies by tax remissions failed to move Treasury.

The Japanese commodity tax was remitted on exports to the United States; it was a classic subsidy that should be countervailed or equalized with a duty imposed under the traditional U.S. countervailing duty statute. This tax remission was one of a long list of subsidies that were described in State Department documents and in a reputable international business publication.[5]

The commodity tax was imposed on the "freely offered" wholesale price in Japan and, therefore, would convincingly reveal the true

Japanese wholesale market price. Thus, the questionable answers the Japanese were giving Treasury could be quickly checked against their commodity tax returns. These were "admissions against interest" and therefore of the highest value as evidence. I had early and futilely urged this approach on Customs and Ritger at Treasury.

Ritger expressed concern about launching any new inquiry, because speed in completing the investigation was his highest priority. With respect to countervailing the subsidies, he admitted with pain and hesitation that some of the alleged subsidies appeared to be of the type that might be countervailed. However, the commodity tax, he believed, was a tax "borne by the product" and not countervailable under his policy. He finally said that Zenith, of course, had a right to file a petition to countervail the subsidies.

I returned to Chicago after this meeting, sadly convinced that Treasury was bent on quickly disposing of the dumping case in a manner that would not offend the Japanese cartel. Accepting worthless letters of assurance from the Japanese cartel that they had not been guilty of dumping, but would never do it again, was absurd to the extreme. I recommended to Zenith president Joe Wright that we file a countervailing duty petition on the commodity tax remission and that we bring this sorry state of affairs at Treasury to the attention of Congress.

Zenith had already vigorously pursued the only other option: entering the Japanese market and thereby forcing the Japanese to abandon their predatory dumping attack on the American industry. The cornerstone of the Japanese strategy was the permanent blockade of import competition from the United States. Again, U.S. government officials were intent on doing nothing to open the Japanese market or to enforce our relevant laws. Even with all the questionable adjustments allowed by Neil Marsh at Customs, Treasury still found dumping margins— although they were obviously far below the actual margins. The real margins were large enough to ensure instant market share for the Japanese interests involved.

THE DUMPING CASE AT TREASURY

In December 1970, Treasury was forced to make a general finding of dumping, that is, "making sales below fair market value" under the Antidumping Act of 1921. This automatically triggered an investigation and hearing before the Tariff Commission to determine whether the dumping was causing injury to the American industry. If it was, Treasury had to determine the margins of dumping on each shipment and offset them with dumping duties.

The staff at the Tariff Commission was in general very able and experienced. The injury investigation was efficiently handled. Public hearings were conducted at which Zenith, a group of companies in the Electronics Trade Association, and a coterie of counsel representing the Japanese companies testified and made written submissions.

To put this narrative in perspective, a brief description of the Tariff Commission is in order. Later renamed the International Trade Commission, the Tariff Commission was an old-line government agency set up by Congress to investigate the effects of unfair and illegal attacks by foreign interests on trade with the United States. Whenever predatory dumping was found by the Treasury Department through its Bureau of Customs, the Commission was empowered to investigate and determine whether the dumping was injuring an American industry. Where injury was found, the Treasury Department was commanded by the Antidumping Act of 1921 to impose an offsetting dumping duty on all relevant imports. The dumping duty was not a fine or penalty, but an amount that merely offset the illegal and unfair competitive advantage provided by the dumping practice.

In the dumping investigation, the Tariff Commission determined unanimously on March 4, 1971, that the American television industry was being seriously injured by the unlawful dumping practices of the Japanese cartel. In its determination of injury, the Commission declared:

In the Commission's judgment, an industry in the United States is being injured by reason of the importation of television receivers from Japan, which are being sold at less than fair value (LTFV) within the meaning of the Antidumping Act, 1921, as amended.

In reaching this determination, three reasons have been persuasive: (1) Imports of television receivers from Japan, determined by the Treasury to have been sold at less than fair value, have increased and now supply a substantial share of the U.S. market; (2) the sellers of the LTFV Japanese receivers have for the most part undersold U.S. manufacturers of television sets in the domestic market; and (3) sales of the LTFV television sets have contributed substantially to declining prices of domestically produced television receivers. [36 Fed. Reg. 4576 (1971)]

The case then went back to Treasury for the imposition of appropriate dumping duties as commanded by the statute. At this crucial point, Japanese interests mounted an intense lobbying campaign to head off the proceedings. The Sarnoff-RCA group, the self-heralded leader of the American industry, avoided participation in the dumping case while quietly supporting its Japanese licensees.

At Zenith, the welcome finding of the Tariff Commission was somewhat encouraging. We were, however, becoming less and less confident that the Treasury Department would follow the law. It was becoming apparent that the lobbyists and law firms representing the Japanese were influencing high-level government officials. Many of these top trade officials were being offered extremely lucrative private-sector jobs as lobbyists for Japanese interests. The temptations were great and overwhelmed a surprising number of "loyal" government servants. This unprecedented movement became the largest and most heavily funded operation to purchase political influence by foreign interests in American history.

One thing the Japanese learned very early was the existence of so-called choke points in the American trade law apparatus. The crucial choke point was usually where fines, duties, or the levels of retaliation for illegal trade practices were formulated. Such work was done by politically appointed officials of the federal government, who rarely stay in their jobs longer than two years. This systemic weakness in the U.S. bureaucracy was exploited in every major Japanese market-capture program. Japanese interests were able to neutralize the remedies provided by law to besieged American industries with nearly 100 percent success.

Following the formal dumping finding on March 10, 1971, the case remained strangely dormant at Treasury and Customs, cloaked in deep secrecy. It took years of efforts by the dying American television industry and the oversight efforts of an angry Congress to get even pitifully inadequate responses from the administration.

While this remedy was delayed, almost the entire American television manufacturing industry was bled to death or was acquired by Japanese interests.

ABROGATION OF TIMELY REMEDY

The unmistakable disloyalty of U.S. trade officials was clearly revealed in the giveaway settlement of the government's dumping case, which was announced on April 28, 1980, ten full years after the Customs Bureau found dumping. As will be shown, the secretly negotiated political settlement of the entire dispute was arranged allegedly for only $77 million for dumping duties and Customs fraud penalties. Zenith conservatively estimated it should have fallen in the billion-dollar range. Zenith was constrained to challenge this obviously bad-faith settlement in the United States Customs Court in Washington, D.C.

On June 27, 1980, Zenith filed a motion and lengthy brief with supporting evidence showing that the settlement was illegal. Section 617 of the Tariff Act, a general provision permitting the settlement of government claims, was not intended by Congress to abort the required assessment of antidumping duties. Section 617 had never before been invoked by Customs in dumping cases. Congress had directed specific procedures to determine and fairly equalize dumping. In addition, the Zenith submissions illustrated with specificity how U.S. government officials had acted arbitrarily in bad faith and unlawfully in arriving at the settlement. The Zenith petition is set forth in this book as Appendix VII.

Among the many evidentiary exhibits in support of the Zenith motion was an affidavit of Zenith's chairman, Joseph S. Wright, and an accompanying analysis by John Nevin, Zenith's president. These documents are reproduced here because, together with Appendix VII, they graphically show the plight of the American television industry. In addition to the Wright and Nevin documents (Exhibit 4.1) there were fifty other exhibits to Zenith's brief in support of its move to have the Customs Court declare the settlement void.

CARTEL LOBBYISTS AND LAWYERS
SCUTTLE LAW ENFORCEMENT

Desperate members of the besieged American television industry had brought two more cases under other federal statutes. In 1976, COMPACT (a group of manufacturers led by Corning Glass) filed a new proceeding under the so-called Section 201 of a law Congress had provided to protect any new or struggling industry. Japan's new army of lobbyists found the new 201 proceeding an ideal opportunity for mischief. The so-called Section 201 case provided a protectionist emergency remedy to shelter new or fragile industries from foreign competition. The television industry was mature and vibrant, but it was under a crippling and unlawful siege. The 201 case was hardly an appropriate remedy.

The 201 case was simple to establish, by merely showing that increased imports were harming a U.S. industry. When COMPACT asked Zenith to join in its 201 petition, I recommended to management that joining this "protectionist" move would be contrary to all our pleas

(text continues on p. 148)

Exhibit 4.1
Affidavit of Joseph Wright and Analysis by John Nevin

UNITED STATES CUSTOMS COURT

ZENITH RADIO CORPORATION,   :
                                             :
                    Plaintiff,   :
                                             :   Civil Action No. 80-5-00861
     v.   :
                                             :
THE UNITED STATES,   :
                                             :
                    Defendant.   :

STATE OF ILLINOIS)
) SS
COUNTY OF COOK   )

AFFIDAVIT OF JOSEPH S. WRIGHT

     Joseph S. Wright, being first duly sworn on oath, deposes
and says:

     I am Chairman of the Board of Directors and Chief Executive
Officer of Zenith Radio Corporation and for the past twenty-seven
years, I have served in the following positions at Zenith:

     Member of the Board of Directors - 1953 to date

     Vice President and General Counsel - 1953-1958

     Executive Vice President - 1958-1959

     President and General Manager - 1959-1968

     Chief Executive Officer - 1965-1976; 1979 to date

     Chairman of the Board of Directors - 1968-1976; 1979 to date.

     By 1968, the massive dumping of Japanese radio and television
receivers on the United States market had destroyed the radio manufacturing business in the United States and was severely impacting
the television manufacturing business to such an extent that the

Exhibit 4.1 (continued)

television dumping proceeding was initiated. On behalf of Zenith, as an interested party, I participated in that proceeding and testified in the Tariff Commission proceeding which culminated in an unanimous determination that the importation of TV receivers from Japan into the United States at less than fair value was causing injury to our industry.

When the dumping finding was officially published by Treasury and timely procedures for specific assessment of dumping duties were to be initiated, we were encouraged that the Treasury's anti-dumping proceeding, as well as the long overdue revaluation of the yen which had just occurred, would make a tremendous difference in the industry's ability to compete and, as a result, Zenith cancelled plans to abandon two major TV plants here in the United States in favor of offshore facilities — plans that had been forced upon us by the unfair dumping practices of the Japanese manufacturers and their U.S. importers.

On August 10, 1972 I wrote to George P. Shultz, the then-newly appointed Secretary of Treasury, calling his attention to the importance of effective law enforcement in stopping predatory dumping practices violative of federal statutes and expressing our appreciation for the Government's progress in this regard. We were further encouraged by his reply of August 31, 1972 in which he stated:

> "The way to achieve broad agreement on international rules of fair trade is to defend vigorously U.S. interests against unfair trade practices on a case-by-case basis. Complaints against unfair trade practices cannot be bargained away. Be assured that the decisions to be reached will be based upon a thorough review of the facts in each case." 1/

1/ Copies of the correspondence between Secretary Shultz and me are attached hereto as Exhibits A and B.

Exhibit 4.1 (continued)

During the next eight years, however, Mr. Shultz's assurances
and predictions did not prove to be valid, as is shown in the
article attached hereto as Exhibit C 2/ which outlined the highly
irregular events that finally culminated in what we believe to be
an illegal attempt on the part of our Government to "settle" the
dumping case on outrageous terms that would greatly injure Zenith.
We are confident we will be able to show in the instant litigation
that the purported "settlement" involves an illegal forgiveness of
liability for hundreds of millions of dollars in dumping duties that
the law requires the Government to collect. The result of such a
"settlement" would be to permit the offending companies to release
all the reserves, either set aside for dumping duty assessment or
to be looked to for this purpose, to fund further unfair predation
in the United States market.

The Government's unwarranted eight year delay in assessing
and collecting dumping duties has not only defeated the purposes
of the antidumping statute but by allowing the dumping duties to
cumulate to huge amounts and then "settling" at what appears to
be approximately ten cents on the dollar would, in effect, provide
a huge bonanza to the law violators. The "settlement" would, in
effect, amount to an outrageous governmental subsidization of
unfair practices condemned by federal law.

2/   "Enforcing the Antidumping Laws: The Television Dumping Case"
      by John J. Nevin, Chairman of the Board, Zenith Radio Corporation,
      Reprint from May, 1979 issue of the Journal of Legislation,
      University of Notre Dame Law School.

Exhibit 4.1 (continued)

It is for these reasons that Zenith felt compelled as an interested party in the dumping case to file the instant action and seek under law to forestall the injury to our business that the attempted "settlement" would surely entail.

Further affiant sayeth not.

Joseph S. Wright

Subscribed and sworn to
before me this 22ᵗʰ day
of September, 1980.

Notary Public

My commission expires
November 26, 1983.

Exhibit 4.1 (continued)

August 10, 1972

Honorable George P. Schultz
Secretary of Treasury
Washington, D. C.

Dear George:

Please accept my belated congratulations on your new
responsibilities. It must seem ages to you since you left
that cloister on the West Coast!

You will recall that more than two years ago I called on you in
Washington and discussed with you the problems of the American
electronics industry and later called on Dave Kennedy for the
same purpose.

At that time we had suffered a very severe erosion of market
share and very substantial reductions of our work force here in
the United States and were in the process of rapidly finding
production facilities outside of this country to serve this market.

At about this time the Treasury Department began serious work
on a dumping complaint which had been pending before it for more
than a year and ultimately did suspend customs valuations and
find dumping on TV receivers from Japan, but the final determination of the amount of dumping has not yet been made.

The real encouragement to us was, of course, the action of the
President and Secretary Connally in bringing about a revaluation
of the yen in terms of the dollar. This was a bold stroke and
while many people complained of its shock and brutality, I don't

Exhibit 4.1 (continued)

know how it could have been accomplished, at least in terms
of Japan, by more diplomatic means. We were encouraged
that the Treasury's anti-dumping proceding and the revaluation
of the yen would make a tremendous difference in our ability
to compete in this market and as a result cancelled plans to
abandon two major plants here in the United States in favor of
similar offshore facilities. As a matter of fact we are now
planning not only to retain these plants but to build a new facility
here in the Chicago area. Our employment is beginning to turn
upward, although not yet to its former levels.

About two years ago we also filed a petition with the Treasury
Department asking it to investigate and proceed under the
countervailing duty law, pointing out the massive Japanese
government subsidies to her electronic industries under the
Electronics Industry Development Emergency Law of 1957 and
the successor act of 1971, together with various other Japanese
government subsidies to the electronics industry, including the
remission of substantial commodity taxes. On May 19, 1972
Treasury announced an investigation of the matters alleged in our
petition and in a more recent petition filed by Magnavox, and has
called for comments.

Naturally, the dumping and countervailing duty matters have been
resented very deeply by our Japanese friends and I am sure that
tremendous pressure has been put on your office and the White
House to sweep them under the rug. My purpose in writing to
you is to tell you how much we appreciate the action by the
Department in getting into these matters under Assistant Secretary
Rossides and his staff and to express the hope that they will be
finally determined on the facts in the record rather than, as has
sometimes happened in the past, be bargained away in high level
trade talks.

I have no doubt about the ability of our highly competitive and
inventive industry to continue to grow and to reflect its burgeoning
technology, in better products at lower prices to the public. We

Exhibit 4.1 (continued)

---

don't need a warm blanket of protection with quotas and Smoot-
Hawley tariff walls to keep out imports. But we do need the kind
of intelligent attention our government has displayed over the
last 18 months in seeing to it that the game is played according
to the basic rules.

With kindest regards, I am

                                      Respectfully yours,

                                      Joseph S. Wright

JSW/lkb

Exhibit 4.1 (continued)

THE SECRETARY OF THE TREASURY
WASHINGTON 20220

AUG 31 1972

Dear Joe:

Thank you for your letter of August 10, 1972,
regarding the countervailing duty and antidumping
investigations of Japanese electronic products. These
cases are understandably important to Zenith, as one of
the leading manufacturers of electronic products in the
United States.

The way to achieve broad agreement on international
rules of fair trade is to defend vigorously U.S. interests
against unfair trade practices on a case-by-case basis.
Complaints against unfair trade practices cannot be
bargained away. Be assured that the decisions to be
reached will be based upon a thorough review of the
facts in each case.

With best regards,

Sincerely yours,

George P. Shultz

Mr. Joseph S. Wright
Chairman of the Board
Zenith Radio Corporation
1900 North Austin Avenue
Chicago, Illinois 60639

Exhibit 4.1 (continued)

ENFORCING THE ANTIDUMPING LAWS:
THE TELEVISION DUMPING CASE

John J. Nevin *

    Dumping is the practice of selling products in an export market at a price below the price at which a comparable product is sold in the home market or selling a product in an export market at a price below its cost of production. Article VI of the General Agreement on Tariffs and Trade (GATT) states: "dumping . . . is to be condemned if it causes or threatens material injury to an established industry in the territory of a contracting party . . . ."[1]

    No American industry has been more characterized by employee layoffs, widespread plant shutdowns, financial losses, mergers and corporate liquidations than has the American television industry. More than a decade ago American television producers concluded that it was the dumping of Japanese television receivers in the American market that was causing the financial distress in the domestic industry and turned to the Government of the United States for the protection against dumping supposedly afforded by the Antidumping Act of 1921.[2]

    As required by the Antidumping Act of 1921, American television manufacturers, in March of 1968, submitted their dumping complaint to the U.S. Treasury.[3] Treasury took almost three years to respond but in December of 1970 advised the U.S. Tariff Commission (later the International Trade Commission) that Japanese television receivers were being dumped in the United States.[4] Three months later the Tariff Commission found that the American industry was being injured by the dumping.[5] Upon being advised of the injury finding, the Secretary of the Treasury became responsible for assessing a special dumping duty in the amount of the difference between the "purchase price" of the dumped merchandise in the United States and the "foreign market value" of that merchandise.[6]

    The three years between the submission of the dumping complaint in 1968 and the Tariff Commission's injury finding in 1971 were years of financial crisis for American television producers. In 1968, nine of the sixteen American producers lost money. In 1969, eight of the remaining fifteen U.S. producers lost money. In 1970, ten of the fifteen U.S. producers lost money.[7]

    Despite the economic chaos that was apparent in the television industry a decade ago, Treasury has done essentially nothing to collect the television dumping duties that are mandated by law. The television dumping case is

---

* Chairman of the Board, Zenith Radio Corporation.

1.   General Agreement on Tariffs and Trade, March 1969, art. IV, para. 1.
2.   Antidumping Act of 1921, ch. 14, § 201, 42 Stat. 11 (codified at 19 U.S.C. §§ 160-172) (1978).
3.   Under 19 U.S.C. 160(c)(1) information may be given to the Secretary in order to initiate an investigation. Through its attorneys, the Imports Committee, Tube Division, Electronic Industries Association notified the Commissioner of Customs of the antidumping violations in a letter dated March 22, 1968.
4.   35 Fed. Reg. 18,768 (1970).
5.   News Release, United States Tariff Commission, Determination of Injury in Investigation No. AA1921-66 (March 4, 1971).
6.   The amount of the duty to be collected by the Secretary of the Treasury on such merchandise is set forth in 19 U.S.C. § 161 (1978).
7.   TC Publication 436 (1971).

Exhibit 4.1 (continued)

2   *Journal of Legislation*   [Vol. 6: 1

a ten-year long story of false and fraudulent submissions made by television importers to the Government of the United States and of unconscionable delays on the part of those importers in providing information that had been requested by the U.S. Government. The television case also provides instances in which the U.S. Treasury itself has been as deceitful as the importers and as responsible as they for long delays in the enforcement of the law.

THE HISTORY OF THE DUMPING CASE

When the Tariff Commission reached its injury finding in 1971, the Customs Service, which reports to Treasury, undertook to determine television dumping margins by establishing the difference between the "purchase price" of imported Japanese television sets and their "foreign market value." The effort was concentrated on establishing the foreign market values for Customs assumed that the purchase prices had been correctly stated on Customs documents submitted at the time television sets had been imported. That assumption would later prove to be invalid.

In 1963, the Japanese television manufacturers, with the approval of Japan's Ministry of International Trade and Industry (MITI) entered into written agreements establishing, among other things, the minimum prices at which Japanese television receivers would be sold to American purchasers.[8] The minimum prices became known as check prices. For many years the documents submitted to Customs by large importers of Japanese television receivers almost invariably showed purchase prices that were the same as the minimum prices listed in the Japanese check price agreements.

In 1970, Zenith Radio Corporation advised Treasury, in a confidential meeting, of its belief that the check prices being used by importers on Customs documents were not in fact the real prices at which imported Japanese television receivers had been purchased. Zenith Radio Corporation supported its assertion with an independent consultant's report stating that Japanese television manufacturers were offering substantial rebates to American purchasers who had ostensibly purchased at the check prices.[9] By failing to report the rebates to Customs, the American importer could avoid television dumping penalties that might later be assessed.

Zenith urged Treasury in 1970 to investigate the financial records of large American television importers to determine the validity of the rebate assertions. Treasury refused to pursue the matter. Some years later, however, a document produced in International Trade Commission hearings[10] would show that, within a few months of the supposedly confidential meeting in Treasury, manufacturers and importers of Japanese television sets were warned by a U.S. attorney for the Electronic Industries Association of Japan that Zenith was "placing pressure on the U.S. Treasury Department" to investigate double pricing. The document, dated October 22, 1970, noted that: "Zenith had not produced any substantiating data to backup the charges." It went on to sāȳ: "Whether our files of

8.   These agreements are explained in a statement submitted by the Japanese Ministry of International Trade and Industry (MITI) to the United States District Court for the Eastern District of Pennsylvania in the case of *In re* Japanese Electronic Products Antitrust Litigation, 402 F. Supp. 244 (E.D. Pa. 1974).
9.   Mentor International, Report on Imported Television Set Pricing Phase II (Sept. 19, 1969) (Prepared for Zenith Radio Corporation).
10. *Television Receivers, Color and Monochrome, Assembled or not Assembled, Finished or not Finished, and Subassemblies Thereof: Hearings Before the United States International Trade Commission* 1340-41 (Jan. 21, 1977).

Exhibit 4.1 (continued)

1979]   Enforcing the Antidumping Laws   3

correspondence and old purchase orders should be purged will have to be discussed with our legal people."[11]

Between March of 1971 and April of 1972 Treasury collected about $1 million in television dumping duties.[12] In March of 1972, however, the assessment of dumping duties on Japanese television receivers was stopped and not resumed until March of 1978. At no time during the six years from March of 1972 until March of 1978 did Treasury acknowledge that the assessment process mandated by American law had been halted. The six-year interruption has never been explained.

The Congress, in the Trade Act of 1974, authorized the International Trade Commission to investigate unfair trade practices allegations either in response to a complaint from an American manufacturer or on its own initiative.[13] Early in 1976 GTE-Sylvania filed an unfair trade practices complaint against Japanese television manufacturers with the International Trade Commission.[14] The Sylvania complaint alleged "the existence of predatory pricing schemes resulting in below-cost and unreasonably low-cost pricing of such television sets in the United States." A few months later the International Trade Commission announced a broader investigation of possible violations of American antidumping, customs fraud and antitrust laws associated with television importation.[15]

The two ITC investigations became immersed in delay and controversy. Japan's Foreign Office refused for an extended period of time to grant visas to a team of Sylvania lawyers and accountants seeking to gather evidence in Japan. The Departments of State, Treasury and Justice moved in concert to restrict severely the proposed unfair trade practices investigations. Treasury claimed sole responsibility for investigating dumping and related customs fraud allegations and refused to permit ITC investigators to see Customs' files. Justice similarly claimed exclusive responsibility for antitrust investigations.

In September of 1976, the Secretary of the Treasury wrote to the Commission explaining the reasons for Treasury's refusal to cooperate with Commission investigators. With reference to the television dumping case, the Secretary said: "As required by the Act, dumping duties are being, and will continue to be, assessed on merchandise subject to the finding so long as it is sold at less than foreign market value or, as appropriate, constructed value."[16] The Secretary's assertion was totally inaccurate and completely misleading. At the time the letter was written, four and one-half years had elapsed since Treasury had last assessed a television dumping duty.

While the authority of the ITC to investigate unfair trade practices associated with television importation was being debated in 1976, color television imports from Japan jumped from 1,044,000 units in 1975 to 2,530,000 units

11. This document was originally produced in response to a subpoena duces tecum served by Zenith Radio Corporation on The Magnavox Company in the course of discovery proceedings in *In re* Japanese Electronic Products Antitrust Litigation, 402 F. Supp. 244 (E.D. Pa. 1974).
12. *Assessment and Collection of Duties Under the Antidumping Act of 1921: Hearing Before the Subcomm. on Trade of the House Comm. on Ways and Means*, 95th Cong., 2d Sess. 14 (1978) (statement of Robert Mundheim, General Counsel, Department of the Treasury).
13. Trade Act of 1974, 19 U.S.C. §§ 2101-2487 (Supp. 1978).
14. GTE-Sylvania filed its complaint on January 15, 1976. The United States International Trade Commission issued a Notice of Investigation No. 337-TA-23 on March 29, 1976.
15. 41 Fed. Reg. 14,949 (1976).
16. Letter from William Simon, Secretary of the Treasury, to Will E. Leonard, Chairman of the United States International Trade Commission (received September 24, 1976).

Exhibit 4.1 (continued)

4   *Journal of Legislation*   [Vol. 6: 1

in 1976.[17] As a result, COMPACT[18], a group representing American television industry labor unions and manufacturers petitioned the International Trade Commission for tariff or quota protection against the flood of color television imports from Japan. Late in 1976 the Commission voted to hold hearings on the quota petition and to suspend its investigations of unfair trade practices with respect to television importation.

In January of 1977 Zenith, although not a member of COMPACT, testified on behalf of the petitioners.[19] In its testimony Zenith demonstrated, from television sales brochures obtained in Japan, that the least expensive 19-inch color television receivers available for sale in Japan were priced at 150,000 yen or something over $500 at the then existent exchange rate of about 300 yen to the dollar. Zenith also showed an advertisement for a 19-inch color television imported from Japan and offered for sale in the United States at a price under $300. Zenith submitted to the Commission engineering analyses that showed that the Japanese receivers sold in the home market for over $500 were essentially identical to the Japanese receivers being sold in the United States for less than $300.

Zenith recommended in the hearings that any tariff or quota protection provided the American television industry be limited to the time period necessary to determine the validity of the unfair trade practices allegations. Following the hearings, however, the United States negotiated a television Orderly Marketing Agreement with Japan.[20] Sylvania's unfair trade practices complaint was settled through a consent decree.[21] The broader unfair practices investigation proposed by the Commission itself was terminated despite the unchallenged charges of dumping and other unfair trade practices that had been presented to the Commission.

A little more than a year after the OMA had been negotiated, the Special Representative for Trade Negotiations gave to the Trade Subcommittee of the House of Representatives a copy of a side letter that had been provided to the Government of Japan at the time the Orderly Marketing Agreement was signed.[22] The side letter had not previously been made public. In the side letter the Japanese Government was assured by the United States that the International Trade Commission would be urged to terminate its investigation of television dumping and leave the dumping issue entirely in the hands of the Department of Treasury. The Government of Japan was also assured that "The Treasury Department will carry out these efforts in strict conformity with the International Antidumping Code."

---

17. United States Department of Commerce statistics.
18. The members of COMPACT are: Industrial Union Department, AFL-CIO; Allied Industrial Workers of America, International Union; American Flint Glass Workers Union of North America; Communications Workers of America; International Association of Machinists; International Brotherhood of Electrical Workers; International Union of Electrical, Radio & Machine Workers; United Furniture Workers of America; United Steelworkers of America; Corning Glass Works; GTE-Sylvania Incorporated; Owens-Illinois, Inc.; Sprague Electric Company; and Wells-Gardner Electronics Corporation.
19. *Public Hearing on Investigation No. TA-201-19 Before the United States International Trade Commission* (January 8, 1977).
20. The Orderly Marketing Agreement (OMA) provided for a voluntary limitation of color television exports to the United States. Orderly Marketing Agreement, March 22, 1977, United States-Japan.
21. *In re* Certain Color Television Receiving Sets, Consent Order, 337 TA 23, United States International Trade Commission (July 29, 1977).
22. Letter from Robert S. Strauss to His Excellency Fumihiko Togo, Ambassador Extraordinary and Plenipotentiary of Japan (May 20, 1977). The contents of the letter were read into the record at the hearing. *Multilateral Trade Negotiations: Hearing before the Subcomm. on Trade of the House Comm. on Ways and Means*, 95th Cong., 2d Sess. 16 (1978) (statement of Ambassador Robert Strauss).

Exhibit 4.1 (continued)

The Congress, almost ten years earlier, had categorically rejected the International Antidumping Code.[23] In Title II of the Renegotiation Amendments Act of 1968 the Congress had directed the Secretary of the Treasury to "resolve any conflict between the Antidumping Code and the Antidumping Act, 1921, in favor of the Act . . . " and to "take into account the provisions of the International Antidumping Code only insofar as they are consistent with the Antidumping Act, 1921."[24] If the side letter represented an effort to evade the intent of Congress, it is highly improbable that the Special Representative for Trade Negotiations was himself responsible for that effort. He had, at the time the side letter was signed, held his position for less than three months and would have had no reason, from his prior experience, to be familiar with the 1968 Congressional action.

In early 1977, as the International Trade Commission hearings were ending, the U.S. Customs Service obtained information indicating that the purchase prices declared on Customs documents at the time television receivers had been imported into the United States may have been falsely stated. According to a report directed to the Commissioner of Customs: "A voluntary tender of duties was made by an importer (Gambles) in early 1977. The importer's records show that the Japanese manufacturer Mitsubishi was engaged in 'double pricing,' *i.e.,* presenting Customs an invoice showing one price while the actual or true price was in fact lower. Such a practice effectively reduces or eliminates dumping duties."[25]

The disclosure led Customs immediately to review records available to the public in an antitrust case Zenith had filed in 1974.[26] Customs learned from that review that other importers had also been engaged in double pricing. According to the report to the Commissioner of Customs: "Subsequent to the double invoicing disclosure, the Office of Investigations undertook a massive inquiry of large importers of TV's including large mass retailers as well as subsidiaries of Japanese TV producers. The investigation revealed rebate schemes as well as other practices directed to the masking of potential antidumping duties."[27] In March of 1978 the U.S. Customs Service turned over to the Criminal Division of the Department of Justice evidence, with respect to undisclosed kickbacks and rebates, that it had accumulated to support possible prosecutions for fraud.

Early in 1979, in a front page story on the television dumping case, the *New York Times* quoted from an internal Customs memorandum in which a senior Customs officer had written: "the U.S. Customs Service has at present in its possession documented evidence that Japanese producers of television receivers, in concert with certain U.S. purchasers, have engaged in double invoicing to circumvent the provisions of the U.S. antidumping statutes."[28] The *Times* reported that grand juries were then considering evidence in what was described "as the largest fraud inquiry in the recent history of the Customs Service." As many as eighty American companies were reported to be under investigation including three of this country's leading retailers.[29]

23. S. Rep. No. 1385, 90th Cong., 2d Sess. 4539 (1968).
24. Renegotiation Amendments Act of 1968, Pub. L. 90-634, 82 Stat. 1345 (1968).
25. Memorandum from V. Hann, Acting Assistant Commissioner (Operations), Department of the Treasury, United States Customs Service, to the Commissioner of Customs (April 1978).
26. *In re* Japanese Electronic Products Antitrust Litigation, 402 F. Supp. 244 (E.D. Pa. 1974).
27. *See* note 25 *supra.*
28. Hersh, *Inquiry Told of Customs Fraud in Imports of Japanese TV Sets,* The N.Y. Times, Jan. 24, 1979, § 1, at 1, col. 1.
29. *Id.*

Exhibit 4.1 (continued)

6 *Journal of Legislation* [Vol. 6: 1

On March 30, 1979, the *New York Times* reported that Alexander's Inc., a department store chain, had pleaded guilty in federal court to a customs fraud charge involving the importation of thousands of television sets from Japan.[30] Alexander's was reported by the government to have submitted an invoice indicating it had paid $72.00 for each Japanese television it had imported. In fact, Alexander's had paid about $47.00 for it had obtained a rebate of approximately $25.00 per set.[31] The fact that eighty American companies, including three of this country's largest retailers, were involved in customs fraud investigations suggested how pervasive the dumping and customs fraud schemes had been. The disclosure that Alexander's had obtained rebates approximating $25.00 from a price reported to have been $72.00 suggested how predatory those schemes had been.

The evidence indicating that many importers had deceived Customs, with respect to the prices at which Japanese television sets had been purchased in the United States, led Customs to investigate intensively the accuracy of information that had been submitted by importers with respect to the foreign market values of those receivers. Reporting on that investigation to the Under Secretary of the Treasury, the Commissioner of Customs said: "In the television case we have uncovered considerable evidence that the basic information submitted by a number of Japanese television manufacturers is false."[32]

A Customs officer, explaining the results of the investigation to a large group of attorneys for television importers, was more specific. He noted that Customs had found that "a significant number of the foreign market value submissions appeared questionable on their face when compared to cost of production submissions," and that when Customs had formally requested access to Japanese cost of production data that had been submitted to the International Trade Commission, the manufacturers had "either refused to supply the information, or refused to respond at all . . . "[33]

The Customs Service borrowed technical experts from the International Trade Commission and the Federal Communications Commission to check the data the manufacturers had submitted to pair sets imported into the United States with sets sold in Japan. The experts concluded that "in a substantial number of cases the sets identified by the manufacturers as the sets sold in the Japanese home market most comparable to the sets exported to the United States were, in fact, not the most comparable, but, rather, quite different."[34]

Labor in Japan is paid on the basis of seniority. It is possible for a long service employee to be paid twice or three times as much for the same work as is paid to a very short service employee. According to Customs, the Japanese manufacturers had claimed that "only the most experienced workers were used to manufacture sets sold in Japan, while the relatively inexperienced workers were used in producing sets exported to the United States." Customs investigators found this claim "virtually impossible to verify."[35]

30. Lubasch, *Alexander's Guilty Plea on Imports*, N.Y. Times, March 30, 1979, § D, at 1, col. 6.
31. *Id.*
32. Memorandum from Robert Chasen, Commissioner of Customs, to Bette Anderson, Under Secretary of the Treasury, and Robert Mundheim, General Counsel of the Department of Treasury (October 18, 1977).
33. Disclosure Meeting Regarding the Japanese T.V. Dumping Cases, May 13, 1978 (statement of Irving W. Smith, Jr., Chief of the Value Division).
34. *Id.*
35. *Id.*

Exhibit 4.1 (continued)

In late 1977 the Commissioner of Customs concluded that information submitted by the television manufacturers could not be relied upon to establish foreign market value in the television case. He concluded those values could be developed quickly and accurately by using information derived from Japanese Commodity Tax reports. In a letter to the Under Secretary of Treasury the Commissioner supported his decision to adopt the Commodity Tax approach when he said:

> aside from the question of the integrity of the information received, we are also of the opinion that the existing administrative procedures necessitating the collection and analysis of vast amounts of commercial information before an antidumping appraisement can be performed represents a perversion of the intent of the Act, in that delays for unreasonable periods of time negate the remedial protection intended by Congress for the affected United States industry.[36]

The Government of Japan levies a Commodity Tax on all television receivers produced for sale in the Japanese market. The Japanese Commodity Tax law stipulates that the tax is to be based on the freely offered selling price of the product "for sales to all purchasers in ordinary wholesale quantities and in the ordinary course of wholesale trade . . . ."[37] The American Antidumping Act of 1921 defines the foreign market value as the price at which the product is offered for sale "in the principal markets of the country from which exported, in the usual wholesale quantities and in the ordinary course of trade for home consumption . . . ."[38]

The two definitions were so nearly identical as to lead the Commissioner of Customs to conclude that the task of establishing the foreign market value of Japanese television receivers imported into the United States could be accomplished with speed and accuracy by using the representations as to home market wholesale prices the Japanese manufacturers themselves had made to the Government of Japan. By mid-December, the Commodity Tax approach to establish foreign market values had been approved by the responsible legal authorities in both Customs and Treasury. On March 17 the Customs Service took action to assess $400 million of television dumping penalties covering receivers imported during the period from April of 1972 through early January of 1977.

On March 27, 1978, Minister Yoshio Kawahara delivered to the Treasury Department a copy of a note addressed to the State Department from the Government of Japan.[39] The note strongly protested the method Customs had used to establish dumping duties. Following the meeting with Kawahara, Treasury decided to delay the assessment of all but $46 million of the television dumping penalties.

The $46 million assessment covered a time period from the beginning of 1972 through June of 1973. The Treasury's decision to limit assessments to the period ending in June of 1973 was made despite a strenuous written recommendation by the Commissioner of Customs that the Treasury proceed

---

36. *See* note 32 *supra.*
37. Commodity Tax Law (Japan), § 11(1) and (2).
38. 19 U.S.C. § 164 (1978).
39. Note from the Government of Japan to the United States Department of State (received by the Department of the Treasury, April 27, 1978).

Exhibit 4.1 (continued)

8   *Journal of Legislation*   [Vol. 6: 1

with the previously approved plan to assess television dumping duties through January of 1977.[40]

On March 30, 1978, telegrams were sent to all U.S. Customs field offices directing that television dumping assessments relating to shipments made subsequent to June of 1973 be deleted from notices that were to be posted on March 31, 1978.[41] The necessary deletions were made by hand by Customs field personnel before the bulletins were posted. Treasury then announced that the Customs Service had assessed dumping duties of $46 million against importers of Japanese television receivers.[42]

On April 10, 1978, Congressmen Charles A. Vanik and Dan Rostenkowski released a statement to the press challenging the action Treasury had undertaken. They said:

> We understand that the department limited its original action in this long drawn-out case to one year of assessments so as to minimize the adverse impact on importers—and, probably, to avoid banner headlines on the extent of Japanese dumping in the American market. But the magnitude of the present dumping liability on imported Japanese televisions is a problem of Treasury's own making, since it is responsible for its failure to enforce the antidumping act in a vigorous and timely fashion.
>
> The history in this particular case of the lack of enforcement of the law as it was written calls for a reconsideration by the Congress of where the responsibility for administering the act should be placed. The degree to which counsel for importers have been permitted to tie the hands of government counsel in procedural snarls raises serious questions as to whether Treasury intends to enforce the antidumping act at all. It is unfortunate that the Treasury Department thought it appropriate to consult both with counsel for the importers and representatives of the Japanese Government as to its proposed action in this case but did not see fit to consult with Congress or representatives of the domestic industry.[43]

The Congressmen's concern with respect to the impact of private meetings between Treasury officials and representatives of Japanese manufacturers was echoed in an April 18, 1978 memorandum written by U.S. Customs Office of Regulations and Rulings attorneys to the Assistant Commissioner of Customs. The Customs attorneys had been asked to hold disclosure conferences with attorneys for television importers, Japanese manufacturers and certain Japanese Government officials. The memo said:

> Our difficulties at these meetings have been compounded by the fact that Treasury has issued vague and conflicting information to the affected importers/manufacturers/Government of Japan officials, concerning particular facets of its policy, while again providing very little direct communication with Customs. Effectively, Customs has been placed in the position of discovering Treasury policy through the often dubious representations of the affected parties.
>
> The entire range of problems which have surfaced during the disclosure conferences (especially the conference with Japanese Government officials)

---

40. Memorandum from Robert Chasen, the Commissioner of Customs, to the General Counsel of the Department of the Treasury (March 1978).
41. Telex dated March 30, 1978 to all Regional Commissioners, District Directors, and Area Directors of the United States Customs Service.
42. News Release, Department of the Treasury (March 31, 1978).
43. News Release, Congressmen Charles Vanick and Dan Rostenkowski (April 10, 1978).

Exhibit 4.1 (continued)

1979]   Enforcing the Antidumping Laws   9

seem to be related to the parties' understanding that the liquidations of March 31 were in some way considered to be 'provisional' in nature, that Treasury took this action primarily because of Congressional pressure, and that Treasury does not expect that the $46 million in dumping duties assessed to date in any way represents a final ascertainment of the liability due and owing.

Rather, those affected anticipate that the assessed amount will be mitigated through informal government-to-government negotiations, or relatively informal contacts between manufacturers and Treasury.[44]

In July of 1978 the legal advisory and review function of the Customs Office of Regulations and Rulings was transferred from the Commissioner of Customs to Treasury's Chief Counsel.[45] At the same time the recommendation function of the Commissioner of Customs, in connection with dumping cases, was transferred to Treasury's General Counsel. The reorganization effectively removed from the Bureau of Customs the authority and responsibility for recommending or initiating action to enforce American antidumping laws. By year end, however, it would be clear that the Office of Regulations and Rulings attorneys had been correct in discerning that an effort would be made to settle the television dumping case informally rather than in the manner anticipated in the antidumping law.

The effort in 1977 and early 1978 to collect the $400 million in television dumping duties had been code named "Project Omega" by the Customs officers involved. Following the decision to reduce the assessments from $400 million to $46 million, however, the "Project Omega" task force was disbanded. The Senior Customs Attorney who had led the task force described the Treasury action for *Time* magazine as follows: "Treasury pulled the plug. Out of the blue they disbanded us. When I protested they told me I would be fired if I continued to protest." *Time* reported that that attorney "who spent 13 years working on antidumping matters, was moved to a new job: processing Freedom of Information Act applications."[46]

In September of 1978 the House of Representatives Subcommittee on Trade held oversight hearings on the Assessment and Collection of Duties Under the Antidumping Act of 1921. At the time of the hearings no effort had yet been made to collect the $46 million in dumping duties that had been assessed six months earlier. In response to a question from Congressman Rostenkowski as to when Treasury would collect the $46 million, Treasury's General Counsel testified: "I would say we are right on the threshold of it."[47]

In regard to when action would be taken to assess duties on television sets imported after June 30, 1973, Treasury's General Counsel said: "First, the Customs Service will move promptly to assess another portion of the backlog, including all televisions imported up to January 1975." He then added: "Two, the Customs Service will thereafter assess the remainder of the backlog as rapidly as its ability to process the full case permits." The Commissioner of Customs later presented a chart to the subcommittee that showed the $350 million in potential television dumping duties for the period June 30, 1973

---

44. Memorandum from Customs Attorneys to the Assistant Commissioner (Regulations and Rulings) (April 18, 1978).
45. Memorandum from Leonard Lehman, Assistant Commissioner, (Regulations and Rulings), United States Customs Service, to all attorneys of the Office of Regulations and Rulings (July 17, 1978).
46. Time, March 26, 1979, at 64.
47. See note 12 supra.

Exhibit 4.1 (continued)

10   *Journal of Legislation*   [Vol. 6: 1

through January of 1977. He advised the committee that Customs planned to clean up that backlog in about six months.

Treasury's General Counsel explained to the subcommittee that if an importer could establish that there were differences in the cost of producing television sets sold in Japan and sets sold in the United States, or that there were differences in certain circumstances of sale (such as advertising costs or warranty costs) then appropriate adjustments would have to be made to wholesale prices before establishing dumping margins.

The General Counsel's testimony included comments on Customs past experience with submissions previously made by Japanese television manufacturers to support claims for cost of production or circumstance of sale adjustment. He said that for the period 1972 through July of 1973 "information submitted by all but one manufacturer was unreliable or incomplete or both." He went on to say: "the Customs Service has concluded that the claims for adjustments for differences in costs of production and circumstances of sale submitted by the manufacturers during the July 1973 to January 1975 period are not reliable and should not be allowed in computing the dumping duties." The General Counsel then articulated Treasury's policy with respect to future claims for adjustment saying: "the Customs Service will consider evidence of adjustment claims as sufficiently persuasive only if that evidence is prepared with express reference to manufacturers' documentation . . . and only if all of the documentation is subject to satisfactory field verification."[48]

In late December of 1978, however, Treasury's General Counsel sought the support of Congressmen Charles Vanik and Dan Rostenkowski for a proposal to settle the television dumping case for about $50 million.[49] Television dumping penalties for receivers imported between March of 1972 and January of 1977 had been estimated to total $400 million. Because of the rapid change in the yen-dollar relationship, dumping penalties for receivers imported in 1977 and 1978 were expected to total an additional $200 million. The $50 million settlement would have amounted to less than ten cents on the dollar.

The Treasury proposal also contemplated that civil penalties that might be assessed for the failure to disclose rebates and kickbacks would be settled for an additional $5 to $10 million. If the kickbacks and rebates were as widespread as many suspect, the civil penalties that could be assessed to importers would approximate $200 million. The settlement of the possibly very substantial civil penalties, before grand juries acted in the criminal cases, would have permitted importers to plead guilty or nolo contendere to criminal charges, pay the criminal penalties, which are normally less severe than the civil penalties, and avoid a public trial.

Congressmen Vanik and Rostenkowski flatly rejected the proposal. Congressman Vanik told the *New York Times:* "I certainly don't think we should compromise grand jury proceedings, and it would compromise them to try to dispose of this claim before the grand jury has settled the issue of fraud."[50]

In the months following the September Trade Subcommittee hearings, virtually no action was taken to assess the $350 million in dumping duties on receivers imported between June 30, 1973 and January of 1977 despite the assurances offered in the hearings that the backlog would be cleaned up in about six months. Shortly after the September hearings, Treasury did set

48. *Id.*
49. Hersh, *supra* note 28, at 1.
50. *Id.*

Exhibit 4.1 (continued)

November 27, 1978 as the due date for payment of the $46 million in dumping payments that it had told the Subcommittee it was "on the threshold" of collecting. The November due date was later extended to December 27, 1978, the December due date was then extended to January 27, 1979 and the January due date was finally extended to March 12, 1979.

On March 13, 1979, the Customs Service announced that importers would have to pay the $46 million in dumping penalties that had been assessed but as yet had not been collected.[51] The importers were told, however, that only part of the payment need be made in cash and that the remainder of the obligation could be fulfilled with promissory notes. There was no mention in the March announcement of what, if any, action would be taken to assess the still unliquidated dumping duties for imports after June 30, 1973.

The March announcement stated that the Customs Service expected by August 1, 1979 to complete its review of protests importers had filed to support their claims that the $46 million assessment of dumping penalties should be reduced or eliminated. The importers had been permitted to support the protests with new documentation to replace the documentation that had previously been found by Customs to be unreliable.

Treasury, having disbanded the "Project Omega" task force, assigned a new group of nine staff attorneys to the task of dealing with the collection of the $46 million in dumping duties that had been assessed on March 31, 1979. The group had been asked to "formulate 'estimates' of the amounts by which the dumping duties assessed on March 31, 1978, will be reduced." In a memorandum dated March 2, 1979 and signed by the nine staff attorneys, the group stated that:

> It is our understanding that these 'estimates' will be used to help determine the portion of outstanding dumping duties which will be collected in March of this year. We understand that the amount of duty remaining after the 'estimated' circumstance of sale adjustments have been made, on a manufacturer by manufacturer basis, will be collected in cash. The balance is to be secured by promissory notes.[52]

The attorneys summarized their concern with the possibility that their work might be misunderstood or misused with the statement:

> [T]he entire 'estimate' exercise is premised upon a number of factual assumptions. Foremost among these assumptions is that all claims for adjustments will be established by the manufacturer to the satisfaction of Customs. We wish to point out that the figures derived during this exercise cannot, under any circumstances, be construed as having been accepted as substantiated to the satisfaction of the undersigned staff attorneys.[53]

Each time the word "estimate" had been used in the memorandum, it had been placed in quotation marks. The memorandum suggested strongly that the new group of attorneys enlisted to replace Customs veterans in the television case were as determined as their predecessors to enforce the antidumping laws. As the claims for adjustment were being considered by Customs officers, the Japanese manufacturers launched public protests against the dumping assessments.

51. News Release, Department of the Treasury (March 13, 1979).
52. Memorandum to File from Staff Attorneys, Department of the Treasury, United States Custom Service (March 2, 1979).
53. *Id.*

Exhibit 4.1 (continued)

12   *Journal of Legislation*   [Vol. 6: 1

In newspaper advertisements and in other appeals for support spokesmen for the Japanese television manufacturers asserted that the Customs decision to base dumping duties on "foreign market values" arrived at by using Japanese commodity tax information was unfair.[54] They asserted that adoption of the commodity tax formula represented "changing the rules after the game has started" for they had been previously led to believe that "foreign market values" in the case would be based on documentation they themselves had submitted to Customs. The opposing view, of course, contended that the long history of false and/or fraudulent submissions made to Customs by the manufacturers fully justified the adoption of an alternate approach to determining home market prices. The opposing point of view also contended that the values the Japanese manufacturers had assigned to television sets in paying taxes to their own government represented the best evidence available for establishing home market prices.

The newspaper advertisements and other appeals for support also asserted that Customs having adopted the commodity tax formula in 1978 had unfairly "made it retroactive—assessing penalties for the years 1971-'73." The opposing view contended, that the long delay in establishing assessments was attributable largely to deceit and delay on the part of the importers and manufacturers themselves and, thus, that delay could hardly be accepted as grounds for reducing the assessments. In addition the opposing view contended that the deceit and delay had already provided the importers and manufacturers with handsome returns for they had not yet paid in 1978 monies that might readily have been collected as early as 1972. With interest costs in the 8-10% range during the period the long delay had produced a substantial monetary benefit for the importers.

Eight years after the Tariff Commission had published its television case injury finding in 1971 it was still unclear as to whether the dumping penalties assessed in the television case would ultimately be determined by enforcement action undertaken by the Customs Service, by an agreement negotiated officially or unofficially by American and Japanese diplomats or by litigation. The long history of the television case had certainly made it clear, however, that the United States did not possess the will or the means to enforce its antidumping laws.

THE CONSEQUENCES OF DUMPING

When the Tariff Commission concluded in 1971 that the American television industry had been injured by dumping, it also concluded that the sellers of dumped Japanese receivers "have for the most part undersold U.S. manufacturers of television sets in the domestic market" and that sales of the dumped television receivers "have contributed substantially to declining prices of domestically produced television receivers."

The failure during the past eight years to impose the dumping penalties mandated by law has permitted importers of Japanese television sets to continue dumping. The dumping, in turn, has made it impossible for American producers to raise prices. (Appendix A)

In the last decade the prices of industrial commodities and the hourly earnings of American workers have doubled. Television prices have increased

54. The Washington Post, February 6, 1979, § A, at 8-9, col. 1.

Exhibit 4.1 (continued)

by about 2%. Had American television producers raised their prices sufficiently to recover even a portion of the skyrocketing material and labor costs they were incurring, they would have been driven from the American television market by the importers of Japanese receivers as completely as they had some years earlier been driven from the American radio market.

The cost-price squeeze caused by the inability to raise prices has had a catastrophic impact on United States television industry earnings. In the ten years 1968-1977, American television producers other than Zenith earned pretax profits amounting to 2.1% of sales. In the five-year period, 1973-1977, American producers other than Zenith earned pretax profits averaging only 0.4% of sales. Pretax profits in American manufacturing industries other than the television industry have averaged approximately 8% of sales. (Appendix B)

In the five-year 1973-1977 period, some 60,000 jobs were eliminated in the American television industry.[55] About twenty American communities experienced the human and economic dislocations associated with the shutdown of a major television manufacturing facility.

Since 1973, five of America's best known television manufacturers have been forced into acquisitions or liquidation. In late 1973, Admiral was acquired by Rockwell International. In 1974, Motorola's television business was sold to Matsushita, the largest of the Japanese television companies. Later in 1974, Magnavox was acquired by an American affiliate of N.V. Philips Gloeilampenfabrieken of the Netherlands, Europe's largest television producer. Still later in 1974, Ford Motor Company sold its Philco television brand name and distribution assets to GTE-Sylvania. The Philco manufacturing assets were liquidated. In 1976, Warwick, a company that had supplied private-brand television products to Sears, was acquired by Sanyo of Japan. During 1978 General Electric sought, but failed to obtain Justice Department acceptance of a proposal to merge its television business with that of an American affiliate of Hitachi of Japan. By the end of 1978, Rockwell International had announced it would liquidate the Admiral television business it had acquired five years earlier.

The explanation for the financial difficulties of American television producers is not to be found in inadequate management. The explanation is to be found in the long continued dumping of Japanese television receivers in the American market.

Ford Motor Company, Motorola and Rockwell International have impressive records of efficiency and profitability in other industries. Each, however, incurred sizable losses in the American television market. General Electric is regarded to be among the best managed of American companies but after years of inadequate profits it found it necessary to seek to merge its television business with that of Hitachi of Japan.

In March of this year the least expensive 19-inch television receivers available for sale in Japan were still priced at about 150,000 yen. At the current exchange rate of about 200 yen to the dollar, that amounted to $750. Comparable receivers imported from Japan for sale in the United States are priced under $350. The least expensive large screen furniture models in Japan are now priced at about 390,000 yen or just under $2000. Consoles with

55. *In the Investigation on Television Receivers and Certain Parts Thereof Pursuant to Section 201 of the Trade Act of 1974; Hearing Before the United States International Trade Commission*, January 18, 1977 (statement of I. W. Abel).

Exhibit 4.1 (continued)

14   *Journal of Legislation*   [Vol. 6: 1

comparable features and screen sizes are readily available in the United States at prices of about $750.

No nation has benefited more than Japan from the willingness of other nations to relax import restrictions and to encourage a free exchange of goods. Japan, however, while exploiting opportunities in the markets of its trading partners, has persisted in pursuing a protectionist policy at home. In 1976, color television sales in Japan exceeded 5 million units; fewer than 500 of those units were imported. (Appendix C)

The exclusions of foreign competition from the Japanese market is an essential part of an export strategy based on dumping. It has provided Japanese television producers with profits substantial enough in their home market to permit them to sell their products in the American market at prices so low as to displace and/or destroy domestic competitors. Television dumping on the scale that we have witnessed in the United States simply could not have been continued without the financial support resulting from very sizable profits in a protected home market.

CONCLUSION

Zenith has concluded from years of direct involvement in the television dumping case that policy-level officials of the U.S. Government have regarded the American television industry to be a pawn that might readily be sacrificed in order to avoid a diplomatic confrontation with Japan or to accomplish some other diplomatic objective. As a result of Treasury's avoidance for more than a decade of its responsibility to enforce the antidumping law, the stockholders and employees of American television companies have been effectively deprived of their right to the protection afforded by that law. The television case should, therefore, be of great concern to any who believe that this is a nation ruled by law and not by men.

The television dumping case raises serious economic issues that should be of concern to those interested in preserving this country's free enterprise system. In the last decade five major American producers have abandoned the television industry and other American producers have been so scarred by unlawful dumping as to be left far less competitive in the American market than they might otherwise have been.

If a firm is to prosper or even survive in the American enterprise system it must be able to invest in laboratories to improve technology and in plant and equipment to improve productivity. The funds required to support these investments must come either from corporate profits or from investors who believe that their investments will generate an adequate future return. An industry confronted with the predatory pricing associated with the dumping can neither earn the profits nor obtain the investor confidence needed to finance those investments.

Dumping has already produced economic chaos in the American television industry and in the American steel industry. The American semiconductor, computer and automobile industries are today, in varying degrees, threatened with that kind of chaos. Unless this country demonstrates the ability to enforce vigorously and quickly its antidumping laws, dozens of other American industries will be left exposed to assaults like that which has been mounted against the American television industry.

American trade deficits with Japan have jumped sharply since the oil crisis.

Exhibit 4.1 (continued)

In 1974 and again in 1975 the U.S. trade deficit with Japan totaled $1.7 billion. In 1976 the deficit rose to $5.4 billion, in 1977 to $8.1 billion and in 1978 it totaled $11.6 billion.[56] The rapidly growing deficits with Japan have not occurred because of a sudden change in the relative productivity of Japanese and American manufacturers.

On the issue of productivity, many Americans have been confused by Department of Labor reports that manufacturing output per man-hour increased by 82% in Japan from 1967 to 1975 and by only 16% in the United States. The slower growth in American productivity and the low prices of imported television receivers and steel in the American market have apparently led many to conclude that the United States is at a productivity disadvantage. (Appendix D)

In 1975, the last year for which measurements are available, manufacturing output per man-hour in Japan was 64.9% of manufacturing output per man-hour in the United States. Expressed differently, in 1975 the average American manufacturing employee produced about 50% more per hour worked than did his counterpart in Japan. It is the absolute level of productivity, not the rate of productivity growth that determines a nation's ability to compete in world markets. America is certainly not at a productivity disadvantage.

In 1978, the American trade deficit totaled a staggering $29 billion. Some $14 billion of that deficit was incurred in trade with the thirteen members of the Organization of Petroleum Exporting Countries (OPEC); almost $12 billion was incurred in trade with Japan alone and a $3 billion deficit was incurred in trade with the rest of the world.[57]

Official Washington apparently continues to believe that vigorous enforcement of this country's antidumping laws would be regarded by our trading partners to be protectionist and would, therefore, threaten the world trading system. A strong case can be made that nothing would threaten the world trading system more than the continuation of American trade deficits of the magnitude experienced in 1978 and the continuation of the instability in the value of the American dollar that has resulted from our 1977 and 1978 deficits.

Dumping can no more be tolerated than bribery as a tactic for increasing sales in a export market. Either dumping or bribery will improve the position of the user in the short term. Their long-term impact, however, is to weaken the confidence of the peoples of the world in the trade system and to generate the protectionist reactions that might ultimately destroy that system.

The $400 million dumping finding suggests that during the 1972 to 1977 period, the average Japanese television set had been imported into the United States at about $40 under its fair market value. A $40 advantage at the time of importation would give the Japanese television sets a retail price advantage, relative to the products of domestic producers, of $65 to $75. That price advantage did not result because the Japanese were more efficient than their U.S. competitors, but rather because they had been able to violate American antidumping statutes with impunity for more than a decade.

There is a startling difference between the manner in which the American public and American leaders perceive the importance of foreign trade problems. The Chicago Council on Foreign Relations commissioned the Gallup organization, in late 1978, to measure the attitudes of the American public and American

56. United States Department of Commerce statistics.
57. *Id.*

Exhibit 4.1 (continued)

---

leaders on a variety of foreign policy questions.[58] The two groups were asked to rate various foreign policy goals in terms of whether those goals were very important, somewhat important or not important. The 13 goals included: "Keeping up the value of the dollar, Securing adequate supplies of energy, Protecting jobs of American workers, Worldwide arms control, Containing Communism" and eight other items.

The goal of "Protecting jobs of American workers" was perceived by 78% of the American public to be very important; only 34% of the American leaders perceived that goal to be very important. Among the American public only one foreign policy goal "Keeping up the value of the dollar" was seen to be more important than protecting American jobs. Among the American leaders only four of the thirteen foreign policy goals were perceived to be less important than protecting American jobs. Among the American public, 45% of the respondents perceived "Protecting interests of American business abroad" to be very important; only 27% of the American leaders perceived that goal to be very important.[59]

The attitudes of American leaders on foreign trade questions continue to be based on a Marshall Plan mentality that sees Europe and Japan as being so weak in economic matters as to require continuing American concessions and that sees the United States as being so strong as to be immune from economic injury no matter what trade concessions are made by its government. Treasury's long avoidance of its responsibility to enforce the antidumping laws in the television case is only one example of the American Government's willingness to wink at unfair and unlawful acts in foreign trade in order to avoid diplomatic confrontation. There are growing signs, however, that the United States Government is losing the support of the American public on trade matters. In August of 1978 the Harris Survey reported that by a margin of 61%-33% the American public now favors a greater restriction on imports rather than a continuation of this country's traditional policy of freer trade with most countries of the world.[60]

Vigorous enforcement of American laws designed to control dumping and other unfair trade practices can be urged solely on the grounds that American stockholders and employees are entitled to the protection afforded by law. Vigorous enforcement of those laws can also be urged because dumping and other unfair trade practices constitute an intolerable threat to this country's free enterprise system and appear to have contributed substantially to our staggering trade deficits in recent years.

In the Harris Survey in which Americans by a 61%-33% margin favored a greater restriction on imports, the respondents agreed by a margin of 64%-26% with the statement: "We have been made suckers by other countries which restrict U.S. goods, but whose goods are free to come into this country." In commenting on the survey Lou Harris, however, noted: "There is a fundamental feeling in this country that if artificial barriers against American goods were removed or tempered, then our products could compete on a profitable basis."

---

58. Gallup, *Foreign Policy Goals for the United States—1978*, in American Public Opinion and United States Foreign Policy 1979, at 12 (John E. Reilly ed. 1979).
59. *Id.*
60. Harris, *Protectionist Sentiment is Growing on Imports*, The Harris Survey (August 10, 1978).

Exhibit 4.1 (continued)

1979]   Enforcing the Antidumping Laws   17

There is considerable reason to believe that what has been described as "protectionist sentiment" in the Congress and in the American public is not a cry for help from people who are unwilling or unable to compete. That so-called "protectionist sentiment" is in large part an angry reaction from citizens who believe the United States is being injured by unfair trade practices that its government has been unwilling or unable to control. A continued failure on the part of the United States Government to enforce laws prohibiting dumping and other unfair trade practices can have no other result than to lead increased numbers of Americans to withdraw their support from this country's traditional position of encouraging freer trade throughout the world.

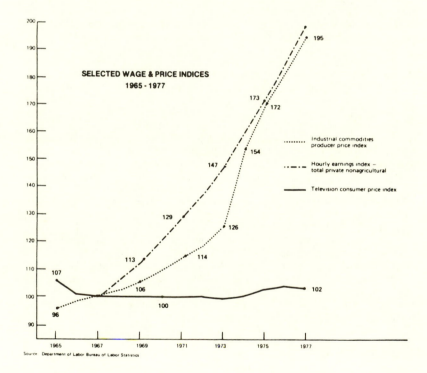

SELECTED WAGE & PRICE INDICES
1965 - 1977

Industrial commodities producer price index

Hourly earnings index – total private nonagricultural

Television consumer price index

Source: Department of Labor Bureau of Labor Statistics

Exhibit 4.1 (continued)

18   *Journal of Legislation*   [Vol. 6: 1

DOMESTIC TELEVISION INDUSTRY PROFITABILITY
(Dollars in Millions)

	SALES	PRETAX OPERATING PROFIT	PROFIT AS PERCENT OF SALES
TEN YEARS 1968 – 1977			
ZENITH	$ 8,096	$ 669	8.3%
ALL OTHERS	17,638	366	2.1
TOTAL INDUSTRY	25,734	1,035	4.0
FIVE YEARS 1973 – 1977			
ZENITH	$ 4,732	$ 284	6.0%
ALL OTHERS	8,376	34	0.4
TOTAL INDUSTRY	13,108	318	2.4
1977			
ZENITH	$ 966	$ 39	4.0%
ALL OTHERS	1,942	42	2.2
TOTAL INDUSTRY	2,908	81	2.8

Source: U.S. International Trade Commission

Exhibit 4.1 (continued)

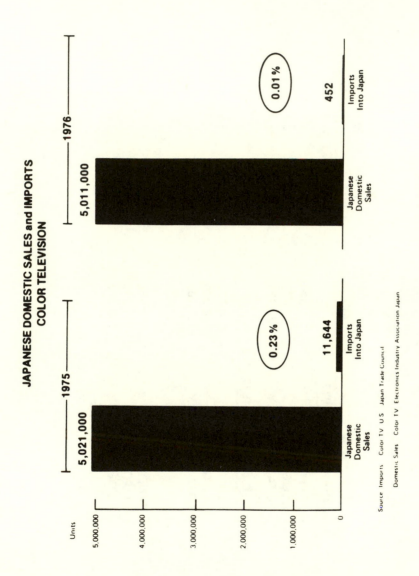

JAPANESE DOMESTIC SALES and IMPORTS COLOR TELEVISION

1976

0.01%

452 Imports Into Japan

5,011,000 Japanese Domestic Sales

1975

0.23%

11,644 Imports Into Japan

5,021,000 Japanese Domestic Sales

Units
5,000,000
4,000,000
3,000,000
2,000,000
1,000,000
0

Source Imports Color TV U S Japan Trade Council

Domestic Sales Color TV Electronics Industry Association Japan

Exhibit 4.1 (continued)

20 *Journal of Legislation* [Vol. 6: 1

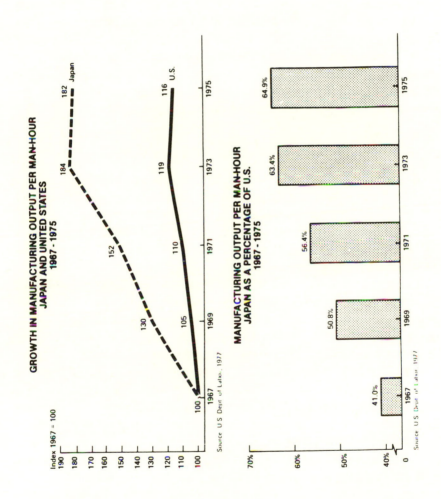

GROWTH IN MANUFACTURING OUTPUT PER MAN-HOUR
JAPAN AND UNITED STATES
1967 - 1975

Index 1967 = 100

Source U.S Dept of Labor, 1977

MANUFACTURING OUTPUT PER MAN-HOUR
JAPAN AS A PERCENTAGE OF U.S.
1967 - 1975

Source U S Dept of Labor, 1977

to government. The correct approach was to restore free trade by eliminating the predatory dumping by the cartel and opening up the Japanese
market to break up the Japanese cartel.

Zenith management took a defensive compromise position. Zenith's
chief executive officer, John Nevin, testified very effectively in the 201
case before the International Trade Commission, showing how badly
the American television industry was being harmed by the flood of
Japanese television receivers. But Nevin pointed out in this testimony
and in written submissions that Zenith did not want a protectionist remedy such as a quota to combat the anticompetitive tactics of the cartel.
Zenith wanted the anticompetitive dumping scheme stopped under the
antidumping and antitrust laws. We only asked for such interim Section
201 relief as would be necessary until the dumping was stopped by the
assessment of long-overdue dumping duties.

JAPAN'S NEW POLITICAL INFLUENCE APPARATUS

The massive increase in TV imports by the Japanese cartel and the
damage done to beleaguered American manufacturers was so obvious
that the cartel interests practically had to concede the issue in the 201
case. The required findings of increased imports causing injury were
easily found by the International Trade Commission (ITC), and the case
went to the President for action.

President Carter's new administration had been heavily infiltrated
by Japan's new agents of influence, who were anxious to deliver to
their new employers. As President Carter's newly appointed Special
Trade Representative, Robert Strauss was given the assignment of
negotiating an Orderly Marketing Agreement in the television industry
with the Japanese. Strauss was the former chairman of the Democratic
Party. He was famous for his political know-how, fatherly charm, and
ability to get things done. In a March 1977 issue of *Newsweek*, Strauss
was quoted as saying, "I know something more than absolutely nothing,
but less than a little [about trade negotiations]."

An anticompetitive Orderly Marketing Agreement was negotiated
with the Japanese government in secret parlays that committed the U.S.
government to settle out. None of the American television producers
were ever informed of this secret document. The agreement was engineered by the first and most important of Japan's new high-powered
lobbyists, Harold Malmgren. He had been Deputy Special Trade Representative under William Eberle, the Special Trade Representative during the Nixon and Ford administrations. When they left office, both

went to work as highly paid consultants to Japanese commercial interests. Malmgren obtained a very lucrative contract to help the Japanese television cartel overcome the dumping, subsidy, and restraint of trade charges.

Malmgren was intimately familiar with the U.S. television industry's problems. He had worked with Eberle in the Nixon-Tanaka summit meetings of 1972, at which the U.S. television industry was allegedly traded off for agriculture, uranium, and aircraft concessions. (See Appendix VII at original pages 14–18.) Malmgren's fees were notoriously high and tempted many other U.S. trade officials to hit the revolving door. He "consulted" with Robert Strauss, Carter's new Special Trade Representative, and his staff in working out the Orderly Marketing Agreement and the drafting of the secret side-letter that pledged an end to U.S. government law enforcement efforts. (See Appendix VII at original pages 19–25.)

Shirley Coffield was an influential member of the Strauss team that negotiated the Orderly Marketing Agreement. She is said to have composed Strauss's secret side-letter to the Japanese government pledging to (1) eliminate the antidumping attacks on the cartel, and (2) have the Supreme Court reverse the countervailing duty case Zenith had won in the Customs Court.[6] All branches of the federal government faithfully and successfully performed under this disloyal and secret pledge of cooperation.

The quota agreement that emerged from the negotiations in Japan had two layers. One was the publicly announced "orderly marketing" quota, which restricted exports to the United States to a yearly maximum of 1.75 million units for a three-year period. It is important to note that this agreement did not affect output from the American television companies the Japanese had recently bought up. The second layer was secret and not visible. It was in effect a pledge to get rid of all the dumping proceedings and related attacks on the cartel members in the United States. Particular emphasis was placed on Zenith's countervailing duty case. In this case the Customs Court had found the remission of commodity taxes on exports to the United States to be a subsidy that was required to be countervailed under well-settled federal law.

The existence of this secret layer came to light a year later, when Robert Strauss was testifying before the trade subcommittee of the House Ways and Means Committee. In answer to a fortuitous question by Representative Rostenkowski, Strauss revealed the existence of the side-letter. When asked if he would produce it, he shrewdly said that he would. Now the cat was out of the bag.

The secret side-letter virtually guaranteed the Japanese that the U.S. government would side with Japanese interests and do everything possible to abrogate the dumping levies, Zenith's lawsuit, and an ITC unfair trade investigation. In short, this letter marked the first time that a U.S. trade official assured the government of Japan not only that the U.S. government would step aside and allow Japan to capture an entire industrial sector, but that the U.S. government would willingly aid and abet that effort in any way it could. The impact of Strauss's letter was phenomenal:

- ITC dropped its unfair trade investigation, which had been initiated by Sylvania.
- Customs appealed the Zenith countervailing duty ruling.
- Justice ruled that there was no conspiratorial dumping restraining trade in violation of the antitrust laws.
- Robert Mundheim, general counsel for the Treasury Department, counseled the Japanese on how to abrogate the dumping levy problem.
- An aide to Mundheim coached the Japanese on how to sidestep paying the levies while the matter was being appealed.
- Treasury recalled liquidation notices imposing dumping duties.
- Congressman Jim Jones tried to introduce an amendment that would grant retroactive immunity from levies to Japanese television companies.
- Treasury granted interest-free delays on dumping duties and fines to Japan.
- Treasury settled for $77 million in dumping duties and fines. Ten years later, only $16 million had been collected. It was conservatively estimated that absent the settlement, over $1 billion should have been recovered and criminal prosecutions for customs fraud should have been initiated and vigorously pursued.
- Most significant, the settlement agreement contained the following fatal and false declaration at the secret urging of the Japanese cartel and its highly paid American lobbyists and lawyer insiders:

  The United States knows of no violation of law relating to or arising from the importation, sale or exportation of television receivers by the . . . [importers] or the Japanese manufacturers/exporters from which [they] have purchased or will purchase.[7]

The U.S. government thus—incredibly—abandoned its constitutional and statutory duty to enforce the civil and criminal laws of the land. In effect, the rule of law was declared to be inapplicable to the pernicious and predatory assault on the American industry and its workers. It explains our government's later deceitful and fraudulent representations to the Supreme Court in the Zenith lawsuits described in the following chapters.

NOTES

1. 395 U.S. 100, 23 L.Ed.2d 129 (1969); 401 U.S. 321, 287 L.Ed.2d 77 (1971).

2. These documents and others cited or quoted in the following paragraphs were not of public record.

3. Quoted in Kenneth Bilby, *The General: David Sarnoff and the Rise of the Communications Industry* (1986), p. 222.

4. Any attack on the cartel would threaten their multimillion-dollar income from the Japanese as the cartel's riskless partner furnishing patent and technical aid to the Japanese; that is, for a healthy percentage of all the cartel's sales, RCA understandably considered that any attack on the Japanese would threaten its huge royalty income.

5. All were identified in Zenith's Petitions for Countervailing Duties.

6. See original pages 23–25 of Appendix VII, where the cartel's influence on Shirley Coffield is described.

7. See original pages 38–40 of Appendix VII.

5

Japanese Government Subsidies

ZENITH PETITIONS FOR THE LEVY
OF COUNTERVAILING DUTIES

For years, Zenith had pleaded in vain with the Treasury Department to offset the subsidies the government of Japan had granted cartel members to aid their dumping attack on the American market. In our visits to the various government offices in Washington, I found a reluctance by officials to discuss or disclose the widespread subsidies conferred on cartel members by the Japanese government. The petition, therefore, became necessary to force the government to act officially so that we could appeal any denial of relief to the courts. We had to seek out evidence of the subsidies from sparse sources we found available to us, as stated in the petition. Zenith's petition and amendment letter are set out here as Exhibit 5.1.

After interminable delays at Treasury that were never explained, in an unprecedented action Congress angrily enacted a deadline giving Treasury one year to resolve this matter. Treasury officials waited out every day of the year allowed and then simply denied the Zenith petition [41 Fed. Reg. 298 (1976)]. Under the regulations, the denial of the countervailing duty petition was officially subject to comments by interested parties before becoming final. Zenith filed its official comments on March 3, 1975, preparatory to challenging the ruling in court. The Zenith submission is reproduced as Exhibit 5.2 to illustrate the plight of an American industry in real jeopardy.

Exhibit 5.1
Zenith's Petition for the Levy of Countervailing Duties;
and Amendment to Petition

ZENITH RADIO CORPORATION
1900 NORTH AUSTIN AVENUE • CHICAGO, ILLINOIS 60638 • PHONE (312) 745-2000

April 3, 1970

The Honorable Myles J. Ambrose
Commissioner of Customs
Bureau of Customs
2100 K Street, N. W.
Washington, D. C.   20226

Petition for the Levy of
   Countervailing Duties

Dear Sir:

     Petitioner, Zenith Radio Corporation, having good and suffi-
cent reason to believe that bounties and grants are being paid
or bestowed, directly or indirectly, upon the manufacture, production and export of dutiable merchandise, listed on the attached
Exhibit A, continuously being imported into the United States in
vast quantities from Japan hereby respectfully requests that the
Secretary of the Treasury investigate, ascertain and determine
or estimate the net amounts of each such bounty and grant and levy
appropriate countervailing duties in accordance with the mandate
of Section 303, Tariff Act of 1930 (19 U.S.C. 1303).

Statement of Reasons for
Petitioner's Belief as
Required by 19 CFR 16.24(b)

     Attached hereto as Exhibit B is a copy of a Department of
State memorandum under date of November 6, 1968, on the subject
of "Japan's Export Promotion Techniques" briefly detailing some
of the various bounties and grants which, it is submitted, are

Exhibit 5.1 (continued)

The Honorable Myles J. Ambrose
Page 2

clearly encompassed by Section 303, Tariff Act of 1930.

Summary of Known Tax
<u>Incentives for Exporting</u>

The following tax incentives, described briefly in Exhibit B,
are currently in effect and should be countervailed as required by
the countervailing duty statute.

1.   <u>Special Depreciation Allowances</u>

Article 46-(2) of the Japanese Special Taxation Measures Law
Relating to Exceptions to the Corporation Tax Law (1969-1970)
provides that firms manufacturing and producing for export may
take depreciation at a rate in excess of the regular rates for
plant and equipment set out in the statutory tax rules. This
measure insures a greater internal cash flow and in conjunction
with the Reserve for Export Market Development described in
paragraph 2 below effects very substantial tax savings as an
incentive for exporters.

Pursuant to Article 46-(2), items 1 and 2 of the Special
Taxation Measures Law, as of April 1, 1968, the accelerated depreciation system was geared up to permit major exporters to apply
a multiplier to their export ratios. In order to participate,
firms are classified as either "B" exporters or "A" exporters. To
qualify as a "B" exporter, a company is required to increase the
value of its exports by 1% or more over two successive accounting
periods (i.e. in one six month period compared to the previous
one). To qualify as an "A" exporter, a company must meet this
same goal, but without its export ratio falling. Alternatively,
it must show a growth in its exports equal to at least 66% of the
total increase in Japan's exports in the period concerned.

2.   <u>"The Overseas Market Cultivation Reserve."</u>

Article 54 of the Special Taxation Measures Law provides an
advantage accompanying the provision in paragraph 1 above that
permits both manufacturers and exporters to set aside a part of
their gross export proceeds as reserves to develop overseas
market. The normal percentage of gross export proceeds is 0.5%
for major trading companies, 1% for those with less capitalization
and 1.5% for manufacturers.

The 0.5% of gross earnings that a major trading company can

Exhibit 5.1 (continued)

The Honorable Myles J. Ambrose
Page 3

put into its foreign market development reserve becomes a 0.65% if
it qualifies as a "B" exporter and 0.3% if it qualifies as an
"A" exporter. For smaller trading companies that qualify as
exporters, the rate becomes 1.3% and for those qualifying as
"A" exporters, the rate is 1.60%. For manufacturers, the rates
are multiplied to 1.95% and 2.4% respectively. These reserves are
deducted from net taxable income after all business expenses. When
merchandise passes from the manufacturer to an exporter, both are
permitted to set up reserves based upon the same transactions.

The very favorable results produced for exporters by these
incentives and subsidies are illustrated by the following example
from page 6 of the State Department's memorandum, Exhibit B,
attached:

In the example given, Company "Y" is a Japanese manufacturer
selling only in the home market and Company "X" qualifies as an
"A" exporter. The system works as follows:

	"Y"	"X"
Gross Sales Revenue	100	100
Costs		
Material, labor, etc.	70	70
Depreciation	10 80	19.6* 89.6
Gross profit	20	10.4
Reserve for o/seas market devel.	--	2.4**
Adjusted gross profit	20	8.0
Tax at 50%	10	4.0
Tax saving	--	6.0

 * As explained above, company X gets 96% acceleration of
   depreciation.

** As an "A" exporter, company X can set up a reserve equal to
   2.4% of gross export proceeds.

Exhibit 5.1 (continued)

The Honorable Myles J. Ambrose
Page 4

3.   Overseas Investment Less Reserve.

To stimulate exports, Article 56 of the Special Taxation
Measures Law permits Japanese firms to accumulate a fund equal to
50% of its investments abroad as a reserve against losses. As
stated in the State Department memorandum, Exhibit B, at page 7,
paragraph (D):

> "Because the GOJ must approve and license such
> investments, this incentive is allowed only
> when Japanese exports will be stimulated or
> other favorable balance of payments will be
> achieved."

4.   "Exceptional Rules of Taxation Respecting Overseas
Transactions in Technology.

Article 58 of the Special Taxation Measures Law provides for
special deductions from taxable income for Japanese firms which
have earned foreign currencies through the export of technical
services, patent rights, copyrights, etc.   The utilization of
this law in connection with the exportation to the United States
of the dutiable merchandise which is the subject of this complaint
should be investigated.

5.   "Entertainment Expenses."

Article 38, items (1) and (2) of the Special Taxation Measures
Law provides preferential tax treatment of "expenses" incurred
overseas in "entertaining" foreign buyers.

The use of this broad incentive in the sale and exportation
to United States buyers of the subject merchandise should be
investigated.

6.   Tariff Rebate to Exporters

The customs drawback system, as indicated in paragraph (G),
page 8 of the State Department memorandum, Exhibit B, is administered with respect to items selected on the basis of "what
practical value their export would have for Japan." It is submitted that this familiar area for concealed bounties and the use

Exhibit 5.1 (continued)

The Honorable Myles J. Ambrose
Page 5

of the formula referred to in the State Department memorandum
should be investigated.

Financial Incentives*

7. Japanese firms by virtue of an elaborate system of governmental financial bounties and incentives, as described in the
footnote references, are able to operate on a vast scale with very
high debt: equity ratios far beyond that possible in the United
States or other countries. The debt component is frequently four
or five times the equity. (See the analysis by James C. Abegglen
in the March, 1970 edition of Scientific American at pages 31-37,
attached hereto as Exhibit D.)

Against this background, the spread between the discount rate
on export trade bills and the on commercial paper provides a
strong incentive to export.

The export advance bill system together with the policy and
practices of the Japan Export-Import Bank and the related financial
incentives and subsidies described in Section II of the State
Department memorandum are powerful subsidies clearly encompassed
by our countervailing duty statute.

Export Insurance System

8.   The Ministry of International Trade and Industry has
described this phase of the Japanese export bounty system in a
memorandum entitled "A Brief Introduction to the Export Insurance"
dated November, 1966, and attached hereto as Exhibit E.   The
system is also described in Section III of the State Department
memorandum Exhibit B.

The purpose and effectiveness of this government subsidy is
described by MITI itself at page one of its memorandum as follows:

----

*A copy of a section of the Japan Foreign Trade News
 describing these incentives in general is attached
 hereto as Exhibit C. The State Department memorandum,
 Exhibit B, also describes these incentives in some
 detail at pages 8-11.

Exhibit 5.1 (continued)

The Honorable Myles J. Ambrose
Page 6

>"The Government of Japan underwrites, by
itself, export insurance policies to insure
perils and risks which are brought about by
export transactions or other overseas transactions conducted by traders and manufacturers
who are engaged in pursuit of foreign trade
and production of goods for export and which are
not insurable through the existent private
insurance institution at present. Export
insurance thus aims at protecting those concerns who are engaged in foreign trade activities
and enabling them to undertake their activities
without fear to bear loss by themselves.

>   *   *   *

>"This brief pamphlet aims at sketching
the whole picture of the government export
insurance system which plays a useful and con-
structive role in export selling of international
trade."

<u>Japan External Trade Organization</u>

9.   Another most effective export subsidy is provided by the
highly organized government owned corporation known as JETRO
(Japanese External Trade Organization). The extremely valuable
marketing research, promotion, design, advertising and other
services provided by this organization are briefly described in
Section IV of the State Department memorandum, Exhibit B.

<u>Tax Credits for Research</u>

10.   Incentives in the form of tax credits for research, a
function essential to the business of every exporting manufacturer
of the products referred to herein, are also a part of the Japanese
bounty program. Effective for accounting periods beginning on or
after June 1, 1967, a corporation increasing its expenditures for
research and experimental projects as compared to the immediately
preceding period is allowing a tax credit in an amount equal to
25% of the incremental change up to 10% of the corporation tax due.

Exhibit 5.1 (continued)

The Honorable Myles J. Ambrose
Page 7

The Commodity Tax Law
Exemption for Export

    11. So called "indirect taxes" provide over forty percent of total national revenues in Japan - approximately three times the ratio of "indirect taxes" to total national revenues in the United States. A principal source of these taxes in Japan is provided by the Commodity Tax Law. Under this statute, with certain exceptions made from time to time, Japanese manufacturers are taxed on the manufacture and sale of the subject products at varying rates from 5% to 20%.

    As an important part of the overall Japanese system designed to induce exportation by providing incentives therefor, as well as to subsidize exports and conceal dumping of consumer electronic products, Japan exempts from such taxes all exports of the subject merchandise. The exemption from those taxes provides an effective subsidy by excusing such exports from their proper share of the overall general tax burden.

    The "plain, explicit, and unequivocal purposes" of our counter-vailing duty statute was set forth in <u>Nicholas & Co.</u> v. <u>United States</u>, 7 St. Cust. Appls., 97, 106, T.D. 36426 (1916), affirmed (1919) 249 U.S. 34, as follows:

> "* * * Whenever a foreign power or depen-
> dency or any political subdivision of a govern-
> ment shall give any aid or advantage to exporters
> of goods imported into this country therefrom
> whereby they may be sold for less in competition
> with our domestic goods, to that extent by this
> paragraph the duties fixed in the schedule of
> the act are increased. It was a <u>result</u> Congress
> was seeking to equalize regardless of whatever
> name or in whatever manner or form or for what-
> ever purposes it was done. The statute inter-
> prets itself as a member of an act calculated
> to maintain an accorded protection, incidental
> or otherwise, as against payments or grants
> of any kind by foreign powers, <u>resulting</u> in an
> equalization thereof to any extent directly or
> indirectly. * * *

*   *   *

Exhibit 5.1 (continued)

The Honorable Myles J. Ambrose
Page 8

> "* * * The sole inquiry is, do the results of
> such acts stimulate exportation or give a
> special advantage by affording aid from the
> public treasury whereby such goods may when
> exported be sold in competition with ours
> for less. * * *"

As the Supreme Court unequivocally stated in <u>Downs</u> v. <u>United
States</u>, (1903) 187 U.S. at pages 513, 515:

> "* * *if a preference be given to·merchandise
> exported over that sold in the home market, by
> the remission of an excise tax, the effect
> would be the same as if all such merchandise
> were taxed, and a drawback repaid to the
> manufacturer upon so much as he exported. * * *

> *   *   *

> "The details of this elaborate procedure
> for the production, sale, taxation, and exporta-
> tion of Russian sugar are of much less impor-
> tance than the two facts which appear clearly
> through this maze of regulations, <u>viz.</u>: that
> no sugar is permitted to be sold in Russia
> that does not pay an excise tax of R. 1.75
> per pood, and that sugar exported pays no tax
> at all. . . When a tax is imposed upon all
> sugar exported, then, by whatever process, or
> in whatever manner, or under whatever name,
> it is disguised, it is a bounty upon exporta-
> tion."

In the Nicholas case the Supreme Court quoting from <u>United
States</u> v. <u>Passavant</u>, (1898) 169 U.S. 16, explained the equitable
basis and need for countervailing duties in such tax remissions
for exports as are involved here:

> "* * * We . . . said, through Mr. Chief
> Justice Fuller, that 'the laws of this country
> in the assessment of duties proceed upon the
> market value in the exporting country, and
> not upon the market value less such remission
> or amelioration as that country chooses to
> allow in accordance with its own views of
> public policy.' And this conclusion was

Exhibit 5.1 (continued)

The Honorable Myles J. Ambrose
Page 9

> reached upon the effect of the remitted tax,
> and not upon the word used to designate it.
> In other words, the decision was not deter-
> mined by a consideration of costs of manu-
> facture of their reimbursement, nor by the
> requirements of the policies of the export-
> ing country. It regarded the fact and effect
> of the remitted excise." (249 U.S. at pages
> 40-41)

The efforts of the Treasury Department to have Congress amend Section 303 to exclude from its coverage all exemptions of exported articles from taxes imposed on like articles destined for consumption in the country of origin failed. It is submitted that Section 303 as written and as clearly interpreted in relevant rulings in Nicholas and Downs should not be ignored in the circumstances of the instant case. The Japanese commodity tax scheme is an integral part of their extensive bounty and grant program and clearly should be countervailed.

Shipping

An investigation should also be made as to the existence and effect of subsidization in the Japanese shipping industry which may disclose the need for countervailing duties to equalize the following unfair disparity between ocean freight rates applicable to shipments between Japan and the United States:

> For the subject merchandise valued over $500 per ton,
> the rate from Japan to the United States is $40 per 40
> cubic feet or per ton whichever is greater, while the
> freight rate on the same merchandise from the United States
> to Japan is $70.

Failure to Report
Bounties and Grants

There is another aspect of this matter that should be given expeditious attention. Customs form 5515 requires answers to the following question:

> "6. Are any rebates, drawbacks, bounties, or
>   other grants allowed upon the exportation
>   of the goods? [] Yes   [] No.   If so,

Exhibit 5.1 (continued)

The Honorable Myles J. Ambrose
Page 10

      have all been separately itemized? [] Yes
      [] No."

    On information and belief knowledgeable importers of Japanese electronics products have been evading this question despite the sanctions provided in 19 U.S.C. 1592 and 18 U.S.C. 1001.

<u>The Urgency of This Petition</u>

    While Section 303 does not require any showing of injury, the urgency of this matter and the need for an·expeditious investigation and compliance with the mandate of the statute is apparent from the following facts:

    Beginning in the 1950's, the Japanese participation in the United States electronics market has not been in any sense a matter of free trade. It has been a calculated predatory invasion based upon the following factors:

1. An elaborate government subsidy program.
2. Subsidized know-how and patent arrangements with certain experienced American companies.
3. A protected home market, effectively closed to American and other competition, where prices are controlled by trade associations and maintained at artificially high levels.
4. A dumping program eagerly patronized by large American merchandisers.

    In the late 1950's, millions of excessively low priced transistor radios were dumped into the United States. By 1960, 55 percent of all portable radios sold in the United States were of Asiatic origin. By 1968, this figure rose to almost 95 percent and by the last quarter of 1969 to approximately 97 percent. For total radios, including portables but excluding automobile radios, imports accounted for approximately 88 percent of the market in 1969 and approximately 90 percent in the fourth quarter of 1969. Except for certain specialty types, the manufacture in the United States of radios was made economically impossible within ten years of this predatory invasion.

    Having thus captured virtually the entire radio market and employing the same predatory tactics and aids described above, the

Exhibit 5.1 (continued)

The Honorable Myles J. Ambrose
Page 11

Japanese manufacturers began in the 1960's to seize the American
television market and make economically impossible the American
manufacture of television receivers. From only 2 percent of the
United States market in 1962, imported black and white television
receivers rose to over 29 percent of the market in 1968 and in
the fourth quarter of 1969 accounted for 50 percent of the entire
American market. Imported color television which rose to 11 percent of the market in 1968, has risen in 1969 to over an 18 percent share of the market in the fourth quarter of 1969 and has
accounted for more than 1 out of every 6 color television receivers
sold in the United States. When color and black and white television statistics are combined, imports account for over 35 percent
of the total television receiver market for the fourth quarter of
1969. For the same fourth quarter, the market share held by
imported phonographs rose to over 34 percent and the share of the
market held by imported home magnetic tape recorders rose to
approximately 93 percent.

    During this period of time many American manufacturers, in
order to survive, were forced by this subsidized and predatory
Japanese competition first to purchase components from Japanese
sources and, when this measure proved insufficient, to make or
procure their radio and television chassis or complete sets in
Japan, Hong Kong, and Taiwan. An alarming movement of American
plants to Asia has taken place, and Taiwan and Mexico, providing
subsidies and incentives as well as cheap labor, have become the
new sites of many former American based factories. This trend
for survival against unfair subsidized competition by moving
American plants abroad is continuing at an alarming rate. It
is conservatively estimated that over 45,000 jobs have already
been lost to American workers in this industry as it rapidly
retreats to foreign manufacturing sites. Many of them are blacks
and members of other disadvantaged minorities trained or in the
process of being trained for productive employment in this industry pursuant to suggested Government programs.

    Petitioner favors and has always favored free and fair inter-
national trade. It cannot, however, continue to manufacture its
products in this country unless the predatory incursion briefly
described herein is stopped by the effective and expeditious
enforcement of our relevant laws.

Exhibit 5.1 (continued)

The Honorable Myles J. Ambrose
Page 12

    It is respectively submitted that in the context of this
industry crisis this petition for full and expeditious enforcement of Section 303 of the Tariff Act of 1930 should be favorably
considered.

                        Respectfully submitted,

                        ZENITH RADIO CORPORATION

                    By_____
                            Philip J. Curtis
                            Vice President and
                            General Counsel
PJC/nc
Attachments

Exhibit 5.1 (continued)

___

The Honorable Myles J. Ambrose
Commissioner of Customs
Bureau of Customs
2100 K Street, N.W.
Washington, D.C. 20226

Amendment to Petition for the Levy
of Countervailing Duties

Dear Sir:

. . . Since the filing of the Petition, the existence of bounties and grants within the provisions of Section 303, Tariff Act of 1930, in addition to those listed in the Petition, have been brought to Petitioner's attention and are set forth below in this Amendment to the Petition.

The 1957 Law for the Development of the
Japanese Electronics Industry

In 1957, as a part of its subsidy programs, the Japanese government enacted a law to serve as the basis for government financial assistance and guidance to the Japanese electronics industry. A copy of this law, as translated by the Library of the Congress, is attached as Exhibit A. There is no question that this law and the bounties and grants it provided has significantly contributed to the market disruption and injury to domestic industry Japanese consumer electronics imports into the United States has caused in recent years.

Under this law the Japanese government provided its electronics industry with massive financial assistance in the form of loans and subsidies for development of this industry. Low-interest, long-term loans extended to the Japanese consumer electronics industry under this law totaled billions of yen during the period 1957 to 1970. This was in addition to the many direct financial benefits, including subsidization of research and development, provided to industry members.

Attached as Exhibit B is a copy of a study independently prepared by Arthur D. Little, Inc., showing some of the products benefiting from the financial assistance measures provided for under the 1957 law and the specific objectives established for such products. In some cases, the specific amount of financial assistance is set out.

Attached as Exhibit C is a two-part study, with appendix, which also sets out some of the products covered by the 1957 law as well as the amount of the subsidies and low-interest loans provided to the Japanese electronics industry

Exhibit 5.1 (continued)

---

for such products. The appendix portion of Exhibit C discloses the various sources, including official documents of the Japanese Ministry of International Trade and Industry (MITI), of the information contained in Exhibit C. Hill & Knowlton of Japan independently prepared Exhibit C at our request.

The 1971 Law for the Development of the
Japanese Electronics Industry

In 1971, the Japanese government enacted the Specified Electronics Industry and Specified Machinery Industry Promotion Temporary Measures Law, a translation of which, prepared by the Department of State, is attached as Exhibit D. The newly enacted law, which is to run to 1977, also contains the authority for overall policy direction and financial assistance to the electronics industry and also exempts this industry from the anti-cartel provisions of the Japanese Monopoly Law. The new law provides for the establishment of a combined Machinery and Electronics Deliberation Council, composed of industry and academic leaders, who will work with MITI on specific policies. The new law provides for the sharing of patented technology and under it, MITI continues to afford advice and assistance to firms planning new or expanded production.

Specifically under the new law, MITI and the Council set out research and development schedules with target years for completion and establish the amount of funding required for such research and development. With respect to the initiation of commercial production, the target year to begin commercial productions is established along with the type and amount of equipment to be newly installed. The amount of funding necessary to initiate commercial production or increase production volume is also determined. Performance or quality levels in the target year are established for the rationalization of production. The type and amount of equipment to be newly installed along with the amount of funds necessary for improving production efficiency are also determined.

Attached as Exhibit E is a list, prepared by the Department of State, of some of the products covered under the 1971 law, while Exhibit F is a study, also prepared for us by Hill & Knowlton of Japan, showing additional products, target guidelines, loans, tax treatments and subsidies under the 1971 law. Another independent study, attached as Exhibit G, also discloses similar subsidization under the 1971 law.

The above bounties and grants resulting from direct Japanese government subsidies and low-interest loans are in addition to those set out in our original Petition. In its report of last November to the President in the television receiver case, TEA-I-21, the United States Tariff Commission, while not finding that television receivers were, as a result in major part of concessions

Exhibit 5.1 (continued)

---

granted under trade agreements, being imported into the United States in such increased quantities as to cause or threaten to cause serious injury to our industry, did find that imports from Japan were increasing as a result of other factors including export incentives. As reported by the Commission, Japanese government export incentives were significant for Japanese exporters of television sets. We have no reason to believe that the bounties and grants bestowed upon exported products as set out in our original Petition do not continue to exist.

It is respectfully submitted that a persistent failure effectively to enforce the countervailing duty statute together with other relevant federal laws will continue to do extreme harm to our domestically based industry. American enterprise in the lawful pursuit of free trade cannot possibly compete against the Japanese government and a heavily subsidized Japanese industry cartelized and officially protected in a closed market at home, particularly when our own government is so inexplicably reluctant to even seriously consider the enforcement of our U.S. laws.

Almost two years have passed since the filing of the Petition. On April 20, 1970, in a letter signed by Mr. Neil J. Marsh, Assistant Director, Technical Section, we were advised:

> Careful consideration will be given to the facts you have presented in your petition. You will be advised when a decision is reached as to whether or not a full scale investigation is warranted.

If you reached a decision that the Petition did not even warrant the investigation referred to by Mr. Marsh, we would appreciate being advised of that fact and the basis for that decision. . . .

Very truly yours,

ZENITH ELECTRONICS
CORPORATION

By _____
　　　Philip J. Curtis
　　　Vice President and
　　　General Counsel

PJC/bjp
attachments

Exhibit 5.2
Official Comments Submitted by Zenith to Commissioner of Customs

ZENITH RADIO CORPORATION
1900 NORTH AUSTIN AVENUE · CHICAGO, ILLINOIS 60639 · PHONE (312) 745-2000

PHILIP J. CURTIS
VICE PRESIDENT AND GENERAL COUNSEL

PHONE (312) 745-5133

March 3, 1975

Honorable Vernon D. Acree
Commissioner of Customs
2100 K Street, N.W.
Washington, D.C. 20229

　　　　Re:　FR Doc. 75-3160 - CERTAIN CONSUMER ELECTRONIC
　　　　　　　　　　　　　PRODUCTS FROM JAPAN

Dear Mr. Commissioner:

　　　　Pursuant to notice at 40 F.R. 5378, dated February 5,

1975, the attached comments are submitted on behalf of

petitioner, Zenith Radio Corporation.

　　　　　　　　　　　　　Respectfully submitted,

　　　　　　　　　　　　　ZENITH RADIO CORPORATION

　　　　　　　　　　　　　Philip J. Curtis
　　　　　　　　　　　　　Vice President and General Counsel

PJC/bjp
Attachment

Exhibit 5.2 (continued)

In the
DEPARTMENT OF THE TREASURY
Bureau of Customs

FR Doc. 75-3160 - CERTAIN CONSUMER ELECTRONIC
PRODUCTS FROM JAPAN

Comments by petitioner, Zenith Radio Corporation, invited by the Bureau's notice are difficult to address to the Commissioner for two important reasons:

A. The tentative ruling, issued after the lapse of nearly five years, does not respond to our 1970 petition or our 1972 amendment in any revealing way except to deny the petition as if it had been filed in 1975 and related only to current bounties and grants. The tentative ruling also completely ignores the Japanese Commodity Tax Law Exemption for Exports and refers only to three present bounties in 1975 which are said to be de minimus, as argued by the Electronic Industry Association of Japan (EIA-J) and such large American customers as Sears, Roebuck & Co. and companies such as General Electric, the largest single stockholder in Tokyo Shibaura Electric Co., Ltd. (Toshiba). 1/ Nothing is said about the variety of effective bounties and grants in existence before and at the time of the filing of our petition and amendment. Nothing is said about the cumulative effect of those bounties

---

1/ Compare the revealing analysis (copy attached as Exhibit A) by Mr. F. J. Borch, then Chairman of the Board, General Electric Company, addressed to The Economic Club of Detroit on October 12, 1971, particularly at pages 6-7, with the "official" comments of General Electric dated July 18, 1972 and filed in opposition to the countervailing duty petitions.

Exhibit 5.2 (continued)

and grants now and through the years during which the
related dumping tactics of the EIA-J membership made a
shambles of the electronic manufacturing industry in
the United States, causing permanent loss of thousands of
jobs, as outlined at pages 10-11 of our 1970 petition. [2]/

B. The secrecy surrounding the Bureau's proceedings and
computations makes it impossible to ascertain and comment
specifically on the undisclosed analyses purportedly
supporting its tentative ruling.

These comments, therefore, are limited to three important
considerations involved in the proposed ruling that the Bureau
must have either ignored or silently rejected:

1. The Commodity Tax Exemptions for Exports, as pointed out
at pages 7-9 of our 1970 petition, is a very large bounty
clearly required to be countervailed under the Nicholas
and Downs decisions of the Supreme Court. [3]/ Nevertheless,
the Bureau has failed to give any satisfactory explanation
for its refusal to follow these decisions in this proceeding.

It must be remembered that commodity taxes in Japan provide
a very substantial proportion of total national revenues
and should not be viewed as mere indirect "excise taxes."

---

[2]/ See also the Tariff Commission's findings in investigations
numbered TEA-I-21, dated November 1971, and AA1921-66, dated
March 1971.

[3]/ Nicholas & Co. v. United States, 249 U.S. 34 (1919); Downs v.
United States, 187 U.S. 496 (1903).

-2-

Exhibit 5.2 (continued)

Average unit profit margins on total production in Japan have been increased by the remission of these taxes on exports to the United States. More importantly, this tax remission has significantly aided Japanese manufacturers in maintaining crippling dumping margins in their anti-competitive export offensive against the United States electronic manufacturing industry. It should further be remembered, as pointed out at page 9 of our 1970 petition, that the Treasury Department failed in its efforts to have Congress amend §303 of The Tariff Act of 1930, 19 U.S.C. 1303, in order to exclude such tax remissions from §303 coverage and thereby legislatively repeal the law as applied in the Nicholas and Downs decisions. 4/ We again direct the Bureau's attention to the detailed submissions made in support of the petitions to counter-vail this bounty and grant.

The effect of the Treasury Department's refusal to counter-vail this bounty and grant has been further aggravated by its concomitant insistence in the dumping case upon adding the amount of the remitted commodity tax to the United States price as a phantom factor, thereby ignoring a large percentage of the true dumping margins. In a case of this magnitude and importance, this drastic dual action of the Department should be accompanied by a full explanation.

4/   Hearings on H.R. 1535 Before House Ways and Means Comm., 82d Cong., 1st Sess., 2 (1951).

-3-

Exhibit 5.2 (continued)

2. The tentative ruling, as previously noted, refers only to
    current bounties and grants without any discussion of the
    many other bounties and grants that were detailed in our
    1970 petition and our 1972 amendment. It is submitted
    that there has been a significant cumulative effect of
    all bounties and grants received and employed by the EIA-J
    membership since 1970 and before to aid their dumping
    activities in restraint of trade in the American market.
    All such bounties and their cumulative effect should be
    examined and properly assessed before any final decision
    is made. 5/

3. At pages 9-10 of our 1970 petition and at pages 1 and 4 of
    our 1972 amendment, the Commissioner's attention was called
    to the fact that on information and belief importers of
    Japanese electronic products were not reporting any of the
    bounties and grants, detailed in our petition, on Special
    Customs Invoice Form 5515 as required by paragraph 6 of
    that form. 6/ In this connection, we also brought to the
    attention of the Bureau on January 23, 1970 the related

5/ The Tariff Commission, in its Report to the President on
    Investigation No. TEA-I-21, dated November 19, 1971, stated
    at page 6: "Besides [dumping], the following factors stimu-
    lated increased U.S. imports of television receivers: A
    variety of export incentives on the part of the Government
    of Japan and the Japanese television industry to bolster
    production well in excess of home market requirements...."

6/ "6. Are any rebates, drawbacks, bounties, or other grants
    allowed upon the exportation of the goods? /_/ Yes /_/ No.
    If so, have all been separately itemized? /_/ Yes /_/ No."

-4-

Exhibit 5.2 (continued)

---

matter that on information and belief secret rebates in significant amounts were being passed to large American buyers by EIA-J manufacturers in Japan and were not being reported on Form 5515 and other entry documents in order to conceal the true margins of dumping.

It is significant that neither the EIA-J nor the large American customers of their members who submitted comments to the Commissioner concerning our 1970 petition and our 1972 amendment denied or in any way commented upon the allegation that the bounties and grants had not been reported as required. The tentative ruling is silent on the matter. There has been no indication of any action on the related matter of concealment of rebates on the same form. This is a serious matter coming within the ambit of at least two important penal statutes, 7/ as pointed out at page 10 of our 1970 petition. We submit that any final ruling on the petitions should reveal the results of the Department's disposition of this matter.

Petitioner is concerned that the Bureau may have by inadvertence or oversight condoned or excused inaccurate answers and omissions in answers to paragraph 6 of Form 5515 in its application to both rebates and bounties- and grants. It has recently come to our attention that the following letter was purportedly sent by the Bureau in answer to an inquiry about the matter:

7/ 19 U.S.C. 1592, and 18 U.S.C. 1001.

-5-

Exhibit 5.2 (continued)

C O P Y

THE DEPARTMENT OF THE TREASURY

(SEAL)   BUREAU OF CUSTOMS

Washington, D.C.

Oct 21, 1971

Refer To

EV 332.1 MK

Bruce E. Clubb, Esq.
Baker & McKenzie
Attorneys at Law
815 Connecticut Avenue, N.W.
Washington, D.C. 20006

Dear Mr. Clubb:

This refers to your letter of October 5, 1971, inquiring
whether the acceptance of rebates (in yen) by your client's
office in Japan, through which it places orders for
television sets with a Japanese producer would involve
the buyer in a violation of any law enforced by Customs.
These rebates would be made after receiving the MITI
check price in dollars and clearing the shipment through
Japanese authorities.

The above-described procedure would not, in our opinion,
violate any law which Customs administers. Inasmuch as
the status of MITI check prices as the basis of appraisement is presently being litigated, we take no position
on the effect of such rebate procedure on appraisement of
the merchandise. We suggest that Customs offices at the
ports of entry be advised of the rebate procedure, as
this may affect the basis of appraisement.

Our opinion does not extend to any questions in the
area of dumping.

Sincerely yours,

/s/ Raymond E. Turner

RAYMOND E. TURNER
Director, Division of
Entry Procedures and Penalties

Reply To: Commissioner of Customs, Washington, D.C. 20226

-6-

Exhibit 5.2 (continued)

It thus appears that the Bureau was aware of the rebate procedure since at least as early as 1971 and that the answers elicited by paragraph 6 of Form 5515 with respect to imports of Japanese television receivers by large American buyers should have been examined. If neither bounties and grants nor rebates were appropriately revealed in the relevant answers to paragraph 6 of Form 5515 by importers of Japanese television receivers, petitioner respectfully suggests that this proceeding should in no event be terminated in the manner proposed but that appropriate procedures should be initiated immediately under 19 U.S.C. 1592 or 18 U.S.C. 1001. */

Respectfully submitted,

ZENITH RADIO CORPORATION

Philip J. Curtis
Vice President and General Counsel

PJC/bjp
Attachment

[*/ Civil and criminal laws providing forfeiture of the value
     of offending imports and criminal fines and imprisonment
     for convicted offenders.]

ZENITH FILES SUIT OVER THE COMMODITY TAX SUBSIDY

After Treasury's denial of our countervailing duty petition, we filed
suit in Customs Court to require Treasury to countervail the commodity
tax remission subsidy that was helping to fuel the predatory dumping
scheme of the cartel. We limited the suit to the commodity tax subsidy
because during the five years of neglect at Treasury, a number of the
other subsidies had been altered—thereby making obsolete the petition
relating to them. When the negative determination was first announced,
the law did not provide for retroactive countervailing duties. Treasury's
unconscionable delay thus effectively defeated the purpose of the
statute in this respect. Therefore, to hasten the adjudication, Zenith limited its suit to the commodity tax subsidy.

Because of the importance of the Customs Court case, a three-judge
panel was assigned. Zenith, as plaintiff, and the Justice Department, as
defendant in frantic opposition to Zenith's case, thoroughly briefed and
argued the cause. The panel of three veteran judges gave the matter full
and careful consideration. Each of the three judges wrote a separate
scholarly opinion in which they unanimously declared the commodity
tax remission to be a subsidy the Treasury would have to countervail
under the plain language of the statute, and in accordance with the clear
holdings of Supreme Court decisions detailed in the Zenith petition.

With respect to Treasury's recalcitrance and claimed right to refuse
to impose the required countervailing duty, the court stated:

The basic question before us is whether the Secretary of the Treasury shall
have the right and be permitted to continue to interpret the provisions of our
countervailing duty statute contrary to its explicit and unambiguous language
and contrary to the interpretation and construction previously placed thereon
by the highest court of our land. The answer can only be, No. [430 F.Supp.
242, 250 (1977)]

The unheard-of disloyalty and abrogation of government process was
so outrageous that it was finally beginning to attract attention.

The ruling of the Customs Court alarmed the cartel and its legion of
lobbyists in and out of government. The deep shock and concern of the
Japanese interests was conveyed to all levels of the U.S. government,
from the White House to the State Department, to Treasury and the
Department of Justice.

At State Department meetings, we outlined and gave a short written
review of our position: that if there had been law enforcement during
the past fifteen years, the current inappropriate and protectionist quota

case would not have been necessary. Further, we explained to them that we were active free traders and had proceeded against cartels that had inhibited free trade ever since the birth of our industry. I explained that one old-fashioned world cartel had been supplanted by a more modern Japanese cartel, aided and assisted by American members of the earlier cartel—namely, RCA and David Sarnoff.

Zenith pleaded with Julius Katz, Assistant Secretary of State, Bureau of Economic and Business Affairs, that in our judgment the State Department should not in any way cooperate with or encourage unlawful activities of foreign cartel members who exploit the U.S. market. Later, Katz would not only become a powerful lobbyist for Japanese interests but would reenter government as George Bush's Deputy Trade Representative! This would be one of the first instances of the revolving door going all the way around, placing former Japanese lobbyists in high trade positions.

Katz solemnly disavowed any policy of encouraging or approving dumping and other illegal practices. I indicated to him that that was our only concern; that is, that he or others at State not attempt to defend or protect the Japanese cartel and its members from any law enforcement activities by any other branch of the federal government. Katz launched into a tirade on how the Zenith countervailing duty case had immense adverse implications that had "disturbed" the government in Washington "at the highest levels." He said that the principle of our case "if upheld upon appeal" would cause chaos in U.S. international relations, because of its effect on huge industries such as steel, automobiles, computers, and the like.

He also emphatically stated that the quota case currently before the President was presenting the world with a "protectionist" attitude by the U.S. government and was "alarming" the international economic community. I told Katz that had the federal laws been enforced against the Japanese cartel, a quota case would never have arisen and that what he called the new protectionist posture revealed in the quota case was the direct result of the government's failure for the past fifteen years to enforce the customs and antitrust laws. His only answer was that if the government were to lose the Zenith case on appeal, the entire structure of U.S. international commercial arrangements would be shattered and all the government could do would be "to pick up the pieces and start all over." I indicated politely that perhaps that would be in the best interest of the country.

Julius Katz later passed through the revolving door of government to his reward as head of General Research Corporation, a Washington lobby whose generous clients included the Japanese government, Hitachi, and Toyota. President Bush later chose Katz to be one of two senior Deputy United States Trade Representatives (USTR) under Carla Hills. Interestingly, prior to entering office, Hills had been business and legal advisor to Matsushita Corporation, a founding leader of the Japanese cartel; and her husband, Roderick Hills, represented C. Itoh, one of Japan's largest trading companies. Along with Katz, Bush chose as Hills's other Deputy USTR one S. Lynn Williams, whose immediate prior position was a leading partner in Gibson, Dunn & Crutchen, one of the leading law firms in Los Angeles. He had opened the Tokyo office for the firm, representing its Japanese clients' business interests in the United States.[1]

The U.S. Trade Representatives' office is responsible to the President for developing and coordinating U.S. trade policy and for leading all trade negotiations. It sits at the President's elbow in the Executive Office of the President. Thus, it could be said that the Japanese cartels had influential friends in the highest echelons of our government.

In response to a frantic appeal by the government, the Court of Customs and Patent Appeals split 3-to-2 in favor of the Justice Department. The administration argued that its "foreign policy" and "practices" required a reversal of the Customs Court decision. The majority opinion reflected the strain required by the reversal. It noted in passing that the difference the government was urging between direct taxes (income tax) and indirect taxes (so-called sales or consumption taxes "borne by the product") was in a sense "chimerical" (i.e., a creature of the imagination) [Zenith v. United States, 562 F.2d 209, 215]. The dissenting opinion urged that the Customs Court had very accurately applied the law to the subsidizing tax remission in accordance with settled Supreme Court law and the plain language of the governing statute [Zenith v. United States, 562 F.2d 1209–1220]. The Supreme Court, recognizing the importance of the case and its international significance (which had been urged upon it by the Justice Department), granted certiorari, agreeing to review it.

THE SUPREME COURT REVIEWS THE CASE

Now the Japanese interests pulled out all the stops. The government briefs were rife with innuendo that the government's foreign trade policy would be reduced to chaos if Zenith were to prevail. (This reminded us of Julius Katz's lecture to Zenith at the State Department meeting.)

In addition to the briefs, the position of the government of Japan in the form of a threatening official note was surreptitiously slipped to the Supreme Court—in bold defiance of the rules. The State Department sent the note to Wade McCree, then the Solicitor General, requesting that he circulate it to the Court. McCree had Michael Rodak, the clerk of the Supreme Court, quietly pass it on to each of the Justices despite the fact that it was grossly improper to do so. Rodak wrote the following note to McCree, ostensibly to provide some cover for his own hide in the event the ploy was exposed:

I am not aware of any rule of this Court which would permit correspondence of this nature to be received and distributed to this Court. If the Government of Japan wished to express its views concerning this case, it should have filed a printed brief . . . as provided for in Rule 42 of the Rules of this Court.

Of course, the secret note was not served on Zenith. A *proper* "friend of the court printed brief" would have been under the rules, but Zenith had no opportunity to respond to this outrageously *improper* communication.

The clandestine note was a threat to the Supreme Court that unless it ruled for Japan, it would be guilty of causing a breakdown of world trade generally and would seriously damage U.S.–Japanese trade relations. In addition, the note predicted that a ruling in Zenith's favor "could bring about a breakdown of the General Agreement on Tariffs and Trade (GATT) system itself and seriously impair the chances for success in multilateral international trade negotiations."

When Solicitor General McCree personally argued the case in the Supreme Court, Justice Blackmun felt compelled, apparently, to clear the air on this delicate matter. The following exchange occurred:

[JUSTICE BLACKMUN]: Mr. Solicitor General, could I ask a question which perhaps I shouldn't ask. It may be a little delicate, but at the request of the Department of State you distributed a communication for the government of Japan in this matter. . . . What does this mean vis-à-vis this case?

MR. McCREE: I don't think it means anything as far as the duty of this Court is concerned here today. . . .

[JUSTICE BLACKMUN]: You do not regard it as a threat to this Court?

MR. McCREE: I do not and I certainly circulated it only because it had been forwarded to us from the Department of State and we circulated it for what it was worth. . . .

[JUSTICE BLACKMUN]: In any event, you are here in good faith doing your best to uphold the position espoused by the government of Japan anyway?

MR. McCREE: Well, if the Court please, I regard my role here as seeking to uphold the construction that the Congress, [I mean] that the Secretary of the Treasury has placed upon the statute committed to you to administer, and the client of the government here is the Secretary of State and not a foreign prince or potentate.

The Supreme Court, if not intimidated, was at least given pause by the government of Japan's note and the Department of Justice's briefs, both of which reflected the Japanese government's legal position. This special, illegal pleading to the Supreme Court by the government of Japan was unprecedented; it indicated the level of involvement and the importance of the television manufacturing market capture program to the Japanese government. In effect, the Japanese government was saying, "surrender your television manufacturing industry to us."

The Supreme Court bowed to the foreign policy position of the President, and Justice Thurgood Marshall was designated to write the opinion. He adopted for the Court the government's arguments in an attempt to justify the political decision. He struggled through a recitation of abstruse legal reasons for "legalizing" the subsidy conferred on the cartel [*Zenith v. United States,* 437 U.S. 443, 459–462]. Three points can be made regarding his reasoning.

1. As the government had frantically urged, Marshall declared that the executive branch's "long-standing" practice of refusing to countervail remissions of taxes on manufacturers' sales of exports to the United States was "entitled to considerable weight." He gave not even a passing nod to the exclusive power of Congress, which had declared the law and its intent in the plain language of the statute. He reasoned that since the General Agreement on Tariffs and Trade (GATT), a voluntary association composed of many trading nations, had recommended that a foreign nation's taxes computed on sales could be remitted on exports without treating the remission as a subsidy, it was "far from unreasonable" for the Treasury to follow this recommendation despite the fact that Congress had emphatically declared that U.S. law prevailed over GATT recommendations. In the event of conflict, our federal statutes had to be given effect by the executive branch. Justice Marshall conceded that the government was not openly contending that GATT supersedes our law. He added, however, that U.S. law "could not be disturbed except for cogent reasons"—reasons that he claimed had been found by Treasury. Cited as authority for this doublespeak was Marks and Malmgren, "Negotiating Non-Tariff Distortions to Trade," 7 L. & Policy in International Business 327.[2]

2. Having thus judicially legislated the GATT rule as an amendment altering the plain language of the countervailing duty statute, Marshall made a brief concession that modern economic theory does suggest that remission of indirect taxes "creates an incentive to export." He did not go on to explain the unfair advantage such remissions of indirect taxes on exports to the United States provides to foreign manufacturers. The U.S. tax system is based on income, whereas the Japanese and European systems designedly produce principal revenues from commodity and other so-called indirect sales taxes. Because imports in the United States are not burdened by sales taxes at our borders, the Japanese television cartel paid little or no taxes anywhere on the products exported to the U.S. market. Their American competitors, however, were burdened with income taxes. The Japanese subsidiaries in the United States also made sure that they paid no taxes by the use of so-called transfer prices, which were carefully constructed by their parents in Japan to produce little or no taxable income here.

3. Justice Marshall had one final minefield to avoid in his tip-toe passage around the countervailing duty statute. He had to find a way around the plain language of the statute an earlier Supreme Court had unequivocally declared to cover such tax remissions. This was not an easy assignment. As the veteran three-judge panel of the Customs Court had so clearly held, the Treasury Secretary had no right to interpret the clear language of the statute contrary to its explicit language and contrary to the construction of the Supreme Court in prior governing cases.

With the help of the Solicitor General's brief, which was full of theory that the "agents of influence" had successfully planted in the administration, Justice Marshall proceeded to distinguish the famous *Downs* case [437 U.S. at 459–462] in the Supreme Court "on the facts." Microscopic examination of all the facts in *Downs,* he said, revealed that a benefit in addition to the remission of taxes could be detected. Its use was deceptively employed to support an argument that *Downs* was not factually "on all fours" with the Zenith case and thus could be ignored.

The *Downs* case involved the remission of a tax on the sale of sugar in Russia prior to World War I. The tax was remitted on exports, and the Supreme Court had unequivocally held the remission to be a bounty that the plain language of our federal statute required to be countervailed. Marshall noted that in addition to the tax remission, a Russian exporter was given a certificate entitling the bearer to sell in Russia a quantity of sugar equal to the amount exported. This extra benefit was blown into a distinction entitling the Court to ignore *Downs,* because no such certificate or added benefit was involved in the Japanese remission of the commodity taxes. This excess benefit found lurking in the facts in *Downs* was an "excess remission" under the GATT rule and could be countervailed, Marshall reasoned. The Japanese remissions, however, could not be countervailed under Treasury's "reasonable interpretation," Marshall concluded.

Nothing was said under this distinction about the fact that in the dumping case, Treasury was adding the Japanese home market tax (computed as a percentage of the sale prices, 50 percent or more higher than the U.S. export prices) to the U.S. price in its dumping margin determinations. Computation of the actual tax remitted on exports should have produced only half the amount of tax paid on the high, fixed prices for the same merchandise sold in the Japanese market. However, Treasury was adding the full Japanese market tax to the export price in computing dumping margins. This was an excess remission of tremendous value when applied to the hundreds of millions of dollars in exports involved in the government's dumping case.

Despite the plain language of the law and Congress's refusal to amend the law as clearly interpreted by the Supreme Court in the *Downs* case, there did not seem to be any way of winning against the combined financial might and determination of the cartel's agents of influence and an administration that was hell-bent on protecting the so-called bastion of our defense against communism in the Far East, the government of Japan. Sarnoff's highly profitable patent licensing scheme with his cleverly shaped Japanese cartel seemed destined to be, in effect, judicially declared to be impregnable to the attack of any rule of law.

As we have been reminded in earlier chapters, for many years such infamous claims of immunity from the law successfully delayed its application against the original American radio cartel members: GE, RCA, Westinghouse, and AT&T. That claim of immunity was based upon the deceptive assertion that the government not only sponsored the cartel in the public interest but requested GE to form it. Years of struggle were required to expose the fallacy of that assertion. It is hoped that some day, years of struggle will expose the fallacy of the Japanese cartel's legal position despite the Supreme Court's political decision in the Zenith countervailing duty case.

NOTES

1.   Another senior partner of Gibson, Dunn & Crutchen was President Reagan's attorney general, William French Smith, when the government so brazenly defended the Japanese cartel in Zenith's antitrust and antidumping suit.

2.   Both Marks and Malmgren had become agents of influence working as Japanese lawyer-lobbyists and "experts" in the TV cases. Their pro-Japanese stance while working for the government continued after they left government service to become effective, highly paid Washington lobbyists and insiders.

6

The Final Battle: *Matsushita et al. v. Zenith*

In 1974 the giant Matsushita, leader of the Japanese cartel, acquired the color television business of the pioneer American manufacturer, Motorola. This was an ominous move that alarmed Zenith management, not only because of the frightening future it portended for Zenith but because of the improper political reception it received at the Department of Justice. Three years later, in commenting (at a Zenith distributors' convention) on the sustained attack of the cartel on the American market, Zenith's Chairman, John Nevin, described Matsushita's acquisition of Motorola: "Zenith has alleged that the Japanese, in addition to entering into unlawful agreements to fix prices and allocate customers, have conspired to gain control of American television companies." The story behind this particular phase of the conspiracy begins in 1973.

In the fall of 1973, the Department of Justice was advised that Matsushita, reportedly the world's largest producer of television receivers, proposed to acquire Motorola's television business. Matsushita was known by the Justice Department to have been involved in the dumping of television receivers on the U.S. market. In addition, Matsushita had an established position in the U.S. television market with its Panasonic brand. The effect of the proposal by Matsushita to acquire the television segment of the Motorola business would be to give Matsushita ownership of two television businesses. Combined, this would account for 9 percent of the American color television market and almost 14 percent of the American black-and-white television market. The Justice

Department elected to study that proposal in secrecy and made no public announcement until March 1974.

Meanwhile, in December 1973, White Consolidated, a relatively small American company, entered into negotiations with Ford Motor Company to buy the Philco consumer electronics business. White was not involved in consumer electronics in the United States market, nor was White involved in consumer electronics elsewhere in the world. Philco's consumer electronics business was a small fraction of the size of Motorola's. The antitrust division of the Department of Justice advised Ford and White that their negotiations would have to be publicly disclosed, because in order to investigate the proposal thoroughly the Department of Justice wanted to seek the views of executives in the American consumer electronics industry.

On February 1, 1974, Zenith was asked by the Department of Justice to express a view as to whether Zenith considered White to be a potential entrant into the consumer electronics business. That information was sought by the Department because the courts had earlier determined that a company capable of entering an industry on its own might be behaving in an anticompetitive manner if it sought to enter that same industry through acquisition. Zenith's Nevin responded:

The only inquiry Zenith received in the Matsushita case was a telephone call asking for information with respect to Zenith sales volumes. The caller carefully avoided providing any information as to the reason why the inquiry was being made. The Antitrust Division has never attempted to explain the very different handling of these two concurrent investigations of proposed television acquisitions.

We do not believe that the Department of Justice's investigation of the Motorola acquisition was adequate and we have, therefore, challenged that acquisition in the courts. Zenith reached a similar conclusion with respect to the adequacy of the Department of Justice's subsequent investigation of Sanyo's proposal to acquire the Warwick television assets. We have also taken action to challenge that acquisition in the courts.

Zenith management believed that the Motorola acquisition had a special significance in the cartel's strategy. The cartel members had successfully captured a very large share of the American market through a "predatory" or "malignant" dumping scheme. Having acquired a foothold in the large American chains and discount houses, the Japanese cartel was beginning to acquire besieged American manufacturers, whose stock had dropped as a result of losses inflicted by the cartel. These companies would be hollowed out by their new Japanese owners. The companies would simply market and distribute Japanese television receivers under American brand names. Further, they would almost certainly be used as political platforms to attack any industry-wide opposition to Japan's market capture attempt. The Matsushita acquisition of Motorola signaled the beginning of this mopping-up exercise, and Zenith felt compelled to challenge it in court as a part of the overall predatory dumping scheme.

ZENITH FILES TREBLE-DAMAGE CASE

On September 20, 1974, Zenith filed a treble-damage case in the United States District Court in Philadelphia against principal members of the cartel doing business in the United States. The suit challenged the dumping scheme as a violation of the Sherman Act and the Antidumping Act of 1916.[1] The Philadelphia federal court had an excellent reputation, as did its supervising court of appeals for the Third Circuit. The famous antitrust "electrical equipment cases"[2] of the 1960s had been successfully tried there.

The case was assigned to Judge A. Leon Higgenbotham, a scholarly, no-nonsense district judge who had the experience, knowledge, and talent to handle complex litigation in a remarkably efficient manner. The assignment obviously displeased the coterie of New York and Washington law firms representing the defendants. They immediately moved the Judicial Panel on Multidistrict Litigation in Washington to transfer the case to Judge Biuno in New Jersey. Biuno had allowed the defendants' counsel in the parallel NUE (National Union Electric) case there to delay interminably NUE's efforts to get discovery of evidence under the Rules.[3] Zenith opposed the motion to transfer in order to avoid being bogged down in a New Jersey court that was apparently either incompetent to handle or sympathetic to defense counsels' dilatory strategy there.

The Judicial Panel had been set up by Congress (28 U.S.C. 1407) to prevent duplication of judicial effort in related complex cases filed in different federal districts. The matter of transfer was heard by the Panel in Washington, D.C. On the basis of the briefs and oral arguments, the Judicial Panel (apparently disturbed by the strange lack of progress in the NUE New Jersey case, which was then four years old) not only denied the defendants' motion to transfer the Zenith case to New Jersey but, on its own motion, ordered that the NUE case be "transferred from New Jersey to Judge Higgenbotham in Philadelphia where both the Zenith and NUE cases could be more efficiently handled together in their pretrial preparation" (388 F.Supp. 565, 567). Although they were obviously dismayed by the turn of events, the teams of New York and Washington defense counsel did not give up their attempts to obstruct the litigation.

They filed a series of dilatory motions on every conceivable grounds. For example, in January 1975 they filed a series of motions—including claims disputing venue and the jurisdiction of the court over the defendants—claiming that the defendants were Japanese companies not doing business in the United States and that therefore they could not be sued in this country; that the court's processes could not reach them. They also attacked the constitutionality of the 1916 treble-damage, antidumping statute, saying that to them it was "void for vagueness."

Judge Higgenbotham disposed of the jurisdiction and venue questions in a thorough opinion rejecting the defendants' false contentions that they were not doing business in the United States (402 F.Supp. 262). He also upheld the constitutionality of the 1916 antidumping statute in a scholarly analysis (402 F.Supp. 25). He directed the defendants to produce their submissions to the Treasury Department in the government's administrative antidumping proceeding under the 1921 Antidumping Act and cleared out all their other dilatory motions.

With our discovery finally well under way, the lawyers for the cartel did not give up trying to block a trial. They filed a frivolous counterclaim against Zenith, making the hilarious claim that Zenith's marketing of its higher-priced products somehow had impeded their dumping activities. The counterclaim was filed in late 1975, shortly before Judge Higgenbotham was promoted to the court of appeals and a new judge, Edward R. Becker, was assigned to replace him in the litigation. The implication of the timing of Higgenbotham's political appointment to the higher court would not be obvious until Becker's presence was felt.

Judge Becker began a process of "chipping away," as he said, at our case with the help of the cartel lawyers, to whom he displayed a strange and admiring deference. He interspersed this deference with sardonic humor directed against our case. He seemed to encourage another round of frivolous motions, which greatly burdened our efforts to get to trial. The unconscionable delays were apparently worth the high fees they brought to the cartel's legal armada. Meanwhile, the cartel continued to ravage the market, driving the remnants of the U.S. television industry to the wall, and a number of them out of business.

In addition, cartel counsel launched a nationwide deposition campaign directed at Zenith's wholesale customers. Nine teams of lawyers drawn from the battery of the twenty law firms representing cartel members set out to harass Zenith in a nationwide campaign relating to their specious counterclaim. Beginning in 1977, these nine teams rifled the files of Zenith and 32 of Zenith's independent distributors, deposed 49 officials, and generated 10,093 pages of transcripts and 2,851 pages of exhibits. Hundreds of thousands of documents were subpoenaed by the cartel's lawyers. Some of these harassing maneuvers were conducted in different parts of the country at the same time. Their campaign lasted three years.

The new wave of groundless motions and the national harassment of Zenith's customers was such an obvious abuse of process that it was laughable, as well as painfully diverting and expensive. But rather than waste time in futile efforts to get Judge Becker to control the campaign to delay trial, we met all the cartel's frivolous demands until they tired of the game. Meanwhile, when they examined distributor officials, we were able on cross-examination to show how the predatory dumping campaign was greatly injuring competition and seriously affecting the business of Zenith and its wholesale customers. Their sword had two edges, and much came out that the nine teams of cartel counsel had apparently not contemplated.

Zenith's attorneys went to Japan and obtained a wealth of evidence about the conspiracy, despite the fact that quantities of relevant documents had been apparently suppressed or destroyed. Also, we were able to subpoena a number of the big American retail chains and buyer groups that were promoting the sale of huge quantities of the Japanese cartel members' cut-rate television receivers. One U.S. cartel customer prudently confessed to the Securities and Exchange Commission and to Customs that it had participated with Japanese suppliers in filing false prices with Customs on their imports of Japanese television receivers.

The cat was finally out of the bag after years of government suppression of the evidence. Now the policy of the Treasury to avoid any inquiry of the big buying chains and groups of discounters became embarrassing to Customs and had to be ostensibly replaced with some show of law enforcement activity to save face. So the Commissioner of Customs appointed a team of Customs agents to follow up on our campaign to expose the massive fraud and investigate some of the buyers' fraudulent Customs submissions.

Conservatively, it was estimated that over a billion dollars should have been collected by the government as a minimum fine and recovery for the criminal, predatory dumping conspiracy. In addition, prosecutions and jail sentences were more than warranted; but the Justice Department refused to act effectively. The weight of evidence was swinging in Zenith's direction, but the cartel, through its lobbyists, was able to put in a political "fix" at high government levels, settling out all aspects of the government case. The infamous government settlement of the dumping and fraud cases had reduced what should have been a billion-dollar figure to about $77 million, only $16 million of which was reportedly ever collected. Zenith officials were shocked at such blatant influence peddling and widespread government disloyalty.[4]

Meanwhile, at Zenith, we had taken depositions and subpoenaed documents in a nationwide discovery campaign exposing the massive fraud and cover-up. The Japanese documents had to be laboriously translated by translators cleared by the court. In addition, the plaintiffs' two top economic experts had to be found qualified by the court and cleared to analyze the evidence, most of which had been put under a blanket of secrecy to prevent any public disclosure.

Judge Becker became increasingly active in keeping us heavily burdened with diversionary tactics in the litigation. Any suggestion that the array of dilatory motions continuously filed by cartel counsel were an abuse of the processes of the court were met with the judge's comment, "You will have to put more people on the case"—a polite rejection delivered with what appeared to us to be inappropriate and sardonic humor. Judge Becker also began dropping veiled hints that he was writing an opinion on the summary judgment motions that might be favorable to the cartel members. He appointed a Norfolk judge to preside over sessions wherein the parties might negotiate a settlement that would get the case off his calendar. It became obvious to us that Judge Becker would never permit a public trial. These settlement sessions produced no offers whatsoever from cartel counsel, who had been emboldened by what we believed to be Judge Becker's friendly attitude toward them.

At a final session in Philadelphia before the settlement judge, counsel for Mitsubishi (a co-defendant member of the cartel) appeared in the company of a high official of Mitsubishi from Japan. The meeting seemed to be directed by Mitsubishi toward some kind of surrender by Zenith that would let Mitsubishi out of the case for a nominal amount. Zenith's chairman, Joseph S. Wright, appeared and the Mitsubishi team confronted him with a hint of some kind of nuisance settlement in the area of $1 million. While his counsel spoke, the Japanese official sat silently with a facial expression we interpreted as condescendingly hostile. When Wright politely indicated that a full discussion of the importance and scope of the case could not be avoided by a nuisance settlement approach, the lawyer for Mitsubishi, pointing his finger at

Wright, shouted in a warlike manner, "We are going to destroy you." This, of course, ended the meeting.

After that, Judge Becker proceeded to throw the case out of his courtroom by granting the motions for summary judgment. He explained, in a very lengthy and grotesque opinion [513 F.Supp. 1100 (1981)] that most of the evidence would be inadmissible in any trial before him and that there was not enough admissible evidence left to warrant a trial. Zenith and NUE, of course, immediately filed notices of appeal. The United States Court of Appeals for the Third Circuit, recognizing the importance of the case, assigned its venerable and highly experienced Chief Judge, Collins J. Seitz; Circuit Judge John J. Gibbons, a brilliant and scholarly member of the court; and Circuit Judge Thomas J. Meskill, an experienced and respected judge of the Second Circuit, to hear and determine the appeal.

The record of evidence for review was compacted into several dozen printed volumes. The court of appeals heard two full court days of argument, a highly unusual occurrence. Six weeks later on December 3, 1983, nine years after Zenith had filed its suit, the court of appeals unanimously ruled that there was ample admissible evidence in the pre-trial record to make out a case of conspiracy in restraint of trade in violation of the Sherman Antitrust Act and a violation of the 1916 Antidumping Act.

The case was remanded to the trial court with directions to give it a jury trial, as provided by the law and the Constitution. The ruling came in two thorough and complementary opinions: one written by Chief Judge Seitz covering the violations of the 1916 Antidumping Act, and the other written by Judge Gibbons showing the same facts to constitute a violation of the Sherman Antitrust Act [723 F.2d 238 (3rd Cir. 1983)]. The appellate court soundly reversed Judge Becker's incredible holding that much of the evidence was inadmissible. It also reversed a ruling by Judge Becker that the Japanese sets sold in Japan were so technically different from those sold in the United States that the Antidumping Act of 1916 could not apply.

HOW THE CARTEL OPERATED

From a distillation of the record evidence, I will set out here, as briefly as possible, the basic structure of the highly organized Japanese cartel. A variety of government subsidies were granted. Free or extremely low interest rate loans were provided to fund the building and expansion of factories under the technical guidance of RCA and

Philips of Holland, RCA's former cartel partner in Europe. GE, a holder of 10 percent of Toshiba stock, was also a cooperative licensor of the cartel membership.

In many respects, the newly formed industry resembled the American trusts and price-fixing pools J. P. Morgan and others had created in the latter part of the nineteenth century and the early 1920s. The new cartel had all the elements characteristic of the universally condemned predatory and malignant dumping scheme so clearly described by Jacob Viner in the leading classic on the subject, *Dumping: A Problem in International Trade* (1966). The highly organized cartel was put in complete control of the Japanese market. Tariff and nontariff barriers, including control of all distribution channels, were erected to keep out all foreign competition and protect the very high pricing levels needed to help subsidize exports to the United States.

The members of the newly created cartel formed a Market Stabilization Council in 1956 to fix and maintain very high monopoly price levels for TV receivers, radios, and other electronic appliances in the closed Japanese market. Through this body, the cartel policed its members' secret pricing agreements by using boycott and other punitive tactics to command obedience. The combined power of the monopoly was apparent from a casual scrutiny of the six cartel members named as defendants in the Zenith case: Matsushita, Toshiba (the largest stockholder being GE), Hitachi, Sanyo, Sharp, and Mitsubishi. Their combined annual sales exceeded $67 billion and their assets $65 billion. They employed more than 500,000 persons. Matsushita became the largest television manufacturer in the world, accounting for over 20 percent of all television sales worldwide.

The defendants in the litigation included closely affiliated and controlled trading companies. One of them, the Mitsubishi Corporation (affiliated with the Mitsubishi Group), had annual sales of $66.9 billion. In addition, all the defendant TV manufacturers had subsidiaries and distribution systems in the United States. Matsushita bought Motorola's color TV business in 1974, and Sanyo bought out Sears' American TV supplier, Warwick Electronics Inc. Magnavox, another troubled victim of the Japanese cartel, was purchased by Matsushita's partner, Philips.

The fixed price levels of TVs and other electronics appliances in Japan came to the attention of the Japanese Fair Trade Commission, an alleged enforcement agency with jurisdiction to investigate price fixing and other antitrust violations of law. It had been set up following World War II to emulate the U.S. Federal Trade Commission. On several occasions the Fair Trade Commission found the cartel guilty of price fixing in Japan; but there was no penalty or injunctive process to deter continuation of the violations, so they continued.

The Japanese manufacturers' cartel continued to fix prices in Japan and regulate production in order to mount the massive dumping scheme in the United States. By 1964, they were arranging regular clandestine meetings of the chairmen and presidents of the cartel members. This high-level club was called the Okura Group by its members, because it held secret monthly meetings in the Okura Hotel in Tokyo. The group had the last say on fixing the high price levels for TV products in Japan as well as total production levels for both the home market and the amount of dumped exports allocated to each member. Formed by Konosuke Matsushita, founder of the huge Matsushita complex of companies, this committee followed the founder's often-expressed philosophy:

We must not have excessive competition for plants and facilities even if we do enter a period of prosperity. But in the future, expansion that produces the effect of competition among rival companies must not be permitted. In a Japanese wrestling match, victory or defeat is important. But we do not compete for victory in business. [513 F. Supp. 1100 (1981) at 1205]

Konosuke Matsushita admonished the cartel that its members must act always "as one body" in both national and international operations. The record evidence was replete with expressions of this philosophy as well as the methods of enforcement that made the classic predatory dumping scheme work.

Another group, the Tenth Day Group, was composed of television department managers of the principal cartel members: Matsushita, Toshiba, Hitachi, Sharp, Mitsubishi, and Sanyo. Two- and three-hour meetings were held secretly as frequently as twice a month. They were held on a rotation basis in each of the member's offices. At these meetings elaborate data and proposals on all phases of production, inventory, pricing, and profits were exchanged and discussed. Production quantities, pricing, and profits at all levels were debated and resolved. All pledged to act "as one body" in all phases of production, marketing, pricing, and wholesale and retail profit margins.

All decisions and problems were reported to the Palace Group (a secret appellate and supervisory court), which in turn reported to the Okura Group, the "Supreme Court" of the conspiracy. The relationship between home market prices and export prices to the United States were an important subject of these secret discussions and agreements.

Concerned that the large dumping margins between the high fixed prices in Japan and the much lower prices charged by the members on exports to the United States might be noticed in government statistics, the cartel members agreed, beginning in December 1966, to report false statistics to the Japanese government.

With all distribution channels tightly controlled by the cartel membership, all pricing—even the profit margins allowed wholesalers and retailers—was rigidly fixed (e.g., 20 percent for retailers and 8 percent for wholesalers). In 1956 the cartel established a secret specialized enforcement body known as the Market Stabilization Council. This group policed the clandestine price-fixing agreements in the Japanese market. The policing of the agreements in Japan included a program of boycotts of offenders and a repurchase of any discounted merchandise discovered in the market. All the "dirty tricks" of America's infamous robber barons had apparently been studied and emulated with an unparalleled efficiency and discipline.

The plan to capture the highly competitive American radio and TV consumer electronics market required a complex program involving a cover-up of the dumping required to establish large market shares. To provide the cover-up, the industry inspired passage of the Japanese Export and Import Trade Act in 1952. The law carved out an exemption from the Japanese antitrust law that had been transplanted to Japan during the American occupation following World War II. Applications for such exemptions by the cartel had to contain a cosmetic representation and agreement that in their export activities, the members would not engage in "unfair business practices." Under the act, MITI was empowered to approve such application if:

1. "there is no fear of violating treaties and other arrangements concluded with foreign Governments or international agencies such as GATT,"
2. the "interests of importers or enterprises concerned at the destination is not injured," and
3. "participation in or withdrawal from the agreement is not unjustly restricted."

In this way the cartel obtained approval to regulate its members' exports free from the interdictions of Japanese antitrust laws and any unfriendly government supervision.

Check Prices

In an attempt to cover up the big margins of dumping and provide a "defense" to antitrust and antidumping law violations under U.S. statutes, the cartel created a facade in the form of rules for its export committees, the TV Export Council and the TV Export Examination Committee. Having been granted the right to set minimum export prices by its license from MITI, the Japan Machinery Exporters Association (JMEA) in private session established what became known as check prices. The check prices, which were proclaimed as minimum prices (allegedly to prevent predatory dumping), were determined through study of the pricing levels in the American market and pursuant to legal advice from a coterie of American lawyers. The check prices were set well below U.S. market price levels. This required the American lawyers to claim all kinds of mythical adjustments in the form of alleged discounts and fictional allowances granted in the Japanese market.

In practice, the check prices were little more than "reference" or "opening asking" prices, fraudulently listed as actual prices in official documents submitted to the Japanese government and on official U.S. Customs entry documents. They were also fraudulently represented as true prices in submissions to Customs in the government dumping case and in sworn answers to our written interrogatories in the Philadelphia litigation. Although a number of fictional allowances and adjustments were accepted by Customs to lower the Japanese market prices in the government dumping case, nothing below the U.S. check price levels was either reported to Customs or used in computing the dumping margins found by Customs.

In 1976, eight years after the government dumping case was begun, Zenith served subpoenas in its Philadelphia suit on a number of big chains, such as Sears and Penney's, and other large buying groups. Documents and testimony that followed uncovered massive fraud. Customs was compelled to assign its fraud unit to investigate, after one of the smaller American wholesalers voluntarily admitted receipt of "secret rebates" not disclosed in the import entry documents. But Customs had based its dumping findings on years of false pricing submissions by the Japanese. Recalculating the entire investigation after years of misguided effort seemed beyond the Bureau's manpower resources.

The infamous government settlement described earlier relieved the government from this responsibility and provided a cosmetic disguise for the vast cover-up of hundreds of millions of dollars worth of televisions illegally dumped on the American market. The actual Japanese prices of U.S. imports were substantially lower than the check prices. Their true levels were concealed and held secret by the elaborate criminal rebate scheme.

As Viner explained in his classic treatise, if the cartel members competed against each other in the United States, their overall profit from the combined operation in both markets would be impaired, if not eliminated. They provided the machinery for this phase of their predatory dumping plan in the agreements and rules that required each member to submit to the Export Examination Committee a so-called Application for Validation of Shipment, in which all the details of every proposed sale to the U.S. market had to be disclosed in advance. No sale could be finalized without the cartel's secret permission!

Under a flexible so-called Five Company Rule, allocation of U.S. customers in accordance with the vote of the members was strictly made and carefully supervised. The Export Council and the Export Examination Committee had the power (1) to investigate any cheating or attempts to compete among fellow cartel members, and (2) to punish violators. This was a highly organized and disciplined combination and conspiracy. It was remarkably similar to the American trusts, pools, and combinations of the last century.[5] Japan had thus become Americanized in the worse sense.[6]

Difference Money

RCA's and GE's licenses and technical aid agreements with the cartel produced "royalties" that were computed as a percentage of the selling prices of total production for both markets. Thus, it is reasonable to believe that their strict royalty collection audits, which were well known for their effectiveness, gave them knowledge of the true, concealed dumping margins. Yet Treasury consistently refused to accept this method in its investigation.

The huge royalties RCA received from the cartel members put it on the side of the Japanese cartel in all the dumping cases in the United States. David Sarnoff was even a decorated hero of the industry in Japan and was decorated by the Emperor himself with the highest award available to a foreigner. GE, another long-time benefactor and licensor, found itself in a quandary regarding the dumping cases. Its position was best expressed by a GE executive in a memorandum produced for Zenith in the Philadelphia litigation. Explaining why GE could not sue the cartel as NUE and Zenith had done, he wrote: "one of the defendants [Toshiba] is a corporation in which we own 10 percent of the stock and the other defendants are both customers and licensees."

Evidence showed that the Japanese cartel had organized and successfully implemented a complex scheme to conceal the ruthless predatory dumping assault on the American industry. The American side of the operation had a number of carefully integrated facets:

- Large, potential quantity buyers in the United States—such as retail chains, huge buying groups, and eventually even some U.S. manufacturers—were secretly offered prices so far below competitive levels in the United States that the temptation to buy became irresistible, despite the fact that criminal law violations were involved.
- Potential U.S. customers were secretly assigned to particular members in the cartel. This ensured that the prices offered would be just low enough to take away business and market share from U.S. manufacturers.

To camouflage the predatory levels of the dumping, the cartel adopted a series of methods of concealing the true prices:

- All Japanese export and U.S. import documents had to be falsified to show that all U.S. imports were priced at or above the check prices.
- The difference between the true, concealed prices and the check prices produced what was termed "difference money" by the cartel members. This had to be refunded to the U.S. buyers in a carefully concealed way to prevent discovery.

An array of secret methods of refunding the difference money was developed by the cartel. This was done with the cooperation of the big American buyers who had been seduced by the bargains:

- Several companies used the Swiss Bank Corporation in Basel, Switzerland, to transfer difference money to an account held by the buyer. For example, Sears received such transfers from Sanyo; cartel member General made such transfers to Midland (a very large American wholesaler).
- Credits falsely labeled as "tooling costs" or "free spare parts" were entered on the books of the seller and buyer.
- Where large buyers such as Sears were purchasing other Japanese products not related to the consumer electronics area, the difference money was passed on as a credit to purchases of the unrelated products.
- Under a cover of what is known as "usance," cartel members allowed extended payment terms and permitted the buyer to retain accumulated interest on his letter of credit made out at the excessive, false check price.

The seller then credited this amount against the difference money owed the buyer.

• Another common method of paying back the difference money was to deposit it in the U.S. buyer's yen account in a bank in Japan.

In 1970, Zenith submitted to Customs a private report disclosing the existence of such "difference money" activities and asked that Customs use its processes on large American buyers to uncover the violations. Customs replied that the official policy of the Treasury Department was not to bother any American customer of the Japanese!

In mid-1976, Zenith was able to serve extensive compulsory demands on the large retail chains and members of buying groups. Zenith was seeking evidence from their files on the purchasing details of their transactions with Japanese cartel members. These huge retailer chains and wholesalers included companies such as Sears, Penney's, Montgomery Ward, and Midland (Western Auto and Gambles). Examining the large quantity of company records was like opening up a huge can of worms. The detailed evidence to conceal the dumping was abundant and compelling. It took several months to sort out the evidence and cross-examine knowledgeable executives. The evidence confirmed everything Zenith had told Treasury and Customs six years earlier in 1970.

In addition, we examined the relevant files of U.S. manufacturers Motorola, Magnavox, and GE. These companies were having receivers made for them in Japan by cartel members at prices below their cost of manufacture in the United States. As expected, the same coordinated Customs fraud was being employed.

Some of the material revealed the cartel's reaction to Zenith's efforts to stop this criminal operation.

In late 1970—after my meetings with Marsh and Ritger at Customs and Treasury, during which I had urgently requested Customs to investigate the dumping scheme—William Tanaka, the cartel's main Customs counsel in Washington, sounded an alarm. It took the form of a confidential letter to the cartel's New York branch, the Japan Light Machinery Information Center. The document, produced in 1977 pursuant to our discovery subpoenas, read in part:

More recently I have heard that Zenith has been giving currency to the story that Magnavox has been a party to alleged double-invoicing and other illegal practices involving the importation of television receivers from Japan. . . . Let me say again that this is all hearsay and I have no direct basis to evaluate such hearsay information. I am only passing this information on so the E.I.A.J. [the cartel] members will be fully aware and be prepared to meet any of these allegations should any of them be made during the forthcoming meeting before the Treasury Department or to the press.

It was reasonable to conclude that Tanaka had been told at Customs and Treasury about Zenith's requests for an investigation of the scandal. It was a shock, if not a surprise, to learn that Ritger left his position as Treasury's chief Customs counsel to join Tanaka's firm as a partner— with his name boldly emblazoned on the firm's new escutcheon, Tanaka, Walders & Ritger.

Files produced in the Zenith litigation revealed a number of secret meetings held by the cartel members and their large U.S. customers during 1970. They met to formulate plans to deflect the government's dumping investigation from their concealment of the cartel's criminal scheme. A Montgomery Ward memo described a secret meeting held in New York on October 26, 1970, during which Ira Millstein, lead counsel for Matsushita and the cartel, discussed a proposed "legal maneuver" that might prevent the Customs Bureau from investigating the cover-up scheme.

Millstein solicited attendees, including large cartel customers, to join in a suit he proposed to file against Treasury, challenging its price determinations in the dumping case on "procedural due process grounds." He defended this solicitation with the reasoning that such a litigation might provide protection against double pricing exposure, that is, discovery of the real prices they had concealed by submitting to the government the mythical check prices. Millstein said that "the government would be in a poor position to press double-pricing charges because this would amount to a second attack on the same prices after the first attack failed, opening possibilities of abuse of process or malicious prosecution."

The veteran three-judge panel of the court of appeals ruled that the bulk of the evidence was admissible. Two concurring opinions, one by Chief Judge Seitz and the other by Judge Gibbons, unanimously held the evidence ample to support a finding that the conspiratorial scheme violated both the Sherman Antitrust Act and the Antidumping Act of 1916. The jury trial we had requested was accordingly ordered.

THE TWICE-AMBUSHED TRIAL

The cartel's lawyers and lobbyists pulled out all the stops in their frantic efforts to prevent a public trial of the scandal. Aided by a shockingly partisan amicus curiae filing by the Justice Department, they cleverly petitioned the Supreme Court to review the antitrust segment of the case on the vague grounds that the court of appeals had not applied a proper standard of review. The result was a highly unusual and peculiar grant of a writ of certiorari (decision to review). This was limited, in accordance with the government's request, to questions of whether there was a "genuine issue of material fact" under the rules requiring a trial of the antitrust part of the case.

The objective of the defense was always to evade and avoid confrontation with the overwhelming record evidence of the predatory dumping scheme and its criminal concealment. Two full days of argument had been allotted to the court of appeals for deep consideration of all the issues. Two full opinions explaining its unanimous ruling were filed, one on the antidumping violations and the other on the antitrust violations.

To avoid the threat of public exposure that a jury trial would produce, the cartel lawyers, working with suspiciously sympathetic Justice Department personnel, had developed a strategy to evade consideration of the evidence in any Supreme Court review. In their filings with the Supreme Court, the government and cartel counsel resurrected an old and often-rejected sleight-of-hand argument. They dismembered the conspiratorial dumping scheme, artificially separating it into two supposedly unrelated conspiracies: a Japan-side conspiracy involving fixed high prices in a market that was closed to imports, and a United States–side conspiracy. They treated the United States–side as the only relevant conduct to be considered under the antitrust laws; the Japan-side conduct was treated as some "other conspiracy" not legally involved in the antitrust litigation.

Their next sleight-of-hand maneuver was to persuade the Supreme Court to agree to review only the Sherman Antitrust Act portion of the case, completely disregarding the Antidumping Act evidence. They attempted this despite the fact that there was only one inseparable set of operational facts involved in the violation of both statutes.

They introduced another deceptive argument that had great psychological force. They put forward the seductive notion that American consumers were being benefited by the low prices of Japanese imports! Quoting from a radical school of economists and "econo-lawyers," they then argued that low pricing benefited consumers and was, therefore, the very goal of U.S. antitrust laws. Evidence of very low pricing, they maintained, was more consistent with a finding of competition than with a finding of unfair restraint of trade.

Finally, they asserted that no trial should be allowed, because under the summary judgment rule there was "no genuine dispute as to relevant material facts."[7] They argued that the evidence, which was artificially limited to the low pricing in the U.S. market, could be viewed as more consistent with a finding of fair competition than with a finding of predatory conspiracy to injure American manufacturers. Using an old trick of the ancient Greek sophists and certain modern economists, they quietly injected a false assumption into their argument. They contended that Zenith and NUE were basing their entire argument on the contention that the cartel members had been selling below cost in the United States for over twenty years, allegedly losing large sums of money with no reasonable prospect of achieving the monopoly that would be necessary to fix high prices in order to compensate for the huge losses. Achieving the required monopoly, it was argued, would be impossible—because even if a monopoly were temporarily achieved and prices artificially raised, new entrants would appear in the market and quickly destroy the monopoly price structure!

In sworn analysis of the evidence, *our* expert witnesses had made it very clear that Zenith and NUE *did not* contend that the concerted, below-cost dumping was anything but a profitable dynamic. The below-cost selling in the United States produced huge increases in sales and was easily subsidized by the high fixed prices in the closed market of Japan. The resulting dynamic growth in production in turn greatly lowered the per unit costs of the entire production.

Based, as the case had to be, on an artificial dismemberment of the predatory dumping scheme, the Government and the cartel had to ignore a long line of relevant cases. For example, the Supreme Court had repeatedly warned in the past:

- [T]he character and effect of a conspiracy are not to be judged by dismembering it and viewing its separate parts but only by looking at it as a whole" [*United States v. Patten*, 226 U.S. 525, 527 (1913); *Continental Ore Co. v. Union Carbide and Carbon Corp.*, 370 U.S. 690 (1962)].

- "The fact finder, be it a jury or a court [where a jury is not demanded by a party], must look at the whole picture and not merely at the individual figures in it" (*id.* at 370 U.S. at 699).

- The plaintiffs must "be given the full benefit of their proof without tightly compartmentalizing the various factual components and wiping the slate clean after scrutiny of each" (*id.* at 699).

- The Supreme Court in the past had further warned lower courts that in determining summary judgment motions they are "bound to view the evi-

dence in the light most favorable to [plaintiffs] and to give them the benefit of all inferences which the evidence fairly supports, even though contrary inferences might reasonably be drawn" (*id.* at 696).

Yet in an action clearly indicating high-level political interference, the
Supreme Court favorably responded to the cartel members' petition.
Adopting the Justice Department's recommendation, the Court granted
review limited to the Sherman Act antitrust aspects of the case. The
predatory scheme was thus dismembered, by unexplained fiat in the
writ granting limited review. The evidence to be considered must be
improperly limited to pricing activity in the United States, and the cartel lawyers were freed to advance their scurrilous defense.

There were no cases that could be cited to support this astonishing
argument. But to ensure a credible appearance to their defense, the cartel and government lawyers needed backing by a scholar, someone
allegedly writing dispassionately in legal or economic journals for the
guidance of the courts. We began to see why the defendants had talked
District Judge Becker out of requiring them to name their proposed
economic experts. Both the plaintiffs and the defendants had been
required to do so under Judge Becker's original pretrial order. Any
expert they named would have been subject to our cross-examination
and any partisan status would be revealed. A jury would have to decide
which experts were more credible; therefore, an open trial could not be
avoided in any summary judgment out of sight of the facts.

When defendants brought the case before the Supreme Court, they
hurriedly filed an article by Frank Easterbrook that had suddenly
appeared in the *Texas Law Review*,[8] just in time to be filed by the cartel
with its Reply Brief in the Supreme Court. The Supreme Court majority
five later adopted Easterbrook's radical theory in its search for an
excuse to agree with the administration's "foreign policy" arguments
and to reject "settled" antitrust principles. A brief look at Easterbrook's
campaign against the antitrust laws is quite revealing.

Easterbrook was a well-publicized member of a radically conservative group of scholars known as the Chicago School. This group regularly published works on antitrust matters that were hailed by business
interests. Knowing that repeal of antitrust and related antidumping laws
was next to impossible in Congress, the Chicago School set out to
preach for judicial repeal. Easterbrook himself had a meteoric rise as a
legal scholar and teacher at the University of Chicago. He was a
Republican whose views were well received in the party and fit the
"Reagan Revolution" line perfectly. Easterbrook had served briefly as a

Deputy U.S. Solicitor General and, with Robert Bork, advocated the Reagan administration's position attacking the "misguided" antitrust decisions of allegedly liberal judges of the past.

Easterbrook produced an extremely timely article criticizing the court of appeals decision in the Zenith case against Matsushita. The cartel lawyers had inspired him to prepare this working paper, distribute it in a program at the Chicago Law School, and have it printed in the *Texas Law Review*. Fifteen copies of the working paper draft dated March 30, 1984, had to be filed to make the deadline for the defendant-petitioners' Reply Brief. When the Court split bitterly in the 5-to-4 voting, Justice Powell, assigned by Chief Justice Burger to write the majority's opinion, used Easterbrook's article as the entire basis for the majority's decision in favor of the cartel. Espousing Easterbrook's sophistry in the face of a forty-volume record of evidence of unfair conspiratorial predation, Justice Powell wrote in pertinent part:

Stating the facts of this case is a daunting task. The opinion of the Court of Appeals for the Third Circuit runs to 69 pages. . . . In addition, the parties have filed a forty-volume appendix in this Court *that is said to contain* the essence of the evidence on which . . . the Court of Appeals based their . . . decisions.

We will not repeat what these . . . opinions have stated and restated, or summarize the mass of documents that comprise the record on appeal. Since we review only the standard applied by the Court of Appeals in deciding this case, and *not the weight assigned to particular pieces of evidence, we find it unnecessary to state the facts in great detail.* (emphasis added) [475 U.S. at 1351]

There was no way Justice Powell could face and explain away the compelling record evidence on which the court of appeals had properly based its decision.

The entire holding of the majority opinion was based on Easterbrook's concocted analysis. Justice Powell wrote:

Professor Easterbrook, commenting on this case in a law review article, offers the following sensible assessment:

"The plaintiffs [in this case] maintain that for the last fifteen years or more at least ten Japanese manufacturers have sold TV sets at less than cost in order to drive United States firms out of business. Such conduct cannot possibly produce profits by harming competition, however. If the Japanese firms drive some United States firms out of business, they could not recoup. Fifteen years of losses could be made up only by very high prices for the indefinite future. (The losses are like investments, which must be recovered with compound interest.) If the defendants should try to raise prices to such a level, they would attract new competition. There are no barriers to entry into electronics, as the proliferation of computer and audio firms shows. The competition would come from resurgent United States firms, from other foreign firms (Korea and many other nations make TV sets), and from defendants themselves. In order to recoup, the Japanese firms would need to suppress competition among themselves. On plaintiffs' theory, the cartel would need to last at least thirty years, far longer than any in history, even when cartels were not illegal. None should be sanguine about the prospects of such a cartel, given each firm's incentive to shave price and expand its share of sales. The predation-recoupment story therefore does not make sense, and we are left with the more plausible inference that the Japanese firms did not sell below cost in the first place. They were just engaged in hard competition." Easterbrook, The Limits of Antitrust, 63 Texas L.Rev. 1, 26–27 (1984) (footnotes omitted). [437 U.S. at 590–594]

Justice Powell, fully embracing Easterbrook's analysis for the majority five, mistakenly held that the plaintiffs' entire case was based on the "senseless" theory that the cartel members had lost large sums of money "selling below cost" in the United States for twenty years. Plaintiffs' claims were thus "economically implausible" and there was no apparent "motive to conspire," said Powell, citing Easterbrook. The majority five, adopting Easterbrook's reasoning and conclusion that the cartel was lawfully engaging in "hard competition" protected—not proscribed—by the antitrust laws, ordered summary judgment in favor of the cartel.

The shock and disbelief of the four dissenters, Justices White, Brennan, Blackmun, and Stevens, was expressed in an opinion by Justice White. Herein he lambasted the majority five for improperly substituting their own peculiar economic "theory" for the record evidence, which raised genuine issues of fact "regarding the harm to respondents caused by Japanese cartelization and by agreements restricting competition among petitioners in this country" (475 U.S. at 603).

White took apart the majority opinion in every respect, plainly accusing Powell of "overturning settled law," making unfounded assumptions at violence with the evidence, and unlawfully invading the province of the factfinder (in this case, the jury). He further pointed to the DePodwin report [475 U.S. at 601–605], in which the evidence was expertly reviewed, and to other record evidence as fully supporting the carefully considered opinion of the court of appeals:

The Third Circuit twice specifically noted that horizontal agreements allocating customers, though illegal, do not ordinarily injure competitors of the agreeing parties. . . . However, after reviewing evidence of cartel activity in Japan, collusive establishment of dumping prices in this country, and long-term, below-cost sales, the Third Circuit held that a factfinder could reasonably conclude that the five-company rule was not a simple price-raising device:

> [A] factfinder might reasonably infer that the allocation of customers in the United States, combined with price-fixing in Japan, was intended to permit concentration of the effects of dumping upon American competitors while eliminating competition among the Japanese manufacturers in either market.
> . . .

I see nothing erroneous in this reasoning.

The Court's second charge of error is that the Third Circuit was not sufficiently skeptical of respondents' allegation that petitioners engaged in predatory pricing conspiracy. But the Third Circuit is not required to engage in academic discussions about predation; it is required to decide whether respondents' evidence creates a genuine issue of material fact. The Third Circuit did its job, and remanding the case so that it can do the same job again is simply pointless.

I use the Third Circuit's analysis of the five-company rule by way of example; the court did an equally careful analysis of the parts the cartel activity in Japan and the check prices could have played in an actionable conspiracy. [*Matsushita et al. v. Zenith,* 475 U.S. 574, at 605–606]

Justice White made it clear in the dissenting opinion that "the academic discussion" of price predation engaged in by the majority when it adopted the Easterbrook theory related fundamentally to a far different and simpler pricing practice than the predatory dumping scheme employed by the cartel. The Court's minority examined the evidence; the majority five read and adopted the Easterbrook article in lieu of undertaking what Justice Powell described as the "daunting task" of reading the evidence. The plaintiffs' theory, reasoned Justice Powell, was, in light of Easterbrook's analysis, "implausible." The "predation-recoupment" claim was bereft of any "rational motive"(*id.* at 590–594)!

This bizarre reasoning was based on the assumption that the cartel was losing money. But the U.S. operation was only half of the overall operation. The high prices charged in Japan's protected market offset the losses in the U.S. market. The point of the assault was to capture an entire industry. The heavily subsidized cartel members were making an overall profit on their entire production of 10 percent to 15 percent, as demonstrated by Zenith's experts' analyses of the evidence in the record. Profits would even be increased over a much longer period of time. What was important was market domination and market control.

The predatory dumping scheme as disclosed in the record evidence was a classic example of the predatory and malignant type of dumping described by the leading expert on the subject, Jacob Viner (1966). According to Viner, a cartel, having a monopoly in its home market (which is closed to imports), fixes very high domestic prices and ravages competition in an open market by dumping products at whatever price is necessary to take the business away from local manufacturers. The motives for such an unfair and rapacious commercial campaign are listed by Viner: (1) to eliminate competition in the target market; (2) to maintain full production from plant facilities; and (3) to obtain the economies of larger-scale production. The greater the quantity of exports over imports (i.e., the greater the balance of trade in favor of the home country), the greater the growth, employment, prosperity, and wealth of the nation at the expense of the target country (Chap. 2).

Easterbrook and the majority five further theorized that predatory dumpers must reasonably expect to achieve a monopoly in the targeted market in order to recoup the "losses" suffered. But Viner notes the following on the basis of the long history of predatory dumping in international trade:

A producer may engage in export dumping primarily with a view to maintaining full production, but he may at the same time deliberately manage his dumping so that it will inflict as much injury as possible upon his foreign competitors. Moreover, the predatory dumper may not expect that he will succeed in wholly eliminating the competitors against whom he is dumping. (1966, p. 122)

The theory that the cartel members were losing money was also false. DePodwin's sworn analysis of the evidence demonstrated that the cartel's scheme had produced an overall profit of 5 to 10 percent. In addition, the growth in gross national product, the full employment, and the tremendously favorable balance of trade helped to produce wealth and prosperity for Japan at the expense of American industry and its workers. The overall profit of 5 to 10 percent was far greater than that available to any of the American manufacturers. They were all reduced to a loss position in profits and market share.

Fully 50 percent of the color TV business was quickly diverted from the market shares of the American industry. Every radio and black-and-white TV manufacturer in the United States had already been taken over in the stage-by-stage offensive. Justice White commented on the obvious growth objective of the unfair dumping scheme:

The Court, in discussing the unlikelihood of a predatory conspiracy, also consistently assumes that [the cartel] valued profit maximization over growth. . . . I believe that this assumption should be argued to the factfinder [the jury], not decided by the Court. [475 U.S. 574, at 605]

The predatory dumping scheme was shown in the evidence to have as its major goal the industrial growth it produced in the Japanese electronics and television manufacturing industries. The below-cost sales in the United States, in turn, produced huge increases in volume, which enabled the Japanese factories to enjoy significantly lower per unit costs produced by economies of scale. Every doubling of total production produced a 20 percent to 30 percent lowering in overall per unit costs. Each market thus benefited the other to produce great growth and a reasonable overall profit.

The seduction of the majority five to the Easterbrook heresy was a puzzlement to the dissenting minority four, as Justice White, with a struggling self-restraint, expressed in his opening statement in the dissenting opinion:

It is indeed remarkable that the Court, in the face of the long and careful opinion of the Court of Appeals, reaches the result it does. The Court of Appeals faithfully followed the relevant precedents, including *First National Bank of Arizona v. Cities Service Co.*, 391 U.S. 253 (1968), and *Monsanto Co. v. Spray-Rite Service Corp.*, 465 U.S. 752 (1984), and it kept firmly in mind the principle that proof of a conspiracy should not be *fragmented*, see *Continental Ore Co. v. Union Carbide & Carbon Corp.*, 370 U.S. 690, 699 (1962). After surveying the massive record, including very significant evidence that the District Court erroneously had excluded, the Court of Appeals concluded that the evidence taken as a whole creates a genuine issue of fact whether petitioners engaged in a conspiracy in violation of 1 and 2 of the Sherman Act, and 2(a) of the Robinson-Patman Act. In my view, the Court of Appeals' opinion *more than adequately supports this judgment.*

The DePodwin Report *alone* creates a genuine factual issue regarding the harm to respondents caused by Japanese cartelization and by agreements restricting competition among petitioners in this country. No doubt the Court prefers its own economic theorizing to Dr. DePodwin's, but that is not a reason to deny the factfinder an opportunity to consider Dr. DePodwin's views on how petitioners' alleged collusion harmed respondents.

The Court, in discussing the unlikelihood of a predatory conspiracy, also *consistently assumes that petitioners valued* profit-maximization over growth.

In light of the evidence that petitioners sold their goods in this country at substantial losses over a long period of time, see Part III-B, *infra*, I believe that this is an assumption that should be argued to the factfinder, not decided by the Court. (emphasis added) [*Matsushita et al. v. Zenith*, 475 U.S. 574, at 598–599, 603]

But the majority five prevailed despite the invalidity of their analysis. Speaking for the majority, Justice Powell ruled:

On remand, the Court of Appeals is free to consider whether there is other evidence that is sufficiently unambiguous to permit a trier of fact to find that petitioners conspired to price predatorily for two decades *despite the absence of any apparent motive to do so*. The evidence must "tend to exclude the possibility" that petitioners underpriced respondents to compete for business rather than to implement an economically senseless conspiracy. *Monsanto*, 465 U.S., at 764. In the absence of such evidence, there is no "genuine issue for trial" under Rule 56(e), and petitioners are entitled to have summary judgment reinstated. (emphasis added) [*Matsushita et al. v. Zenith*, 475 U.S. 574, at 597, 598]

The following conclusion of the Easterbrook analysis became the law of the case, binding the court of appeals on the remand:

The predation-recoupment story therefore does not make sense, and we are left with the more plausible inference that the Japanese firms did not sell below cost in the first place. They were just engaged in hard competition. [*id.* at 586]

The Supreme Court had ruled that the Japanese cartel was not credibly shown to have engaged in any illegal activity; it was, therefore, as Easterbrook said, "just engaged in hard competition," and the majority five made it plain that the Sherman Act promoted and protected such competition. Therefore, the court of appeals also had to throw out the 1916 Antidumping Act count, which the Supreme Court had refused to review at the urging of the Justice Department. The act required an "intent to injure" or "to restrain trade." No such intent could be ascribed to anyone merely engaging in competition. The law protected such competition. Any injury sustained as a result of such lawful competition was, therefore (in legal jargon, *Damnum absque injuria*) damage resulting from legal activity encouraged by the law and thus not compensable at law.

The amazing and tragic result left us wondering what could have propelled the majority five into what we believed to be such improper judicial legislation. The cartel's rapacious conduct was, in effect, now sanctioned and encouraged by the Supreme Court of the United States!

THE AFTERMATH

After the ruling, two events occurred that shed considerable light on the matter. *First,* Clyde V. Prestowitz, an experienced former counselor to the Secretary of Commerce, wrote an informative book entitled *Trading Places: How We Allowed Japan to Take the Lead* (1988). In it he displayed extensive knowledge of the *Matsushita* ruling and described the tragedy of the result in a very able criticism. The author observed:

The U.S. Justice Department filed an amicus curiae (friend of court) brief [in the Supreme Court in the *Matsushita* case] on behalf of the Japanese—*an astonishing step . . . it was well known to the U.S. Government that the Japanese had in fact colluded.* Secretary [of Commerce] Baldwin strongly opposed the Justice Department action, but the State Department and Treasury supported it. They were afraid that a ruling against the Japanese would invalidate the legal basis for the voluntary restraint Japan had placed on its auto exports from time to time. *In effect, the United States supported unfair trade in order to preserve the agreements that were in part its result.* (emphasis added) (pp. 205–6)

This shocking revelation may explain why the government, in its brief and oral argument, urgently persuaded the majority five to adopt Easterbrook's "timely" work. In adopting it, the majority five were probably motivated by a desire to do deference to the "foreign policy" of State and Treasury.[†]

Second, the suspicious timing and appropriateness of Easterbrook's article was cleared up by information provided to William Roberts, a leading partner in the plaintiffs' Philadelphia law firm. In private com-

---

[†]The incredible back-room politicking of Edwin Meese in the Reagan White House that brought about this ill-conceived Japanese "voluntary" quota policy is exposed by David Stockman, Reagan's Office of Management and Budget director, in his book *The Triumph of Politics* (1986), pp. 153–58:

Meese was trundling around the White House, doing what he did best: quietly pounding square pegs into round holes, convincing himself and the President that all we had to do to maintain our free trade position was to convince the Japanese "voluntarily" to restrict their own exports.

And so the essence of the Reagan Administration's trade policy became clear. Espouse free trade but find an excuse on every occasion to embrace the opposite. As time passed we would find occasions aplenty.

ments to Harry First, a law school professor, Easterbrook admitted that he was a consultant to the Japanese companies in the case and had reviewed the record evidence before he wrote his article! Roberts requested an affidavit from First disclosing his conversation with Easterbrook, and it was willingly furnished (see Exhibit 6.1). Professor John Flynn, who is mentioned in the affidavit, also furnished an affidavit corroborating First's recollection of Easterbrook's statements.

Our curiosity about this matter was further stimulated by a letter that counsel for the cartel had sent to the court of appeals at the time the court was about to comply with the Supreme Court's mandate. In that letter, cartel counsel falsely represented to the court that Easterbrook's law review article was a "non-commissioned learned professional paper," in contrast to the sworn analysis of plaintiffs' experts. No mention was made of the fact that Easterbrook's article was neither under oath nor timely filed, as required by Rule 56 of the Federal Rules of Civil Procedure. Failure to disclose the compelling fact that Easterbrook was partisan and consultant to the cartel members in the case was a repeated deception that worked a crucial fraud on the federal courts.

As has been noted, on remand the court of appeals understandably felt constrained to obey the Supreme Court's direction that the cartel was, as Easterbrook had described it, commendably engaged in lawful competition, not "irrational conduct," and that plaintiffs were not even entitled to a trial of the case. The cartel's letter to the court supported their position that the Supreme Court opinion and mandate, based as it was on Easterbrook's "non-commissioned" law review article, commanded dismissal of the entire case.

The affidavits of professors First and Flynn that Easterbrook had confessed to them that he was a consultant to the cartel and, therefore, a paid partisan in disguise disclosed a deceptive, unethical misuse of Rule 56 of the Federal Rules of Civil Procedure. That rule was carefully drawn under the Supreme Court's supervision pursuant to a law of Congress and was then made law by an act of Congress. It reads in pertinent part:

(c) . . . The [summary] judgment [in this case for the cartel] shall be rendered forthwith [without trial] if the pleadings, depositions, answers to interrogatories, and admissions on file, together with affidavits, if any, show that there is no genuine issue as to any material fact and that the moving party is entitled to a judgment as a matter of law. . . .

Supporting and opposing affidavits shall be made on personal knowledge, shall set forth such facts as would be admissible in evidence, and shall show

Exhibit 6.1
Affidavit of Harry First

AFFIDAVIT OF HARRY FIRST

COUNTY OF NEW YORK   :
                     : ss.
STATE OF NEW YORK   :

HARRY FIRST, being duly sworn according to law, deposes and says:

1.   I am Professor of Law at New York University School of Law, New York, New York. I make this affidavit at the request of attorneys for Zenith Radio Corporation and National Union Electric Corporation, plaintiffs in In Re Japanese Electronic Products Antitrust Litigation, M.D.L. 189, which I understand is presently pending in the United States Court of Appeals for the Third Circuit at Nos. 80-2080 and 81-2331/81-2332/81-2333. Having read the decision of the Supreme Court of the United States in this case, Matsushita Electric Industrial Co., Ltd., et al. v. Zenith Radio Corporation and National Union Electric Corporation, No. 83-2004, 54 U.S.L.W. 4319 (March 26, 1986), I contacted counsel for the plaintiffs to obtain information concerning aspects of the Supreme Court's decision. In the course of those conversations, I had occasion to refer to the law review article by Frank W. Easterbrook entitled "The Limits of Antitrust," 63 Texas L.Rev. 1 (1984), to which the Supreme Court Majority opinion in Matsushita referred. I commented that it was my recollection that the author of that article had told

Exhibit 6.1 (continued)

---

me that he was a consultant for the defendant companies in that
case. As a result of that conversation, I have been asked to
provide this affidavit, and I provide the information contained
herein to the best of my personal knowledge, recollection and
belief.

2.   At a meeting which I attended in January 1985 of the
Association of American Law Schools in Washington, D.C.,
Professor Frank Easterbrook, the author of the article referred
to above, was a speaker before the Antitrust Section of the
Association, and during the course of his speech referred to the
Japanese Electronic Products Antitrust Litigation and to certain
of his opinions with respect to issues in that case. Since I
had recently returned from Japan, where I had spent my
sabbatical year studying Japan's antitrust law, I was interested
in the basis of certain of Professor Easterbrook's views. I
spoke with him about the case after his speech. In the course
of our discussion of the business practices of Japanese
corporations and Professor Easterbrook's views concerning that
case, it is my recollection that Professor Easterbrook stated
that he was a consultant for the Japanese companies who were
defendants in the case and that his views of the practices of
these corporations was supported by the record, which he had
reviewed.

3.   It is my recollection that Professor John Flynn of the
University of Utah College of Law was also present and heard my
conversation with Professor Easterbrook. I have since confirmed

-2-

Exhibit 6.1 (continued)

my own recollection by speaking with Professor Flynn, who stated
to me that he also recalls Professor Easterbrook's making a
statement to that effect.

3.   I have never been retained by either of the plaintiffs
in that litigation and have volunteered this information.

_____
HARRY FIRST

SWORN TO AND SUBSCRIBED
before me this 29 day
of September, 1986.

_____
NOTARY PUBLIC

Jan 31, 1989

affirmatively that the affiant is competent to testify to the matters stated therein.

The cartel's motion for summary judgment was, as required, originally filed in the district court. This motion was not supported by any evidence; it merely challenged the sufficiency of plaintiffs' evidence, and the cartel was mysteriously excused from a pretrial order requiring them to file their experts' analyses under oath.

With the cartel's experts undisclosed and in hiding, Judge Becker had to strain illegally to rule the bulk of the plaintiffs' vast evidentiary record "inadmissible in evidence." The court of appeals had soundly rejected this gross abuse of discretion; and the Supreme Court was not asked by the cartel (wisely) to review this ruling, nor did it question the court of appeals action on that vital point. Rather, the cartel lawyers filed no affidavits or evidence of any kind. They merely made arguments that were based entirely on Easterbrook's belatedly published law review article.

If Easterbrook was a consultant to the cartel or its lawyers, his analysis should have been submitted under oath as testimony of an expert witness for the cartel. This would have clearly raised an issue of material fact, conflicting as it did with the sworn reports of plaintiffs' experts. A trial at which all the experts could testify would have been required without question.

If Easterbrook's true status—as well as the concealed reason why the government sponsored the cartel's deceptive argument—had been timely admitted, the highly questionable tactic of using his unsworn analysis in the Supreme Court as the unbiased work of an independent scholar seeking to guide the Court in the public interest would have been fatally exposed.

JUSTICE THURGOOD MARSHALL'S TRAGIC SWING VOTE

Prior to the oral argument in the Supreme Court, there was reason to believe that on well-settled principles, the Supreme Court would be constrained to affirm the thorough opinions of the unanimous court of appeals. The fact that the Reagan-Meese Justice Department had successfully urged the Supreme Court to review the case could explain the Court's unexpected decision to do so. At the oral argument, however, Justice Marshall's startling remarks concerned me almost to the point of despair. With Burger, Powell, Rehnquist, and O'Connor probably being more than inclined to adopt the administration's political position, it seemed that Marshall could be the swing vote against us. His remarks at the argument were very disturbing: "As a consumer, why am I worried about a drop in prices?" (referring to the predatory prices in the United States), and "Am I worried about the prices in Japan?" (referring to the very high monopoly pricing of televisions in Japan). Marshall's deciding vote swung the Supreme Court into a decision that favored a foreign cartel whose predation in the United States had directly resulted in widespread unemployment of minorities in the American consumer electronics industry.

It was shocking to learn that Marshall, the first black judge ever to be elevated to the Supreme Court and an appointee of President Johnson during his war on poverty, had joined the Nixon-Reagan segment of the Court. In casting his swing vote, Thurgood Marshall aided in approving the most rapacious and illegal attack on competition since the robber barons' trusts. Had Marshall voted with White, Brennan, Blackmun, and Stevens, the Rule of Law would have prevailed and our constitutional right to a jury trial would have been upheld. A jury's common sense, we were convinced, would right the wrong; and a justly revived American industry would again be able to provide jobs for many Americans.

Speaking for the government, Charles Rule also explained away the embarrassing evidence that the cartel had criminally concealed the vast extent of the predatory dumping by falsifying U.S. Customs entry documents on hundreds of millions of dollars worth of imports. He blithely disposed of these felonies, which were flagrant violations of federal civil and criminal statutes, as having been committed in the public interest! At the oral argument, Rule repeated this shocking argument from the government and cartel briefs. He said:

The third fact is the secret rebates that were not disclosed by petitioners. In effect, the petitioners engaged in, so the court [of appeals] said, more than twenty-five different rebate schemes. . . .

Again, this is more indicative of individuals evading regulatory constraints that hampered their individual efforts to try to compete in the marketplace and sell at the lowest price possible.[9]

Such invalid reasoning of the end justifying the means may also have helped in Marshall's seduction. Nowhere in the briefs of the cartel and government or in Justice Powell's opinion was the basic definition of "conspiracy," which is condemned in the Sherman Act, ever noted or confronted.[10] For years after passage of the Sherman Act, the Supreme

Court again and again recited this fundamental precept, repeating it with vigor:

No conduct has such an absolute privilege as to justify all possible schemes of which it may be a part. The most innocent and constitutionally protected of acts may be made a step in a criminal plot, and, if it is a step in a plot, neither its innocence nor the Constitution is sufficient to prevent the punishment of the plot by law. [*Aikens v. Wisconsin,* 195 U.S. 194, 206 (1904); *Loewe v. Lawlor,* 208 U.S. 274, 299 (1908)]

This timeless principle, long-established in both English and American law, was eloquently expressed in England in 1817 by Lord Stowel:

To press forward to a great principle by breaking through every other great principle that stands in the way of its establishment . . . to procure an eminent good by means that are unlawful, is as little consonant to private morality as to public justice. [Re: Le Louis (1817) 2 Dods 210, 257]

The great benefit allegedly brought by the cartel's predatory dumping scheme to American consumers in the form of low prices could not excuse the cartel's criminal plot under well-settled principles. To give the government what it wanted for concealed policy reasons, the majority five had to evade confrontation with settled principles of law.

Any post-mortem review of the tactics employed by the cartel's lawyers and their colleagues at the Department of Justice should include their grossly improper and false representations to the Supreme Court that Zenith was not damaged by the cartel's assault. At the oral argument, lead counsel for the cartel, Mr. Zoeller, lied to the Court about the record evidence of damage to American industry inflicted by the cartel:

The undisputed facts of this case are that from the beginning of the alleged period of conspiracy when these companies entered the United States market with zero market shares, on through roughly twenty years covered in this case, the two market leaders in the United States, Zenith and RCA, remained the two market leaders . . . [and] lost none of their market shares.[11]

Justice Stevens,[12] who obviously had read the record evidence, confronted Zoeller directly on this unethical misrepresentation, exposing its impropriety on two counts:

[Justice Stevens]: Is it true that some seventeen or eighteen companies have gone out of business in the American market?

Mr. Zoeller: Oh, I don't know how many companies have gone out of business. I do know this, your honor, the record shows that the rate of failure . . . before the Japanese entered and the rate of failure afterward was greater before than after.[13]

Then Justice Stevens lowered the boom on Zoeller's improper and false representations:

Question: What about the other plaintiff [NUE].

Mr. Zoeller: The other plaintiff had gone out of business in the year 1970. . . .

Question: As I read the Court of Appeals opinion, they say that you conceded the fact of damage; that there was enough evidence. I don't mean you conceded on the merits, but that you didn't contend that the record was deficient with regard to the proof of damage. Is that right?

Mr. Zoeller: On this record, your honor, we have argued on summary judgment only the issue of liability. We have not addressed the issue of damage either in the court below or in the Court of Appeals, or not do we address it in this court! It simply is not raised by the motion for summary judgment which raises itself to the more basic issue of liability.[14]

Thus, Zoeller was adroitly forced to confess not only that he and his government cohort, Charles Rule, were misrepresenting the record evidence, but that they were concealing the fact that the cartel lawyers had admitted the damage to Zenith, NUE, and the American industry when they brought their motion for summary judgment.

Nevertheless, RCA's David Sarnoff got his revenge on Zenith for breaking up his original international patent racket. By arming the cartel at its birth with advice and America's technical know-how and fueling it from RCA's laboratory in Japan, he was generously rewarded as the hero of the cartelized Japanese industry and appropriately decorated by the Emperor himself. RCA's more practical reward, of course, was the percentage share of the sales prices of the cartel's entire production—a sum approximating $200 million a year in 1985.

The Marshall Documents

After a draft of this book had been submitted for publication, release of the late Justice Thurgood Marshall's files was announced by the Library of Congress. Examination of those files confirmed my belief that there is a mystery surrounding Marshall's swing vote in favor of the Japanese cartel's legal position. The documents reveal the highly unusual path the case took in the Supreme Court process.

1. See the copy of an Order reproduced in Exhibit 6.2. This document raises the question of why the Solicitor General or one of his experienced staff did not argue this important case on behalf of the administration. Perhaps the Solicitor General was aware of the secret reason why the government supported the cartel. The Easterbrook scam, which was concocted to shield this embarrassing secret from the plaintiffs and the Court, may have been too "rich" for the Solicitor General's office—which is supposed to be independently professional, as well as counsel to the Court, when it presents legal arguments for the administration in the Supreme Court.

2. Also reproduced in Exhibit 6.2 is a letter from Justice Powell to Chief Justice Burger describing the drastic change in the outcome of the case caused by Marshall's unexplained decision to change his vote. But for Marshall's now newly revealed and unexplained postconference vacillation, the opinion of the court of appeals would have prevailed and the industry could have been saved.

3. However, another Marshall file document (reproduced in Exhibit 6.3) reveals that on March 3, 1986, over two months after changing his vital vote, Justice Marshall wrote on the front of Justice White's circulated dissenting opinion draft, "BRW. Please join me in your dissent. TM." Conceivably, Marshall had forgotten that his was the key swing vote and that his joining Justice White's analysis would, in effect, transform White's dissenting opinion into the majority view. This must have caused alarm and concern in the Burger and Powell offices.

4. What happened to bring Justice Marshall back again does not appear to be recorded in his files. But his mysterious reconversion is noted on a document dated March 6, 1986 (also reproduced in Exhibit 6.3).

The documents thus show that in a matter of months following his official conference vote to allow the court of appeals ruling to stand, Marshall changed his vote three times with no recorded explanation. To surmise about the causes of his mental gyration is tempting but would serve no useful purpose unless more facts are found. One thing seems reasonably certain, however: had the Prestowitz revelation and the Easterbrook scam been revealed to the Court before any vote took place, the opinion of the court of appeals would have been unanimously allowed to stand and a great American manufacturing industry would have been enabled to survive.

Exhibit 6.2
Order of October 31, 1985; and Justice
Powell's Letter of November 18, 1985

Supreme Court of the United States
Washington, D. C. 20543

CHAMBERS OF
THE CHIEF JUSTICE

October 31, 1985

MEMORANDUM FOR THE CONFERENCE

Subject: Report on Conference Actions on Miscellaneous Motions,
            Submitted with other Non-Discuss Matters for the
            November 1, 1985 Conference

  1.   No. 83-2004, Matsushita Electric Industrial Co.,
                     Ltd., et al. v. Zenith Radio
                     Corporation, et al.

            Motion of the SG to permit Dep. Asst. Atty.
            Gen. Charles F. Rule to argue pro hac vice on
            behalf of the Government.

                  --Charles Rule is a 1981 graduate of the
                  University of Chicago Law School. He served
                  as a law clerk to Chief Judge Daniel M.
                  Friedman (then of the Court of Claims) and
                  was admitted to practice in the District of
                  Columbia in 1983. Mr. Rule served as the
                  Acting Asst. Attorney General in charge of
                  the Antitrust Division from April to
                  September 1985. He is thoroughly familiar
                  with this case and had substantial
                  responsibility for preparing the
                  Government's brief. The SG believes that
                  Mr. Rule is especially qualified to present
                  the Government's amicus argument in this
                  case.

                                                          GRANT

  2.   No. 84-773, Bender, et al. v. The Williamsport Area
                   School District, et al.

            Motion of petrs for leave to file post-argument
            brief.

Exhibit 6.2 (continued)

Supreme Court of the United States
Washington, D. C. 20543

CHAMBERS OF
JUSTICE LEWIS F. POWELL, JR.

November 18, 1985

83-2004 Matsushita Electric v. Zenith

Dear Chief:

        Thurgood's note to you of November 15 has just come to my attention. He advises that, after careful reexamination, his vote now is to reverse.

        As I now understand the situation, Thurgood's vote provides a majority of five who would reverse and remand: You, Thurgood, Bill Rehnquist, Sandra and me.

        According to my Conference notes, after our considerable discussion (and I must say, possibly some confusion), those who voted to DIG or affirm were Bill Brennan, Byron, Thurgood, Harry and John. On the basis of this vote of five Justices to DIG, as we left Conference I understood it was agreed that Bill Brennan would write a brief explanation of why the Court was dismissing the case as improvidently granted. In walking down the corridor with Bill after the Conference, I said that given the five votes to dismiss I would not write in dissent.

        I have just discussed this situation with you on the telephone, and I agree with you that in light of Thurgood's letter we now have five votes to reverse and remand.

        Sincerely,

Lewis

The Chief Justice

lfp/ss

cc: The Conference

Exhibit 6.3
Justice Marshall's Handwritten Comments
on Draft Opinions, March 3 and 6, 1986

To: The Chief Justice
Justice Brennan
Justice Marshall
Justice Blackmun
Justice Powell
Justice Rehnquist
Justice Stevens
Justice O'Connor

From: **Justice White**

Circulated: _____ MAR 3   1986 _____

Recirculated: _____

BYW

Please join me in your dissent

Jn!!

1st DRAFT

SUPREME COURT OF THE UNITED STATES

No. 83-2004

MATSUSHITA ELECTRIC INDUSTRIAL CO., LTD.,
ET AL., PETITIONERS *v.* ZENITH RADIO
CORPORATION ET AL.

ON WRIT OF CERTIORARI TO THE UNITED STATES COURT OF
APPEALS FOR THE THIRD CIRCUIT

[March ——, 1986]

Join

JUSTICE WHITE, dissenting.

It is indeed remarkable that the Court, in the face of the long and careful opinion of the Court of Appeals, reaches the result it does. The Court of Appeals faithfully followed the relevant precedents, including *First National Bank v. Cities Service Co.*, 391 U. S. 253 (1968), and *Monsanto v. Spray-Rite Corp.*, —— U. S. —— (1984), and it kept firmly in mind the principle that proof of a conspiracy should not be fragmented, see *Continental Ore Co. v. Union Carbide & Carbon Corp.*, 370 U. S. 690, 699 (1962). After surveying the massive record, including very significant evidence that the District Court erroneously had excluded, the Court of Appeals concluded that the evidence taken as a whole creates a genuine issue of fact whether petitioners engaged in a conspiracy in violation of §§1 and 2 of the Sherman Act, and §2(a) of the Robinson-Patman Act. In my view, the Court of Appeals' opinion more than adequately supports this judgment.

The Court's opinion today, far from identifying reversible error, only muddies the waters. In the first place, the Court makes confusing and inconsistent statements about the appropriate standard for granting summary judgment. Second, the Court makes a number of assumptions that invade the factfinder's province. Third, the Court faults the Third

Exhibit 6.3 (continued)

03/05

Stylistic Changes Throughout.

and pp. 7, 12, 18

To: The Chief Justice
Justice Brennan
Justice White
Justice Marshall
Justice Blackmun
Justice Rehnquist
Justice Stevens
Justice O'Connor

From: **Justice Powell**

Circulated:_____

Recirculated:_____ MAR 6 1986

4th DRAFT

SUPREME COURT OF THE UNITED STATES

No. 83 2004

MATSUSHITA ELECTRIC INDUSTRIAL CO., LTD.,
ET AL., PETITIONERS *v.* ZENITH RADIO
CORPORATION ET AL.

ON WRIT OF CERTIORARI TO THE UNITED STATES COURT OF
APPEALS FOR THE THIRD CIRCUIT

[March ——, 1986]

JUSTICE POWELL delivered the Opinion of the Court.

This case requires that we again consider the standard district courts must apply when deciding whether to grant summary judgment in an antitrust conspiracy case.

I

Stating the facts of this case is a daunting task. The opinion of the Court of Appeals for the Third Circuit runs to 69 pages; the primary opinion of the District Court is more than three times as long. 723 F. 2d 238 (CA3 1983); 513 F. Supp. 1100 (ED Pa. 1981). Two respected District Judges each have authored a number of opinions in this case; the published ones alone would fill an entire volume of the Federal Supplement. In addition, the parties have filed a forty-volume appendix in this Court that is said to contain the essence of the evidence on which the District Court and the Court of Appeals based their respective decisions.

We will not repeat what these many opinions have stated and restated, or summarize the mass of documents that comprise the record on appeal. Since we review only the standard applied by the Court of Appeals in deciding this case, and not the weight assigned to particular pieces of evidence, we find it unnecessary to state the facts in great detail. What follows is a summary of this case's long history.

GE AND RCA EXPLOIT THE JUSTICE
DEPARTMENT'S "ANTI-ANTITRUST" POLICY

Although GE had earlier sought to sell its then-profitless consumer electronics division to one of its Japanese licensees, it failed to obtain Justice Department approval while the Zenith litigation was flaring. In 1985 the administration's "anti-antitrust" law enforcement policy encouraged GE to concoct a new way to legally reacquire RCA, an organization GE had formed in 1919 to control the emerging consumer electronics industry in the United States pursuant to the GE, Westinghouse, AT&T conspiracy.

On December 12, 1985, on the front page of the Business section the *Chicago Tribune* prominently printed news of the GE–RCA merger:

RCA Corp. agreed to be acquired by General Electric in a friendly all cash transaction. The two companies which together have revenues exceeding $40 billion have common interests in business including commercial and consumer electronics, defense [government contracts in huge defense programs], broadcasting [including RCA's National Broadcasting Company] and satellite communications. . . . The transaction would be the biggest non-oil merger ever. . . . A Justice Department spokesman said the agency didn't have any comment.

The newspaper further described the details of the merger:

The surprising merger will create a diversified high-tech conglomerate . . . General Electric . . . is widely diversified and one of the nation's largest industrial concerns. G.E. boasts of $27.9 billion in sales . . . with $24.7 billion in assets and earnings of $2.28 billion. . . . In 1984 RCA earned $341 million on revenue of $10.1 billion. [RCA had over $1 billion in cash reserves.]

Like RCA, G.E. is a leading defense and aerospace company. It also makes or markets large appliances, consumer electronics, lighting products, electric motors, turbine power equipment, locomotives, and construction equipment. . . .

[T]he merger will require approval . . . by various federal agencies including the FCC because RCA owns five TV stations and G.E. owns one. . . .

Presumably the merger proposal also will be reviewed for antitrust implications [by the Justice Department], though approval along these lines isn't expected to be a major problem. Adopting the policy that U.S. firms are engaged in a world market, the Reagan administration hasn't pressed antitrust policy hard on American companies.

What appeared to be a flagrant violation of the antitrust laws, which the Justice Department surely would not dare to approve, was explained away in the following comment that also appeared on the front page of the Business section of the *Chicago Sun Times* on December 12, 1985:

The G.E.–RCA merger . . . has touched off only minimal antitrust controversies, in part because the Justice Department has taken a hands-off attitude about even the largest mergers and takeovers. . . .

Both companies have huge defense related electronics and aerospace, and G.E. said it would not willingly forfeit those or the sale of N.B.C. without rethinking the deal. *But a spokesman said the merged firm would be willing to forsake the consumer electronics industry.* . . .

Before the merger G.E. said it would get out of the consumer electronics business [manufacture and sale of television sets, parts and picture tubes], and begin buying television sets and stereos carrying its brand name. (emphasis added)

There was no mention of the federal court consent decrees that had been entered in government proceedings brought against both RCA and GE in 1932 and again in 1958, after Zenith's successful lawsuit against them had resulted in a substantial financial settlement that included royalty-free, worldwide licenses. *TV Digest,* a leading trade publication, explained how the shocking merger was orchestrated in the face of federal court decrees:

It is only coincidence, says RCA, that it picked this year [1985] to seek termination of a 53-year-old consent decree that otherwise would have kept G.E. from making the takeover offer. . . .

On petition from RCA filed early this year and without objection from the Justice Department, the U.S. District Court, Wilmington, Delaware, terminated that order . . . and a 1958 order [entered in a government antitrust case after the Zenith case had been settled in 1957[15]].

Orders were still in force November 6 [1985] when G.E. and RCA heads say they held their first meeting to explore the merger. (December 1985, p. 2)

Earlier press reports revealed a previously secret, well-planned program at high levels of both RCA and GE looking toward a merger (which would be flagrantly violative of the antitrust laws) that would not be attacked by the Reagan administration (whose refusal to enforce those laws was notorious). William French Smith, Reagan's personal lawyer and Attorney General, retired as Attorney General in *February, 1985* to rejoin his former California law firm (Gibson, Dunn &

Crutcher, a leading law firm representing Japanese business interests) and on *March 6, 1985,* became a director of RCA! In its 1985 report to stockholders, RCA was required by Securities and Exchange Commission (SEC) rules to list its directors and disclose any outside business relationship each director had with the company. At page 6 of this legalistic report, the following was vaguely admitted:

Gibson, Dunn and Crutcher: The law firm of Gibson, Dunn and Crutcher of which Mr. Smith [the newly appointed director] is a senior partner, renders legal advice and services to RCA and its subsidiaries.

The SEC did not require disclosure of the nature of the services or the amount of compensation involved. However, it was apparent that the required discreet cooperation of the Justice Department in its approval of the GE–RCA merger had been (with good reason) confidently relied upon by the heads of both companies during their secret planning sessions.

The segments of RCA that GE wanted in the acquisition—and those it did not want—could be discerned in the legally required proxy statement accompanying a Notice of Special Stockholders Meeting for February 13, 1986, to approve the merger. At page 15 of this 120-page tome, stockholders were informed that the deal would not go through if "any necessary governmental or regulatory action required divestiture of any assets that would have a material adverse effect on (a) the Aerospace Business Group of General Electric, (b) the Electronics Segment *(other than Consumer Products and Services)* of RCA, (c) General Electric . . . taken as a whole, or (d) NBC and its subsidiaries taken as a whole" (emphasis added). General Electric, for good reason, did not want RCA's then-profitless consumer electronics manufacturing business.

Then, in July 1987, the true scope of GE's merger strategy became discernible. The July 23, 1987, edition of the *Wall Street Journal* reported the following:

New York: General Electric has agreed to sell its consumer electronics business to French electronics giant Thomson S.A. in return for Thomson's medical equipment business and a cash sum G.E. said was "significantly more than $500 million and less than $1 billion." (p. 1)

GE further noted to the press that Thomson's medical equipment business was an excellent fit in a business GE viewed as among its fastest growing.[16] GE was thus rid of the profitless television set business but not RCA's Japanese patent licensing bonanza, which was netting in the area of $200 million annually. Every consumer electronics unit entering the United States from abroad for years has brought a rewarding royalty under an RCA license. Likewise, through licensing fees, every unit sold in Japan at prices fixed at subsidizing levels 40 percent or more over prices to U.S. buyers have produced profit-sharing income to RCA and GE.

Before the sale, GE had already reduced RCA factories from 23 to 17 and eliminated 23 percent of salaried workers. All this illustrated GE's philosophy of avoiding fields of business that had been invaded by the Japanese, with whom it has historically cooperated and whom it has licensed in the electrical power fields. The sale reflected GE's policy of emphasizing high-profit areas of manufacture, service, and defense outside Japan's targeted areas here. In addition, GE acquired the power and prestige of the highly profitable National Broadcasting Company. The trade press observed that all this fit well with the plans of GE management, who between 1981 and 1986 had closed 73 facilities and 30 manufacturing plants, cut employment of over 132,000 American workers, and sold off 232 businesses or product lines while acquiring 338. Jack Welsh, GE's current Chairman, well deserves the nickname "Neutron Jack," which is familiarly applied to him by the press and the thousands of American workers who have been "nuked" by his managerial savagery.

CONCLUSION

The tragic result of the fraudulently induced *Matsushita* heresy in the Supreme Court is the message it gives to the trading nations of the world. Indeed, Japan's successful abrogation of U.S. trade law has led to many emulations by the newly industrialized countries of Asia. The message was loud and clear:

- If you want an industrial sector in America, simply copy the rapacious trade scheme set forth in the record evidence on file in the *Matsushita* case.
- Exploit the revolving door of political appointees in and out of the U.S. government.
- Be generous with the "lobbyists" and "experts" when they solicit you, and retain leading public relations firms to promote your dumping venture as a project to benefit American consumers.

- Be generous in your contributions to American think tanks, which are expert at rationalizing unfair trade tactics.

- Read Pat Choate's *Agents of Influence* (1990) and Clyde V. Prestowitz's *Trading Places: How We Allowed Japan to Take the Lead* (1988). These excellent works provide an accurate overview of America's systemic weaknesses in government.

- Last and most important, invest in lobbyists who are well known for their influence in the U.S. trade establishment.

NOTES

1. The Sherman Act and the Antidumping Act of 1916 overlap to a degree and are complementary one to the other. The Sherman Act requires a "contract, combination or conspiracy" in restraint of trade. The Antidumping Act of 1916 does not. The latter can be breached by a single company or companies not necessarily combining or conspiring with another and requires evidence of a specific "intent to injure."

2. These were successful antitrust treble-damage actions in which customers of heavy electrical equipment alleged and proved that General Electric, Westinghouse, and some twenty-five other manufacturers had conspired to fix prices and allocate markets for practically all equipment utilized in the generation, transmission, and distribution of electricity in the United States. A court that handled *that* famous litigation was well equipped, we believed, to handle the Zenith case.

3. NUE was a successor to the pioneer Emerson radio company.

4. See details of the "settlement" in Appendix VII at original pp. 37–41. Zenith and other industry members' efforts to attack the settlement were unsuccessful. The courts avoided having to review the massive fix by alluding to the power of the executive branch "to settle claims."

5. For example, in 1906 during the high tariff era in America, Mr. Gary of the infamous Steel Trust defended its notorious predatory dumping activities in foreign markets: "Of course we are pressing this export business because we want a place to put our goods, as it so materially affects the employment of our labor and also because it so materially affects our balance of trade. . . . We want to bring all the foreign money we can into this country." *Iron Age,* April 1906, p. 1324.

6. See Jacob Viner, *Dumping: A Problem in International Trade* (1966), pp. 80–93.

7. Rule 57 of the Federal Rules of Civil Procedure.

8. 63 Texas L.R. 1 (1984).

9. Transcript of the oral argument in the Supreme Court at pp. 20–21.

10. The Supreme Court had accurately defined "conspiracy" in a number of antitrust cases throughout the decades, beginning in 1893, as "a combination of two or more persons, by concerted action to accomplish a criminal or unlawful purpose or some purpose not itself criminal or unlawful, by criminal or unlawful means." *Pettibone v. United States,* 148 U.S. 197, 203 (1893); *Duplex Printing Press Co. v. Deering,* 254 U.S. 443, 465–466 (1921); *Truax v. Corrigan,* 257 U.S. 312, 327 (1921).

11. Transcript of the oral argument in the Supreme Court at p. 7.

12.   Stevens was a well-known and respected antitrust scholar and lawyer at the time he was appointed to the Court by President Ford.

13.   Transcript of the oral argument in the Supreme Court at p. 47.

14.   Ibid.

15.   These decrees were entered in civil proceedings by consent of RCA to avoid a public trial with all the embarrassing evidence that would have reached the press. The 1958 consent decree was entered after RCA had pleaded nolo contendere (unwilling to contest) in a companion criminal case in which it had been indicted for criminal violations of the antitrust laws.

16.   A Salomon Brothers analyst observed, "G.E. is a giant in the diagnostic-imaging market and it sounds as if they're going to be a bigger and more formidable giant."

Afterword

Few, if any, of the trading nations of the world have not engaged at some time in predatory dumping. Regarding the United States, Jacob Viner states: "Export dumping on a continued and systematic scale was a common practice of American manufacturers since at least the late eighties of the last century."[1] Indeed, the predatory dumping tactics of our infamous trusts and combinations on would-be competitors were condemned throughout the world. Even England, which has often been praised as a champion of free trade, was not above predatory dumping at times. Before World War I, American predatory dumping gave rise "in foreign countries to more vigorous protest and to more countervailing legislation than the export dumping of any other country."[2] Canada passed the first general antidumping law in 1904, directing it primarily at the American predatory dumping schemes. Other nations soon followed. In the United States, the Antidumping Act of 1916 was passed to counter the predatory dumping of Germany's chemical *Kartell* and to guard against other nations' predatory dumping. Japan enforces its antidumping law vigorously where a few foreign products are allowed to be imported. Of course, many manufactured products in important industries are not allowed to be imported. As we have seen, Zenith was totally blocked from importing into Japan.

When viewed against history, it is interesting to observe that the predatory dumping scheme of the Japanese cartel, which has now been sanctioned by a Supreme Court vote of 5-to-4, replicates an unfair trade practice that was well known and universally outlawed almost a century ago. When the Supreme Court's blunder in legalizing this universally condemned trade practice is recognized by the public and the Congress, a proper legislative remedy will become apparent. The gaping hole blasted in the Sherman Act and its companion Antidumping Act of 1916 by the Supreme Court must be repaired in the public interest.

No American industry can survive, however efficient and productive, if it is targeted by a foreign cartel practicing the predatory dumping scheme that is now sanctioned by a divided Supreme Court. Two-way free trade in international commercial relations with America must be restored in place of the unfair predation of our vital industries and their workers by foreign cartels. As Adam Smith, the father of economics, wrote in 1776:

The obvious and simple system of natural liberty establishes itself of its own accord. Every man, *as long as he does not violate the laws of justice,* [must be] left perfectly free to pursue his own interest his own way, and to bring both his industry and capital into competition with those of any other man or order of men.[3]

Justice is defined as fairness and fair play. In free trade, as in any competitive contest, the discipline of fairness and fair play is essential. Without that enforced discipline, "contracts, combinations, and conspiracies in restraint of trade" quickly arise to seek unfair advantages, restrain free trade, and attempt to monopolize. "Play fair" is the clear commandment in our antidumping, countervailing duty, and antitrust laws. No amount of sophistry and rationalization, however brilliantly spun into impressively abstruse legal and economic theories, can validly excuse violations of that commandment.

Tragically, hundreds of thousands of manufacturing and related jobs have been moved from America to foreign soil as a result of inexcusable law enforcement failures and corrupt influences. By the end of the 1980s, over forty American factory complexes manufacturing consumer electronics products in the United States had been forced to close as a result of the cartel's lawless, predatory assault. Many of the world's leading pioneers in the field had thus been put out of business or taken over by cartel members, a tragedy incredibly promoted by our own faithless servants in government. By 1992, a badly wounded Zenith was the sole survivor of the perfidious assault. But Zenith, despite its famous low-cost efficiency, faced continuing losses. The cunningly promoted assault, now sanctioned by the Supreme Court, finally drove

Zenith to move television manufacturing to Mexico in a desperate effort to remain alive.

The American public must again be awakened as it was in the 1880s, when cries for reform created the Sherman Act and provided a disciplined free trade that was protected against industrial gangs whose tyranny destroyed competition and restrained trade. Failure to act will continue to permit the erosion of America's great industrial base and the loss of its vital jobs. The country may well slide into the status of a formerly great industrial nation controlled by foreign interests.

When scholarly historians in the distant future review this era and the tactics employed by the government and cartel lawyers in the *Matsushita* case, they may be reminded of what the historian Edward Gibbon wrote in his eighteenth-century classic, *The History of the Decline and Fall of the Roman Empire:*

but in the decline of Roman jurisprudence, the ordinary promotion of lawyers was pregnant with mischief and disgrace. The noble art, which had once been preserved as the sacred inheritance of the patricians, was fallen into the hands of freedmen and plebians, who, with cunning rather than skill, exercised a sordid and pernicious trade. Some of them . . . [prepared] a harvest of gain for themselves or their brethren. Others, recluse in their chambers, maintained the gravity of legal professors, but furnishing a rich client with subtleties to confound the plainest truth, and with arguments to colour the most unjustifiable pretensions.[4]

NOTES

1.   Jacob Viner, *Dumping: A Problem in International Trade* (1966), pp. 80–93.
2.   Ibid.
3.   Adam Smith, *An Inquiry into the Nature and Causes of the Wealth of Nations* ([1776] 1937), Vol. 1, Book 1, Chapter 9.
4.   Edward Gibbon, *The History of the Decline and Fall of the Roman Empire* (1909), Vol. 2, p. 185.

Appendices

Appendix I
Sherman Antitrust Act

"SHERMAN ANTITRUST ACT
July 2, 1890
Ch. 647, 26 Stat. 209

"An Act to protect trade and commerce against unlawful restraints and monopolies.

"Be it enacted by the Senate and House of Representatives of the United States of America in Congress assembled, [1.1]
"SEC. 1. Every contract, combination in the form of trust or otherwise, or conspiracy, in restraint of trade or commerce among the several States, or with foreign nations, is hereby declared to be illegal. [1.2] Every person who shall make any such contract or engage in any such combination or conspiracy, shall be deemed guilty of a misdemeanor, and, on conviction thereof, shall be punished by fine not exceeding five thousand dollars, or by imprisonment not exceeding one year, or by both said punishments, in the discretion of the court. [1.3]
"SEC. 2. Every person who shall monopolize, or attempt to monopolize, or combine or conspire with any other person or persons, to monopolize any part of the trade or commerce among the several States, or with foreign nations, shall be deemed guilty of a misdemeanor, and, on conviction thereof, shall be punished by fine not exceeding five thousand dollars, or by imprisonment not exceeding one year, or by both said punishments, in the discretion of the court.
"SEC. 3. Every contract, combination in form of trust or otherwise, or conspiracy, in restraint of trade or commerce in any Territory of the United States or of the District of Columbia, or in restraint of trade or commerce between any such Territory and another, or between any such Territory or Territories and any State or States or the District of Columbia, or with foreign nations, is hereby declared illegal. Every person who shall make any such contract or engage in any such combination or conspiracy, shall be deemed guilty of a misdemeanor, and, on conviction thereof, shall be punished by fine not exceeding five thousand dollars, or

---

[1.1] The language "That this Act may be cited as the 'Sherman Act'" was added by the Hart-Scott-Rodino Antitrust Improvements Act of 1976, Pub. L. No. 94-435, §305(a), 90 Stat. 1397.
[1.2] Section 1 of the Sherman Act was amended by the Miller-Tydings Act of 1937, ch. 690, tit. VIII, 50 Stat. 693, which inserted two provisos between the two original sentences of the Sherman Act, permitting resale price maintenance by owners of trademarked goods where state fair-trade laws authorized such contracts. This statute was subsequently repealed by the Consumer Goods Pricing Act of 1975, Pub. L. No. 94-145, 89 Stat. 801.
[1.3] Sections 1, 2 and 3 of the Sherman Act were first amended to increase the criminal penalties from $5,000 to $50,000 by the Act of July 7, 1955, ch. 281, 60 Stat. 282. These sections have recently been further amended by section 3 of the Antitrust Procedures and Penalties Act of 1974, Pub. L. No. 93-528, §3, 88 Stat. 1708, which increased the offenses from misdemeanors to felonies, increased the maximum fine to $1 million for corporations and $100,000 for any other person, and increased the maximum term of imprisonment to three years.

47

by imprisonment not exceeding one year, or by both said punishments, in the discretion of the court.

"SEC. 4.   The several circuit courts [1.4] of the United States are hereby invested with jurisdiction to prevent and restrain violations of this act; and it shall be the duty of the several district attorneys of the United States, [1.5] in their respective districts, under the direction of the Attorney General, to institute proceedings in equity to prevent and restrain such violations.   Such proceedings may be by way of petition setting forth the case and praying that such violation shall be enjoined or otherwise prohibited.   When the parties complained of shall have been duly notified of such petition the court shall proceed, as soon as may be, to the hearing and determination of the case; and pending such petition and before final decree, the court may at any time make such temporary restraining order or prohibition as shall be deemed just in the premises.

"SEC. 5.   Whenever it shall appear to the court before which any proceeding under section four of this act may be pending, that the ends of justice require that other parties should be brought before the court, the court may cause them to be summoned, whether they reside in the district in which the court is held or not; and subpoenas to that end may be served in any district by the marshal thereof.

"SEC. 6.   Any property owned under any contract or by any combination, or pursuant to any conspircy (and being the subject thereof) mentioned in section one of this act, and being in the course of transportation from one State to another, or to a foreign country, shall be forfeited to the United States, and may be seized and condemned by like proceedings as those provided by law for the forfeiture, seizure, and condemnation of property imported into the United States contrary to law.

"SEC. 7.   Any person who shall be injured in his business or property by any other person or corporation by reason of anything forbidden or declared to be unlawful by this act, may sue therefor in any circuit court of the United States in the district in which the defendant resides or is found, without respect to the amount of controversy, and shall recover three fold the damages by him sustained, and the costs of suit, including a reasonable attorney's fee. [1.6]

"SEC. 8. [1.7] That the word "person," or "persons," wherever used in this act shall be deemed to include corporations and associations existing under or authorized by the laws of either the United States, the laws of any of the Territories, the laws of any State, or the laws of any foreign country."

[1.4]   By the Act of March 3, 191, ch. 231, §291, 36 Stat. 1167, jurisdiction in cases arising under the Sherman Act was vested in the district courts, instead of the circuit courts, of the United States.
[1.5]   By the Act of June 25, 1948, ch. 646, §1, 62 Stat. 909, effective September 1, 1948, the title "United States attorneys" was substituted for "district attorneys of the United States."
[1.6]   Repealed by the Act of July 7, 1955, ch. 283, §3, 69 Stat. 283. Original section 7 had been reenacted with some modifications as section 4 of the Clayton Act of 1914, ch. 323, §4, 38 Stat. 731, 15 U.S.C. §15 (1970).
[1.7]   Present section 7."

Appendix II
Judge Leahy's Opinion in
Zenith Radio Corp. v. Radio Corp. of America

**ZENITH RADIO CORP. v. RADIO CORP.
OF AMERICA et al.**

Clv. A. No. 1098.

United States District Court
D. Delaware.

June 13, 1952.

———•———

Arthur G. Connolly, Wilmington, Del., Willis H. Taylor, Jr., and R. Morton Adams, of Pennie, Edmonds, Morton, Barrows & Taylor, New York City, Burton K. Wheeler and George F. Hirmon, Washington, D. C., Irving Herriott and Francis W. Crotty, Chicago, Ill., Thomas Reddy, Washington, D. C., for plaintiff.

Caleb S. Layton, of Richards, Layton & Finger, Wilmington, Del., Stephen H. Philbin, of Fish, Richardson & Neave, John T. Cahill and John W. Nields, of Cahill, Gordon, Zachry and Reindel, William H. Davis and Brian Forrow, New York City, for defendant Radio Corp. of America.

William Prickett, Wilmington, Del., John E. F. Wood and Henry R. Ashton, of Fish, Richardson & Neave, New York City, for defendant Western Electric Co., Inc.

John J. Morris, Jr., of Hering, Morris, James & Hitchens, Wilmington, Del., Albert C. Bickford and Thomas Thacher, of Simpson, Thacher & Bartlett, New York City, for defendant General Electric Co.

LEAHY, Chief Judge.

This is an action for judgment that defendants' pooled patents be declared unenforceable against plaintiff. Defendants counterclaimed charging infringement on specific patents. In 1946 plaintiff was a licensee under defendants' patents. Plaintiff brought its first declaratory judgment suit and this particular action came at issue. Then, after the license had expired plaintiff brought its second and the present suit. A statement is made that a motion will come later to consolidate.[1] The second complaint, substantially similar to the first, recites that the license has ended.

The action here is by Zenith Radio Corporation against Radio Corporation of America, Western Electric Company, Incorporated, and General Electric Company.[2] Zenith filed its complaints seeking a declaratory judgment of non-infringement, invalidity, and unenforceability of defendants' patents. Defendants—RCA, WE and GE—counterclaimed on infringement of 40 specific patents.[3] Although some of the patents involved are concerned with television receivers using cathode ray tubes, RCA brought another action in Chicago in 1948 alleging infringement because of manufacture and sale of cathode ray tubes for television receivers. The action was brought against Zenith, plaintiff here, and its subsidiary, Rauland Corporation. To that action plaintiff here plead invalidity and non-infringement, and it also raised the same issue of unenforceability because of misuse.

The complaint alleges pooling of thousands of patents and a blanket assertion against Zenith for infringement. The vital allegation, for present purposes, is that none of the pooled patents "can be validly asserted against plaintiff as infringed by plaintiff's radio apparatus." The justiciable controversy asserted is broad and without limitation. Plaintiff wants to know whether the manufacture and sale by it of its radio apparatus constitutes infringement of any valid patent rights owned by defendants; and whether any of defendants may in any way use their patents to interfere with the continuance of plaintiff's business.

---

1. Plaintiff's reason for filing the case at bar was the lurking defect in the first action, i. e., as licensee, plaintiff may have been estopped to challenge validity and hence there would have been no justiciable controversy between the par-

2. In the matter at bar, defendants American Telephone and Telegraph Company, Bell Telephone Laboratories, Inc. and Westinghouse Electric Corporation are outside the jurisdiction of this court.

3. 24 patents are specified by RCA; 10

As stated, defendants RCA, GE and WE filed answers and counterclaims.[4] The existence of a justiciable controversy is admitted with respect to the 40 identified patents. Plaintiff's reply denies infringement, charges invalidity, and claims the specified patents are unenforceable for the reasons stated; in fact, it is charged *all* of defendants' patents were acquired "as part of a plan and conspiracy to dominate and monopolize in violation of the antitrust laws". As a result, says plaintiff, by virtue of unlawful monopoly and practices, defendants are abusing the privileges of the patent system and therefore they should be barred from enforcement of their patents.

Much pretrial discovery has occurred as well as many pretrial conferences. Defendants utilized interrogatories in order to require plaintiff to particularize the allegations of invalidity. Answers to these have been made. Plaintiff has asked for the right to inspect certain writings relating to the origin and history of the inventions. I allowed this inspection by order of May 7, 1951. Defendants have stated that it will take many more months before they will be able to collect the remainder of these particular documents. It is planned depositions will follow the disposition of the questions raised by the interrogatories. The latest group of interrogatories, the ones which become pertinent for discussion at this time, will be described later.

One of the major problems for decision is the parties are apart on the frame of reference—plaintiff seeks to go back to 1919 at the time of the formation of RCA in order to show an original conspiracy, among the defendants, to illegally pool patents and to show, also, divisions of territories as well as divisions of use.

The present matter originally arose by a blanket objection on the part of defendants to plaintiff's interrogatories. These interrogatories are voluminous. They run to 166 printed pages, comprising 419 numbered interrogatories; and, by looking at the independent paragraphs, it may be said that some 1,185 separate queries have been

put. For example, RCA claims that interrogatory 356 asked for a total of more than one million items respecting defendants' patents, many of which have expired and have nothing to do with the patents in suit. In short, the interrogatories seek, in detail, the business, management and affairs of more than 20 corporations over a period of 30 years. After a pretrial discussion on the problems surrounding the questions raised by the interrogatories, defendants filed a motion under Fed. Rules Civ.Proc. rule 42(b), 28 U.S.C. and asked for an order granting a separate trial of the issues of validity and infringement of the patents specified in the counterclaim.

A pretrial conference was noted, at which time an attempt—it was hoped—would be made to limit the issues. Plaintiff's position is that defendants' motion is premature for the reason that a pretrial conference directed to a determination of the issues to be tried should not be had until all discovery is completed. Plaintiff objects to the attempt on the part of defendants to limit the issues to the apparatus alleged to infringe in the counterclaim.

One of the questions which must be met is whether defendants, having been brought into court, can say they charge plaintiff with an infringement of 40 patents, and whether that is the issue raised by the declaratory judgment suit; or whether plaintiff can say it has the right during pretrial discovery procedures to go back 30 years in order to demonstrate misuse or violation of the antitrust laws in order to establish defendants' inability to charge infringement, not only as to the 40 patents mentioned, but also as to some 10,000 patents which are owned by all defendants.

[1-4] The nature of plaintiff's proposed interrogatories may be found by succinct exposition. Interrogatories 1 through 196, for example, are concerned with ancient agreements entered into before 1923. Interrogatories 197 through 308 cover the period from 1925 to the consent decree of 1932 (which will be explained later). Interrogatories 309 through 354 deal with

---

4. As noted, the other defendants, A T & T, BL and Westinghouse, have not accepted the invitation to appear in these proceedings.

other consent decrees and certain activities pursuant to those decrees through 1935. All the interrogatories are, in the main, concerned with radio broadcasting, and international radio telegraph traffic. In this connection, interrogatories 341–43 call for all contracts and documents relating to the negotiation of all contracts and the identification of all personnel engaged in the negotiation of such contracts with respect to the transmission of wireless messages by RCA between the United States and Poland, Argentina, Chile, Brazil, Belgium, China, Czechoslovakia, The Dutch West Indies, The States of the Levant Under French Mandate, Italy, Indo-China, Japan, Liberia, The Netherlands, The Dutch East Indies, Portugal, Surinam, Siam, Spain, Sweden, Costa Rica, Turkey, Russia, Venezuela, Australia, Germany, France, Bolivia, Canada, Cuba, Switzerland, Territory of Hawaii, The Fiji Islands and Tahiti. With respect to interrogatories 355 through 419, they are addressed to patents but they make no mention of the patents in suit; instead they relate to all patents ever owned or licensed by RCA. I have no intention of going through all of the 419 interrogatories[5] with their 1,185 subdivisions and discussing them in detail.[6] The 166 pages of interrogatories, while put, I believe, in good faith by plaintiff's counsel, nevertheless, I have concluded, to permit them to be used would be to expand this case by a length and breadth of oppressive detail which the courts, if not in the past, should refuse to countenance.[7]

I shall refer to substantial portions of the record taken at the pretrial conferences. The matter to be determined is of much

5. Post-argument, plaintiff urged the application of Caldwell-Clements, Inc. v. McGraw-Hill Publishing Co., Inc., S.D.N.Y., 12 F.R.D. 531. That authority has been studied at length, but I shall not pause to distinguish it, on its facts, from the matter at bar.

6. F.R. 33 does not sanction oppression by interrogatories. Many courts have struck interrogatories less burdensome than these here present. E. g., Hercules Powder Co. v. Rohm & Haas Co., D.C.Del, 3 F.R.D. 328; Porter v. Montaldo's, D.C., 71 F.Supp. 372; Aktiebolaget Vargos v. Clark, D.C., 8 F.R.D. 635; Tivoli Realty, Inc. v. Paramount Pictures, Inc., D.C.Del, 10 F.R.D. 201; Dipson Theatres, Inc. v. Buffalo Theatres, Inc., D.C., 8 F.R.D. 86; Cinema Amusements, Inc. v. Loew's Inc., D.C. Del, 7 F.R.D. 318; Walling v. Parry, D. C., 6 F.R.D. 554; Jones v. Pennsylvania Railroad Co., D.C., 7 F.R.D. 662.

In addition, there is authority that interrogatories will be stricken if they are excessive in number. Wright v. R. & L. Market, D.C., 9 F.R.D. 539 (31 too many). Compare also the following cases decided before the effective date of the 1946 amendment to F.R. 33; Batemore, Inc. v. Standard Brands, Inc., D.C., 7 F.R.D. 455 (65 too many); Checker Cab Mfg. Corp. v. Checker Taxi Co., D. C., 2 F.R.D. 547 (79 too many); Brightwater Paper Co. v. Monadnock Paper Mills, D.C., 2 F.R.D. 547 (55 too many); Stewart-Warner Corporation v. Staley, D.C., 2 F.R.D. 199 (33 too many); New England Terminal Co. v. Graver Tank & Mfg. Corporation, D.C., 1 F.R.D. 411 (88 too many).

Again, in the absence of a strong showing of relevance a party will not be required to disclose confidential information.

Interrogatory 414 requires a complete breakdown of RCA's volume of business in dollars, net profits and royalties according to various areas of activity. This information is confidential and is not relevant at all. The interrogatory is clearly improper. Wagner Manufacturing Co. v. Cutler-Hammer, Inc., D.C., 10 F.R.D. 348; Canister Co. v. National Can Corporation, D.C.Del, 8 F.R.D. 408; Cities Service Oil Co. v. Celanese Corporation of America, D.O.Del, 10 F.R.D. 458; Hirshhorn v. Mine Safety Appliances Co., D.C., 8 F.R.D. 11; and cases there cited.

7. In the Report of the Committee of the Judicial Conference of the United States in the matter of Procedure in Antitrust Cases (p. 12), the boundaries of proper discovery in an action such as this should be established by the issues as specified at pretrial conferences. So narrowed, these issues fix the subject matter for decision. And only such matters relevant to that subject matter are valid discovery under F.R. 26–33.

GE points out that while plaintiff contends other patents and apparatus are in the case at bar, plaintiff has, in fact, commenced in this court two other actions (our C.A. 982ª and 1247) seeking vital interest to the parties, for the decision which is made now will direct the course of this large and complex litigation. Many difficult and troublesome questions arose at pretrial. For example, I attempted to have counsel give me the legal distinction between the "misuse of a patent monopoly" and a "use" which was in violation of the antitrust laws. The following occurred:

"Mr. Adams: Assuming we prove that they have just taken this blanket of patents and said to Zenith, 'We have a blanket of patents and we are going to get you. You are the only one in the industry who refuses to take our license. You are the only one that refuses to pay us a tax for the privilege of doing business.' That is what we say they say.

"Now, I would expect, if we are right about it, your Honor would also find that that mass of patents which they used as a mass was part of a scheme, was created as part of a scheme to violate the antitrust laws. Therefore your Honor would hold that they cannot enforce any of them against us and your Honor would hold that you therefore do not need to go into the questions of validity or infringement of any of them.

"The Court: It is your thesis, then, that this is what I have sometimes referred to as an *in terrorem* approach on the part of RCA?

"Mr. Adams: It certainly is, your Honor, and we think they have done exactly that, and that is what we allege in our compaint, and that is what we offer to prove, and we have asked these interrogatories in order to get the evidence.

"Now, your Honor will understand if we are right about that there is no occasion to even discuss the other side's proposition that it should be limited to particular patents. It is just off the beam. Naturally enough, sure, I can understand it. They would love to limit it to particular patents, just as they would like to get rid of the charge of antitrust violation; and they keep using the term 'misuse' as though a violation of the antitrust laws by means of patents was not a misuse of patents.

"The Court: You heard the question Mr. Nields along that line this morning and I would like your version. I would like your help because I don't get the distinction as yet between misuse as distinguished from a violation of the antitrust laws.

"Mr. Adams: I don't either, your Honor, in a sense, but what has happened is this, and I think it goes back to the very earliest of the cases, the motion picture patents case. [Motion Picture Patents Co. v. Universal Film Mfg. Co., 243 U.S. 502, 37 S. Ct. 416, 61 L.Ed. 871.] This is my own explanation of how it comes into the law.

"Whoever argued that case was confronted by the fact that the Supreme Court of the United States had 5 to 4 established a contrary doctrine in the A. B. Dick case [Henry v. A. B. Dick Co., 224 U.S. 1, 32 S.Ct. 364, 56 L.Ed. 645], namely, that a patent owner could restrict the use of his patented machine to unpatented articles supplied by and used therewith. So it was urged in the motion picture patents case that whatever the law was in the Dick case it was changed by the Clayton Act [15 U.S.C.A. § 12 et seq.], so that it now became or his conduct became illegal as a violation of the Clayton Act. What the Court said was we don't have to go into the question of whether it is a violation of the Clayton Act. We find you can't do that with a patent.

"Now, as recently as the Morton Salt case [Morton Salt Co. v. G. S. Suppiger, 314 U.S. 488, 62 S.Ct. 402, 86 L.Ed. 363]

similar declaratory relief against other patents of defendants with respect to other specific home receiver apparatus which in those actions plaintiff here alleges it is making.

The Report of the Judges' Committee to the Judicial Conference shows the concern of the judiciary with the Gargantuan proportions of present-day trials and the caveat against much of the man-

ner and techniques which have been utilized in cases decided in the past. For example, so far in my trial of the antitrust case of U. S. v. E. I. duPont de Nemours & Co., which is still active (trial started January 17, 1951 and still in process), I have, in the course of the trial, been required to write six trial opinions.

*See 78 F.Supp. 591.

the Supreme Court again had occasion to say the same thing, because in the Morton Salt case the case went to the Supreme Court as a result of a motion for summary judgment and the defendant or rather the party who owned the patent in that case urged that no summary judgment should be granted because it ought to be given an opportunity to put in evidence to show that what it was accused of doing was not a substantial restraint of competition and hence could not be a violation of the antitrust laws. The Supreme Court, however, disposed of that and said we don't need to go so far as to say it is a violation of the antitrust laws; all we have to do is to say you can't use a patent this way.

"Now, the Courts have also said, of course, that if you do go so far as to violate the antitrust laws of course there is a misuse of patents, but they have recognized that there may be acts which do not fall within the four corners of the antitrust laws which are nonetheless contrary to public policy. I think the Supreme Court has repeatedly stated that in its opinions, that it is contrary to the purpose of the patent system and it is contrary to public policy to try to use a patent so as to create a monopoly which the Patent Office never intended to give, and they have said that that public policy was so great that even the doctrine of *res adjudicata* must yield to it. So that doctrine of misuse crept in in order to establish that there may be cases which are short of a violation of the antitrust laws. I think that is why our opponents here would like to talk about it. They use it as a means of trying to limit it to something other than the violation of the antitrust laws, and yet we think and we allege that they have misused by violating the antitrust laws, as well as otherwise.

"Now, have I—

"The Court: You have very clearly explained it to me, yes.

"Mr. Adams: Now, as far as the interrogatories themselves are concerned, I think perhaps the best way to approach them as throwing light on this particular issue is for me to very briefly state what we think of as the violation of the antitrust laws and the conspiracy which we are at-

tempting to prove. I think with that in mind the interrogatories are almost self-explanatory. When we drew them up we tried to divide them into sections. We tried to give them titles. We tried to make the things flow in a very orderly way so as to fit into what we thought of as the simplest method of approaching this antitrust violation.

"Now, the story briefly, your Honor, is this: During World War I, I think it became evident to a great many people in this country that there were two dominant radio companies in the world, particularly in this country. One of them is the British and the other was the German. The Alien Property Custodian seized the German interests, not only seized them, but sold them to the Navy, I may say for an oddly small amount. That left only the British and they were in the dominant radio position. Well, under those circumstances, it occurred to the General Electric Company that radio is destined to be a great industry. Now, they then organized the Radio Corporation of America to be the dominant radio company, but under their control.

"The Court: Who are 'they'?

"Mr. Adams: The General Electric Company. Now, at that time we think that the complete plan was established and that it was a question of separate months or maybe separate years to bring it into fruition. But in any event one of the first steps was to organize RCA. I think even before that the groundwork was laid and that GE had made arrangements with the British interests to buy out their U. S. dominating position.

"In any event, as soon as GE had caused RCA to be organized it also caused RCA to buy out the British interests.

"Then what happened was that they made arrangements for domination of the world radio.

"Now, the reason that becomes important to us is two-fold. In their deals whereby they divided territory with the British and with the Germans and with the French, and later with the Dutch, in their deals whereby they divided up the entire South American territory, there were two characteristics: one of them was that this illegal division of territory and trade was cast in the guise of patent licenses. The other was that they contained provisions for a self-perpetuating funneling into a pool of patents, and mind you none of these patents was disclosed in the documents and arrangements, none of the cross license agreements and none of the funneling provisions ever had to talk about particular patents, because the scheme was set up on the basis 'You have a mass of patents, we have a mass of patents, and if a third party hasn't got a mass of patents he better go get him some and then he can get into the deal, and we will justify it all on the basis of patent licenses.'

"We say that that has permeated this scheme from the outset and continues to permeate it today.

"Gradually, I think within a very few months, A T & T was brought into it. And mind you also that in these agreements what they did is they would allocate a certain field to GE, they would allocate a certain field to A T & T, and they would allocate a certain field to RCA. Later when Westinghouse came in it got part of the field.

"The Court: What do you mean by a field?

"Mr. Adams: Well, for example, they would say to the A T & T, 'You can have telephone communication.' GE said, 'We want electronic purposes other than radio communication, but we want to be the one that makes all the apparatus for RCA.' So when Westinghouse came in they shared their so-called nonradio eletronic field with Westinghouse and they also shared the making of the radio apparatus for RCA. RCA presumably was given the field of radio communication, but then they had a little trouble distinguishing that from the telephone company field and so they limited it to telegraph instead of telephone. But it was that kind of a division, not of territory—the territorial division was international—but what we call the field of use territory was within the United States, among companies who thereby were prevented from competing. We say that some of their own operations which have been —true, by hearsay disclosed to us—re-

veal that they got into squabbles among themselves as to who got what, and they had arbitration proceedings even to fight it out, and some of the statements made in the arbitration proceedings we think are quite revealing. We think a good many of the items that we have asked for here will be revealing as to the true intent to perpetuate a vast scheme of monopoly by means of patents and by means of undisclosed patents, and that part of the scheme is to set up organizations where they could take the income from the royalties which they eventually collected from the industry to create research laboratories to create still more patents, and this, mind you, goes on forever.

"The agreements that are in existence today appear to have a termination date, but as I read them they end only if somebody wants to exercise the termination date, and a notice has to be given some three years in advance, and furthermore even under the agreements they continue to apply as long as any patent exists for which the application is now in the Patent Office.

"The Court: Didn't the Department of Justice catch all that business in its 1932 decree?

"Mr. Adams: It certainly did not, your Honor, none of it.

"The Court: Why not?

"Mr. Adams: In the first place, because we say the only charge that was made— and let me recite them briefly—one, I think the parties who owned the stock in RCA divested themselves of that kind of control of RCA, and I don't know that that continues any longer. We assume it doesn't. Another thing that happened was that they said they would give up their exclusive rights. Now, that was. for the United States and also for abroad, and I think that is the thing that the other side would point to as being the great change.

"Now, a third thing that happened was that each party recaptured enough of what had previously been granted so that it could operate under its own patents in these fields which had previously been given exclusively to the other fellow.

"Now, you would think that on the surface that that would work out to clean up the monopoly and to destroy the scheme.

"The Court: Is it your contention they outsmarted the Department of Justice?

"Mr. Adams: Yes, your Honor, and we think the Department of Justice came into this Court later and said so and wanted to reopen the decree.

"The Court: That was a matter before Judge Maris, wasn't it?

"Mr. Adams: Yes, your Honor, and I think the holding in that case was that the Department of Justice stood in the same position as a private litigant, that having made and signed a decree it could not change it later. But I point to the fact that the Department of Justice itself came in and wanted to reopen it as evidence that it found out that it had been outsmarted.

"The Court: I am sorry I used that word. I don't like to use it.

"Mr. Adams: Well, I shouldn't have myself.

"Well, we think there is a great deal going to be revealed in the answer to these interrogatories as to what happened in that Department of Justice arrangement. We have asked very pointed and specific questions so we will find out what happened. What the other side is asking your Honor to do is before anybody knows the facts to say we cannot prove that case. That is all they are asking. They want to knock that issue out of the case before they have to state any facts.

"Now, just to look at the interrogatories, the first set concerns the organization of RCA by GE. It seems obvious from what I have stated that that is the conspiracy, that is the origin of it. We want to know— in fact, we ask a very pointed question: Why did GE organize RCA?

"Then in the next set we ask inquiries concerning the acquisition of the Marconi interests by RCA. Then we ask about how did RCA happen to combine with GE and what was the deal between them. Then we ask about these combinations with the British and the French and the German companies.

"Let me add to what I said a moment ago about the significance of that to Zenith. RCA put itself in the position with these foreign deals so that it could not grant Zenith the right to export its apparatus. It could not give any license to Zenith with respect to operations in foreign countries; and, furthermore, put the world in the condition so that when Zenith exports its apparatus it butts right into another pool in the foreign countries, a pool of patents of exactly the same type as the pool we are talking about here.

"Now, these things are directly relevant to the charge that we make and to the position in which we find ourselves where they are asserting this blanket and trying to, as I say, levy a tax on us for the privilege of doing business.

"Now, I could go through the interrogatories. We come to the South American consortium. I have already referred to that. That was a flagrant manifestation, we think. Let me say this also—

"The Court: I have listened to that word for nearly a year now.

"Mr. Adams: Well, maybe I should use a more modern term, but the fact, we think, is the same, and that is that in these deals in the answers to the questions that we have asked will be found proof of their intention, their purpose, and the scheme by which they intended to carry it out and to perpetuate it.

"The Court: Mr. Adams, have I got your thesis correctly? You walk into the courtroom when you start your trial and don't go into any technical discussions of the patents at all; is that correct?

"Mr. Adams: None, none. I can imagine that we might pick out some particular phony patent of theirs just to show that it was phony. For example, Mr. Nields says why do we ask for them to tell us about the cases where they have two patents with the same claims. We think they have that information or they documented. We think that is the kind of organizations they are where they keep information like that available. If they don't know, just let them say they don't know. He talks about these million items. You know what he did with that one?

"The Court: That frightens me.

"Mr. Adams: Surely, me, too; but it is not true.

"The Court: Why isn't it?

"Mr. Adams: Number one, it is the kind of information that they have already tabulated. That is the way they do their business. Again, if they don't have it, if they have a blanket of 10,000 patents and don't know what they are, just let them say so, if that is what they are asserting. But it is not that kind of a thing.

"Now, to build up the figures what he does is to slip in the word repetitious. He multiplies them all by 30, because we ask for that information each year, and I suppose it has not occurred to him that he could say in one year 'Ditto for the year 1950 so and so', having given it all for the previous years.

"Now let me say a word about this order of trial. I am conscious of the fact that we would like to dispose of the case as soon as we can, and Mr. Nieids has said to your Honor they would like to have the patent issues tried first and promptly. We think that the antitrust issue is the only issue that can dispose of the case. We think, as we stated to your Honor before, that even if we meet them on their patents as they have asserted in their counterclaim, and if we prove every one of them invalid and every one of them not infringed, we still have not secured the protection we started out to get, and we still have to go through the litigation on that issue. We say that being so, let us do it first.

"The Court: Well, why wouldn't you be satisfied to win your own private war? Why do you want to destroy the whole empire the defendants have created?

"Mr. Adams: That seems to us to be the only way we could get the protection, your Honor. You see, they have this mill going. The patents are popping up all the time, every week.

"The Court: In other words, you may be sued in 1953 or 1954?

"Mr. Adams: Surely, or tomorrow.

"Specifically—maybe this is completely a digression—but on the patent end of it I would say that they have not—and this is something for independent argument—they have not complied with the order of this Court to produce the information and documents that we ask for under Rule 34, and I am sure we are going to have to take depositions in order to compel them to do it, just as we are taking depositions on similar matters in the Chicago case, where we had to even go to the Court to get them to identify documents that they were withholding. We had to bring a motion to get the judge to order them to identify them, and yet they will say they want to try the case. Of course they want to try it before they give us the facts. But, as I say, that is a separate matter.

"As far as the interrogatories are concerned, we put in a lot of time trying to make them pertinent, clear, to bring out the evidence which we think we have to have in order to prove our case. I completely sympathize with the point of view of the Courts that when it comes to the trial of the case they don't want to be burdened with masses of evidence. We as lawyers don't want to be burdened with it, but the time to face what goes into evidence at the trial I think comes at the time when the discovery is completed. Certainly we as competent counsel are going to be able to eliminate the irrelevant material. Certainly that is our intention. But we can't unless we have it.

"Mr. Wheeler: First I want to be sure that it is clear in the mind of the Court what happened with reference to these agreements originally, because that is extremely important in order to understand the fundamental principles of why and how they set up this monopoly.

"The Court: What year are you starting with?

"Mr. Wheeler: 1919. On October 17, 1919, they organized RCA. On October 17 of 1919 the agreement was made with the American Marconi, and on November 21 RCA and the British Marconi entered into an agreement whereby RCA granted an exclusive license to all of the patents that she had, and British Marconi granted a license to RCA to all the patents that they had. Thereby they excluded RCA from manufacturing or selling in England, because if RCA did attempt to do it they would be not only violating—they would not only be violating the British patent, but they would also be violating their own patents, and the same thing would occur with the British Marconi. They could not come to the United States and manufacture or sell, manufacture with just their own patents. They completely excluded and divided up the territory in that way.

"Now, then, the same thing happened, the identical same thing happened with the French agreement. When they talk about what relation has the communications agreements with the manufacture of radio sets, I call your attention to the fact that the same agreement that they made with the British Marconi included everything for radio purposes. That included devices and everything of the kind. So that the one agreement included and set up the pool and was part of the very pool as it was originally organized, and it is the very part of the pool at the present time. That is why they accumulated the 10,000 patents that they have in this pool.

"Now, when they got these agreements then they gave—subsequently after criticism in Congress of the policy of RCA then they started to give licenses, and Zenith was the first one to take a license. At the outset I think they charged something like —I know of five per cent, because that came up before a Committee of Congress and was criticized in Congress because of the amount that they charged, and they not only charged on their particular patents, but they charged also on the cabinet that went over in which the radio was encompassed. In that agreement they limited Zenith and all of the rest of the companies in the United States to the United States alone. Why did they do that? Because of the fact that they had given the exclusive licenses to the British, to the French, to the Dutch, and to the Germans, and so they said to every American 'You cannot go in and set up a manufacturing plant, nor can you sell your products in Great Britain,

Germany, France, Czechoslovakia, Holland, or any other country'.

"We talk about the bad effects of a high tariff. Here was an instrument that excluded, definitely excluded every manufacturer in this country from extending its business, and also excluded any German company, any French company, or any English company from coming over here and selling its products in the United States.

"The Court: How about Tahiti and the Fiji Islands?

"Mr. Wheeler: The Fiji Islands, let me say, was part and parcel of the pool, was part and parcel of the pool that was set up, and the Fiji Islands is not important excepting in the sense that it was part and parcel of the whole scheme that was set up.

"Then they came along until 1932. They say they purged themselves in 1932. Well, first of all, they did not purge themselves in 1932. First of all, they did not purge themselves because of the fact that in their contracts they did not purge themselves of a division of the field, nor did they purge themselves of the division of the territories; and where they set up and divided the territories the Supreme Court of the United States has repeatedly held that a division of the territories is a violation of the Sherman Anti-Trust Act [15 U.S.C.A. §§ 1–7, 15 note], likewise a division of the field. They did not purge themselves of that.

"Secondly, these contracts co⁻ 1in funneling provisions which the Supreme Court of the United States has repeatedly said, and Judge Knox has said in the Carboloy case [U. S. v. General Electric Co., D.C., 80 F.Supp. 989], that where there is a funneling provision in an industry that dominates that industry, and that is of itself a violation of the Sherman Anti-Trust Act; and in the Transrap case [Transparent Wrap-Machine Corp. v. Stokes & Smith Co., 329 U.S. 637, 67 S.Ct. 610, 91 L.Ed. 563] Justice Douglas said that in that particular case where it was a small matter and they did not dominate the industry, he said that was not a violation of the Sherman Anti-Trust Act per se, but he was explicit to say that where it was an industry that was dominated it would be a violation of the Sherman Anti-Trust Act.

"As Mr. Adams has pointed out, every one of these contracts contains that funneling provision, and they contain that funneling provision even after the agreements expire.

"Secondly, they did not purge themselves of prohibiting the American companies from engaging in the manufacture of radio sets in England or in these other countries.

*   *   *   *   *   *

"Mr. Bickford: I thought I might say a few words to you, your Honor, addressing myself to what I consider is the purpose of this visit here, and that is to try to find some way of making this case manageable from the standpoint of the Court and the parties.

"As stated by our friends the plaintiffs the case is simply unmanageable and we are striving to make it manageable and bring it down to the issues that are real, the real issues between the parties, and that is simply the enforcement or threatened enforcement of patents which the plaintiff claims will injure it in its business if they were enforced against it. That is the real issue.

"The defense that has been pleaded and which I assume they will try to prove is, as Mr. Adams has stated, a simple misuse of patents. He says by violation of the antitrust laws, but it is a misuse defense no matter what he calls it by addition and explanation as to what the acts were which he claims constitute the misuse.

"Now, if any misuse still exists it must be apparent from evidence of things that are actually going on—and you should not have to go back to 1919 and probe the intentions and purposes of the parties in making agreements such as Senator Wheeler has outlined to you—if there is any contemporaneous misuse it must be apparent now. It does not make any difference whether that amounts to the stature of an antitrust violation or whether it is something less than that. But even if the antitrust violation were in the case and if it were an antitrust defense as distinguished from something else, that alone does not assist the plaintiff nor assist the Court or us in arriving at the solution that we are here to try to arrive at.

An antitrust violation *per se* in private litigation is not a defense to a case. That antitrust violation must be directly related to some injury or threatened injury to the plaintiff. Accordingly, purported defenses of this kind have been held inapplicable in actions of private litigation where contractual obligations, statutory remedies, and so forth, are in issue.

"The notable case is Bruce's Juices case [Bruce's Juices, Inc., v. American Can Co., 330 U.S. 743, 67 S.Ct. 1015, 91 L.Ed. 1219] decided last year or the year before in the Supreme Court where an antitrust violation was held to be no defense on a contract right. Here the antitrust violation with respect to patents not in issue can have no relevancy to the complaint that the plaintiff has made here in a declaratory judgment action that certain patents are being threatened to be enforced against them and in his reply by saying that the defendants should be enjoined from asserting these patents.

"So I reach the point of why we are here. We are here, as I said before, to try to cut down the preparation for trial and the issues in the trial and the evidence in the trial to that which is really relevant to the cause of action pleaded in the complaint and the reply and to the patents which the defendants have concededly threatened against the plaintiff.

"Now, concretely, your Honor, if you will look at the index to these interrogatories it is not until Interrogatory 355, appearing on page 6 of the index, under item XVIII, that anything subsequent to 1932 is sought. Everything on page 1 is 1919. Everything on page 2 is 1919. Everything on page 3 is 1921. On page 4 item VIII is 1920; item IX is 1925; item X is 1923. On the next page item XI is 1926; item XII is 1929; item XIII is 1930; and the first four items on page 6 are 1932, and 1932 is the time when the consent decree in the Government's suit which alleged all these things with which the earlier interrogatories are concerned was entered into. I don't think that it lies well in the mouths of the plaintiffs here to say that the Government was overreached in that suit. The Government was represented by four different Assistant Attorneys General; John Lord O'Brien,

Judge Olney, who was special counsel brought in from California, and two others over a long period of time; and Judge Nields in this Court has held that that decree was entered into in the public interest. The mere fact that subsequent Assistant Attorney General Thurman Arnold made the bald statement in this Court that it was not in the public interest can have no effect here where the Court before whom that remark was made said that that was insufficient to establish the fact.

"So I ask your Honor at least in this situation here where we are now to strike out those interrogatories prior to 1932 which I have indicated, and, as I say, to me it doesn't make any difference whether they say this is a misuse defense because of an antitrust violation or a misuse defense because of some other thing. I still think that for the purposes of this hearing we should be able to arrive at a sensible cutting down of the work involved and that we have proposed to your Honor a sensible plan and a workable solution such as Mr. Nields has outlined to you and such as I have added to in the striking out of these interrogatories at least down to 1932.

"The Court: Mr. Adams, our discussion this morning has been about the interrogatories. At least that has been the basis of our approach. We have left that field to a certain extent. During the recess I checked with the Clerk and you have no motion before me for trial of the separate issue under Rule 42. Do you propose to file one?

"Mr. Adams: Well, it had not occurred to us, your Honor. I did not know that that kind of issue was being presented.

"The Court: I thought you wanted that tried first. I thought you and Senator Wheeler suggested—

"Mr. Adams: What we were saying, your Honor, was the other side had this morning said to your Honor that they wanted the patent issue tried first and were asking for a date, and we were countering that by saying it seemed to us that that was out of order, that the real thing to be tried first was the other issue because that was the one which would dispose of the case.

"The Court: Then maybe, Mr. Nields, you ought to file a motion for separate trial of the patent issues?

"Mr. Nields: Perhaps I should.

"The Court: Then I could make definitive ruling on that.

"Mr. Nields: We would be happy to file that.

"The Court: And it may be that that would need be disposed of either for or against you before I come to the interrogatory question.

"Mr. Adams: Well, if I may say a word on that, it would seem to us that whichever aspects of the case were tried first it would still have to go ahead with discovery on the other issues, because, as we said, even if we establish—

"The Court: Not necessarily. If we try the patent question first and I find the 40 patents which the defendants apparently rely on to be invalid, you go home happy.

"Mr. Adams: No, we don't, your Honor.

"The Court: No?

"Mr. Adams: No. That is just the point.

"The Court: What do you want, perpetual insurance against litigation? Very few people have the ability to enjoy that attribute.

"Mr. Adams: That is the case we pose to your Honor, is that here is an illegal scheme being used against us and we want relief from it. As I said to your Honor, it is not merely the patents that they pick out. We like any other manufacturer change our apparatus. We are in business. They have patents, as I say, that come up every week. Some of them come from these foreign agreements, some out of their mutual agreements here in this country, and some of them out of the laboratories they maintain out of the millions of dollars they collect from the industry under this scheme, and I mean it, millions every year which they use to perpetuate the scheme. Now, we are not content to just take their say-so on a particular patent that they choose to assert against us by counterclaim. We want freedom in our business from this vicious scheme, and I say the way we will be happy is when they purge themselves of it."

Defendants' position was made clear by the following:

"The Court: Mr. Nields, clear this for me, please. Is your frame of reference as far as this litigation is concerned 1932–1951 or December 1946–1951?

"Mr. Nields: My frame of reference from the point of view of time within which these misuse issues could be relevant, if they existed, is December, 1946, to the present, but I go back a year of that to give leeway and perspective to whatever facts there may be. From the point of view of the pool, however, I don't think that plaintiff is concerned with anything except what existed as of the day the suit was brought. That is not a distinction with much of a difference, but it is just that you either have a pool or you don't and it is either legal or it is not legal. So that from the standpoint of RCA's ownership from the point of view of time I think the Court is concerned only with the state of facts as of the date the suit was brought and thereafter, but I also wish to point out in that connection that when we give the plaintiff and when the plaintiff chooses to give you the facts with respect to our ownership of patents as of the date the suit was brought, to all intents and purposes the plaintiff automatically goes back to 1932, because the major agreements of which the plaintiff complains were entered into as a result of the consent decree entered by this Court in 1932. So that from the point of view of this great conspiracy to pool patents and all of that, my very I hope accurately worked out logic still lets the plaintiff go back to 1932.

*   *   *   *   *   *

"We calculate that if we assume that the alleged patent pool had a total of 5,000 patents for each of these 30 odd years the interrogatory would call for 150,000 separate items, most of which would deal with patents which have long since expired and with patents that have nothing to do with home receivers.

"Interrogatory 356 asks for a total of over one million additional items with respect to patents, most of which are long

since dead, and most of which have nothing to do with home receivers.

"The Court: Do I understand you correctly? You say one million items?

"Mr. Nields: One million items it would call for. Now, these items, your Honor, would be duplicates in a large part, because he is asking for us to list across the board the patents we owned each year, so that there would not be one million separate answers, there would be a million separate items, many of which would be repetitious. But that would give your Honor, in my judgment, a fair view of the scope of these interrogatories, and of the lengths to which plaintiff seeks to go, as we respectfully submit, to no useful end so far as establishing the enforceability of the patents in suit is concerned.

"In addition, if your Honor would turn to Interrogatory 418 and 419 you will find that we are asked to list all the patents owned by A T & T, Western Electric, Bell Laboratories, GE and Westinghouse which contain a claim or claims identical or substantially identical to the claim or claims contained in any other patent owned by any of these companies. We would not know how to go about answering such an interrogatory. If there are identical claims apparently the Patent Office didn't find them. The patents are equally available to the plaintiff, and who is to say what claims are substantially identical, and to what end?

"I would like to have your Honor keep in mind that it is not any part of the purpose of this pretrial to limit any issue with respect to the validity and infringement of the patents in suit. If the plaintiff can establish or thinks he can establish that they have claims identical with each other or what not, that is completely another matter. This is a part of this large alleged misuse defense, which we respectfully submit has sprawled all over the place, way beyond what this Court or the defendants should be called upon to cope with.

"It is not feasible to go through all the interrogatories and all the subdivisions and show why they are improper, and it is not my understanding that that is what your Honor wishes to discuss at this time. We do wish to emphasize through the interrogatories, however, that the scope of the misuse defense should and must drastically be cut down, (a), in point of time to our use of patents since January 1, 1946, and our ownership of patents as of the date the suit was brought, in each case home receiver patents, and from the point of view of the subject matter to our use of the patents in suit and our ownership of home receiver patents."

The plaintiff stated its position at length:

"Mr. Adams: At the outset let me say, your Honor, that it seems to me the real difficulty we are having here is that the defendants are really trying to avoid meeting what we consider the issue tendered by Zenith in its complaint. In re-reading the discussion we had before I was very much struck by the statement which was made when we pointed out that there was no surprise at all to the other side that that was the issue tendered. I in fact quoted one of the counsel as accusing us of having brought that issue into the Court, and then I think it was Mr. Nields interrupted and said 'Yes, but it is our purpose to knock that issue out of the case.'

"Now, that seems to me to be a very fair statement of what they are attempting to do. The issue is in their case and what they are attempting to do by a pretrial conference is to knock it out of the case so that they won't have to meet it. Now, I think they do that by the familiar device of anybody that is accused of unethical conduct, and that is they try to divide it into a lot of parts and say as to that part you see nothing wrong and as to this part you see nothing wrong, and they try to avoid facing the whole picture. It seems to me that is the essence of it.

"They keep talking about limiting it to patents. It is not the kind of controversy we tendered, and let me try to crystallize it in this way:

"If we are right about this and if the evidence which we have asked them to produce and which I might say is wholly in their possession, not ours, I would imagine that the Court would enter a judgment substantially as follows:

"Zenith is a radio manufacturer in the business of making and selling broadcast apparatus in this country and abroad. The defendants have asserted and threatened to assert against Zenith and its jobbers and dealers and customers a mass of undisclosed patents.

"The Court: Is that accurate?

"Mr. Adams: That is what we allege and I believe it is true. That is specifically alleged in the complaint.

"The Court: In other words, you say we go beyond the limitation of 40 patents as suggested?

"Mr. Adams: The 40 patents have nothing to do with it, your Honor. That is a separate controversy."

1. The crux of the matter is RCA is confronted with an investigation into its entire corporate life since 1919 to the present, circa 1952. It is, indeed, difficult to appreciate such an investigation when the main problem for determination calls for a consideration of a misuse defense to specific patents (40) which defendants seek to enforce against specific apparatus. The theory urged by plaintiff, I conclude, should not be a precedent, for no corporation of any size would be able to sue an infringer unless it opened up its corporate files from the date of its charter existence and was made to answer searching and minute inquiries about transactions which could be ancient. From the paper record, I see RCA was organized in 1919, at the request of the Government, so as to provide an American transoceanic radio communication service. In order to accomplish this, various patent licenses and cross-licenses were necessary. This brought into the picture A T & T, WE, GE and others. All of this administration has been examined in the past by various Governmental Agencies. This brings into focus facts of critical significance. For example, RCA's patent position was investigated, as is found in a report of the Federal Trade Commission (December 1, 1923), which resulted in a complaint filed by FTC on January 24, 1924; FTC dismissed the complaint on December 19, 1928. In fact, in this Court the United States brought an action against RCA, A T & T,

WE, GE and others (our No. 793 in Equity). That litigation resulted in a consent decree, filed November 21, 1932. Supplemental consent decrees were entered on May 25, 1934 and June 2, 1935. Then, on July 31, 1942, Assistant Attorney General Thurman Arnold moved, in this Court, to vacate those decrees without prejudice to the Government. Circuit Judge Maris was especially assigned to determine the application. He refused the Government's position and left the consent decrees undisturbed. See United States v. Radio Corporation of America, D.C.Del., 46 F.Supp. 654. An appeal was taken to the Supreme Court, but the appeal was dismissed on the motion of the then Solicitor General. See 318 U.S. 796, 63 S.Ct. 851, 87 L.Ed. 1161. It is to be noted that 45 of the 50 agreements which plaintiff wishes to bring, once again, before this Court, for legal examination, were in existence before the consent decrees. All 50 agreements were known at the time of the Government's motion to vacate the consent decrees.[8]

[5,6]. 2. Ownership of patents—regardless of number—does not constitute misuse. Counsel have drawn the distinction between a misuse defense and issues which arise in an antitrust action. A misuse is a specific defense to an infringement suit, or an action for royalties, and the considerations there involved are different from those in the orthodox antitrust suit. The law of misuse involves unlawful extension of the lawful monopoly conferred by the patent. Morton Salt Co., v. G. S. Suppiger Co., 314 U.S. 488, 62 S.Ct. 402, 86 L.Ed. 363; B. B. Chemical Co. v. Ellis, 314 U.S. 495, 62 S.Ct. 406, 86 L.Ed. 367; Mercoid Corp. v. Mid-Continent Investment Co., 320 U.S. 661, 64 S.Ct. 268, 88 L.Ed. 376; Mercoid Corp. v. Minneapolis Honeywell Regulator Co., 320 U.S. 680, 64 S.Ct. 278, 88 L.Ed. 396. There are differences between a government antitrust suit; a private one, and a misuse defense as to the holder of a patent. These differences are not merely doctrinal. They depend upon the facts of

each case. No private litigant has the right to take upon himself the role of the Attorney General in the enforcement of the antitrust laws. If such was fact, the legal life of the judiciary would be intolerable.

[7] It is the Attorney General who applies for enforcement of the antitrust laws in the public interest. When the private litigant sues, he must establish his right to redress for the particular wrong done to him.

[8] The task, here, is made easier by a concession made by RCA. It is willing to have the scope of the issues include its use of the patents in suit since 1946 with respect to any apparatus in controversy. It makes this concession, however, without prejudice to its position that its use of such patents with respect to apparatus other than the home receivers is irrelevant. The issues, then, with respect to RCA's ownership of patents should be confined to all license agreements for the manufacture and sale of home receivers under home receiver patents as of January 1946. This, of course, also covers any discussion of ownership of home receiver patents.

[9] 3. Misuse issues are different from validity and infringement. The documentary proof is different. I conclude a trial of both issues would impose a heavier burden than one has the right to ask of any single judge.[9] This present complex litigation comes precisely within the authorization of F.R. 42(b). In fact, in infringement suits of lesser complexity antitrust or misuse issues have been separated for trial apart from patent issues. For example, in Container Co. v. Carpenter Container Corp., D.C.Del., 9 F.R.D. 89, 91–2, my colleague Judge Rodney said:

> "It seems clear that the issues, proof and witnesses in the anti-trust claim are substantially different from and foreign to the issues, proof and witnesses in the patent infringement claim.
> * * *

---

8. Plaintiff's desire to probe into the corporate history of defendants shows it is not until page 126 of the 166 pages of interrogatories plaintiff reaches the mat-

ter which was argued before and decided by Judge Maris.

9. See fn. 7, supra.

"Rule 42(b) justifies separation to further convenience or avoid prejudice. Since it appears from the record that the issues, proof and witnesses will be substantially different for each claim, the convenience of both the parties and the court will be served by separation. Insofar as Container and Continental are concerned, counsel trying the anti-trust claim will not try the patent infringement claim, and Continental is not concerned as a party with the latter claim. Convenience to these parties would thus be served by separation for this reason also."[10]

[10] As I remarked in Canister v. National Can Corp., D.C., 3 F.R.D. 279, at page 280:

"I am fully aware that issues should not be tried piecemeal unless necessary to prevent undue delay or to promote the interest of justice. Rickenbacher Transp. Inc. v. Pennsylvania R. Co., D.C., 3 F.R.D. 202. But, in the case at bar, it is obvious the interest of the parties will best be served by ascertaining if we have a contract upon which an action may be maintained before we direct our attention to the large issues of breach and damages. Hence, defendant's motion under Rule 42(b) is granted."

In Hazeltine Research, Inc. v. Automatic Radio Mfg. Co., Inc., D.C., 77 F.Supp. 493, 498, Hazeltine sued Automatic Radio on a patent licensing agreement for royalties and an accounting. Automatic interposed various "misuse" defenses. Both parties moved for summary judgment. Hazeltine's motion was granted. Automatic Radio's was denied. The District Court said:

"Defendant's most substantial defense is that set forth in paragraph 10 of its answer to the complaint: 'That the plaintiff, in an illegal endeavor to eliminate all competition and secure an unlawful monopoly in violation of the antitrust laws of the United States, acquired the approximately 425 United States letters patent and the approximately 120 applications for United States letters patent * * * from its employees * * *' (and from other corporations and persons). If the issue of whether a monopoly existed was relevant to this case, I would not decide the question on summary procedure, but would require that it be submitted for trial. However, in this case, it is not necessary to decide the question. The license contract involved here is entirely separate from any action of plaintiff to eliminate competition or engage in a monopoly. Assuming, arguendo, it was engaged in an unlawful scheme to maintain a monopoly, the contract here was not an integral part of it. The contract in suit did not help to promote any monopoly plaintiff had established. See American Refining Co. v. Gasoline Products Co., Tex.Civ. App., 294 S.W. 967. The contract here is complete in itself and enforceable without reference to any contract of the plaintiff with others or of any illegal activity on the part of plaintiff in violation of the anti-trust laws. It being itself a valid contract, collateral activities of the plaintiff do not render it unenforceable. Gasoline Products Co., Inc. v. Champlin Refining Co., D.C., 46 F.2d 511, 514; Walker on Patents, Vol. II, Sec. 409, p. 1590, and cases; cf. Radio Corporation of America v. Majestic Distributors, D.C., 53 F.2d 641. (Compare United Shoe Machinery Co. v. La Chapelle, 212 Mass. 467, 99 N.E. 289, Ann.Cas. 1913D, 715, where the contract in issue was held to be an essential means of maintaining the illegal monopoly of plaintiff.) The defense that plaintiff is using its patents to force others, not the defendant, to assign to plaintiff rights under their patents is rejected on the same ground."

The Court of Appeals affirmed, 1 Cir., 176 F.2d 799, 805-6. Chief Judge Magruder wrote:

10. Compare Society of European Stage Authors v. WCAU Broadcasting Co., D. C., 35 F.Supp. 460; Hall Laboratories, 106 F.Supp.—37

Inc. v. National Aluminate Corp., D.C. Del., 95 F.Supp. 323; Stewart-Warner Corp. v. Staley, D.C., 2 F.R.D. 448, 447.

" * * * From Automatic's somewhat nebulous generalizations, it is difficult to ascertain the precise nature of its argument on this score, though it does concede that the mere accumulation of patents, however great in number, is not illegal per se. Cf. Transparent-Wrap Machine Corp. v. Stokes & Smith Co., 1947, 329 U.S. 637, 67 S.Ct. 610, 91 L.Ed. 563. * * *

" * * * The district court correctly ruled that, even assuming arguendo that Hazeltine was engaged in an unlawful scheme to maintain a monopoly, the license contract in suit was not an integral part of it; that the license agreement, being itself a valid contract, will not be rendered unenforceable by collateral activities of the plaintiff in violation of the anti-trust laws. 2 Restatement, Contracts § 519 (1932); 5 Williston, Contracts § 1661, Rev.Ed.1937; 2 Walker, Patents § 409, Deller Ed., 1937. See, also, Bruce's Juices, Inc., v. American Can Co., 1947, 330 U.S. 743, 754, 755–756, 67 S.Ct. 1015, 91 L.Ed. 1219. Morton Salt Co. v. G. S. Suppiger Co., 1942, 314 U.S. 488, 62 S.Ct. 402, 86 L.Ed. 363, is no authority for the proposition that a contract action for patent royalties may be bogged down by the defendant into a complicated and protracted trial of asserted collateral infractions of the anti-trust laws.\ And see Radio Corporation of America v. Majestic Distributors, D.C. Conn., 1931, 53 F.2d 641, 642–643, and cases cited."

The Supreme Court affirmed (6 to 2) in Automatic Radio Manufacturing Co., Inc. v. Hazeltine Research, Inc., 1950, 339 U.S. 827, 70 S.Ct. 894, 898, 94 L.Ed. 1312. This is the most recent decision on misuse of patents. Mr. Justice Minton indicated the Court's view:

"The mere accumulation of patents, no matter how many, is not in and of itself illegal. See Transparent-Wrap Machine Corp. v. Stokes & Smith Co., 329 U.S. 637, 67 S.Ct. 610, 91 L.Ed. 563. And this record simply does not support incendiary, yet vague, charges that respondent uses its accumulation of patents 'for the exaction of tribute'

and collects royalties 'by means of the overpowering threat of disastrous litigation.' We cannot say that payment of royalties according to an agreed percentage of the licensee's sales is unreasonable. Sound business judgment could indicate that such payment represents the most convenient method of fixing the business value of the privileges granted by the licensing agreement. We are not unmindful that convenience cannot justify an extension of the monopoly of the patent. See, e. g., Mercoid Corp. v. Mid-Continent Investment Co., 320 U.S. 661, 666, 64 S.Ct. 268, 271, 88 L.Ed. 376; B. B. Chemical Co. v. Ellis, 314 U.S. 495, 498, 62 S.Ct. 406, 408, 86 L.Ed. 367. But as we have already indicated, there is in this royalty provision no inherent extension of the monopoly of the patent. * * *" 339 U.S. 834, 70 S.Ct. 898.

There is no attempt, here, to prevent appropriate discovery either as to the patent issues or misuse issues. RCA has said—I think correctly—it has at no time requested the court to enforce any patent, at least, not until after the misuse issues have been tried. Plaintiff's authorities that courts will not enforce patents until misuse issues have been disposed of, do not meet the question as to the order in which courts may try the various issues presented. Enforcement of a patent concerns the misuse defense—this means, there is discretion in the court as to the order in which validity, infringement or enforceability may be tried. Plaintiff's argument rests on the proposition that there is a continuing and unpurged misuse. RCA's position is it has never sought to prevent plaintiff from having the opportunity to establish this defense. This certainly was my understanding of what occurred at the pretrial conferences. The fact is RCA is ready and willing to meet any relevant misuse defense at the proper time and as to the specific patents it claims are infringed. This means it is willing to have the present scope of the misuse defense encompass RCA's administration of its patents, i. e., licensing, litigation or other assertion of all patents with respect to home receivers.

Moreover, RCA does not seek to avoid the issue testing the legality of a "patent pool" or various techniques of "funneling".

As to the *use* or *misuse* of RCA's patents, I conclude plaintiff's defense to the counterclaim charge of infringement should not be concerned with activities prior to 1946. The earliest date upon which RCA rests to enforce its specific patents in suit is December 1946. Nevertheless, I think it necessary to go back to January 1946 to determine if there is any unpurged misuse of patents by virtue of RCA's administration of its patent rights prior to December 1946.

[11] The blueprint for the progress of this litigation should take the following course: Matters relating to patents not in controversy and to the use of patents which are not in suit are not relevant prior to 1946. Consequently, a pretrial order should exclude proof of matters not relating to what has been done with the patents since plaintiff determined not to renew its license in 1946. A declaration may be made, here, with respect to the patents which defendants allege to be valid and infringed by plaintiff's specified apparatus, but no other patents and apparatus should be embraced in any judgment to be entered. The trial should proceed on the basis of an examination of the questions involving infringement and validity and, if counsel will make proper application, the issues involving misuse may follow immediately thereafter; and, before any order is entered directing that any of defendants' 40 patents should be enforced by the injunctive process, or by a finding for damages.

Appendix III
Deposition of Cornelius Mayer

[p. 458] At 10 a.m. on Tuesday, 16th August, 1955, proceedings under the Notice were resumed as follows:

CORNELIUS MAYER, of Lagernstrasse 2, Kloten, Zurich, Switzerland, being recalled and examined on the part of the Cross-Claimants, doth depose and say as follows:—

By THE COMMISSIONER: Are there any preliminary statements to be made before we begin?

By Mr McCONNELL: I want to make this statement for the record. I am proceeding with Commander Mayer in an effort to expedite these proceedings, and I am going to proceed as rapidly with the examination as I can. However, it is perfectly obvious that there are physical limitations on the examination of this witness imposed by the fact that we have now several hundred documents at least produced from the witness's files which I have had no chance to examine. The main purpose of producing the files—or one of the main purposes, at least—at this time was this. I believe I made a statement when the witness was here before that it was impossible to conduct any further examination of this witness until I had the documents from his files. As I say, I am going to try in every way that I know as an advocate to continue as rapidly as physically possible with the examination, but there may be times in the examination when I will want to suspend for 20 or 30 minutes to examine the documents with which to go forward. We will try and work it out so that some of us are looking at the files and extracting what we think are the most pertinent for my use in the examination of the witness whilst I continue the examination, but I cannot do the impossible. All I can do is the best that I can do.

DIRECT EXAMINATION by Mr McCONNELL contd.

Q Commander Mayer, you have been sworn as a witness already in this case, have you not?

A Yes.

[p. 459] Q Since we were here, what have you done with reference to getting together your files in order to produce them at this hearing?

A I received word from Mr Nields that the Chicago Court had ordered that you should have my files in London, so I proceeded to put them into cases and ship them there. I think we got word on Saturday, and we have been shipping the cases since then.

Q Have you gotten together and shipped back to London all the files which you took from London to Zurich last April or any other time?

A Yes.

Q   There has been no editing or no calling-out of those files, so far as
    you are concerned?
A   No. We have not shipped our library, which I also took from Lon-
    don, but we have shipped all the files that I have.
Q   What is the library that you refer to?
A   Technical printed publications, books and periodicals.
Q   Well, so that the record may be clear, we never made any request
    on you to ship the library, but aside from technical treatises, all
    your correspondence and all your agreement files have been
    returned for this hearing?
A   Yes.
Q   Now, when you were here before and I examined you, as I recall
    your testimony you told me that R.C.A. was not a member of this
    patent pool here in London. Is not that what you testified to?
A   That is right.
Q   Did you have some negotiations on that subject with a man by the
    name of Shoenberg?
A   On the subject of our licence agreement with E.M.I.
Q   Did you have some negotiations with him on the subject of
    whether or not your patents were in the pool or were to be in the
    pool?
A   No negotiations, no. We told him at the beginning R.C.A. could
    not participate in any pool arrangement.
Q   "at the beginning." What time was that?
[p. 460] A   I do not exactly remember, but it would be about two years before
    our agreement, I would say; about 1948.
Q   You told him in 1948 that you could not possibly be a member of
    the pool. Is that what you told him?
A   Could not participate in any pool arrangement.
Q   Now, where did you tell him this?
A   In London.
Q   What part of the year 1948?
A   I do not remember exactly. It would have been when our negotia-
    tions first started.
Q   As a matter of fact, your patents were in the pool at that time,
    were they not?
A   The patents under which E.M.I. had the right to grant licences.
    The pre-1945 patents were patents which E.M.I. could grant
    licences under.
Q   They had a right to sub-license those patents?
A   Right.
Q   And they had sub-licensed them by licensing the pool to make
    sub-licences; is that right?
A   I believe they included the R.C.A. patents in the patents which

they put into the pool.

Q   Now, you do not mean to tell me you just believe that. You know that, do you not?

A   Yes, but I did not do it, so I say that is what I understand.

Q   You know that your patents were in the pool, that all your patents up to 1945 were in the pool, do you not?

A   I know that E.M.I. included them in what they put into the pool.

Q   So they were in the pool, were they not?

A   Yes.

Q   And you got royalties from the pool—I mean you, R.C.A., got royalties from the pool—on all the 1945 patents, the patents issued prior to 1945. Is that not so?

A   When are you speaking of?

[p. 461] Q   I am speaking of the time in 1948 when you say you had this talk.

A   No, we had not got an agreement with E.M.I. as I recall at that time.

Q   You were getting royalties from the pool on the 1945 patents?

A   No, Sir.

Q   You were not? Are you certain about that?

A   Not as I recall.

Q   Not as you recall. I am asking you whether you are certain.

A   I say not as I recall. We started to get royalties after our agreement with E.M.I.

Q   You had an agreement which covered the 1945 patents, did you not? I will withdraw the question.

A   Our agreement with E.M.I. was 1950, I think.

Q   E.M.I. had an agreement which came through Marconi Wireless Telegraph Company, did they not, on all your patents prior to 1945?

A   That may be.

Q   Is that not a fact?

A   I do not recall.

Q   You just cannot remember that?

A   No.

Q   You knew it in 1948?

A   Whatever it is, it is in the documents that you have.

Q   I do not care about the documents.

A   There need not be any question about whether it is or it is not.

Q   You told me the last time you were here as a witness that you were not in the pool. That was your testimony under oath, that you were not in the pool.

A   R.C.A. is not in the pool.

Q   We will find out about that.

A Some of the patents of R.C.A. under which E.M.I. had a right to grant licences were included by E.M.I. in the pool, not by R.C.A.

Q And they were included in the pool in 1948, were they not?

A Yes.

[p. 462] Q And they were included in 1945?

A I am not familiar with the older pool arrangements.

Q You were handling them, were you not?

A No.

Q You had negotiations with Shoenberg about it, did you not?

A I did not join R.C.A. until 1947.

Q I know when you joined R.C.A.

A So I was not handling it.

Q After you joined R.C.A., you had negotiations with Mr Shoenberg about whether or not you would be in this pool, did you not?

A Not "whether or not." We told them we could not be.

Q You got into it, did you not?

A We did not get in it.

Q All right; we will find out about that.

By Mr McCONNELL: I ask that this document be marked for identification Mayer Exhibit 5 as of this date.

(The reporter marked the document Mayer Exhibit 5, 16/8/55)

Q I show you a document marked for identification Mayer Exhibit 5, which purports to be a letter under date the 17th November, 1949, to Dr B.E. Shackelford in New York on the subject of E.M.I. Licensing purporting to be signed by C.G. Mayer with copies to Shackelford and Dr. Jolliffe, and I ask you to look at that document and tell us whether or not you wrote it and sent it to the addressee thereof. (Document handed to the witness.)

A Yes.

Q Do you want to look at it and familiarise yourself with it, or are you familiar with it?

A No, I am not.

Q I want to ask you some questions about it.

A It is too long for me to read just now. If you ask the questions, perhaps I can refer to it, if necessary.

Q All right; you can. You said in this letter: "I visited Shoenberg at his place in the country near Eastbourne where he is spending

[p. 463] this week. Dale Harris was also there, and we proceeded to discuss a number of points connected with the proposed agreements." When did you have that meeting with Shoenberg, can you tell us now, approximately? This letter is under date the 17th November, 1949.

A It would have been some time shortly previous to that letter, I would say.

Q Who is Dale Harris?

A An assistant to Shoenberg.

Q And who was Shoenberg?

A Shoenberg was at that time, I think, Director of Research at E.M.I.

Q Now, you say on page 2: "By virtue of his claim for exclusivity under the pre-1945 R.C.A. British patents and in order to safeguard the operation of the pool, Shoenberg previously had asked for the conditions mentioned in paragraph 16 of ref. (a)." Now, what was Mr Shoenberg's claim for exclusivity under the pre-1945 R.C.A. British patents?

A His claim came out of the earlier agreement, E.M.I./R.C.A. agreement—I believe it was the 1935 agreement—under which he claimed that because of our later agreement with Marconi E.M.I. would obtain exclusivity for the R.C.A. patents. We did not agree with him at all at that time or at any other time. That was a bone of contention in our negotiations with E.M.I. as outlined, I think, in the memorandum.

Q Is the 1935 agreement that you refer to the agreement between E.M.I. and R.C.A.?

A Yes. Now, in the last testimony you showed me an agreement which I did not recognise, and since thinking about it that is obviously the agreement of which I had a printed form, but I did not recognise your photostatic copy and I did not read it at the time. It was one of your exhibits on the last occasion.

Q Is that Sarnoff Exhibit 4.Z.10 for identification? (Document handed to the witness.)

[p. 464]

A Yes, I believe this is the agreement. I have not had a chance to compare this with what I have seen, the printed document, but it is the memorandum of 1935.

Q The memorandum of 1935 referred as follows: "The R.C.A.–Marconi agreement of November 21st, 1919, as amended by agreements dated February 10th and October 14th, 1921, and by a certain waiver letter dated May 24th, 1934, with which agreement as so amended and modified the parties are familiar, remains in full force." Now, is that not the agreement which Mr. Shoenberg asserted as giving him the exclusive right to sub-license all R.C.A. patents up until 1945?

A That agreement, as I remember, does not give him the exclusive right for R.C.A. British patents, but arising out of that agreement, and because of our agreement with Marconi, he claimed that he would have the exclusive right to grant licences under R.C.A. patents.

Q I do not know whether you listened to my previous question or not. I will ask the reporter to read it out.

(The reporter read the previous question)

Q   (Continued): I will amend that. Is not the agreement referred to, as amended by agreements dated February 10th and October 14th, 1921, the R.C.A.–Marconi agreement of November 21st, 1919, the agreement to which Mr. Shoenberg referred to as that under which he was basing his rights of his claim to the R.C.A. patents?

A   I believe it was the 1919 agreement.

Q   It was the 1919 agreement, was it not?

A   I think so.

Q   And this agreement acknowledges that those agreements, including the agreement of November 21st, 1919, remain in full force. Is that so?

A   Yes.

Q   And that was the position that Mr Shoenberg took with reference to R.C.A. patents which had been issued prior to 1945, that he had the right to license them regardless of any new agreement. Is not that right?

A   Yes.

[p. 465] Q   As a matter of fact, Mr Shoenberg did put those patents in this pool, did he not?

A   Yes.

Q   And he collected royalties on account of those patents through the pool, did he not?

A   Yes.

Q   And he paid those royalties to R.C.A., did he not, or a part of them?

A   Not that I know of.

Q   You did not think you ever got any royalties from the pool?

A   I do not know. You are talking about at that time, are you not?

Q   Yes.

A   I am talking of later. At that time, I do not know.

Q   You do not know whether R.C.A. got any royalties or not in 1945?

A   I do not know.

[p. 466] Q   Do you know whether they got any royalties from the pool after you came here in 1947?

A   No. We got royalties from the 1950 agreement with E.M.I.

Q   I did not ask you anything about 1950; I asked you about 1947.

A   I do not know.

Q   You do not know whether you got any in 1947. Do you know whether you got any in 1948?

A   No.

Q   You do not know?

A   No.

Q Did you have anything to do with collecting royalties at that time?

A. No.

Q Did you ever have anything to do with collecting royalties for R.C.A.?

A No.

Q In this letter on page 3 you say: "Shoenberg said that they could not agree to license foreign manufacturers to import into Great Britain, and he says this on the basis of his claim for exclusivity." That claim for exclusivity he based upon the 1919 Marconi agreement; is that right?

A Yes.

Q And he made that claim to you at this meeting, did he, at which Dale Harris was present?

A Yes. I think I reported that.

Q And you are reporting it back to New York.

A Yes.

Q Did he tell you that?

A I do not understand what you mean.

Q Did he make that statement to you, that they would not agree to license foreign manufacturers to import into Great Britain?

A If it is in there, that is what he said.

Q Regardless of whether it is in here or not, did he tell it to you? I am asking you now.

[p. 467] A Yes. What I am saying is I do not recall at this stage exactly what he said but I rely on my written report.

Q You would not send something to New York that was not true, would you?

A No.

Q You further said that Mr Shoenberg said: "In their view it would mean the immediate collapse of the whole licensing pool and of the revenue derived from it." Did he tell you that?

A Yes.

Q You also say that he said: "They have always had to refuse to license imports from anywhere." Did he make that statement to you?

A Yes.

Q You also say that he said: "British manufacturers are extremely jealous of importers, and although the Patent Act does not specifically support this attitude, there is no doubt that the old idea of patents giving a monopoly continues today and confirms a basis of a general licensing policy in Britain of using patents to build up trade and keep out cut-throat competition from foreign countries where prices may be cheaper." Did he make that statement to you?

A   Yes.

Q   And you retaled [*sic*] that on to New York?

A   Yes. He did not make that statement; that was an observation of my own. May I just go back a moment there? I think you have said the whole paragraph and asked me whether he made that statement.

Q   All right. I do not care what the fact is, just so I get the fact. I am not asking these questions to try to force you into a position; I want to know what the fact is. Is this your view and not his, or are you quoting him?

A   I am making an observation of what I found in Britain.

Q   And that observation has no reference to anything that Mr Shoenberg told you in the conversation?

[p. 468]   A   Yes, but I would not say that is exactly what he said.

Q   You are not quoting him?

A   No, I am not quoting him.

Q   Are you giving to Mr Shackelford the benefit of a substance report of what he said?

A   Yes.

Q   So this was discussed, then, in your conversation with Mr. Shoenberg out in the country at Eastbourne?

A   That last observation?

Q   Yes.

A   I would say No.

Q   That is just something that you threw in of your own, is it?

A   I think so.

Q   Are you sure about it?

A   Yes.

Q   This was written in 1949. You had been here two years. Does this summarise your observation of British manufacturers during your two years observation here in England?

A   That summarises, I should say, the attitude of some of the people who licensed under their patents in Britain.

Q   In other words, you had gotten that attitude from your licensees; is that right?

A   No, I had not.

Q   Where did you get it?

A   Out of my head, my observations.

Q   You do not get things just out of your head. Where did you get it? What observation did you make?

A   It did come out of my head.

Q   You just invented it; is that right?

A   You are twisting it when you say I invented it.

Q   Whether I am twisting it or not, I want to find out what you based that observation on.

A   I based it, I would say, on the agreement which the pool put out.

[p. 469]   Q   In other words, reading their own agreement, that was the only logical conclusion you, as a layman, could come to, was it not?

A   Yes.

Q   That that was their attitude?

A   Yes.

Q   Did anybody in the pool tell you that they wanted to keep out cut-throat competition?

A   No.

Q   You just inferred that from the way they acted; is that it?

A   Not from the way they acted; from what I observed and what I read.

Q   You had to see them do something or say something, did you not?

A   No. I could read what was in their document.

Q   Did you read anything else except their pooling agreement?

A   No.

Q   That was enough to satisfy you that this statement was true; is that right?

A   Yes.

Q   On page 4 of this letter you state: "With regard to the conditions of Article II, it is doubtful whether they are met by the licences granted by the pool, and E.M.I. would be unwilling to commit themselves to the conditions for anything more than the licences under R.C.A.'s British patents which would be made available by the proposed sub-licensing agreement. In carrying out the conditions, therefore, it would probably be necessary to have a separate licensing form for the R.C.A. patents (which, according to E.M.I., would not include those for which they claim they already have licensing rights)." What were the conditions of Article II to which you refer?

A   I would need to look at it.

Q   Where would you look? Do you want to look at this letter?

A   No. Article II of whatever it is.

Q   What is it?

A   I do not know.

Q   Look at the letter and tell us, if you can, what you are referring

[p. 470]   to. That is the question.

A   That is Article II of the draft sub-licensing agreement, which states that "E.M.I. shall not restrict any licensee, by written agreement or otherwise, in regard to exports or imports to or from any country."

Q   That is Article II of the pool sub-licensing agreement; is that it?

A   No; of the R.C.A.–E.M.I. draft sub-licensing agreement.

Q   And that was in conflict with the provision of the pool licensing agreement?

A   Yes.

Q   And you are so reporting it?

A   Yes.

Q   What did you suggest to do to remedy that situation?

A   I think what you read out. It was not entirely my suggestion, but it was one by our law department, which suggested we put forward a separate document under which E.M.I. would grant R.C.A. licences in Britain, in which document there would be no restrictions of any kind. It would be non-exclusive, non-discriminatory and non-restrictive.

Q   And those agreements only covered the patents subsequent to 1945; is that right?

A   It was R.C.A.'s contention that what Shoenberg claimed, exclusivity on the pre-1945 patents, was not so.

Q   You knew he was claiming that?

A   Yes.

Q   I am reading to you from a document which has been marked here Luscombe Exhibit 5, which was a letter from Mr Topham of the 1st July, 1954, to Philco (Overseas) Limited, in which he says: "E.M.I. (as one of the said grantors) is in a position to offer you a licence under R.C.A.'s patents for Great Britain and Eire on inventions made after 1944, but can only offer it in accordance with enclosed form 'X.I.' (Patents on R.C.A. inventions made

[p. 471]   before 1945 are already included in your A.7 licence.)" You knew that the pool was licensing your pre-1945 patents under their standard licence form, did you not?

A   Yes, but what we contended was that—

Q   I do not care what you contended. I did not ask you the question. Just listen and answer what I ask you.

A   May I say something?

Q   No; you will answer my question.

By Judge THOMPSON: I object to the beligerant [sic] attitude of Counsel. He is trying to twist the documents. They speak for themselves, and it is unfair to the witness, and Counsel knows it.

By Mr McCONNELL: It is not unfair to the witness.

By Judge THOMPSON: The witness has got a right to complete his answers and not submit to Counsel trying to put words in his mouth. The documents speak for themselves.

By Mr McCONNELL: This witness has attempted to create an utterly false impression of the relationship of R.C.A. to this pool, and I am going to show what the truth is.

By Judge THOMPSON: Counsel is attempting to create an utterly false impression with respect to the documents and agreements, which speak for themselves, and he knows it, and his conduct is unprofessional.

By Mr McCONNELL: Any time you have any complaint of my professional conduct, there is a place where you can go, and when you get there, you will be in it, too; I will tell you that. I have a right to cross-examine this witness to get the truth, and I certainly am going to do it.

(The Reporter then read: "(Q) You knew that the pool was licensing your pre-1945 patents under their standard licence form, did you not? (A) Yes, but what we contended was that—")

A (Continued). May I be permitted to finish?

Q No. I asked you a question and you answered it.

A I did not answer it.

[p. 472] Q You said Yes, you knew it.

A My answer was not complete.

Q If you want to make something else in addition to it, make it with your own Counsel when I get through with my examination. You have answered my question.

A I would like to put on the record that it is not an answer.

Q That your answer is not true; is that what you are trying to tell us?

A No; that you prevented me from completing my answer.

Q All right; you put it on the record. Knowing that the pool was licensing your patents prior to 1945, you suggested a separate licence agreement for the patents subsequent to 1945; is that right?

A No.

Q That is not right?

A No.

Q Did you suggest a separate licence for your patents after 1945?

A The licence which we suggested was a licence under R.C.A. patents without respect to date.

Q Have you a copy of that?

A You have it, I think.

Q Do I? I do not know.

A Yes.

Q Is it in the documents which you have sent here?

A It is the Exhibit A to the R.C.A.–E.M.I. sub-licensing agreement.

Q While that is being looked for, you referred to the legal department. Did the legal department suggest this idea of this separate licensing agreement?

A I do not know where it came from.

Q You volunteered that it was something that had to do with the legal department.

A Yes.

Q Was that where you got the information?

A The legal department prepared the document.

[p. 473] Q Did they prepare it for some reason which they expressed to you in any way?

A As part of our agreement with E.M.I.

Q No other reason given for this separate agreement?

A Certainly.

Q What?

A Because R.C.A. would not be able to participate in the pool and that we would not put any restrictions on the grant of licences under R.C.A. British patents or any other patents.

Q In other words, this was so that you would not participate in the pool; is that it?

A Right.

Q You mean, by "participate in the pool," not to receive any benefits from it?

A No. We received our revenue from E.M.I.

Q You knew E.M.I. was getting the revenue from the pool, did you not?

A Yes.

Q You knew that?

A Yes.

Q In other words, you wanted to get the revenue from the pool?

A We wanted to get the revenue to which we were entitled for the grant of licences under our patents.

Q Which were granted through the pool?

A Which were granted under a document without any restrictions, using E.M.I. as an agent.

Q But you already told us that the patents prior to 1945 were licensed by E.M.I. irrespective of any such agreement.

A Yes, because E.M.I. had a right under the previous agreement to license under R.C.A. pre-1945 patents; but the agreement which R.C.A. proposed, and which you have as Exhibit A, covered all R.C.A. patents, and we were and we are willing to grant licences direct to any applicant, and he does not have to go through our agent, E.M.I. in this case.

Q   You referred to Exhibit A, which was attached and was part of the
    Fisk Exhibit 2 for identification. I ask you if that is the document
[p. 474] you are referring to. (Fisk Exhibit 2 handed to witness.)
A   This is an unsigned document. There is a conformed agreement,
    which should be your basis.
Q   You referred to that yourself.
A   Not this. I did not refer to this.

> By Judge THOMPSON: The witness did nothing of the
> kind. He referred to Exhibit A to the agreement with
> E.M.I. and you have had it for two or three months. It
> is no use trying to trick the witness into answering
> something that is based on an assumption without any
> basis.

A   (Continued): I think it is the same, but just for the sake of the
    record, the document I referred to is, of course, the conformed
    agreement.
Q   (By Mr McConnell): You think we have something else besides
    that, do you?
A   No; I think it is the same. That happens to be a photostat.
Q   Did you know that this extra licence agreement, which you desig-
    nate here as Exhibit A, was being issued to these licensees for £1?
A   Yes.
Q   £1 royalty?
A   Yes.
Q   Did you know you did not even collect the pound?
A   I am not sure. No, we did not collect the pound.
Q   And you did not get any pound from E.M.I. either, did you?
A   We got our revenue from E.M.I.
Q   You got the revenue from the pool, did you not?
A   We got the revenue from E.M.I.
Q   From the pool?
A   From E.M.I.'s income out of the pool.
Q   And you knew that all the time, did you not, that E.M.I. was get-
    ting the revenue from the pool?
A   That is right.
[p. 475] Q   You said a moment ago that you knew what the standard licence
    agreement of the pool was?
A   Yes.
Q   That provided for a schedule of royalties based upon the produc-
    tion of sets, did it not?
A   Yes.
Q   As you produced more sets, that provided that you paid more roy-
    alty; is that not right?
A   Yes.

Q That is the way your royalties were figured?

A Yes.

Q They were not figured on the basis of £1, were they?

A Whose royalties are you speaking of here? Are you speaking of the royalties which the set manufacturers in Britain pay as a result of their agreement with the pool?

Q That is right.

A Of which E.M.I. received a share?

Q Yes.

A Under our agreement with E.M.I., that 1950 agreement, we received a proportion of revenue from E.M.I.

Q You knew that the proportion of revenue which you received from E.M.I. represented the proportion of the pool revenue represented by the R.C.A. patents, did you not?

A A proportion of E.M.I.'s receipts from the pool which included some of R.C.A.'s patents.

Q Were there some excluded?

A No.

Q They were all in it, were they not?

A All R.C.A. patents were made available through that Exhibit A. The revenue derived from them went to E.M.I., and we received our share from E.M.I.

Q Let us see the other agreement. Is Mr Topham your R.C.A. agent?

A No.

Q I call your attention to the provision which is contained on page
[p. 476] 2 of Luscombe Exhibit 4, which states: "In consideration of the payment by licensee of one pound sterling (£1.0.0.), receipt of which is hereby acknowledged and of other good and valuable consideration given by the licensee as and for the compensation payable by licensee for the licence granted and agreed to be granted to licensee by E.M.I. under this agreement, no other compensation shall be payable, and no statements or reports shall be rendered by licensee under this agreement with respect to contract apparatus made and used, sold, leased or otherwise disposed of by licensee under the licence so granted and agreed to be granted." Did you know about that provision in this sub-licence?

A I do not know what you are speaking of.

Q Look at it.

A Yes.

Q You knew about that?

A I have seen this document, or I have seen a document like it.

Q They were all like that, were they not?

A Yes.

Q Is your position that this agreement licensed all of the R.C.A. patents?

A Right.

Q And it called for no royalty payments at all?

A I think except the £1 compensation.

Q That is all?

A That is all.

Q That is all you were to receive at any time for the licence to manufacture and sell under all R.C.A. patents without any restrictions; is that right?

A No.

Q That is not right?

A That is not right. Our revenue was derived under our agreement with E.M.I., the sub-licensing agreement of 1950, of which you have a copy.

[p. 477] Q You told us a moment ago, unless I completely misunderstood your testimony, that this licence was irrespective of E.M.I., completely indifferent to E.M.I., without restrictions of any kind, character or description, offered to anybody without any sort of discrimination, and offered to them for £1.

A No; I said nothing of the kind.

Q All right.

A That is an E.M.I. document.

Q That is an E.M.I. document which you prepared and submitted, a form of it, at least, with your agreement Fisk Exhibit 2, is it not? Look at it and see if it is. (Fisk Ex. 2 handed to witness.)

A I referred to the conformed agreement.

Q Compare it if you will and tell us if it is the same thing or something different.

A Why not have the right one, and then you would know. Have you got the conformed agreement there?

Q I am talking about the form of the agreement.

A (After examining exhibit): That is all right; I was looking at the wrong page. You will notice the difference under Article IV on the compensation, in which the E.M.I.–R.C.A. agreement of 1950 in Article IV, relating to compensation, says: "Monetary consideration"—and this is in connection with the Exhibit A of that agreement, which is similar to the X.1 agreement which you have been speaking of—"and terms for payment including statements or reports shall be determined and set forth herein by E.M.I."

Q The only additional compensation that you were to receive aside from the £1 came through the pool, did it not?

A It came from E.M.I.

Q Through the pool?

A   In E.M.I.'s share of receipts from the pool.

By Mr McCONNELL: Let us have a recess.

(A short recess was then taken)

[p. 478]   Q   Returning to this Luscombe Exhibit 4 for identification, which under Article III designates the compensation for the use of all of the R.C.A. patents as £1, after E.M.I. as your agent had executed that agreement, was it your contention that you were entitled to any further royalty for the use of those patents?

A   This is not an agreement between R.C.A. and the licensee.

Q   You have said that several times. E.M.I. was your licensing agent in England, was it not?

A   Yes.

Q   E.M.I. was the agent for R.C.A.?

A   Yes.

Q   Is it your contention that E.M.I. as your agent had no authority to license your patents in England?

A   They had the authority granted to them under our sub-licence agreement with E.M.I.

Q   Did they have authority to execute *that* agreement?

A   They did.

Q   And they executed it as your agent, did they not?

A   They executed it as themselves, so far as I am aware.

Q   It covered all your patents, you just told us.

A   It covers whatever it says in the document.

Q   Did it cover all your patents, or just some of them?

A   I will see what it says. What it says is: "E.M.I. hereby grants and agrees to grant to the licensee a non-exclusive licence under R.C.A.'s patents in Great Britain," etc. Then, if you look under "Definitions" and see what it says about patents, it says: "'Patents' means all letters patent and rights by licence or otherwise to or under letters patent. 'Patents of R.C.A.' means all patents on inventions made by Radio Corporation of America, except patents on inventions made before January 1, 1945, and granted in the name of M.W.T."

Q   Now can you answer my question, whether it included all your patents in England?

A   Except patents on inventions made before January 1, 1945, and granted in the name of M.W.T.

[p. 479]   Q   Then it did not include all your patents?

A   That is right.

Q   It only covered those patents which were after 1945; is that not right?

A   Post-1944, yes.

Q   So that all of your patents prior to 1945 were licensed under the
    standard licence of the pool, were they not?
A   Yes.
Q   Now, as to your patents subsequent to 1945, which you say are
    licensed under *that* agreement, were you entitled to any further
    royalties, other than set forth in that agreement, from that
    licensee?
A   We were entitled to the revenue derived through the agreement
    with E.M.I.
Q   Were you entitled to any revenue from that licensee, other than
    £1, through E.M.I. or any other way?
A   I can only repeat that we were entitled to the revenue which we
    had a right to under our sub-licence agreement with E.M.I.
Q   All right. In that sub-licence agreement with E.M.I. you were enti-
    tled to whatever they got, or a share of it?
A   A share of it.
Q   And they were getting revenue through the pool on not only
    patents prior to 1945 but patents after 1945, were they not?
A   Yes, in so far as licensees had taken the X.1 agreement.
Q   That is the pool agreement?
A   No; this agreement.
Q   You were entitled to the revenue there from licensing of patents
    through the pool whether or not they signed the X.1 agreement,
    were you not?
A   Yes.
Q   It did not make a bit of difference whether they signed the X.1
    agreement or not; you were still entitled to the revenue from the
    pool?
A   Entitled to our share of what E.M.I. got from the pool.
[p. 480] Q   Do you think £1 is a fair valuation for the rights of your patents?
A   No; it does not represent that.
Q   I did not ask you what it represented; I asked you whether or not
    you thought that was a fair value.
A   The question has no meaning.
Q   Can you answer my question?
A   No, I cannot.
Q   You are not going to answer it?
A   I tell you your question has no meaning.
Q   Do you refuse to answer my question?
A   Would you like to repeat your question?
Q   Yes. (To the Reporter): Read the question to the witness, please.
        (The Reporter then read: "Do you think £1 is a fair valuation
        for the rights of your patents?")
A   No.

Q   And you would not license them for £1, would you?

A   No.

[p. 560] Q   Let us have the document. That is the one that was produced from
your files. Now, before we get into the pool agreement, you
apparently thought there was something wrong with restricting
any licensee in regard to exports or imports to or from any country, did you not?

A   Yes.

Q   You thought that might be illegal on the anti-trust laws, did you
not?

A   Yes.

Q   I call your attention to paragraph 7 of the basic pool agreement
which is marked for identification Mayer Exhibit 19, which you
have produced from your files: "Unless otherwise agreed no
licences are hereby agreed to be granted to import radio apparatus
into the United Kingdom or to deal in in the United Kingdom
imported radio apparatus or radio apparatus containing imported
component parts to an extent exceeding in value 10 per cent of the
retail list price of such radio apparatus except in each case sam-
ples and experimental models for the use of the parties hereto."
That was a restriction against the import of these sets into England, was it not?

A   By the pool, yes.

Q   And you knew the terms of that?

A   Yes.

Q   And you knew that your patents were being licensed by that pool?

A   Our patents were not.

[p. 561] Q   Your patents were not being licensed by that pool?

A   Our patents were being licensed by E.M.I. under the document
which you have as Exhibit A. It is true that some of our earlier
patents E.M.I. had certain rights under.

Q   Now, I read you this from page 2 of this agreement. I am reading
from Clause (b) on page 2 under the title "Electric and Musical
Industries Limited and its subsidiaries." (b): "that subject to the
rights, if any, which the U.S.A. Government may have in respect
of patents arising out of Government contracts then and will be
for the period from 1st January, 1953, to 31st December, 1957,
entitled to grant or procure other than to grant licences for radio
broadcast sound receivers and radio broadcast television receivers
for entertainment and education (except in the naval, military,
marine and aircraft fields) under all British patents present and
future on inventions made and conceived by the Radio Corporation of America prior to 1st January, 1945, and further entitled for

the said period to grant licences to others (except E.M.I.'s subsidiaries) under other British patents of Radio Corporation of
America by means of a document identical with Exhibit 'A'
attached hereto." You knew that was in your files?

A   Yes.

Q   And you knew the terms of it?

A   Yes.

Q   And you knew that your patents were being licensed by the pool,
did you not?

A   Some of our patents. The patents which E.M.I. had the right to
grant licences under, pre-1945 inventions. That was a non-
exclusive right that E.M.I. possessed. A licence under all R.C.A.
patents was available and is available to licensees directly from
R.C.A. under conditions of no restriction.

Q   And which you have already told us was never used to license
anyone except through the pool. Is that not right?

[p. 562]   A   We have had no licence in the home entertainment field under
that provision except those which we have made through E.M.I.

Q   Now, under this agreement you concede they were entitled to
license everything prior to 1945. Will you go further than that and
agree that the language that they are "entitled for the said period
to grant licences to others (except E.M.I.'s subsidiaries) under
other British patents of Radio Corporation of America by means
of a document identical with Exhibit 'A' attached hereto" correctly states the fact?

A   E.M.I. had the right to grant such licences?

Q   Under R.C.A. patents, yes.

A   Yes.

Q   Now, in your letter you say "Shoenberg said that they could not
agree to license foreign manufacturers to import into Great
Britain, and he says this on the basis of his claim for exclusivity.
In their view it would mean the immediate collapse of the whole
licensing pool and of the revenue derived from it. They have
always had to refuse to license imports from anywhere." Did he
make that statement to you?

A   Yes.

Q   And he made that statement to you in 1949?

A   If that is the date of that letter.

Q   The letter says on its face "17th November, 1949."

A   Yes.

[p. 604]   A   Well, Exhibit 42 gave Exhibit 46 as ref. (b), and in the paragraph
which we were speaking of earlier, the reference was paragraph 7

of this ref. (b), so perhaps the best thing would be to see what paragraph 7 of Exhibit 46 says.

Q   That is a good starting point.

A   Shall I read it, or will you?

Q   You can read it.

A   "We next discussed at some length whether the licence should be based on all sets manufactured whether a patent of the group was used or not, or whether it had to be worded in such a way that the licensee only pays if a patent is used."

Q   And that was discussed with reference to the Sherman Act, was it?

A   It goes on a little further along: "The question is whether it would be considered a breach of the Sherman Act to collect royalties whether a patent was used or not. Obviously this 'overall' basis had many advantages (as in Britain also), and clearly a lower rate could be offered if the royalty was based on total production than if on sets which only use a patent." So that was the previous occasion when you brought up the word "again."

Q   Had somebody instructed you on the obligations of the R.C.A. company under the Sherman Act with reference to that particular subject of whether royalties could be charged on a group of patents or had to be charged on a particular patent owned by R.C.A.?

A   No, I received no instructions on the matter.

Q   That was your interpretation of the Sherman Act; is that right?

A   No, I cannot say that was my interpretation of the Sherman Act, because I am not familiar in detail with the Sherman Act.

Q   Where were you getting this idea that it might be illegal under the Sherman Act to do this?

A   I suppose it was a matter of common knowledge at that time, that that was a question.

[p. 605] Q   If it was a matter of common knowledge, it was also a matter of your own knowledge at that time, was it not?

A   It was in my head, yes.

Q   You did not do anything to remedy that situation, did you?

A   I raised the question.

Q   You raised the question, but you did not do anything, and R.C.A. did not do anything, so far as you know, to remedy or to meet the question which you raised?

A   Because—

Q   Not "because." Did they do anything?

A   It is not a breach of the Sherman Act.

Q   You are going to rule on the law in this case; is that it?

By Judge THOMPSON: Counsel is forcing the witness to

rule on the law and asking utterly improper questions and asking legal questions of a layman who has no knowledge of the technical aspects of the law. He is certainly not trying to rule on the law, excepting as you are trying to force him to do it by utterly improper questions.

By Mr McCONNELL: Is that a ruling now or an objection? You know, you have been off the Bench a long time. I do not think you are ruling in this case. Mr Reporter, would you read the question to the witness again?

(The reporter read: "You raised the question, but you did not do anything, and R.C.A. did not do anything, so far as you know, to remedy or to meet the question which you raised?")

By Mr NIELDS: The witness made an answer. Could we have that?

(The reporter read: "(A) Because— (Q) Not 'because.' Did they do anything? (A) It is not a breach of the Sherman Act.")

By Mr McCONNELL: I move to strike out the witness's statement about the Sherman Act. The Court is going to determine that.

[p. 606] Q What I want to know is whether R.C.A. did anything to meet the question which you raised.

A I think to get an answer we would have to look at the further correspondence.

Q Do you know of anything which they did at the present moment?

A I think we would have to look at the further correspondence.

Q What correspondence do you want to look at?

A What followed from that letter, Exhibit No.—?

Q Let us see first whether you have to look at any further correspondence.

A What is the reference to that yellow one you have your left hand on?

Q Exhibit 42? Is that the one you want to look at? That is a letter of the 18th January, 1950.

A No. I would have to look to see which one we are talking about now.

Q We will let you look at some correspondence in the recess, but for the moment—

A In order for you to have an answer, you will have to look at the further correspondence.

Q   I do not think so. I think I can find out from you what you know about it. You say on page 2: "It seems clear from the nature of the pool licence that the licensee pays a royalty on all his receivers regardless of whether a patent is used or not." Where did you get that information?

A   From the pool document.

Q   The pool licence?

A   Yes.

Q   And you had a copy of that in your files, did you not?

A   Yes.

Q   You know, you do not have to examine any correspondence to tell me that no change was made in the pool license?

A   No.

[p. 607] Q   There has been no change in that pool licence since that date?

A   No.

Q   Which was the 18th January, 1950. Now, you made the further statement: "Consequently, E.M.I.'s receipts are not dependent on the use of an E.M.I. or R.C.A. patent by the licensee." Was that your conclusion from what you knew at the time?

A   Yes.

Q   Nothing has happened to change that, has it?

A   No.

Q   It is still the same situation?

A   Yes.

Q   Did you do anything on behalf of R.C.A. to attempt to change that situation?

A   No need to.

Q   I did not ask you whether there was any need to. I asked you whether you did anything.

A   I raised the question.

Q   You raised it with Shackelford. Did you raise it with Shoenberg?

A   I must have mentioned it to him.

Q   Do you remember whether you did or you did not?

A   Yes.

Q   You raised it?

A   Yes.

Q   He did not do anything about it, did he?

A   No.

Q   And you still went on and did business with him?

A   Yes.

Q   If you want to look at some correspondence during the recess, you can look at it, any of this correspondence that you want. I am not asking you to. That is up to you.

[p. 543] Q Mayer Bulk Exhibit 33 is interoffice correspondence relating generally to reports of the Dr. Shackelford/Straus trip. Page B is a letter from L. M. Neyhart on the letterhead of the Radio Corporation
of America, International Division, to Mr C. G. Mayer with reference to the trip reports of Shackelford and Straus. 33.C is inter-
company correspondence from Shackelford to a number of people
with reference to the trip report, and it is under date of October
20th, 1953. D is a list of persons who apparently got the trip
reports. E is a memorandum under date of September 23rd, 1953,
with a memo on it with reference to destroying page 1 of the
report. F is under date of 23rd October, 1953, addressed to Shackelford, with reference to the trip report, signed by C. G. Mayer.
When did you receive a copy of this Shackelford/Straus trip
report?

A I think you said it was 1953, did you not?

Q I will give it to you and see if it refreshes your recollection as to
when you received it. Look at the whole bulk exhibit.

A I must have received it about September 1953, I would say. Yes, it
was sent to me in September 1953.

Q How large a document was that report?

A I do not recall, but it was several pages.

Q Did you read it?

A I did at the time.

Q Did you keep a copy of it in your files?

A It was returned.

Q You sent it back to Dr. Shackelford?

A Yes.

Q In this document which is marked for identification Mayer
Exhibit 33.B, Mr Neyhart states: "However, will you note we
received two pages, page 1 'After the writer left Japan' etc. and
page 6 beginning 'For the first time outside of the United States
the entire radio industry has been organised patent licence-

[p. 544] wise'." What was he referring to there; do you know?

A No, I do not know. I do not recall now.

Q In this letter he says: "I checked with Mr Straus's office and they
said that they sent you full copies of the reports. Will you please
see if you do not have the rest of it." Was there something in the
report which you did not send them?

A May I look at that correspondence?

Q Yes. (Exhibit 33 handed to witness.)

A   As I recall, my interpretation of their first request was only for the pages, but evidently they wanted the whole report; so I returned the whole report. I think it says so in that first note there.

Q   That report refers to the statement: "For the first time outside of the United States the entire radio industry has been organised patent licencewise." Is that what the report said?

A   I do not recall the exact words of what the report said, but if there is a quotation in that note there, I suppose that is what it had in it. This was a report of Dr. Shackelford's visit to the Far East and it presumably contains his comments on the situation.

Q   That was his conclusion, was it, that the entire radio industry has now been organised?

A   No, I do not think that was a conclusion at all.

Q   You think that is just a statement?

A   May I see that remark?

Q   Certainly.

A   No, I do not think that was a conclusion. I think that was a remark in the body of the report.

Q   It was not a conclusion; it was just a statement of fact. Is that it?

[p. 545]   A   I do not know whether it was a statement of fact; a statement made in the report.

Q   Under 33.C there is a request to a whole group of people in the International Division apparently to return this trip report to Dr. Shackelford, stating: "We should appreciate it very much if you would return your copies of the above trip report, which were sent to you on September 23rd, 1953." Do you know why they wanted them back in New York?

A   I think there was some management disagreement with some of the views which had been put forward, so the reports were recalled.

Q   So they wanted them all back wherever they were?

A   Right.

Q   Do you recall what that management dispute was about?

A   No, I do not.

Q   Do you recall whether or not the Legal Department had anything to do with that request?

A   I do not know.

Q   On 33.E, which is a memorandum under date of September 23rd, 1953, there is the direction: "Please destroy page 1 of report entitled 'Trip Report, East Asia and Europe' and page 6 of report entitled 'Trip Report Japan' and substitute attached pages." Did you do that?

A   I guess I did.

Q   Do you remember whether you did or not?

A   I do not remember, but I normally would have done it.

Q   You normally destroy things, do you?

A   It was a specific request in connection with that specific report.

Q   What you mean to say is that normally you follow directions; is that right? If they told you to destroy it, you destroyed it?

A   And put in the substitute pages.

[p. 546]   Q   Do you remember what was in the pages that you destroyed?

A   I think there were very little changes, as I recall, from the pages which were substituted for them.

Q   Do you remember what the changes were?

A   No, I do not. There were a few words only.

Q   According to F, you sent your copies of the trip reports back on the 23rd October, 1953. Does that correspond with your recollection?

A   It would have been about that time.

Appendix V
Judge Igoe's Opinion in Radio Corp. of America v. Rauland Corp. and Zenith Radio Corp., *dated March 26, 1956*

[¶ 68,306]   Radio Corporation of America, Plaintiff v. The Rauland Corporation and Zenith Radio Corporation, Defendants.   Zenith Radio Corporation and The Rauland Corporation, Counter-Claimants and Cross-Claimants v. Radio Corporation of America, Counter-Defendant, and General Electric Company and Western Electric Company, Inc., Cross-Defendants.

In the United States District Court for the Northern District of Illinois, Eastern Division.   Civil Action No. 48 C 1818.   Dated March 26, 1956.

Clayton Antitrust Act

Private Enforcement and Procedure—Suit for Civil Damages and Injunctive Relief—Pretrial Procedures—Disqualification of Trial Judge.—In a patent infringement action where antitrust defenses and counterclaims were pleaded, the plaintiff's petition that the trial judge disqualify himself from hearing the case was denied on the ground that the affidavit of personal bias and prejudice did not set forth a sufficient basis for disqualification. A judge has a duty not to disqualify himself, regardless of his personal inclination to do so, where such an affidavit does not set forth a sufficient basis for disqualification. This is particularly true where there is any possibility that the petition is merely a device to secure another judge in the hope that he will rule differently on matters already decided.

See Private Enforcement and Procedure, Vol. 2, ¶ 9013.

For a prior decision of the U. S. District Court, Northern District of Illinois, Eastern Division, see 1955 Trade Cases ¶ 68,144; and for a prior decision of the U. S. Court of Appeals, Seventh Circuit, see 1954 Trade Cases ¶ 67,886.

Opinion re Petition of RCA for Change of Judge and Affidavit of Personal Bias and Prejudice

MICHAEL L. IGOE, District Judge [*In full text*]: There is before me for decision and affidavit of personal bias and prejudice and a petition that I disqualify myself from sitting further in this case, filed pursuant to Section 144 of Title 28 of the United States Code.

Such a petition imposes a very disagreeable duty upon the trial judge, since it requires him to pass upon the question of whether his own conduct, as set forth in the affidavit, is sufficient as a matter of law to constitute bias and prejudice under the Federal statute. While I would much prefer to avoid this unpleasant duty by referring it to another judge or court, the cases are clear that I must myself determine whether or not the affidavit is legally sufficient and timely filed. The only way I can avoid this burden is by disqualifying myself, which would in itself be a determination that the petition has merit.

Another difficult aspect of the matter is that I must treat the facts asserted in the affidavit as true, even though I might know of my own knowledge that such assertions are either incomplete or wholly false. The Court of Appeals has summed up the situation in the leading case of *Tucker v. Kerner*, 186 F. 2d 79, 85 (C. A. 7, 1950):

"... the statute is plain, and a judge when presented with the embarrassing situation of passing on an affidavit charging 'personal bias or prejudice' is entitled to and must look solely to the facts alleged in support of such charge. His duty to deny the affidavit on insufficient allegations is no less imperative than to allow it on sufficient allegations."

[*Affidavit*]

Turning now to the affidavit, itself, it is executed by Frank Folsom, president of plaintiff and counter-defendant Radio Corporation of America, on information and belief. Since it deals almost wholly with matters about which Mr. Folsom could have no direct knowledge, it is a fair assumption that the affidavit represents information related to him by RCA's attorneys in the case.

[*Refusal to Grant Motion*]

In the first place, Mr. Folsom avers that there is personal bias and prejudice shown in the colloquy on December 3 and 14, 1954, when the court refused to grant RCA's motion "to set some limitations to the scope of the depositions" being sought by Zenith Radio Corporation and The Rauland Corporation, the counter-claimants. (Affidavit, pars. 6, 7, 8.)

As the affidavit shows on its face, this request for a pretrial conference to limit the scope of depositions to be taken by Zenith was made only after RCA had sought to stop the taking of any depositions on the counterclaims, resorting to motions in this court, mandamus proceedings in the Court of Appeals, and even to a petition for an injunction in the Supreme Court of the United States. Further, the motion for a pretrial conference to limit the depositions was filed after RCA had notice that the depositions had been scheduled to commence in New York on December 6, 1954. As this court observed at the time, the request appeared to be a dilatory maneuver designed to relitigate what had already been 'decided, namely that counter-claimants were entitled to the usual deposition procedures under the Federal Rule of Civil Procedure.

Clearly this is a decision that a trial judge is entitled to make, as has already been decided by the Court of Appeals in the case of *RCA v. Igoe* [1954 TRADE CASES ¶ 67,886], 217 F. 2d 218 (C. A. 7, 1954), cert. den. 348 U. S. 973 (1955).

Even if my decision to permit Zenith and Rauland to proceed with their depositions was error, as Mr. Folsom avers, it cannot and does not constitute personal bias and prejudice. To hold otherwise would invite a litigant to disqualify any judge whose rulings in interlocutory matters displeased him, and permit "shopping" for a judge who might rule favorably—a procedure which would break down the orderly administration of justice. *Refior v. Lansing Drop Forge Co.*, 124 F. 2d 440 (C. C. A. 6, 1942); *Tucker v. Kerner, supra.*

[Marriage Ceremony]

In paragraph 9 of the affidavit it is stated:

"On information and belief, Mr. W. Donald McSweeney, one of active counsel for Zenith and Rauland in this action, was married on February 18, 1955, and according to the Chicago press the ceremony was performed in the chambers of said Michael L. Igoe."

The above is the complete and total treatment of this subject in the affidavit, although there are inferences in the memorandum filed by RCA with the affidavit that this evidences some improper relationship between the court and counsel. The facts stated in the affidavit itself do not constitute bias or prejudice. However, in view of the suggestion that there may be other facts, not stated, which would lead to a conclusion of improper conduct, I am impelled to state for the record that there is no relationship, of personal friendship or otherwise, between this court and any counsel in the case which would suggest that I disqualify myself.

[Production of Files]

Paragraphs 10 and 11 of the affidavit deal with the circumstances surrounding the court's order of August 10, 1955 requiring the production of certain files which had been removed by RCA from London, England to Zurich, Switzerland after the court had entered orders permitting the taking of depositions in England, France, Germany and Holland—files which RCA refused to produce without an order of court.

This again was an interlocutory order in which the court made its rulings on the basis of briefs and arguments of counsel in open court. It appeared at the time that the order was justified and that the removal of the documents to Switzerland and the refusal to produce them at the depositions in London were unreasonable and dilatory tactics on the part of counsel. Even if this was error it does not constitute bias and prejudice under the cases cited.

[Judge's Conduct]

Paragraph 12 of the affidavit deals with the proceedings on February 10, 1956 when this court set a trial date for the counterclaims for the first week in October, 1956. It is stated that the court "stamped from the bench to his chambers and slammed the door" after making certain remarks to counsel in error.

As to the fact that the court expressed irritation, even anger, on this and other occasions, it cannot be disputed that judges are human beings and therefore subject to the usual human frailties. It has long been recognized that critical comments and expressions of irritation about the tactics of parties or their counsel in the course of judicial proceedings do not constitute personal bias and prejudice. *Refior v. Lansing Drop Forge Co., supra; U. S. v. 16000 Acres of Land*, 49 F. Supp. 645 (D. C. Kansas, 1942). To hold otherwise would deprive the court of its power to control the conduct of litigants in the court room and make it possible for attorneys to remove a judge whose rulings displeased them by resorting to deliberately provocative conduct. Attorneys before this court owe it some measure of courtesy and respect, and can hardly be heard to complain if the judge expresses irritation at being interrupted and contradicted.

[Timeliness of Affidavit]

I must also examine the question of whether the affidavit has been timely filed. The complaint in this case was filed by RCA in December, 1948 and the original counterclaim was filed in November 1949. The amended counterclaim was filed on February 11, 1954. Until June 15, 1954 this court had stayed all proceedings in this case, on request of RCA. The matters of bias and prejudice are said to have arisen in December, 1954 and to have "culminated" on February 10, 1956. It is elementary that an affidavit of this sort must be filed at the outset, and not long after the petitioner has sought and utilized the processes of the court in the proceedings. The sequence of events in this case over a period of many years is completely inconsistent with the argument of petitioner that its affidavit is timely. *Skirvin v. Mesta,* 141 F. 2d 668 (C. C. A. 10, 1944).

By the same token, petitioners argument of prejudice in the mere setting of a trial date on a counterclaim which was originally filed more than six years ago is completely without merit.

[Judge's Duty]

In its memorandum, RCA suggests that I should step aside, regardless of whether the affidavit is legally sufficient, arguing that no judge should continue to sit in a case where one of the parties feels he cannot get a fair trial. I have a great deal of sympathy for this position, and if I were free to follow my own personal inclinations I would step aside. I have no interest whatever in this case or its outcome. It is just another case which was assigned to me in which I am charged to preside. I have made no determination in my own mind of the merits of the action, and the rulings heretofore made have all involved preliminary matters in which I have exercised my best judgment. It is plain from the cases, however, that I have a duty not to disqualify myself, regardless of my inclination to do so, where the affidavit does not set forth a sufficient basis for standing aside. *Tucker v. Kerner, supra.* This is particularly true where there is any possibility that the petition is merely a device to secure another judge in the hope that he will rule differently on matters already decided during the course of several years of litigation. As the court stated in the case of *Benedict v. Seiberling,* 17 F. 2d 831, 840:

". . . to allow a disinclination to further sit in this case to work our voluntary retirement would be to permit the authors of this attack, who, we must assume, are participating counsel alone, to gain unlawfully that which they are not justly entitled to have. This would be unjustifiable from any aspect, and an invasion of the right of the plaintiff to have her case tried, if legally proper, before the judge whose regular assignment of duties is to try the cases brought into the court over which he regularly and immediately presides. Our oath of office is, among other things, to administer justice between litigants before us without fear or favor. If we may not now observe this oath in this case, it would be because we have not had the courage to follow its injunctions under all circumstances, and a voluntary withdrawal would give rise to an inference that such was the fact."

[Petition Denied]

For the reasons stated, I conclude that I cannot properly recuse myself and the petition is denied.

Appendix VI

Judge Igoe's Opinion in Radio Corp. of America v. Rauland Corp. and Zenith Radio Corp., *dated May 23, 1957*

[¶ 68,744] Radio Corporation of America, Plaintiff-Counter-Defendant v. The Rauland Corporation and Zenith Radio Corporation, Defendants-Counter-Claimants. Zenith Radio Corporation and The Rauland Corporation, Cross-Claimants v. Radio Corporation of America, General Electric Company, and Western Electric Company, Inc., Cross-Defendants.

In the United States District Court for the Northern District of Illinois, Eastern Division. No. 48 C 1818. Dated May 23, 1957.

Sherman Antitrust Act

Private Enforcement and Procedure—Suit for Civil Damages—Pretrial Procedures—Depositions—Notice—Suppression.—A notice for the taking of a deposition which was served the day before the deposition was to be taken was not unreasonably short where counsel for the parties were all in Oslo, Norway, for the purpose of taking foreign depositions and it was understood that the party serving the notice was to proceed with its depositions at that time. Also, a motion to suppress the depositions of two witnesses because the refusal of two other witnesses to produce certain documents prevented adquate cross-examination of the witnesses whose depositions were taken was denied. The request for the production of the documents was informal, and the witnesses whose depositions were taken had no connection with the witnesses who were requested to produce the documents.

Number 78—117   Cited 1957 Trade Cases   73,047
7-12-57   Radio Corp. of America v. Rauland Corp.

See Private Enforcement and Procedure, Vol. 2, ¶ 9013.775.

For other decisions of the U. S. District Court, Northern District of Illinois, Eastern Division, see 1957 Trade Cases ¶ 68,712, 1956 Trade Cases ¶ 68,475, 68,490, and 68,306, and 1955 Trade Cases ¶ 68,144; and for a decision of the U. S. Court of Appeals, Seventh Circuit, see 1954 Trade Cases ¶ 67,886.

Memorandum Regarding Depositions

[Motions]

IGOE, District Judge [*In full text*]: There are pending motions to suppress the depositions of the witnesses Steen, Broberg and Noren, as well as a motion for the production of documents under Rule 34 of the Federal Rules of Civil Procedure. They have been argued and counsel for both sides have presented very elaborate affidavits and statements of position.

As to the motion for production of documents, sought by RCA, counsel for Zenith have assured the court that except for some documents which are being made available for inspection now, and others which will be made available in connection with the answers to interrogatories, the documents called for have already been produced, to the extent they are available, and have supported this with affidavits. On this showing, the entry of an order would be an empty gesture.

RCA has also moved to suppress the depositions of the witnesses Broberg and Noren, "or in the alternative for an order authorizing RCA to re-examine the witnesses Nygren, Carajo, Broberg and Noren." The grounds asserted are the failure of the witnesses Nygren and Carajo (called by RCA) to produce documents necessary to the cross-examination of the witnesses Broberg and Noren (called by Zenith). The Steen deposition is said to have been taken by Zenith on insufficient notice to RCA.

[Notice of Taking Deposition]

From the affidavits of Messrs. Sokolow and Curtis, it appears that written notice of the Steen deposition was served on counsel for RCA in Oslo, Norway, on February 27, 1957, where counsel for both sides were then engaged in taking depositions in this case. The notice called for the appearance of Steen on the next day, February 28, 1957. Counsel for RCA called counsel for Zenith at about 6:00 p.m. on February 27, and protested the short notice, saying that he would not attend. He did not attend, although he and his associates were in Oslo at a place nearby the American Embassy where the deposition of Steen was taken.

The Federal rules do not specify any minimum notice of the taking of depositions, and the court must determine in any case what is reasonable under all of the circumstances. In this case, counsel were all in Oslo for the taking of the foreign depositions, and it was apparently understood that Zenith was to proceed with its depositions at the time. Under these circumstances it is not clear that the notice was unreasonably short. Certainly there appears to have been no justification for counsel deliberately staying away from the proceedings in order to prevent any taking of the deposition. The motion to suppress the Steen deposition is denied.

[Suppression of Depositions]

RCA moves to suppress the Broberg and Noren depositions, not because of any irregularity in the notice or taking of those depositions, but because it is claimed that the refusal of the witnesses Nygren and Carajo to produce documents relating to the approval of Zenith sets by SEMKO, an organization which has to do with electrical standards in Sweden, prevented adequate cross-examination of Broberg and Noren.

From the conflicting affidavits of Messrs. Sokolow and Curtis, it appears that Zenith radios were approved by SEMKO prior to 1939 but that no tests have been made on them since. SEMKO witnesses refused to produce records relating to the pre-1939 Zenith approval without Zenith's consent. Zenith attorneys consented, subject to the production of similar records regarding approval of RCA sets. This consent by Zenith was withdrawn, and the documents were not produced, when it appeared that similar records relating to RCA could not be located.

According to the testimony, as set forth in the affidavits, the records of SEMKO were incomplete and it would be "fantastic work" to locate the requested records. Apparently the requests for document production were not made in the subpoenas to the witnesses, but were made informally a few days prior to the hearing.

On the basis of these facts the court is asked to suppress the testimony of two other witnesses, who apparently had no connection with SEMKO, but who testified that they had sold Zenith radios, which had been approved by SEMKO.

The motion to suppress the Broberg and Noren depositions is denied, as is also the motion for alternative relief in the form of permission to go back to Sweden for the purpose of re-examining Broberg, Noren, Nyberg and Carajo. To follow the latter course would be to disrupt completely the schedule which this court has already laid down for the commencement of the trial of this action on June 17.

UNITED STATES CUSTOMS COURT
BEFORE: HON. HERBERT N. MALETZ, JUDGE

ZENITH RADIO CORPORATION,	:	
	:	
Plaintiff,	:	
	:	
v.	:	Court No. 80-5-00861
	:	
THE UNITED STATES,	:	Complaint File
	:	
Defendant.	:	

BRIEF IN SUPPORT OF PLAINTIFF'S CROSS-MOTION
FOR PARTIAL SUMMARY JUDGMENT ON ITS FIRST CAUSE
OF ACTION AND IN OPPOSITION TO DEFENDANT'S MOTION TO DISMISS

INTRODUCTORY STATEMENT

Plaintiff is a domestic manufacturer of television receivers. On March 10, 1971, the Secretary of the Treasury caused to be published a finding of dumping with respect to television receivers from Japan (T.D. 71-76), which finding was issued and published pursuant to the Antidumping Act of 1921, as amended (19 U.S.C. §160 *et seq.* (1970)). 36 Fed. Reg. 4597 (1971).

Over the years that followed the publication of the finding, the Antidumping Act was not significantly enforced with respect to Japanese television receivers. By the end of 1979, there existed a backlog of over five years worth of unliquidated entries. Antidumping duties which were assessed in the liquidation of earlier entries were, for the most part, not collected.

Effective January 1, 1980, the determination of antidumping duties on entries of merchandise subject to a finding of dumping and not assessed with antidumping duties as of that date became governed by the procedure specified in section 751 of the Tariff Act of 1930 (19 U.S.C.

§1675), which was added by the Trade Agreements Act of 1979, Public Law 96-

39, §101, 93 Stat. 144, 175 (1979).$\underline{1/}$ Further, section 516A(a)(2)(B)(iii)

of the Tariff Act of 1930 (19 U.S.C. §1516a(a)(2)(B)(iii)), added by sec-

tion 1001 of the Trade Agreements Act of 1979 and also effective on January

1, 1980, provides interested parties with the opportunity and the right to

obtain judicial review of administrative determinations reached under

section 751.

　　　　Effective January 2, 1980, the responsibility for administering

the antidumping law and for acting as the "administrative authority" under

section 751 and other sections of the Tariff Act of 1930 was transferred

from the Secretary of the Treasury to the Secretary of Commerce. Exec.

Order 12188, 45 Fed. Reg. 989 (1980); Reorganization Plan No. 3 of 1979, 44

Fed. Reg. 69273 (1979). On April 28, 1980, the General Counsel of the

Commerce Department made clear that the thousands of unliquidated entries

of television receivers from Japan, which were entered prior to April 1,

1979, were not going to be subject to a section 751 proceeding. *See* Com-

plaint, ¶16, and Collective Exhibit 1 to the Complaint. Although the

Commerce Department had apparently made a determination of the amount of anti-

dumping duties due on said entries (*viz.*, close to $138.7 million; *see* Complaint,

¶17), the procedure mandated by Congress was not to be followed. Instead,

on April 28, 1980, the United States had entered into agreements with

various importers of television receivers from Japan under which alleged

claims by the United States arising out of the aforesaid unliquidated

entries were "settled", allegedly under the authority of section 617 of the

---

$\underline{1/}$　The texts of this and other relevant statutes appear in the Statutory
Appendix to this brief.

Tariff Act of 1930, as amended (19 U.S.C. §1617).[2/] Under these agreements, the United States would receive between $75 and $77 million from the importers, approximately $66 million representing antidumping duties and approximately $9-$11 million representing penalties under section 592 of the Tariff Act of 1930, as amended (19 U.S.C. §1592).

On May 28, 1980, plaintiff commenced this action, pursuant to section 516A(a)(2) of the Tariff Act of 1930, for the purpose of challenging the settlement agreements, including (a) the Commerce Department's determination that the amount of antidumping duties due on unliquidated entries of television receivers from Japan, entered prior to April 1, 1979, was only approximately $138.7 million (less the relatively small amount found due on previously liquidated and protested entries), (b) the Commerce Department's determination to demand only approximately $66 million (less the relatively small amount found due on previously liquidated and protested entries) as antidumping duties for the aforedescribed unliquidated entries, (c) the Commerce Department's determination not to assess any antidumping duties in the individual liquidations of the aforedescribed entries, and (d) the Commerce Department's failure to follow the mandatory procedures set forth in section 751 of the Tariff Act of 1930. *Plaintiff believes that the implementation of the settlement agreements would result in the unlawful forgiveness of hundreds of millions of dollars in antidumping duty liability.*

[2/] The settlement agreements also included (1) claims by the United States arising out of certain liquidations -- some of which claims were asserted in several collection suits in United States District Courts, (2) claims by the United States arising out of an investigation relating to section 592 of the Tariff Act of 1930 (19 U.S.C. §1592), and (3) claims by an importer in an action in this Court challenging the assessment of antidumping duties on two entries. *See* Complaint, ¶16; Collective Exhibit 1 to Complaint. However, it is clear that the most substantial share of the alleged claims subject to the settlement agreements is accounted for by those arising out of the unliquidated entries.

In its Complaint (filed on June 27, 1980), plaintiff pleaded two causes of action: first, the settlement of alleged claims is *ultra vires*, illegal, and void, section 617 of the Tariff Act of 1930 providing no authority for settlement; and second, even assuming, *arguendo*, the existence of statutory authority to settle under section 617, the United States Government officials who recommended and who determined that the alleged claims should be settled acted arbitrarily, in bad faith, and unlawfully.

On July 28, 1980, the defendant filed a motion to dismiss,[3] based principally on the argument that the challenged settlement agreements dealing with alleged antidumping duty claims did not involve a "determination" specified in section 516A but rather were concluded pursuant to proper statutory authority to compromise claims. Plaintiff submits that, for the reasons presented herein, the defendant's arguments are without merit. Moreover, plaintiff submits that this Honorable Court should award summary judgment to plaintiff on the matter of liability pleaded in plaintiff's first cause of action -- to wit, the settlement agreements are *ultra vires*, null and void.

FACTUAL BACKGROUND

1. The Extraordinary Delays in the Assessment of Antidumping Duties.

On December 5, 1970, a notice was published in the Federal Register announcing that the Secretary of the Treasury had determined that television receivers from Japan were being or were likely to be sold at less than fair value ("LTFV") within the meaning of the Antidumping Act of

---

[3]   Appended to the motion to dismiss as Exhibit A, B, and C, respectively, were copies of an affidavit of Robert E. Chasen, Commissioner of Customs ("Chasen Affidavit"), an affidavit of Robert H. Mundheim, General Counsel, Department of the Treasury ("Mundheim Affidavit"), and a declaration of Homer E. Moyer, Jr., General Counsel, Department of Commerce ("Moyer Declaration").

1921, as amended (19 U.S.C. §160 *et seq.* (1970)). 35 Fed. Reg. 18549

(1970). On March 4, the Tariff Commission (now "International Trade

Commission") determined that a domestic industry was being or likely to be

injured by reason of the aforesaid LTFV sales. This determination was

published in the Federal Register on March 9, 1971. 36 Fed. Reg. 4576

(1971). On March 10, 1971, the Secretary of the Treasury, with extra-

ordinary, if not unprecedented, promptness, caused to be published a

finding of dumping covering television receivers from Japan. 36 Fed. Reg.

4597, T.D. 71-76 (1971). As a result of the publication of the finding,

all unappraised television receivers from Japan entered, or withdrawn from

warehouse, for consumption on or after one hundred twenty days prior to the

filing of the original antidumping petition in 1968 became susceptible to

the assessment of antidumping duties.[4] *See* 19 U.S.C. §161(a).

Regrettably, the dumping finding was not enforced; since 1971,

minimal amounts of antidumping duty were assessed and even lesser amounts

were collected, causing the decimation of the domestic television industry[5]

---

[4]   The clear purpose of the Antidumping Act was to provide for the assessment of additional duties designed to offset the margin of unfair pricing,
or dumping. *See C. J. Tower & Sons* v. *United States,* 21 CCPA 417, 424-426,
T.D. 46943 (1934). The Act was thus designed "to protect the producers of
the United States against actual or threatened demoralization of American
markets . . . ." *Ellis K. Orlowitz Co.* v. *United States,* 47 Cust. Ct. 583,
587, A.R.D. 136 (1961), *aff'd,* 50 CCPA 36, C.A.D. 816 (1963). *Accord,*
Timken Co. v. *Simon,* 539 F.2d 221 (D.C. Cir. 1976); *J. C. Penney Co.* v.
United States Department of the Treasury, 319 F. Supp. 1023, 1024 (S.D.N.Y.
1970), *aff'd,* 439 F.2d 63 (2d Cir.), *cert. denied,* 404 U.S. 869 (1971); *SCM*
Corporation v. *United States (Brother International Corporation, Party-in-*
Interest), 80 Cust. Ct. 226, C.R.D. 78-02, 450 F. Supp. 1178 (1978); *City*
Lumber Co. v. *United States,* 64 Cust. Ct. 826, A.R.D. 269, 311 F. Supp. 340
(1970), *aff'd,* 59 CCPA 89, C.A.D. 1045, 457 F.2d 991 (1972).

[5]   *See* Affidavit of plaintiff's Chairman, Mr. Joseph S. Wright, annexed
hereto as Exhibit 1 and made a part hereof.

and extreme public and congressional dissatisfaction with the Treasury
Department. For entries of Japanese television receivers made through
March 1972, a modest amount of antidumping duty was assessed. *See* Moyer
Declaration, Attachment A, page 2. No entry made subsequent to March 1972
was liquidated until six years later, *i.e.*, March 31, 1978. *Id.*

During the six year period between March 1972 and March 1978, the
Customs Service had made repeated requests of manufacturers, exporters, and
importers of television receivers from Japan for information which the
Customs Service needed in order to ascertain the amounts of antidumping
duties to be assessed on entries of television receivers from Japan.
Specifically, the requested information was needed to enable the Customs
Service to ascertain (a) the foreign market value (19 U.S.C. §164) or
constructed value (19 U.S.C. §165) of television receivers from Japan
covered by each entry, (b) the purchase price (19 U.S.C. §162) or exporter's sales price (19 U.S.C. §163) of said television receivers, and (c) the
adjustments, if any, which would be made to the aforesaid foreign market
value (19 U.S.C. §161(b) and (c)). The Customs Service found that the
manufacturers and exporters of television receivers from Japan either refused to submit, or to afford the Customs Service access to, requested
information or were extremely tardy in submitting information, and, addi-
tionally, the information which was submitted was found to be inaccurate,
incomplete, unreliable, and/or false. *See, e.g.,* Prepared Remarks of
Irving W. Smith, Jr., Chief, Value Branch, delivered at a "Disclosure
Meeting Regarding the Japanese TV Dumping Cases" on May 3, 1978. A copy of
these remarks is annexed hereto as Exhibit 2 and is made a part hereof.
*See also Statement of Facts Pertaining to the Finding of Dumping of Tele-
vision Receivers from Japan* (especially pages 31, 90, 95), a copy of which

-6-

is annexed hereto as Exhibit 3 and made a part hereof.[6/]

Eventually, senior Customs Service officers expressed serious

concern over the delays in duty assessment. On November 19, 1976, the

Commissioner of Customs wrote to the Under Secretary of the Treasury, as

follows:

> "[I]t is time to determine what can be done in the
> appraisement area when exporters, importers, or their
> lawyers cause undue delays to take place in a dumping
> situation. We suggest that . . . appropriate steps be
> taken to appraise based on the best information avail-
> able.

> *   *   *   *   *

> [W]e believe that ample opportunity has been given to
> manufacturers to submit relevant data and their re-
> luctance to respond certainly justifies using the best
> information available for appraising under the Antidumping
> Act."

A copy of the Commissioner's memorandum of November 19, 1976, is annexed

hereto as Exhibit 4 and is made a part hereof.

Beginning in December 1976, the Customs Service learned that much

information submitted to it by many of the importers of television re-

ceivers from Japan was false or fraudulent, designed to overstate the

---

[6/]   This document is an expurgated version of a document believed to have
been prepared by Customs Service personnel at some time in late 1978. The
document states, in the section entitled *Introduction:*

> "This paper has been prepared in order to present,
> in a single document, a comprehensive recitation
> of the relevant facts, as perceived by the re-
> sponsible Customs officers (excepting certain
> factual documentation prepared by the Office of
> Investigations and not released to other Customs
> offices for security reasons), pertaining to the
> finding of dumping against television receivers
> from Japan (T.D. 71-76). Accordinly, [*sic*] this
> exposition is intended to be free of opinions and
> conclusions; it is endorsed by the Office of the
> Chief Counsel, Regulations and Rulings, Operations,
> and Investigations."

The expurgated version of the document was obtained from the public reading
file of the Customs Service.

actual purchase price in order to reduce the antidumping duty liability. An

investigation conducted by the Office of Investigations of the Customs

Service revealed that importers, manufacturers, and exporters of television

receivers from Japan engaged in rebate schemes as well as other practices

directed to the masking of potential antidumping duties. *See* memorandum to

Commissioner of Customs from the Acting Assistant Commissioner (Operations),

apparently dated April 1978, a copy of which is annexed hereto as Exhibit 5

and made a part hereof.[7/]

    By late 1977, the Customs Service concluded that information sub-

mitted to the Customs Service by the manufacturers of television receivers

from Japan could not be relied upon to establish foreign market value (19

U.S.C. §164) or their claimed adjustments (19 U.S.C. §161(b) and (c)). On

October 18, 1977, the Commissioner of Customs wrote a memorandum to the

Under Secretary of the Treasury and the General Counsel of the Treasury

Department describing the unfortunate status of the enforcement effort and

---

[7/]   The fraud uncovered was massive and pervasive. One major retailer in
New York City pleaded guilty to an information charging customs fraud.
United States v. *Alexander's Inc.*, 79 Crim. 0194 (S.D.N.Y. 1979). Copies
of the information with notation of plea and transcript of court proceedings of March 29, 1979, are annexed hereto as Exhibit 6 and made a part
hereof. Several federal grand juries were impaneled, one of which has
returned a multicount indictment against the nation's largest mass mer-
chandiser, for customs fraud and for conspiracy to enter Japanese television receivers into the commerce of the United States by means of false
statements. *United States* v. *Sears, Roebuck and Company, Incorporated,* No.
CR 80-183-RJK (C.D. Cal. 1980). A copy of the *Sears* indictment is annexed
hereto as Exhibit 7 and made a part hereof. In fact, in the *Sears* case,
the United States named as unindicted co-conspirators two major Japanese
television manufacturers and their attorneys. *See* Government's Response to
the Court's Request for Further Information Concerning the Issue of Single
Versus Multiple Conspiracies: List of Unindicted Co-conspirators (July 10,
1980), a copy of which is annexed hereto as Exhibit 8 and made a part
hereof. A description of the alleged conspiracy appears in the Government's Opposition to Defendant Sears' Motions to Dismiss the Indictment, at
1-5 (June 2, 1980), a copy of which is annexed hereto as Exhibit 9 and made
a part hereof.

outlining the course of action to be taken to eliminate the swelling back-

log of unliquidated entries. In that memorandum, at 1, Commissioner Chasen

stated:

> "As you are most aware there has been con-
> siderable discussion during the past week, both
> within the Executive Branch and the news media, as
> to the derrogation of our responsibilities in
> administering the Antidumping Act, particularly
> with respect to televisions from Japan. The basic
> facts in respect to televisions are (1) that no
> dumping appraisements have been performed as to
> entries made after the first quarter of 1972, (2)
> that, as of this date, $2 billion worth of tele-
> visions from Japan have been allowed to enter the
> United States market place without regard to a
> determination of liability for dumping duties and
> (3) that the domestic television producing indus-
> try is today distressed (regardless of the attri-
> buted reason therefor).
>
> "In this respect Customs is of the opinion
> that a 5-year delay in performing appraisements,
> which to a large extent is due to present pro-
> cedural requirements, and the collection of anti-
> dumping duties, as appropriate, serves to sub-
> stantially undermine the remedial intent of the
> Antidumping Act - notwithstanding that existing
> bonding procedures may insure collectibility of
> any antidumping duties which may be ultimately
> collected.
>
> "In the eelevision [*sic*] case we have un-
> covered considerable evidence that the basis
> information submitted to Customs by a number of
> Japanese television manufacturers is false.
> Further, aside from the question of the integrity
> of the information received, we are also of the
> opinion that the existing administrative proce-
> dures necessitating the collection and analysis of
> vast amounts of commercial information before an
> antidumping appraisement can be performed repre-
> sents a perversion of the intent of the Act, in
> that delays for unreasonable periods of time
> negate the remedial protection intended by Congress
> for the affected United States industry."

A copy of the Commissioner's memorandum of October 18, 1977, is annexed

hereto as Exhibit 10 and is made a part hereof.

-9-

Among the corrective measures which the Commissioner stated were
being taken were the following:

> "Customs Headquarters will prepare and distribute
> within the next 4 to 6 weeks cognizant field
> officers appraisement information as to all
> backlogged entries concerning the statutory home
> market values as well as related information
> pertaining to rebates and kickbacks on United
> States sales by the involved manufacturers.
> Liquidation of the backlogged entries by the field
> will commence immediately. Should any further
> technical or other assistance be needed, it shall
> be, as appropriate, furnished by Headquarters.
>
> "In contrast to past administrative practices,
> this information will be compiled under the
> authority and mandate of section 209, Antidumping
> Act, and section 500, Tariff Act of 1930, util-
> izing all 'reasonable ways and means' to effectuate
> the necessary appraisements.
>
> "The home market price information will be based
> on the commodity tax report supplied by the manu-
> facturers to the Japanese Government. Both cir-
> cumstances of sale and cost of production adjust-
> ments will be either nonexistent or extremely
> limited. In the case of circumstances of sale
> adjustments, the amount will be limited to the
> amount of the adjustment to the U.S. price. This
> approach will give us an almost immediate access
> to usable foreign market value information, *vis-a-
> vis* the current procedures which now take at best
> 2 to 3 years. This approach of appraisement has
> been cleared by the responsible Customs legal
> authorities . . . ."

Id. at 1-2.[8]

---

[8] The "commodity tax" to which the Commissioner referred is a tax which
is levied on all television receivers produced for sale in Japan and is
based on the freely offered selling price of the product for sale to all
purchasers in the ordinary wholesale quantities and in the ordinary course
of wholesale trade. The Customs Service determined, with the approval of
the Treasury Department, that the foreign market value could be accurately
and properly ascertained by using information derived from Japanese Commodity Tax reports supplied by the Japanese manufacturers to the Japanese
Government. This determination was based upon the following considerations: (a) by statute, Congress had instructed and authorized Customs
Service officers to use all reasonable ways and means to ascertain, estimate, and appraise the foreign market value, and any other fact deemed
necessary for the purposes of the Antidumping Act; (b) the manufacturers of

Footnote continued--

On November 21, 1977, the Commissioner again wrote to the General
Counsel and announced that "we are ready to begin appraisements in accordance
with the plan outlined to you on October 18." A copy of the Commissioner's
memorandum of November 21, 1977, is annexed hereto as Exhibit 11 and is
made a part hereof. The Commissioner also reported:

> "In order to achieve uniformity and promptness
> of appraisement we intend to centralize the appraise-
> ment process at Headquarters or some other central
> location. The appraisement paperwork for all back-
> logged entries will be completed and finally liquidated
> on a single date rather than staggering the appraise-
> ment over a period. We believe that such approach
> will minimize any attempt by the affected importers to
> frustrate the appraisement and liquidation process."

Id. at 2.

On December 6, 1977, Customs Headquarters initiated the so-called
"Project Omega". A telex was issued by the Director of the Duty Assessment
Division to all regional commissioners, all area directors, and all district directors, instructing that "all unliquidated entries of . . . [tele-
vision receivers from Japan] entered thru April 11, 1977, shall be packed
and forwarded to this office immediately." A copy of the telex is annexed

---

Footnote 8/ continued--

television receivers from Japan had consistently failed to furnish the
Customs Service with requested information or else had provided the Customs
Service with information that was incomplete, inaccurate, false, and/or
unverifiable; (c) the long delay in the assessment of antidumping duties
represented a perversion of the intent of the Antidumping Act and a nega-
tion of the remedial protection intended by Congress for the affected
United States industry; (d) the statutory basis for the assessment of the
Commodity Tax in Japan is virtually identical to the statutory definition
of foreign market value in the Antidumping Act; and (e) the statements of
the Japanese television receiver manufacturers submitted to the Japanese
Government for the purpose of assessing the Commodity Tax constitute ad-
missions of said manufacturers as to the foreign market value of the
television receivers. *See generally* Exhibit 3 at 28 *et seq.;* Exhibit 2;
Exhibit 5; Exhibit 10. *See also* expurgated version of memorandum from the
General Counsel of the Treasury Department, dated March 15, 1978, to the
Secretary of the Treasury, a copy of which is annexed to the Mundheim
Affidavit as Exhibit 2.

hereto as Exhibit 12 and is made a part hereof. Subsequently, a task force
of customs officers proceeded to determine the amount of antidumping duties
on the above-described unliquidated entries. In making these calculations,
foreign market value was based on the Commodity Tax Law information. Because
of the unreliability and incompleteness of information submitted in support
of importers' claims for adjustments from foreign market value, under 19
U.S.C. §161(b) and (c), claimed adjustments were not allowed. *See* Exhibits
2 and 5. The stated purchase price or exporter's sales price was based on
information contained in actual invoices, even though by that time the
Customs Service had become aware that double invoicing and rebating were
widespread and that the prices shown on the invoices were frequently overstated. *See* Exhibit 5. *See also* a memorandum dated September 20, 1978,
from Commissioner Chasen to the General Counsel at Treasury (at 12), a copy
of the expurgated version of which is annexed hereto as Exhibit 13. [The
expurgated version was obtained from the Customs Service's public reading
file.] *It was determined that approximately $382 million in antidumping
duties would be assessed in the liquidation of the aforesaid entries.* See
Attachment A (at 2) to Moyer Declaration. On March 20, 1978, the Director
of the Duty Assessment Division, at Customs Headquarters transmitted a
telex to "all district, port and area directors involved in Project Omega,"
advising *inter alia* that (1) the entries of television receivers forwarded
to Headquarters pursuant to the December 6, 1977 telex instructions (*see*
Exhibit 12) were being returned to the appropriate offices, and (2) the
entries "on which antidumping duties have been found to be due . . . have
been liquidated and entered into the automated accounting system . . . [and]
will appear on the bulletin notice of March 31, 1978." A copy of the telex
is annexed hereto as Exhibit 14 and is made a part hereof. The telex

-12-

advice and instructions make clear that the bulletin notices for these
entries were prepared, were dated March 31, 1978, and were to be posted on
March 31, 1978, at customhouses throughout the United States.

However, notwithstanding the above-described developments, the
contemplated March 31, 1978 liquidations did not take place. It is believed that at some time in March 1978, the office of the General Counsel
of the Treasury Department asked the Commissioner of Customs for a statement on the impact on Customs' revenue accounting system of a delay in the
liquidation of Japanese television sets subject to antidumping appraisements then being processed. A response was apparently drafted for the
Commissioner's signature, by Mr. John B. O'Loughlin, the Director of the
Duty Assessment Branch. *See* undated memorandum from the Commissioner of
Customs to the General Counsel, a copy of which is annexed hereto as
Exhibit 15 and made a part hereof. The draft memorandum presented an
extraordinarily vigorous recommendation against delay in liquidation.
Although Commissioner Chasen denies having signed or transmitted the memo-
randum (*see* Chasen Affidavit, ¶38), we believe that the unsigned memorandum
was transmitted by Mr. O'Loughlin to Mr. Jordan Luke of the General Counsel's
office on March 24, 1978. *See* copy of note dated March 24, 1978, from Mr.
O'Loughlin to Mr. Luke, a copy of which note is annexed as Exhibit 16 and
made a part hereof.[9]

On March 28, 1978, the General Counsel of the Treasury Department
met with the First Secretary of the Embassy of Japan and numerous attorneys
for Japanese television manufacturers. *See* Mundheim Affidavit, ¶21. On
March 30, 1978, Customs Headquarters issued telex instructions to all

----

[9]   Copies of the undated draft memorandum (Exhibit 15) and the March 24
memorandum (Exhibit 16) were both obtained from the Customs Service's
public reading file.

-13-

regional commissioners, all district directors, and all area directors,
instructing that all entries of television receivers from Japan entered
subsequent to June 30, 1973, be deleted from the bulletin notices of
liquidations that were to be posted on March 31, 1978. A copy of this
telex is annexed hereto as Exhibit 17 and is made a part hereof. We understand that the deletions were made by hand by Customs Service field personnel before the bulletin notices were posted. On March 31, 1978, the
amended bulletin notices were posted, entries of television receivers from
Japan made prior to July 1, 1973, were liquidated, and approximately $46
million in antidumping duties were assessed thereon. *See* Attachment A (at
2) to Moyer Declaration. With respect to those liquidated duties, normal
collection efforts were not pursued by the Customs Service, as we shall
show *infra*.

2.   Possible Motivation for the Treasury Department's Decision to Abort
      the Liquidations Planned for March 31, 1978.

         We believe that the Treasury Department's eleventh hour decision
to prevent the posting of the notices of liquidation for most of the back-
logged entries resulted from political or diplomatic pressure -- *i.e.*, not
the factors which Congress expected would be considered when it enacted the
antidumping legislation. In fact, as explained below, it appears that
Treasury's actions may have been in furtherance of one or more secret and
illegal arrangements between our Government and the Government of Japan to
frustrate the collection of antidumping duties on Japanese television receivers, in utter disregard of the mandate of the statute.

      A.   The 1972 Honolulu Summit Meeting.

         In the case of *COMPACT et al.* v. *Blumenthal et al.*, C.A. 79-1207
(D.D.C. 1979), *appeal pending sub nom. COMPACT et al.* v. *Miller et al.*,
No. 79-1948 (D.C. Cir.), the plaintiffs therein sought to take the depo-
sition of Alexander Sierck, a high-level official in the Justice Department,

who had reportedly spoken of an understanding reached in 1972 at Honolulu,

Hawaii between President Nixon and Prime Minister Tanaka of Japan, where-

under the United States "'agreed to take a dive on color TV's' in return

for Japanese agreements favorable to certain U.S. exports." The Government

defendants opposed the motion to depose and submitted the affidavit of Mr.

Sierck, who stated:

> ". . . I did not state that the United States 'agreed
> to take a dive on color tv's' in return for concessions
> by the Japanese in such negotiations. I did, however,
> state to Caulfield that I had heard a rumor or 'story'
> to that effect. I did not then, and do not now,
> possess any knowledge, in either my personal or pro-
> fessional capacity, concerning the veracity of that
> rumor or 'story'."

The plaintiffs' motion was denied and the case was dismissed for lack of

subject matter jurisdiction. Copies of the motion to depose with support-

ing affidavit, memorandum in opposition with supporting affidavit, Court's

Order denying the motion to depose, and Court's final Memorandum and Order

are annexed hereto as Collective Exhibit 18 and made a part hereof.

We do not know whether the rumor which Mr. Sierck heard has a

basis in fact, but we are aware of the following facts:

(i) In early 1972, the Japanese Government appears to have been

concerned over the assessment of antidumping duties by United States

Customs on products from Japan. Sentiment was expressed in the Japanese

press that our nation's growing trade imbalance with Japan should not be

corrected by the vigorous enforcement of the antidumping law but rather by

increased exports to Japan, particularly of agricultural products. *See,*

e.g., newspaper articles appearing in the Japan Economic Journal of January

25, 1972, March 21, 1972, April 18, 1972, April 25, 1972, May 23, 1972, and

August 1, 1972, copies of which are annexed hereto as Collective Exhibit 19

and made a part hereof.

-15-

(ii) The Honolulu summit occurred on August 31 and September 1,
1972, and, judging from press reports, trade issues were given high priority
in the discussion. *See, e.g.,* newspaper articles appearing in the Japan
Economic Journal of August 29 and September 5, 1972, the New York Times of
July 24, September 1, and September 2, 1972, and the Washington Post of
September 1 and 2, 1972, copies of which are annexed hereto as Collective
Exhibit 20 and made a part hereof. Apparently, the meeting resulted in an
agreement by the Japanese Government to purchase various American goods and
services, namely agricultural, forestry, and fishing products, aircraft,
and uranium enrichment services. In fact, the anticipated Japanese purchases from the United States of agricultural, forestry, and fishing products during Japan's fiscal year 1972 exceeded $2 billion, making Japan the
United States' largest market in the world for such exports. *See* "Texts of
Nixon-Tanaka Communique and Announcement on Trade in Honolulu," appearing
in the New York Times of September 2, 1972 (part of Collective Exhibit 20).
According to the September 5, 1972 issue of the Japan Economic Journal
(part of Collective Exhibit 20), "[t]he only concession which the Japanese
were able to get from the Americans was their confirmation of the principle
of free trade." Of course, none of the newspapers reported of any secret
deal which may have been struck.

(iii) In 1972 and in years subsequent, the United States Department of Agriculture engaged in an extensive campaign of extolling the
value of United States farm exports to our balance of payments. A recurring theme (stated either explicitly or by strong implication) in that
Department's presentations has been that the United States should produce
and export those products in which it has a comparative advantage, namely,
agricultural products, so that it can pay for those imports which Americans

need in order to maintain their standard of living -- namely, *Japanese television sets,* among other things. *See, e.g.,* address by Secretary of Agriculture Earl L. Butz before the Washington-Agricultural Conference on Trade with Japan at 1 (Washington, D.C.; March 27, 1972), address by Secretary Butz at 36th World Trade Conference at 5-6 (Chicago, Illinois; March 8, 1973), statement by Secretary Butz before the Permanent Subcomm. on Investigations of the Senate Comm. on Government Operations at 3 (July 23, 1973), address by Secretary Butz before the Graduate School of Banking, University of Wisconsin at 9 (Madison, Wisconsin; August 14, 1973), address by Secretary Butz at a Japan Press Club luncheon at 9 (Tokyo, Japan; April 17, 1974), transcript of Secretary Butz's remarks on a television program (September 1, 1975), and U.S. Department of Agriculture, *Foreign Agriculture* at 3 (column 2) (November 24, 1975), copies of which are annexed as Collective Exhibit 21 and made a part hereof.

The following statement appearing at page 9 of Secretary Butz's April 17, 1974 address, *supra,* is typical of the Agriculture Department's rhetoric:

> "For us, Japanese purchases account for about 15 percent of the total volume of U.S. agricultural exports. While we are able to supply you with the products you must have -- feedgrains, wheat, soybeans, cotton, hides and skins and a variety of other products -- you serve as a market of major importance to our farm sector. Because of your efforts to improve the diets of the Japanese people, our rural people are able to eat better.

> "But, as you know, this trade is not one-way. Japan ships to the United States about 30 percent of its industrial exports. For the American family, Japanese products have become an important part of our way of life. An American father, for example, may drive his son to a little league baseball game in the family car -- a Datsun, Toyota, or Honda -- where the son will play ball with a Japanese-made baseball glove, baseball bat, and even the baseball -- while the proud father looks on taking pictures with his Japanese camera. At home, mother may be fixing dinner while she watches her favorite show on her portable Japanese television receiver.

-17-

> "Looking at it another way, one bale of U.S.
> cotton serves as the exchange for a medium priced
> Japanese camera, television set, or tape recorder.
> With about 10 bales of cotton, we can pay for a low-
> cost model of a Japanese car.
>
> "So the trade between Japan and the United
> States is mutually beneficial. Japan needs our
> agricultural exports. The United States needs your
> industrial exports. We are interdependent, and we
> are trading for our mutual advantage."

Another example may be found in the following excerpt of Secre-

tary Butz's August 14, 1973 address (at page 9):

> "We cannot afford the luxury of running away
> from membership in the trading world. We must be
> part of the world economy because the United States
> cannot maintain its current standard of living with-
> out massive imports of fuels, raw materials, bananas,
> coffee, shoes, automobiles, *TV sets, and other low-
> cost consumer items*. Furthermore, we cannot import
> these items if we do not export. This Nation would
> go bankrupt." [Emphasis added.]

Television receivers from Japan had already been found by an

Executive Department of the United States to have been dumped. Was the

Secretary of Agriculture simply exercising monumentally poor judgment in

lauding the importation into the United States of unfairly low priced

articles which were found to have been causing injury to a domestic in-

dustry -- or was the Secretary acting in furtherance of some unlawful deal,

as suggested in Mr. Sierck's rumor, wherein our Executive Branch agreed

to sacrifice our domestic television industry in exchange for a more robust

agribusiness or some other export-oriented industry?

(iv) Finally, not a single importation of television receivers

from Japan entered after the first quarter of 1972 was liquidated during

the balance of the Nixon-Ford administration.

-18-

B.   The Secret Side Agreement of May 20, 1977.

In the early days of the present Carter Administration, the International Trade Commission conducted an "escape clause" investigation involving television receiver sets and, on March 22, 1977, it reported the results of that investigation to the President. U.S.I.T.C. Publication 808, 42 Fed. Reg. 16489 (1977). The Commission determined, *inter alia,* that color television receivers are being imported into the United States in such increased quantities as to be a substantial cause of serious injury to the domestic industry producing articles like or directly competitive with the imported articles. Subsequent to and in view of that finding, the Government of the United States entered into an Orderly Marketing Agreement ("OMA") on May 20, 1977, limiting the export from Japan to the United States of color television receivers (and certain subassemblies thereof) for a period of three years beginning July 1, 1977, to 1.75 million units in each annual restraint period. *See* Pres. Proc. No. 4511, 42 Fed. Reg. 32747 (1977). The OMA was effectuated by an exchange of several notes or letters between Robert S. Strauss, the Special Representative for Trade Negotiations, and Fumihiko Togo, the Ambassador Extraordinary and Plenipotentiary of Japan. Copies of these letters, all of which are dated May 20, 1977, are annexed hereto as Collective Exhibit 22 and are made a part hereof.

However, over a year later, another letter dated May 20, 1977, from Ambassador Strauss to Ambassador Togo, surfaced. This secret side letter to the OMA was made public, for the first time, on July 18, 1978, when Ambassador Strauss appeared before the Subcommittee on Trade of the House Ways and Means Committee and, in response to questions from Congressman Rostenkowski, agreed to make the side letter public. *Multilateral Trade Negotiations: Hearing before the Subcomm. on Trade of the House Comm. on Ways and Means,* 95th Cong., 2d Sess. 16 (1978). A copy of the

-19-

side letter, as reprinted in the aforecited *Hearing* (including the testimony with regard thereto), is annexed hereto as Exhibit 23 and made a part
hereof.

Essentially, the side letter reflects certain commitments undertaken by the United States toward the Japanese Government, apparently in
consideration of the Japanese concessions embodied in the OMA. The commitments all related to matters of great concern to Japanese television manufacturers: (1) the then pending unfair trade practice case brought by GTE
Sylvania Incorporated and Philco Consumer Electronics Corporation against
the Japanese manufacturers pursuant to section 337 of the Tariff Act of
1930, as amended (19 U.S.C. §1337), (2) the countervailing duty litigation
brought by plaintiff herein regarding the forgiveness of the Commodity Tax
on television sets and other consumer electronic products exported from
Japan, and (3) the possibility of dumping duty assessments. The Special
Trade Representative assured the Japanese Government that his office would
urge the International Trade Commission to limit the scope of its unfair
trade practice investigation, and that the United States would vigorously
pursue its appeal from the countervailing duty decision of the Customs
Court.[10]/

With respect to the matter of antidumping duties, assurances were
given that the Treasury Department would liquidate entries promptly in
order to reduce uncertainty, that Treasury would inform the Government of
Japan of any significant developments in pending investigations, and that

---

[10]/ The section 337 case was terminated shortly after the writing of the
side letter, by consent decree. *See* 42 Fed. Reg. 39492 (1977). In the
countervailing duty case, the Government prevailed on appeal before the
Court of Customs and Patent Appeals and on certiorari before the Supreme
Court. *See Zenith Radio Corporation* v. *United States,* 437 U.S. 443 (1978),
aff'g, 64 CCPA 130, C.A.D. 1195, 562 F.2d 1209 (1977), *rev'g,* 78 Cust. Ct.
59, C.D. 4691, 430 F.Supp. 242 (1977).

-20-

Treasury would receive any information which the Government of Japan wished

to provide. More significant, however, was the commitment that "[t]he

Treasury Department will carry out these efforts in strict conformity with

the international [*sic*] Antidumping Code."

This commitment to assess antidumping duties on Japanese tele-

vision receivers in strict conformity with the International Anti-Dumping

Code, 19 U.S.T. 4348, T.I.A.S. 6431 (1967), was contrary to domestic law.[11/]

Specifically, Article 8 of the Code, relating to "Imposition and Collection

of Anti-Dumping Duties" conflicts with section 202 of the Antidumping Act

of 1921, as amended (19 U.S.C. §161). Under that section of the Act,

Congress directed that in the case of all imported merchandise subject to a

---

[11/] It must be remembered that when the U.S. Representative signed the
Code on June 30, 1967, there was no delegated authority to do so. The
Senate was irate with the Executive Branch's overreaching and considered a
proposed resolution which would have provided that the sense of Congress
was: (1) that the provisions of the Code conflict with the Act; (2) that
the Code should be submitted to the Senate for approval as provided by
Article II, section 2, clause 2, of the Constitution; and (3) that the Code
should come into effect in the United States only upon passage of implementing
legislation by Congress. *S. Con. Res. 38,* 90th Cong., 1st Sess. (1967).
When the resolution was referred to the Tariff Commission for comment, that
agency replied that the Code and Act conflicted. *See Report of the U.S.
Tariff Commission on S. Con. Res. 38, Regarding the International Antidumping Code Signed at Geneva on June 30, 1967* (1968) (Committee Reprint of
Sen. Comm. on Finance, 90th Cong., 2d Sess. (1968)). Although the resolution was never acted upon, a rider to a Renegotiation Amendments House
bill, H.R. 17324, 90th Cong., 2d Sess. (1968), was added in the Senate
which would have had the effect of totally nullifying the Code. Finally, a
compromise was reached, in conference, which, while allowing the Administration to save face, clearly carried out substantially the Senate amendment. *See* 114 Cong. Rec. 29888 (remarks of Senator Long) (1968). Public
Law 90-634 (1968) was enacted and directed the Secretary of the Treasury to
"resolve any conflict between the Code and the Act in favor of the Act
. . ." and to "take into account the provisions of the International
Antidumping Code only insofar as they are consistent with the Antidumping
Act, 1921." Pub. L. 90-634, §201, 82 Stat. 1345, 1347 (1968). In short,
any effort to modify the Act was rejected. *See* Pintos and Murphy, *Congress
Dumps the International Antidumping Code,* 18 Cath. L. Rev. 180 (1968); *see
also* Long, *United States Law and the International Anti-Dumping Code,* 3
Int'l Law. 464 (1969).

dumping finding, there shall be levied, collected, and paid a special

dumping duty in an amount equal to the difference between the statutory

foreign market value (or constructed value) and purchase price (or ex-

porter's sales price). On the other hand, Article 8(a) of the Code pro-

vides:

> "The decision whether or not to impose an
> anti-dumping duty in cases where all requirements
> for the imposition have been fulfilled and the de-
> cision whether the amount of the anti-dumping duty
> to be imposed shall be the full margin of dumping
> or less, are decisions to be made by the authorities
> of the importing country or customs territory. It is
> desirable that the imposition be permissive in all
> countries or customs territories parties to this
> Agreement, and that the duty be less than the margin,
> if such lesser duty would be adequate to remove the
> injury to the domestic industry."

Thus, Article 8(a) may be construed in such a way as to suggest that

dumping duties may be eliminated or reduced below the margins of dumping

if some other vehicle, such as a quota or an orderly marketing agreement,

were adopted and were deemed adequate to remove the injury to the domestic

industry.

It appears that the Government of Japan interpreted Ambassador

Strauss's commitment to administer the antidumping law in strict conformity

with the Code in precisely that manner. At least one newspaper reported

that it was the understanding of the Japanese Ministry of International

Trade and Industry ("MITI") that the "problem of TV export to the U.S." was

settled by the OMA. *See* article appearing in Nikkei Sangyo of October 2,

1978 (and an English translation thereof), copies of which are annexed

hereto as Exhibit 24 and made a part hereof. *Indeed, the Treasury Depart-*

ment itself has acknowledged that the Government of Japan has taken the

position that the side letter to the OMA barred further assessment of dump-

ing duties. Administration of the Antidumping Act of 1921: Hearing

on Assessment and Collection of Duties Under the Antidumping Act of 1921

-22-

before the Subcomm. on Trade of the House Comm. on Ways and Means, 95th Cong.,
2d Sess. 262 (1978).

There is yet an additional aspect of the side letter which is
somewhat disturbing. Upon information and belief, the side letter was
drafted by an attorney in the Office of the Special Trade Representative
named Shirley Coffield. Ms. Coffield was then and is now the wife of
Daniel Minchew, who was, at the time of the negotiation of the OMA, the
Chairman of the International Trade Commission. Prior to joining the
Commission, Mr. Minchew was employed by the United States–Japan Trade
Council, Inc., an organization which was charged by the Justice Department
in a civil suit filed in 1976 with filing misleading statements with the
Department under the Foreign Agents Registration Act. *See* Department of
Justice press release dated July 13, 1976, a copy of which is annexed
hereto as Exhibit 25 and made a part hereof.[12/] Mr. Minchew continued to
maintain his liason with Japanese business interests while serving on the
International Trade Commission and, in fact, while still at the Commission,
signed a contract to do consulting work for those interests upon his de-
parture from the Commission. *See* 2 *Investigation of Senator Herman E.
Talmadge: Open Session Hearings before the Senate Select Comm. on Ethics,*
96 Cong., 1st Sess., 678–680, 944–947 (1979); 3 *Investigation of Senator
Herman E. Talmadge: Open Session Hearings before the Senate Select Comm.
on Ethics,* 96 Cong., 1st Sess. 771–773 (printed in 1980). Indeed, the
entire record of the Talmadge investigation casts grave and extraordinary
doubts on Mr. Minchew's integrity and on the propriety of his past conduct

---

[12/] The suit, which alleged that the Council is an organization using a
trade association facade to conceal its foreign agent activities in this
country in representing Japanese governmental interests, ended in a consent
decree. *See* United States–Japan Trade Council Notice, dated September 10,
1976, a copy of which is annexed hereto as Exhibit 26 and is made a part
hereof.

in numerous endeavors.$\underline{^{13/}}$ *See, e.g., 1 Investigation of Senator Herman E.*

Talmadge: Report of the Senate Select Comm. on Ethics to Accompany S. Res.

249, 96th Cong., 1st Sess. 85–101 (Senator Talmadge's motion to dismiss

charges), 122–134 (Senator Talmadge's supplemental brief), and 176 (excerpt

of additional views of Senator Schmitt) (1980). Copies of the cited pages

from the three volumes on the Talmadge investigation are annexed hereto as

Collective Exhibit 27 and are made a part hereof. In fact, last year Mr.

Minchew pleaded guilty to the commission of a felony and was subsequently

incarcerated. *United States* v. *Minchew,* Criminal No. 79-00363 (D.D.C.

1979). Copies of the information, waiver of indictment, judgment and

commitment order, and Government's Statement of Facts are annexed hereto as

Exhibit 28.

          Furthermore, on March 24, 1977, Mr. Minchew, then Chairman of the

International Trade Commission, was, in effect, severely scolded by Congress-

man Vanik during congressional hearings, because of certain remarks alleged-

ly made by Mr. Minchew to the Japanese press with respect to the television

escape clause proceeding, which Mr. Vanik felt were clearly inappropriate.

See Authorization of Appropriations for and Oversight of the U.S. Inter-

national Trade Commission and Comparability of Trade and Production Sta-

tistics: Hearings before the Subcomm. on Trade of the House Comm. on Ways

and Means, 95th Cong., 1st Sess. 78-83 (1977). Copies of these pages are

annexed hereto as Exhibit 29 and are made a part hereof.$\underline{^{14/}}$ Within weeks

---

$\underline{^{13/}}$ Immediately prior to his joining the Commission, Mr. Minchew had been
Senator Talmadge's administrative assistant. Mr. Minchew was a principal
witness in the highly-publicized Senate investigation of Senator Talmadge
in 1979.

$\underline{^{14/}}$ Also of interest is Mr. Minchew's testimony that the United States
embassy in Japan apparently advised Mr. Minchew of the sensitivity in Japan
of issues involving trade in television receivers. *See Hearings* at 79-80.

of this congressional hearing, we understand that Mr. Minchew's wife was in

Japan as part of the United States team involved in the negotiation of the

OMA, including the unfortunate and illegal commitments contained in the

clandestine side letter.

3. Activities at Customs and Treasury Subsequent to the March 31, 1978
    Liquidations.

       The response of principal members of the Subcommittee on Trade of

the House Ways and Means Committee to the Treasury Department's last minute

actions relating to the assessment of antidumping duties was harsh. On

April 10, 1978, Congressmen Vanik and Rostenkowski released a statement to

the press, challenging the action that Treasury had taken. They said:

> "We understand that the Department limited
> its original action in this long-drawn-out case to
> one year of assessments so as to minimize the
> adverse impact on importers--and, probably, to
> avoid banner headlines on the extent of Japanese
> dumping in the American market. But the magnitude
> of the present dumping liability on imported
> Japanese TVs is a problem of Treasury's own making,
> since it is responsible for its failure to enforce
> the Antidumping Act in a vigorous and timely
> fashion.

*   *   *   *   *

> "The history in this particular case of the
> lack of enforcement of the law as it was written
> calls for a reconsideration by the Congress of
> where the responsibility for administering the Act
> should be placed. The degree to which counsel for
> importers have been permitted to tie the hands of
> government counsel in procedural snarls raises
> serious questions as to whether Treasury intends
> to enforce the Antidumping Act at all. It is
> unfortunate that the Treasury Department thought
> it appropriate to consult both with counsel for
> the importers and representatives of the Japanese
> government as to its proposed action in this case
> but did not see fit to consult with Congress or
> representat [sic] of the domestic industry."

A copy of the press release (with attached Treasury Department press

release) is annexed hereto as Exhibit 30 and is made a part hereof.

On April 18, 1978, attorneys of the Customs Service's Office of

Regulations and Rulings sent a memorandum to the Assistant Commissioner,

echoing the Congressmen's concern with respect to the impact of private

meetings between Treasury officials and representatives of the Japanese

interests. The Customs attorneys, who had been asked to hold disclosure

conferences with such representatives, stated:

> "Our difficulties at these meetings have been
> compounded by the fact that Treasury has issued
> vague and conflicting information to the affected
> importers/manufacturers/Government of Japan
> officials, concerning particular facets of its
> policy, while again providing very little direct
> communication with Customs. Effectively, Customs
> has been placed in the position of discovering
> Treasury policy through the often dubious repre-
> sentations of the affected parties.

                    *   *   *   *   *

> "The entire range of problems which have sur-
> faced during the disclosure conferences (especially
> the conference with Japanese Government officials)
> seem to be related to the parties' understanding
> [sic] that the liquidations of March 31 were in
> some way considered to be 'provisional' in nature,
> that Treasury took this action primarily because
> of Congressional pressure, and that Treasury does
> not expect that the $46 million in dumping duties
> assessed to date in any way represents a final
> ascertainment of the liability due and owing.
> Rather, those affected anticipate that the assessed
> amount will be mitigated through informal government
> to government negotiations, or relatively informal
> contacts between manufacturers and Treasury."

A copy of the memorandum is annexed hereto as Exhibit 31 and made a part

hereof.

In September of 1978, the House Subcommittee on Trade held over-

sight hearings on the assessment and collection of duties under the Anti-

dumping Act of 1921. Much of the Subcommittee's attention was focused on

the Treasury Department's delinquencies in administering the television dumping case.[15]/ *See Administration of the Antidumping Act of 1921:*

Hearing on Assessment and Collection of Duties Under the Antidumping Act of

1921 before the Subcomm. on Trade of the House Comm. on Ways and Means,

95th Cong., 2d Sess. 4-24, 40-51, 251-267 (1978). Copies of these pages

are annexed hereto as Exhibit 33 and are made a part hereof. At the time

of the hearings no effort had yet been made to collect the $46 million in

dumping duties that had been assessed six months earlier. In response to a

question from Congressman Rostenkowski as to when Treasury would collect

the $46 million, Treasury's General Counsel testified: "*** I would say

we are right on the threshold of it." *See Hearing* at 42.

> The General Counsel also had the following to say:

> "Customs has concluded that for the period,
> 1972 to January 1975-- for the period 1973, July
> 1973 to January 1975, information submitted by all
> but one Japanese manufacturer was unreliable or
> incomplete or both.

> "Consequently, Customs may appropriately
> look to the best available evidence to determine
> the wholesale price of sets sold in Japan. As
> you know, the wholesale price of that set is com-
> pared to the wholesale price of sets sold in the
> United States.

---

[15]/ In fact, by the time of the hearing the entire Congress had become
aware of and concerned over reports of the pervasive use of false and
fraudulent submissions by importers of Japanese television receivers to
conceal dumping margins. In the Customs Procedural Reform and Simplifi-
cation Act of 1978, Congress took the extraordinary step of explicitly
preventing the more lenient penalty provisions of that law from applying
to alleged violations of section 592 "involving television receivers that
are the product of Japan and that were or are the subject of antidumping
proceedings if the alleged intentional violation-- (i) occurred before the
date of enactment of this Act, and (ii) was the subject of an investigation
by the Customs Service which was begun before the date of enactment of
this Act." Pub. L. No. 95-410, §110(f), 92 Stat. 888, 897 (1978). *See H.R.
Rep. No. 95-1517 (Conference Report),* 95th Cong., 2d Sess. 13 (1978); 124
Cong. Rec. S 9923-28 (daily ed., June 27, 1978; remarks of Senator Morgan).
Copies of the aforesaid Congressional Record pages are annexed hereto as
Exhibit 32 and are made a part hereof.

"If the price in Japan is higher, there is
dumping and the difference between the two wholesale prices is the dumping margin.

"The best available evidence in this case
includes information derived from the administration of the Japanese commodity tax. We can derive the wholesale price of sets sold in Japan
from that information.

"However, the antidumping law requires that
if the importer can establish to our satisfaction
that there are differences in the cost of producing the sets sold in Japan and the sets sold in
the United States, or that there are differences
in certain circumstances of sale, then we must
make adjustments to the wholesale price before
determining dumping margins.

"Now, with that background, I want to report
to you the recommendations that Customs has made
and in which Treasury concurs.

"First, the Customs Service will move promptly
to assess another portion of the backlog, including
all televisions imported up to January 1975.

"Two, the Customs Service will thereafter
assess the remainder of the backlog as rapidly
as its ability to process the full case permits.

"Three, the Customs Service will continue to
rely on alternative sources of evidence, including
information derived from the commodity tax, to
compute the dumping duties due on television
receivers of any manufacturer that has failed to
submit complete and reliable information to Customs
on a timely basis.

"Four, the Customs Service has determined
that for the period, July 1973 to January 1975,
only one manufacturer has submitted complete
and reliable information to Customs on a timely
basis.

"Five, in using alternative sources of evidence, the Customs Service will further refine
the approach that it used in the March 31, 1978,
liquidation by incorporating commodity tax information actually reported by the manufacturer to
the Japanese Government whenever that information
has been made available to the Customs Service
on a timely basis in response to its request.

"Six, the Customs Service has concluded that
the claims for adjustments for differences in costs
of production and circumstances of sale submitted
by the manufacturers during the July 1973 to
January 1975 period are not reliable and should
not be allowed in computing the dumping duties.

"Seven, the Customs Service will inform in
writing the importers that are assessed dumping
duties on the basis of alternative evidence
in this case of that fact, of the Customs Service's
basis for this treatment, and the Customs Service's
willingness to consider in conjunction with the
filing of protests claims for adjustments, if, but
only if, those claims are supported by more persuasive evidence than the manufacturer's [*sic*]
previously submitted to the Customs Service.

"Eight, the Customs Service will consider
evidence of adjustment claims as sufficiently
persuasive only if that evidence is prepared
with express reference to manufacturers' documentation and is accompanied by a suitable undertaking promptly to supply copies of supporting
documentation from purchasers and suppliers of
the manufacturer, where Customs so requests; and
only if all of the documentation is subject to
satisfactory field verification.

"Nine, the Customs Service will promptly
notify the importers that were assessed dumping
duties on the basis of best available evidence
on March 31, that they will have the same opportunity to submit more persuasive evidence promptly
in support of their previously filed protests.

"Ten, the Customs Service will begin collection procedures for each assessment immediately
after it occurs and is reinstituting collection
procedures on the March 31 assessment now."

Id. at 20-22.

The Commissioner of Customs also testified at the September

hearings. He indicated that he felt quite confident that Customs would

liquidate the remaining entries of Japanese television sets through March

1977 within six months and, further, that those entries represented about

$350 million in antidumping duties. *Id.* at 45, 19, 20.

-29-

Regrettably, the Commissioner's and General Counsel's commitments

to the Subcommittee were not fulfilled. The backlog of unliquidated entries

was not cleared.$\underline{16}/$ The effort to collect liquidated duties was simply not

made.$\underline{17}/$ Instead, in late December of 1978, Treasury's General Counsel

sought the support of Congressmen Charles Vanik and Dan Rostenkowski

for a proposal to settle the television dumping case, including the civil

---

$\underline{16}/$ According to Commissioner Chasen's memorandum of February 19, 1980 at
3 (Attachment B to Moyer Declaration), "[t]wo more series of assessments
were made (excluding the one for Sony in December 1979). The first, in
December 1978, was for $3 million on imports by General, Hitachi and NEC
through December 1974. The second in June 1979, was for $29 million on
imports by the other six companies through March 1974."

$\underline{17}/$ Shortly after the September hearings, Treasury went through the motions of setting November 27, 1978 as the due date for payment of the $46
million in dumping duty payments that it had told the Subcommittee it was
"on the threshold" of collecting. The November due date was extended until
December 27, 1978; the December due date was extended until January 27,
1979; the January due date was extended until March 12, 1979. The Commissioner's letter granting the last-mentioned extension stated: "No further
extensions of time are contemplated." *See* letter of January 19, 1979, a
copy of which is annexed hereto as Exhibit 34. On March 9, 1979, the
Commissioner of Customs sent out demands for payment which were not really
demands for payment. Rather the "demand" letter stated that "[i]n lieu of
full payment . . . [the importer] may tender cash in the amount specified
together with a promissory note for the balance . . . ." The letter also
indicated that if the requested cash plus promissory note were tendered,
"no further collection action will be taken at this time." A copy of the
letter of March 9, 1979, is annexed hereto as Exhibit 35 and is made a part
hereof. On April 12, 1979, the Commissioner advised the importers, by
letter, of the amount of money to be paid in cash and the amount to be
covered by promissory note. The letter concluded with the statement:

> "Failure to pay the full amount of the duties
> or the estimated amount accompanied by a promissory
> note and the surety agreement by May 14, 1979, will
> result in administrative collection action and the
> possible referral of the debt to the Department of
> Justice."

A copy of the form letter (and enclosures) of April 12, 1979, is annexed
hereto as Exhibit 36 and is made a part hereof. By May 14, 1979, most of
the importers refused to pay or sign promissory notes, and shortly thereafter the Justice Department initiated (but did not prosecute) collection
actions in several district courts. In fact, within days after the April
28, 1980 settlement agreements, Justice filed stipulations of dismissal with
prejudice in most of those suits, two of which have since been dismissed.
See defendant's motion at 24.

and criminal fraud cases, for about $50 million. *See* article in New York
Times of January 24, 1979, a copy of which is annexed hereto as Exhibit 37
and made a part hereof. The Congressmen flatly rejected the proposal.

Also, notwithstanding the General Counsel's remarks to Congress,
we believe that Treasury made vigorous efforts to reduce unlawfully the
antidumping duty liability on the entries liquidated on March 31, 1978 (and
subsequently protested), and on the entries made subsequent to June 30,
1973. Customs Service attorneys frequently questioned the correctness or
wisdom of the tasks that they were asked to perform. *See, e.g.,* Customs
attorneys' memorandum dated April 18, 1978 (Exhibit 31); Memorandum of
Attorneys Kersner and Altschuler, dated June 1, 1978, a copy of which is
annexed hereto as Exhibit 38 and made a part hereof; memorandum dated March
2, 1979, from staff attorneys to file, a copy of which is annexed hereto as
Exhibit 39 and made a part hereof.

The last memorandum cited was signed by all nine staff attorneys
of the Office of Regulations and Rulings assigned to work on the television
case. This group of lawyers had been asked to "formulate 'estimates' of
the amounts by which the dumping duties assessed on March 31, 1978, will be
reduced." In the memorandum of March 2, 1979, the group stated that:

> "It is our understanding that these estimates
> will be used to help determine the portion of
> outstanding dumping duties which will be collected
> in March of this year. We understand that the
> amount of duty remaining after the 'estimated'
> circumstance of sale adjustments have been made,
> on a manufacturer by manufacturer basis, will be
> collected in cash. The balance is to be secured
> by promissory notes."

The attorneys summarized their concern with the possibility that
their work might be misunderstood or misused with the statement:

> "[T]he entire 'estimate' exercise is premised
> upon a number of factual assumptions. Foremost
> among these assumptions is that all claims for

-31-

> adjustments will be established by the manufac-
> turer to the satisfaction of Customs. We wish to
> point out that the figures derived during this
> exercise cannot, under any circumstances, be
> construed as having been accepted as substantiated
> to the satisfaction of the undersigned staff
> attorneys."

Virtually every time the word "estimate" was used in the memorandum, it

was placed in quotation marks.

Subsequently, the concerns of the nine Customs attorneys were

expressed in very strong terms by Congressman Vanik, in a letter dated

March 19, 1979, to Commissioner Chasen. A copy of this letter is annexed

hereto as Exhibit 40 and is made a part hereof. Among other things, Mr.

Vanik stated:

> "As I understand your proposal, you are
> permitting the importers to pay approximately 25% of
> the total debt in cash and to execute promissory
> notes for the remainder. This exercise is apparently
> based on the belief that the protest review will
> result in a determination that the initial assess-
> ments were too high. For this reason, and because
> the sums involved are so large, the Service is
> unwilling to require the importers to pay the
> full amount owed in cash. I am compelled to
> point out that Customs' solicitous regard for the
> potential adverse impact of full cash collection
> upon importers is completely at odds with the lack
> of concern for the injury to the domestic industry
> which has characterized the entire history of
> this case. However, my objections to your collec-
> tion exercise lie in the unreliability of the
> method and data used. *Furthermore, I am deeply
> concerned that despite the very questionable
> validity of the exercise, it will be used as a
> model for future assessments.*

> "With respect to each Japanese manufac-
> turer, the estimated reduction in dumping duties
> is based on the adjustments claimed for only three
> television models despite the fact that in fiscal
> year 1973 these manufacturers exported nearly 400
> different models to the United States. Moreover,
> the selection was not based on the import volume
> represented by the comparable export model.
> Rather these models were selected because Customs
> and the Japanese producers agreed on their compar-
> ability to the export model. Thus, although there

is no evidence that the models chosen are a
representative sample, the results of the 'estimate' exercise were applied across the board for
each manufacturer. I seriously question whether
the percentage adjustment claimed for a color
television of a particular screen size would match
that for a monochrome of different size. This
would seem especially true for cost of production
adjustments.

"It is my understanding that the eight
attorneys working on the adjustment review seriously question the methodology and the unverified
nature of the data. The 'estimated' reduction
exercise also assumes that the claimed adjustments
will be proven factually valid. Thus far, no on-
site verifications of data submissions have been
made, and I understand that it is your intention
to make any such verifications only on an as-
needed basis. Given the history of this case, I
question the propriety of giving the Japanese
manufacturers the benefit of the doubt in this
manner. I would expect that no claimed adjustments
would be granted as part of the protest review
without a thorough on-site verification of the
relevant submissions.

"I must assume that your reason for proceeding with collection in this manner is based on
a concern for the importers and/or a fear that
unless the immediate impact of collection is
lessened, litigation will result. I have already
stated my view with regard to the former reason.
With regard to the latter, I have heard officials
in both the Treasury Department and the Customs
Service state their belief that the government's
chances of winning in court are not very good. I
must take exception to this view. Adjustments
are to be granted only if they are 'established to
the satisfaction of the Secretary' (Sec. 202(b),
Antidumping Act of 1921). Such a high standard
would be very difficult for an importer to successfully challenge in court.

"*Finally, I am concerned not only with the
immediate results of your actions, but also with
their long-range effects. You have classified
this first assessment as a learning experience
from which you will be able to decide how to
handle future assessments. I would therefore hope
that before any reliquidation takes place following the protest review Customs would take steps to*

-33-

ensure the accuracy and validity of the final
assessment. I would consider it most inappropriate to make further assessments on the basis of
your 'estimated' reductions exercise." [Emphasis
added.]

On March 27, 1979, Commissioner Chasen responded by letter to
Congressman Vanik, assuring that "[t]here is no intent to use our resolution of the protests pending before Customs as a 'model' for further liquidations." A copy of the Commissioner's letter is annexed hereto as Exhibit
41 and is made a part hereof.

In May 1979, Customs lawyers and auditors conducted on-site
verifications (of claims for adjustments) at the facilities of the television manufacturers in Japan.[18/] It is our understanding that most of the
companies did not fare well in this exercise. By June 1979, protest decisions, which, we understand, were not particularly favorable to the importers, were prepared by attorneys in the Office of Regulations and Rulings.[19/]

However, the protest decisions as prepared in June 1979, were
never approved because of opposition by the Office of the Chief Counsel of
the Customs Service. That office reports to the General Counsel of the
Treasury Department. The attorney in the Chief Counsel's office who had
principal responsibility for the television dumping case was one R. Theodore
Hume, who, in June 1978, was transferred from the General Counsel's office

---

[18/] Plaintiff believes that the verification exercise was faulty to begin
with and that the verification program initially recommended by Customs
Service auditors was rejected in favor of a less onerous and less reliable
one.

[19/] In a March 13, 1979 Treasury Department press release, it was announced
that "[t]he Customs Service expects to complete the protest review . . . by
August 1, 1979, including an as-required on-site verification in Japan." A
copy of the press release is annexed hereto as Exhibit 42 and is made a
part hereof.

to the Chief Counsel's office, where he unquestionably emerged as "Treasury's man in Customs," for the purposes of the television case.[20/]

     After Mr. Hume expressed dissatisfaction with the draft protest decisions, the Commissioner, on July 16, 1979, announced the creation of a new Special Task Force on Japanese Televisions, to be headed by Mr. Hume. The task force was given the responsibility for handling all issues relating to antidumping matters concerning televisions.

     We understand that Mr. Hume permitted certain Japanese manufacturers whose claims were rejected in earlier verifications to submit yet additional data and that he ignored opinions of Customs Service lawyers and auditors and of independent auditors that various claims for adjustments were not satisfactorily established. Further, he insisted that a so-called "exporter's sales price offset" adjustment to foreign value should be granted for expenses reflected in home market prices for general and administrative expenses up to the amount incurred in the United States, when the importer is related to the manufacturer. This adjustment is, in our judgment as well as in the judgment of the attorneys of the Office of Regulations and Rulings who were responsible for preparing the protest decisions, absolutely unauthorized by and contrary to the controlling statute. Nevertheless, when the protest decisions were finally issued, this adjustment was allowed,[21/] and, more significantly, was somehow to be computed in the Task Force's planned liquidations (within the next two months) for entries extending into 1977 or beyond.

[20/] Mr. Hume is now Deputy General Counsel, Office of the United States Trade Representative.

[21/] *See, e.g.,* Customs Service press release of October 31, 1979, a copy of which is annexed hereto as Exhibit 43 and made a part hereof. It should be noted, however, that notwithstanding the statement in the press release that the Customs Service has ruled on the protests, subsequently, additional manufacturers' data were considered by Customs, additional on-site verifications were conducted, and, upon information and belief, new protest decisions were issued, resulting in further reduction of duty liability.

By November 14, 1979, it became apparent to Congressman Vanik
that Treasury was engaging in a feverish rush to "wipe the slate clean"
before the end of the year -- at which point, among other things, entries
not yet liquidated would become subject to administrative and judicial
review by domestic interests. On that date, he wrote to the Secretary of
the Treasury, cautioning him not to act precipitously. A copy of the
letter is annexed hereto as Exhibit 44 and is made a part hereof. Specifically, Mr. Vanik said:

> "Given the history of this case, I believe it
> is totally inappropriate for Treasury to make further
> dumping duty assessments in this proceeding. Further
> action should be taken by the Department of Commerce
> after January 1, 1980 and pursuant to Title I of the
> Trade Agreements Act of 1979.

> "I have continually urged Treasury to act ex-
> peditiously with respect to antidumping procedures.
> However, I have never advocated speed at the expense
> of accuracy nor 'settlement' of this case at the ex-
> pense of carrying out the law. Assessments in this
> proceeding within the next seven weeks could only be
> accomplished by taking procedural 'short cuts', e.g.,
> not conducting on-site verification. The importance
> of such verification was emphasized in the Department's
> announcement of its protest decisions. Furthermore,
> the recently enacted Trade Agreements Act of 1979
> clearly reflects the Congressional intention that in-
> formation submitted during the course of a proceeding
> be verified.

> "*In addition to the real danger of making fac-
> tual errors, a hasty assessment effort would have a
> number of other adverse effects. First, it could
> give the appearance that Treasury is trying to evade
> the expanded opportunity for judicial review pro-
> vided in the Trade Agreements Act with respect to
> this proceeding.* Second, to the extent the assess-
> ment involved decisions of a precedential nature,
> the agency losing responsibility for these functions
> could bind the Department of Commerce in its future
> administration of the statute. Finally, a hasty
> assessment, far from providing Commerce with a
> 'clean slate,' could result in more protests and
> litigation than would otherwise occur, thus adding
> to Commerce's burden as it assumes responsibility
> in this area." [Emphasis added.]

As matters developed, Customs did not liquidate any other relevant entries before the end of the year. This backlog, going back to 1974,
then became the responsibility of the Commerce Department.

4.   The Settlement Agreements.

The transfer of functions from Treasury to another department had
been sought by Congress because of Treasury's dismal track record in
enforcing the countervailing duty and antidumping laws. *See S. Rep. No.*
96-402, 96th Cong., 1st Sess. 12, 23-24 (1979); *H.R. Rep. No. 96-585,* 96th
Cong., 1st Sess. 6-7 (1979); *Reorganization Plan No. 3 of 1979: Hearings*
before a Subcomm. of the House Comm. on Government Operations, 96th Cong.,
1st Sess. 174-175, 186, 244-245, 258 (1979); *see also* authorities cited in
Argument I, A, 1, *infra.* The hope had been that Commerce would succeed
where Treasury had failed. Indeed, in response to questions posed at a
congressional budget hearing held on February 7, 1980, a Commerce Department spokesman gave every indication that his department would act expe-
ditiously and responsibly with respect to enforcing then pending dumping
findings, including the Japanese television case. The Director of Commerce's
Office of Budget stated:

> "Review of the current findings will commence on
> the anniversary month of the publication of the
> finding. This system is in compliance with the
> TAA, sections 751 asd [*sic*] 736, and is opera-
> tional. Questionaires [*sic*] have been forwarded
> for January findings. The first reviews should be
> published in June.

> "By definition, this means that cases with anni-
> versary dates in December may not begin the annual
> review cycle until that month in 1980 and must be
> completed not later than the anniversary date in
> 1981. *It is noteworthy that we intend to try to work*
> *off the enormous TV backlog as soon as possible, but*
> *not later than this same two-year period applicable*
> *to the other cases.*

> *"About 40 case analysts will be working on*
> *antidumping annual reviews, of which about 10 will*
> *be devoted to TVs."*

Trade Functions Authorizations for Fiscal Year 1981: Hearings before the

Subcomm. on Trade of the House Comm. on Ways and Means, 96th Cong., 2d

Sess. 86 (1980) [emphasis added].

Further, on March 28, 1980, the Department of Commerce caused to

be published a notice in the Federal Register (45 Fed. Reg. 20511), pur-

suant to section 751(a)(1) of the Tariff Act of 1930, in which it stated

that it was "conducting an administrative review of findings of dumping

under the Antidumping Act, 1921, to determine the foreign market value and

United States price of each entry of merchandise subject to the finding

. . . and to determine the amount, if any, by which the foreign market

value exceeds the United States price." The dumping finding of television

receivers from Japan was listed specifically among those findings for which

the administrative review would be conducted. The notice also stated:

"After providing an opportunity for comment by interested parties, the

Department of Commerce will publish in the Federal Register the results of

such review, together with notice of any antidumping duties to be assessed

and estimated antidumping duties to be deposited."

However, on April 28, 1980, the Commerce Department's General

Counsel, Homer E. Moyer, Jr., announced at a press conference that, on that

date, the Commerce and Treasury Departments had concluded agreements to

settle claims for antidumping duties and penalties related to the importa-

tion of television receivers from Japan during the period 1971 to 1979.

Mr. Moyer cited 19 U.S.C. §1617 as the legal authority for the settlement.

He indicated that agreements had been reached with 22 importers and that

these importers accounted for the great bulk of imported television re-

ceivers subject to the finding, T.D. 71-76. Distributed at the conference

were (a) a press release dated April 28, 1980, (b) a prototype settlement agreement, and (c) a list of the informal names of companies with whom

agreements had been reached. *See* Complaint, Collective Exhibit 1. In-

cluded in the settlement were (a) claims by the United States arising out

of liquidations -- some of which claims were asserted in several collection

suits in United States District Courts, (b) claims by an importer of tele-

vision receivers from Japan in an action in the United States Customs Court

challenging the assessment of antidumping duties on two entries, (c) alleged

claims by the United States for penalties arising out of an investigation

relating to section 592 of the Tariff Act of 1930, and (d) alleged claims

by the United States arising out of unliquidated entries of television

receivers from Japan, entered between July 1, 1973 and March 31, 1979. *Id.*

At the press conference of April 28, 1980, Mr. Moyer indicated

that the Commerce Department had determined that the total amount of anti-

dumping duties on the subject entries of television receivers from Japan

was approximately $138.7 million.[22/] Included in this amount was an amount

found to be due on the previously liquidated and protested entries, which

amount, upon information and belief, was approximately $13 million. *Id.*

Under the terms of the settlement, a total of between $75 and $77

million would be paid by the importers. Approximately $66 million repre-

sented antidumping duties and approximately $9 to $11 million represented

penalties under 19 U.S.C. §1592. In return for these payments (or agree-

ments to make these payments) the responsible agencies of the United States

would: (a) dismiss with prejudice the suits for the collection of duties

assessed upon entries made prior to July 1, 1973; (b) abandon certain

further administrative investigations concerning the possible imposition of

_____

[22/] The questionable method by which Commerce arrived at this figure is
described in Attachment C (at 1-2) to the Moyer Declaration.

Neither plaintiff nor any of its representatives was aware of the
settlement or settlement agreements, or of any of the substantive determinations reflected therein, until the announcement was made thereof at
the aforedescribed press conference.

civil penalties pursuant to 19 U.S.C. §1592; and (c) within ten days, issue
instructions to Customs officers to liquidate entries made prior to March
31, 1979, without assessing any antidumping duties. The settlement agreements also contained such false statements as: "The United States knows of
no violation or potential violation of law relating to or arising from the
importation, sale or exportation of television receivers by the . . . [im-
porter] or the Japanese manufacturer(s)/exporter(s) from which it has
purchased or will purchase . . . ." *Id.*

In reaching or prior to reaching the settlement agreements
discussed above, the Commerce Department did the following: (a) it determined the foreign market value, including adjustments to foreign market
value, and the United States price (*i.e.,* purchase price or exporter's
sales price) for all unliquidated entries of television receivers from
Japan entered prior to April 1, 1979; (b) it determined that the amount of
antidumping duties due on said unliquidated entries was approximately
$138.7 million (less the relatively small amount found due on previously
liquidated and protested entries); (c) it determined that it would demand,
as antidumping duties for the said unliquidated entries, approximately $66
million (less the relatively small amount found due on previously liquidated
and protested entries); and (d) it determined that no antidumping duties
would be assessed in the individual liquidations of the aforesaid unliquidated
entries. Thus, the Commerce Department has made determinations described
in section 751 of the Tariff Act of 1930, although, in failing to give
plaintiff or other interested parties representing the domestic television
industry an opportunity to be heard prior to making such determinations, it
has not followed the procedures mandated by that section or other provisions of law and it has not followed the procedures which it appeared to

indicate it would follow in the Federal Register notice of March 28, 1980.

Moreover, the Commerce Department had made its determination as to the

amount of antidumping duties due well in advance of the settlement of April

28, 1980. Instead of publishing that determination in accordance with

section 751, which would have enabled the plaintiff to contest the deter-

mination promptly in this Court, the Commerce Department engaged in secret

negotiations with representatives of manufacturers, exporters, and im-

porters of television receivers from Japan, which negotiations culminated

in the aforedescribed settlement.[23]/

[23]/ On May 9, 1980, the United States Court of Appeals for the District of
Columbia Circuit, in the *COMPACT* litigation, *supra*, issued, *per curiam*, an
injunction pending appeal, pursuant to the appellants' motion, thereby en-
joining the Customs Service from liquidating entries of television receivers
subject to T.D. 71-76 or from implementing the terms of any of the settle-
ment agreements pending the subject appeal. On May 13, 1980, the appellees
filed a motion to dissolve the injunction, and attached as an appendix the
Moyer Declaration (which is appended to their present motion as Exhibit C).
That motion was denied *per curiam*, in an order entered on May 27, 1980.
Copies of the Orders of May 9, 1980 and May 27, 1980 are annexed hereto as
Collective Exhibit 45 and are made a part hereof. As of this writing, the
COMPACT appeal is still pending and the injunction is still in force.

Bibliography

The forty-volume record of evidence filed in the Court of Appeals and the Supreme Court in the *Matsushita* case. The Supreme Court case is generally known as *Matsushita et al. v. Zenith,* 475 U.S. 574 (1986). In the Court of Appeals, the official citation to the opinion is *Zenith Radio Corp. v. Matsushita Elec. Indus. Co. et al.,* 123 F. 2d 238 (1983). It is also known as the Japanese Electronics Products Antitrust Litigation, 723 F. 2d 238 (1983), 475 U.S. 574 (1986). In the District Court, the case is referred to as *Zenith Radio Corp. et al. v. Matsushita Elec. Indus. Co. et al.,* 513 F. Supp. 1100.

Appleyard, R. *Pioneers of Electrical Communication.* New York: Macmillan, 1930.

Archer, G. *Big Business and Radio.* New York: American Historical Company, 1939.

Baerwald, Hans. *Party Politics in Japan.* Boston: Allen & Unwin, 1986.

Balling, Richard. *America's Competitive Edge.* New York: McGraw-Hill, 1982.

Banning, W. P. *Commercial Broadcasting Pioneer, the WEAF Experiment, 1922–1926.* Cambridge, MA: Harvard University Press, 1946.

Bartlett, Donald L., and James B. Steele. *America: What Went Wrong.* Kansas City, MO: Andrews and McMeel, 1992.

Bilby, Kenneth. *The General: David Sarnoff and the Rise of the Communications Industry.* New York: Harper & Row, 1986.

Brewster, Kingman. *Antitrust and American Business Abroad.* New York: McGraw-Hill, 1958.

Case, Joseph Young, and Everet Needham Case. *Owen D. Young and American Enterprise.* Boston: David P. Godine, 1982.

Choate, Pat. *Agents of Influence.* New York: Alfred A. Knopf, 1990.

Coe, D. *Marconi, Pioneer of Radio.* Julian Messner, 1934.

Crowther, J. G. *British Scientists of the Nineteenth Century.* K. Paul, French, Trubner, 1935.

Deacon, Richard. *Kempei Tai: History of the Japanese Secret Service.* Beafort Books, 1983.

Dunlop, O. E. *Marconi: The Man and His Wireless.* New York: Macmillan, 1937.

Eicles, W. H. *Wireless.* London: Oxford University Press, 1933.

Epstein, Stephanie. *Buying the American Mind.* Washington, DC: Center for Public Integrity, 1991.

Fallows, James. "Playing by Different Rules." *Atlantic Monthly,* September 1987, pp. 22–32.

Gibbon, Edward. *The History of the Decline and Fall of the Roman Empire,* vol. 2. London: Methuen, 1909.

Hadley, Eleanor M. *Antitrust in Japan.* Princeton: Princeton University Press, 1970.

Harvard Business School. *Zenith Radio Corporation v. United States: 1977.* Boston: HBS Case Services, Harvard Business School, 1978.

"Hearings of the Senate Interstate Commerce Committee on the Nomination of Thad H. Brown." Seventy-sixth Congress, Third Session. Washington, DC: U.S. Government Printing Office, 1940.

Jaffe, B. *Men of Science in America.* New York: Simon & Schuster, 1944.

Katz, Donald. *The Big Store.* New York: Viking, 1987.

Kintner, Earl W., ed. *The Legislative History of the Federal Antitrust Laws,* vol. 1. New York and London: Chelsea House, 1978.

Letwin, W. *Law and Economic Policy in America: The Evolution of the Sherman Act.* Westport, CT: Greenwood, 1965.

Lewis, Charles. *America's Frontline Trade Officials.* Washington, DC: Center for Public Integrity, 1991.

Maclaurin, W. *Inventions and Innovation in the Radio Industry.* New York: Macmillan, 1949.

Magaziner, Ira C., and Robert B. Reich. *Minding America's Business.* New York: Harcourt Brace Jovanovich, 1982.

McCraw, Thomas K. *America versus Japan.* Boston: Harvard Business School Press, 1986.

Ozawa, Terutomo. "Japan's Industrial Groups." *Michigan State Business Topics* 28, no. 4 (1980): 33–40.

Pepper, Thomas, Merit E. Janow, and Jimmy W. Wheeler. *The Competition: Dealing with Japan.* New York: Praeger, 1985.

Prestowitz, Clyde V. *Trading Places: How We Allowed Japan to Take the Lead.* New York: Basic Books, 1988.

Report of the Federal Trade Commission on the Radio Industry. December 1, 1923.

Rossides, Eugene T. *U.S. Customs, Tariff and Trade.* Washington, DC: Bureau of National Affairs, 1977.

Seager, H., and C. Gulick. *Trust and Corporation Problems.* New York: 1929.

Segal, Harvey H. *Corporate Makeover.* New York: Viking, 1989.

Sherman, John. *Recollections of Forty Years in the House, Senate and Cabinet.* 1895.

Smith, Adam. *An Inquiry into the Nature and Causes of the Wealth of Nations,* Modern Library ed. New York: Random House, 1937.

Stockman, David A. *The Triumph of Politics.* New York: Harper & Row, 1986.

Suomela, John W., et al. *Foreign Industrial Targeting and Its Effects on U.S. Industries, Phase 1: Japan.* Report to the Subcommittee on Trade, Committee on Ways and Means, U.S. House of Representatives. U.S. International Trade Commission Publication 1437. Washington, DC: 1983.

Tarbell, I. M. *Owen D. Young: A New Type of Industrial Leader.* New York: Macmillan, 1932.

Thorelli, H. *The Federal Antitrust Policy.* 1955.

Viner, Jacob. *Dumping: A Problem in International Trade.* Reprints of Economic Classics. New York: Augustus M. Kelley, 1966.

Walker, A. *History of the Sherman Act.* New York: 1910.

Woodward, Bob, and Scott Armstrong. *The Brethren.* New York: Simon & Schuster, 1979.

Index

ABOUT THE AUTHOR

PHILIP J. CURTIS is a semi-retired corporation and civil litigation lawyer with over forty years of experience. Mr. Curtis was educated at Regis University and at Georgetown University, and he has been active both with the federal government and in private practice. He participated in many of the actions described in this work.